D1156039

THE BEST PLAYS OF 1957–1958

THE BURNS MANTLE YEARBOOK

Illustrated with photographs, and
with drawings by HIRSCHFELD

from "The Dark
at the Top of the
Stairs"

THE BEST PLAYS
OF 1957-1958

EDITED BY LOUIS KRONENBERGER

DODD, MEAD & COMPANY

NEW YORK · 1958 · TORONTO

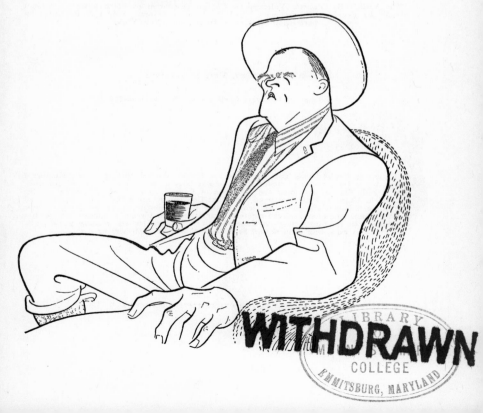

WITHDRAWN

LIBRARY
COLLEGE
EMMITSBURG, MARYLAND

"Look Back in Anger": By John Osborne. Copyright © 1957 by Criterion Books, Inc. Published by Criterion Books, Inc. Reprinted by permission of Criterion Books, Inc., New York, N. Y.

"Under Milk Wood": By Dylan Thomas. Copyright 1954 by New Directions. Reprinted by permission of New Directions, New York, N. Y.

"Time Remembered": By Jean Anouilh, English version by Patricia Moyes. Reprinted by permission of Coward-McCann, Inc., New York, N. Y. "Time Remembered" is the sole property of the authors and is fully protected by copyright. It may not be acted either by professionals or by amateurs without written consent. Public readings and radio or television broadcasts are likewise forbidden. All inquiries concerning rights except stock and amateur rights should be addressed to the author's agent, Dr. Jan van Loewen, International Copyright Agency, 81-83 Shaftesbury Ave., London, W.1. All inquiries concerning stock and amateur rights should be addressed to Samuel French, Inc., 25 W. 45th St., New York 36, N. Y.

"The Rope Dancers": By Morton Wishengrad. © 1958 by Morton Wishengrad. Reprinted by permission of Crown Publishers, Inc., New York.

"Look Homeward, Angel": By Ketti Frings. © 1958 by Edward C. Aswell as Administrator, C.T.A. of the Estate of Thomas Wolfe and/or Fred W. Wolfe and Ketti Frings. Reprinted by permission of Charles Scribner's Sons, New York, N. Y.

"The Dark at the Top of the Stairs": By William Inge. Copyright © 1958 by William Inge. Reprinted by permission of Random House, Inc., New York, N. Y.

"Summer of the 17th Doll": By Ray Lawler. Copyright © 1957 by Ray Lawler. Reprinted by permission of Random House, Inc., New York, N. Y.

"Sunrise at Campobello": By Dore Schary. Copyright © 1957 as an unpublished work by Dore Schary. Copyright © 1958 by Dore Schary. Reprinted by permission of Random House, Inc., New York, N. Y.

"The Entertainer": By John Osborne. Copyright © 1958 by John Osborne. Published by Criterion Books, Inc. Reprinted by permission of Criterion Books, Inc., New York.

"The Visit": By Maurice Valency, an English adaptation of "Der Besuch der alten Dame" by Friedrich Duerrenmatt. © 1956, 1958 by Maurice Valency. Reprinted by permission of Random House, Inc., New York.

© 1958 BY DODD, MEAD & COMPANY, INC.

Library of Congress Catalog Card Number: 20-21432

CAUTION: Professionals and amateurs are hereby warned that the above-mentioned plays, being fully protected under the copyright laws of the United States of America, the British Empire, including the Dominion of Canada, and all other countries of the Copyright Union and the Universal Copyright Convention, are subject to a royalty. All rights, including professional, amateur, motion picture, recitation, public reading, radio broadcasting, television, and the rights of translation into foreign languages, are strictly reserved. In their present form these plays are dedicated to the reading public only. All inquiries regarding them should be addressed to their publishers or authors.

PRINTED IN THE UNITED STATES OF AMERICA

EDITOR'S NOTE

IN editing this forty-first volume in the *Best Plays* series, I find myself once more under very pleasant obligations. Once more my wife, Emmy Plaut, has provided help that is more accurately called collaboration. For editorial assistance, I am immensely indebted to Barbara Kamb. For the use of photographs, I must thank the Editors of *Life* Magazine and Doris O'Neill, and for the use of its tabulation of Hits and Flops, *Variety* and Mr. Abel Green. Particular thanks are due, for their reports and articles, to Miss Cassidy, Mr. Hobson, Mr. Maney and Mr. Sherwood, and for very kindly granting the use of their sketches, to Jo Mielziner, William and Jean Eckart, Ben Edwards, Ralph Alswang, Oliver Smith, Howard Bay, Alvin Colt, Irene Sharaff, Miles White and Raoul Pene du Bois.

And it remains, as always, a great pleasure to be associated in this project with Mr. Hirschfeld.

LOUIS KRONENBERGER

CONTENTS

CONTENTS

THE SEASON IN PICTURES
(Photographs follow page 86)

Peter Ustinov, Gerald Sarracini and Elizabeth Allen in "Romanoff and Juliet"

Outstanding Broadway Performances 1957-1958

Lena Horne, Josephine Premice and Ossie Davis in "Jamaica"

Charles Saari, Pat Hingle and Teresa Wright in "The Dark at the Top of the Stairs"

"West Side Story" costume designs by Irene Sharaff

Model by Oliver Smith for a set in "West Side Story"

Set design by Howard Bay for "The Music Man"

"The Music Man" costume designs by Raoul Pene du Bois

Jo Mielziner's set design for "Look Homeward, Angel"

Set design by Ralph Alswang for "Sunrise at Campobello"

Eli Wallach and Joan Plowright in "The Chairs"

Anne Bancroft and Henry Fonda in "Two for the Seesaw"

Laurence Olivier in "The Entertainer"

"Infernal Machine" costume designs by Alvin Colt

Costume designs by Miles White for "Jamaica"

Set design by Ben Edwards for "Jane Eyre"

Sketch by William and Jean Eckart for a set in "The Body Beautiful"

"Rumble" scene from "West Side Story"

Kenneth Kakos, Ralph Bellamy and Perry Skaar in "Sunrise at Campobello"

SUMMARIES AND COMMENTARIES

THE SEASON ON BROADWAY

THERE was a sense of activity, of aliveness, of special things cropping up, of new names bursting forth, of the vernal rather than the autumnal, about the 1957-58 Broadway season. All this inspired the thought, some of it even furnished the evidence, that '57-'58 must be an outstandingly good season. The thought, when pursued, emerged a little ill-nourished; the evidence, when examined, appeared a trifle scant. If there were hallelujahs to be blown, it must needs be with muted trumpets; if cheers were to be raised, E. M. Forster's two cheers rather than three would be enough. But if it was hardly a season of notable achievement, it was certainly one of continual interest, of conspicuous variety, and in a certain sense of progress. It was a very good dinner-party season, with one debatable play after another to animate the fish course or at times to rattle the dessert plates. It was equally a good season for fairly solemn discussion groups: just how angry was John Osborne—or was *anger* even the right word?; just how mordant was Friedrich Duerrenmatt, just how symbolic *The Rope Dancers,* how genuine a musical-drama advance was *West Side Story,* how exhilarating a musical-comedy retreat was *The Music Man?*

Its variety, I think, was the season's pleasantest merit; and it was a very real merit seeing that what commonly proves so depressing on Broadway is not the percentage of failure but the percentage of formula. Nine-tenths of what turns up in the usual Broadway season can, almost as easily when good as when bad, be put into a very few pigeonholes. This was not true of '57-'58. There was, to begin with, an impressive geographical variety. To take only the Ten Best Plays: seldom does even one of them originate anywhere but in the United States, England or France. Last season three of them did—and from Australia, what is more, and Switzerland and Wales. The variety also included—in addition to assorted dramas and melodramas, comedies and farces—verse plays, real-life documentaries, real-life chronicles, Molnaresque fantasy, Saroyanesque folderol, a two-character play, a sociological musical, a cut-down *Back to Methuselah,* a one-man show, a one-woman show, a Beat-Generation comic, a Sean O'Casey reading, and adaptations from novels as dissimilar as *Jane Eyre, Miss Lonelyhearts* and *Say, Darling.*

3

To be sure, the presence of so much variety—of so many readings, chronicles, documentaries, adaptations and the like—helps to spotlight the absence of widespread creativeness. It stresses the fact that all too much of what is produced on Broadway has merely been processed for it; that no longer is the play the thing; that the show, the theatre piece, the stunt, the cut-down novel, the journalistic paste-up bulk collectively larger. In the popular sense there is nothing wrong with all this; indeed, considering the immemorial lure of the actor, the eternal magic of the limelight, there is something quite natural. Ralph Bellamy's impersonation of F.D.R., Peter Ustinov's gay shenanigans in *Romanoff and Juliet*, the special exuberance of *The Music Man* are the very essence of the theatre. In a critical sense, however, something must always be done, not just to distinguish the production from the play, or what is show business from what is art, but to note how much of the one there is on Broadway as against how much there is of the other. And the proportion, even in a plainly better-than-average season like '57-'58, is not reassuring. Gimmickry much outdistances artistry, the scissors at times seem mightier than the pen; in an age of fantastic progress in transportation, the stage vehicle has still its curiously old-fashioned look, and the director labors not to enhance what has merit but to cover up what hasn't.

Still, in one form or another, we had the work of William Inge, Arthur Laurents, John Osborne, William Saroyan, Dylan Thomas, Maxwell Anderson, Brendan Gill, Carson McCullers, Christopher Fry, Friedrich Duerrenmatt, Peter Ustinov, Jean Anouilh, Aldous Huxley, Sean O'Casey, Noel Coward, Leonard Bernstein, Harold Arlen, Meredith Willson, William Gibson, Morton Wishengrad and Ketti Frings. And though it was the most practiced hands that were on occasion the most faltering, though some of the biggest names provided the worst disappointments, it was never a season when choosing the Ten Best Plays quite equaled the ten labors of Hercules. As it was a season rich in variety, so it was one whose plays, again and again, had scattered virtues. However scored with faults, this one was lively, that one was individual, a third proved amusing, a fourth showed promise. In such a season, some of the chosen ten must squarely face up to how much can be said against them—as some of the rejected may argue how much can be said in their favor. (In one instance, however—that of William Gibson's *Two for the Seesaw*—it was unfortunately not possible for us to make arrangements to include the play among the Ten Best.)

It was a season whose drama conspicuously surpassed its comedy (though on more than one occasion the two were intertwined). In-

Among Broadway first-nighters are: Elsa Maxwell, Bernard Baruch, Marlene Dietrich, the Duke and Duchess of Windsor, Brooks Atkinson, Billy Rose, Leonard Lyons, Moss Hart, Dolly Haas, Margaret Truman and, of course, Mr. Hirschfeld himself

deed, it may partly have been the presence of so much interesting drama that endowed the season with its special aura of merit. No doubt unconsciously, merit tends to go by weight. A season with eight or ten shrewd, gay, stylish comedies—which would constitute a truly exceptional season—might still, in retrospect, seem a little light and frivolous; but any season with eight or ten stimulating dramatic pieces will seem full-bodied and notable for "significance." That sense of significance was apparent last season from the outset, from the late September opening of an exceedingly provocative serious musical—*West Side Story*. Right on its heels, moreover, came a reverberantly serious play, *Look Back in Anger;* and the sense of how much can be harsh, hateful, troubling, buffeting in life; a real sense indeed of the facts of life or (what at times are more sinister) the fantasies, was to persist throughout the season. It was hardly an escapist season that could introduce, again and again, into its plays such subjects as suicide, murder, betrayal, desertion, homosexuality, infidelity, corruption, abortion, arson, drunkenness, physical illness, mental illness, poverty, race prejudice, frigidity and juvenile delinquency. On the other hand, the very fact that these matters cropped up so often may suggest that it was a season over-rich in that near-neighbor or disguised-brother of the escapist—the sensational.

On top of the harsh American rhythms of *West Side Story, Look Back in Anger* spat out in very British accents the most blistering vituperation the stage had encountered in years. Why John Osborne's play had hit England with such a bang the year before was immediately clear: it had not only jabbed some good spiny cactus into England's aspidistra drama, it also clanged a new generation's call to disorder in English life. Something that might pass for the Zeitgeist had united with somebody who, at his best, could be magically defamatory. Hardly had the curtain gone up on the frowsiest-looking attic in years—to reveal Jimmy Porter's better-born wife bent over an ironing board and his working-class friend asprawl among the Sunday papers—for Jimmy himself to let loose his bilious scorn, like a revolving gun turret, on everything within range—art, religion, radio, Sunday, England, mother-in-law, wife. As minutely venomous as a wasp, as sweepingly violent as a whirlwind, his growls subsiding in whines, his mockeries lapped in self-pity, Jimmy brought to a vast repository of grievances a commensurate repertory of abuse.

Postulating a gray-as-ashes England where upper-class loss has not meant lower-class gain, Mr. Osborne wrote of a young intellectual who looks back because he has so little incentive to look ahead, and looks back in anger (or at any rate resentment) because he has no brighter past than future. Exulting in his wrongs rather than crusading for his rights, Jimmy—at least on the surface—is a full-fledged Disorganization Man. But gnawing at him worse than have-not economics is the English intestinal bug of class resentment. Happily, Osborne never lets this become a mere plight in man's clothing: Jimmy is always exasperatingly and most individually alive. He has, moreover, a fine real-life gift for witty excoriation.

Less happily, the best in all this has been largely conveyed by the end of a brilliant, dynamic first act. It may be that the first act's very power of assault lessens the force of what follows. But what follows has also its limitations. That the wife's actress friend, after lashing out at Jimmy and getting his wife to leave his bed and ironing board, should thereupon assume them herself, is both witty and theatrical; and a number of other things are sufficiently lively. But the plot, besides seeming derivative in places, has too little organic development. The play never really advances from a kind of one-man show to an integrated social drama. To be sure, any negativist, no-exit attitude that is in effect disdainful of moral crisis cannot develop very far; but Osborne, having shown how socially resentful Jimmy can be, chiefly shows thereafter how personally irresistible he is; and after raising the question of human plight, bogs down in bohemian mess. The truly commanding merit of *Look Back in Anger* is that not for many years has anyone come out of England with Osborne's talent for throwing stones. The play's very palpable limitation is its much smaller talent for architecture, for placing one stone on top of another.

Opening the same week as *Look Back in Anger, Miss Lonelyhearts* derived from a novel born of something far more genuinely savage and pessimistic. Unfortunately, Howard Teichmann's adaptation could in no way do justice to Nathanael West's book, for one reason because no stage adaptation could. West's story of a young news-paperman who jauntily takes over an agony column, only to grow more and more horrified and sickened by the suffering he encounters in every batch of mail, exhibits an untouchably personal style and a scarcely transferable personal vision. So terse and packed in method as to create in 75 pages the effect of a novel, *Miss Lonely-hearts,* unlike most books, had to be blown up rather than cut down for the stage, and seemed, on the stage, loose, slack and synthetic in flavor. Clearly intending no vandalism, Mr. Teichmann was forced into it through trying to make sense of *Miss Lonelyhearts* in the theatre. And he did not make sense of it for all that. He simplified the story only to complicate the storytelling; yet for all his stage gimmicks his hero seemed wooden, his hero's going to pieces seemed banal, while his ending misrepresented West's meaning. And simplifying in one place, Teichmann softened in another, till theme and story were alike ill-used. What alone came off was the gloatingly malevolent editor, who made a good villain. But the real villain of the book—life itself—never appeared in the play.

In *The Egghead* Molly Kazan wrote a play with contemporary overtones about a not-very-contemporary-minded professor. Hank Parsons is full of highminded intolerances, he grants his seemingly

Robert Preston, David Burns, Helen Raymond, Pert Kelton and

Barbara Cook in "The Music Man"

dumb wife the freedom of thought to think as he does, he chants
ancient war-cries while paying no attention to current wars.   Then
the FBI start investigating a former student of his, a brilliant Negro.
Hank, certain that the student is no Communist and equally certain
that he is being smeared as one, rushes to his defense.   But soon
enough the accusation is proved true.

Almost always interesting, and managing to vitalize its issues while
humanizing its atmosphere, *The Egghead* yet had that crying fault
of a message play—it could not create flesh-and-blood people who
really seem to govern their own lives.   This was partly a matter of
plot: the tale of a cocksure know-it-all who is being royally had is a
staple of artificial comedy.   In *The Egghead* the staple tricks were
very unconvincingly applied to something serious and real; while as
anything but a comic butt the professor seemed hard to accept in
himself.   Moreover, for all her plotting Mrs. Kazan had in time to
abandon action for argument, with a drop in dramatic force.   Though
the last act of *The Egghead* was an animated enough symposium,
there had ceased in any creative sense to be a play.

William Saroyan's first new Broadway work in fourteen years,
The Cave Dwellers, had its decided partisans; for myself it seemed
acutely disappointing.   It told of broken-down performers—a done-
for boxer, a beat old clown, an ailing actress, a man with a bear and
a woman who gives birth to a baby—camping out in a crumbling,
abandoned East Side theatre.   By day they lie abed, or beg in the
streets, or in desperation steal milk; by night they act out their one-
time roles, philosophize, soliloquize, dramatize the day's rebuffs, fall
asleep and dream.   With most of all this Mr. Saroyan was back at
his usual stand making his usual pitch, but with almost none of his
usual showmanship.   If no less soupy and boozy in the old days
about the down-at-heel, Saroyan in the past often showed an alcoholic gaiety and verve, a real gift for brewing instant-vaudeville.
However much the poet in him might slump or the philosopher
gabble, the prankster could shine.

But instead of being a high-spirited toastmaster to waifdom in
The Cave Dwellers, Saroyan was its longwinded poet laureate.   Instead of the old cockeyed and even imaginative variety turns, there
were sad-eyed little gallantries; and even when he half-mocked at
stage doings, Saroyan seemed half mawkish.   His people were not
just too good to be true, they were mostly too good to be interesting.
Their sole message was love, love for one another; all was love, the
secret of the theatre was love, even hate was love.   A fine desidera-
tum, no doubt; but beyond its seeming a very doubtful fact, Mr.
Saroyan could never make any of it soar as poetry or move along

as drama. His words were not only too many, but too vague. Theatrically, it need not have mattered that Saroyan wrote first with an eraser—to wipe out reality—had he afterwards, with a pen, created magic. Unhappily, *The Cave Dwellers* had little magic—only an occasional stab of pathos in a great wilderness of plight; or a flash of humor or poetry amid constant murmuration.

If Dylan Thomas's *Under Milk Wood* classifies a little uneasily as "drama," comedy in any conventional sense is no better for something as often elegiac as farcical. In a certain sense, to be sure, *Under Milk Wood* cannot even be classified as playwriting; it is at most a stage piece. It is something, however, not really meant to be read, something that for a right effect needs to be spoken, to be enacted. It is the work of a very gifted poet on his way to becoming a playwright: it has a good deal of stage life, but chiefly in terms of the caught moment, the fleshed vignette, the animated cartoon. Though essentially storyless, it is not static; but what is dynamic in it derives chiefly from language.

The production, as staged by Douglas Cleverdon, suffered from an attempt to make a rather extraordinary creation resemble an ordinary theatre piece; from making Thomas's people into character actors or vaudevillians who skittered and brayed and struck deliberate ham attitudes; from giving the whole thing, indeed, a suggestion of the mock ten-twent-thirt beer-and-pretzel revivals of old melodrama in the '30s. The proper method, surely, was not assorted shenanigans but a sustained style; something that should endow Thomas's picture of a Welsh community from one midnight to the next with the patterned flow of ballet. What with so much local color (as well as poetic color) in the text, there was no danger of mere flaccid allegory. With the text once again pre-eminent in these pages, I think it possible to surmise what a magician (if also a wastrel) with words Thomas could be. If he had not yet learned, on his way to becoming a playwright, that verbal victories alone are not enough for dramatic triumph, he had achieved the sort of spoken incantations that are among the age-old glories of the stage; he could enkindle moods that are part of the stage's power; he was master of the quick colloquy, of the sharp soliloquy, of exchanges between girl and boy, or husband and wife; and of the speech that brings a sudden lunge of fun or rush of color. Thomas's problem—it is not easy to decide whether he could have solved it—was to shake off much of the verbal seaweed that clung to him so as to create drama with sharper and with swifter strokes.

Compulsion, as dramatized from Meyer Levin's novel about the Loeb-Leopold murder case, re-enacted the grisly tale in 20 explicit scenes. Beginning just after the murder, it proceeded to portray two self-styled young supermen who had dreamed of committing a perfect crime, and to indicate how very imperfect a crime they had actually committed. It showed their dissensions as danger loomed, their behavior as defection narrowed; it described the fantasy worlds they inhabited and, at length, the trial itself, with the prosecution stressing the atrocious nature of the crime, and the defense the compulsive pathology of the criminals. Told in a loose, jagged, episodic form that emphasized its documentary nature, the play had the virtue, as theatre, of being again and again electrifying, as it had the drawback, as drama, of not widening or deepening enough. If the reason for this was partly that factual truth tends to be formless, it was rather more that in *Compulsion* it lacked a sufficiently large frame of reference. Perhaps Hebbel long ago put his finger on why *Compulsion* fails to be truly large and liberating drama with his famous remark that in a good play everyone must seem to be in the right. With the two killers of *Compulsion* this was not possible, less because of how hideous their crime was than of how gratuitous. It lacked an understandably human motive. Clinically, the crime could be explained: given a lawless Jazz Age, two spoiled rich men's sons, a homosexual neurosis and a Nietzschean intellectual arrogance, and such a mixture may explode into murder-for-a-thrill. But the case is too special to induce audience identification in the theatre; it seems like Grand Guignol in real life. Moreover, with everything already made clear, the terribly protracted trial scene became a weapon for hitting the audience about three times too often over the head.

Monique was a child of the same French novel that inspired the film *Diabolique,* though the two were by no means twins. As a chiller *Monique* was inferior, partly because of production. If not for a long time had any Broadway melodrama shown so much plot this was fortunate, for not for a long time had one displayed such strenuous overacting. But though the whole thing had all the subtlety of a burglar alarm, it did have a requisite amount of suspense, as well as a passable surprise at the final curtain.

Carson McCullers' *The Square Root of Wonderful* exhibited a talent in hopeless disarray. The author of *The Member of the Wedding* this time wrote on a variety of themes, in a variety of tones, at a variety of tempos. A work containing enough material for several plays emerged, for lack of integration, no play at all. The parts were not only greater than the whole; they destroyed the whole.

The play made clear (not least through hate) that the square root of wonderful is love. There were Tennessee-Williams overtones,

Julie Harris in "The Country Wife"

now from *The Glass Menagerie,* now from *Cat on a Hot Tin Roof.* A genteelly despotic Southern mother has made an all-tied-up-in-knots old maid of her daughter, a psychotically bitter and frustrated writer of her son. The son in turn has hurt and made unhappy his simple young wife; divorced from her now, he tries to shatter her romance with an uncomplicated architect. But amid so many fractured lives there is much leisurely showing of the farcical side of family existence. The farce moments were sometimes amusing, the old-maid daughter was not only amusing but touching. But so abruptly did things shift focus, so wildly did they change tone, that farce firecrackers negated real bullets, and the play's virtues were turned into faults. Jangling with false notes, *Square Root* could not mate humor with horror, or get its varied themes to coalesce; and in the attempt, Miss McCullers' genuine individuality and special feeling for life became sadly blurred. What emerged was a square root in a round hole.

That once-or-twice-a-season sort of play that is very "interesting" without being successful, that insists on going its own way even though it lose its way, turned up in Morton Wishengrad's *The Rope Dancers.* Laid in a turn-of-the-century Manhattan tenement, the play was a stubbornly harsh tale of a lacerated family; of a rigid, arrogant, unappeasably bitter woman with a lazy, feckless would-be writer of a husband, and an eleven-year-old daughter born with six fingers on one hand. The mother, beyond having brought up the daughter to feel like someone with two heads, does not know how to convey her own love to the child. As the central figure in the play, the mother emerges no mere victim, no strong woman exacerbated by a weak husband and a hard fate. Hers is a willful strength gloating over weakness in others, a puritan nature full of repressed sexuality, a guilty mind attributing misfortune to sin. Seen as a pathological figure, Margaret is valid and often effective. But, even in Siobhan McKenna's tight, unbending portrayal, Margaret seemed more than a psychological study. Mr. Wishengrad seemed to identify her with something in life itself, perhaps with something that gnawed at his own insides. He pushed on, as a result, toward rather grandiose tragedy, toward loud-pedaled moments that never quite rang true. In Wishengrad's pessimistic geography, where exactly (one wondered) was east, and where was west; what was determinism, what was pathology, what was sin? The more, in any case, he tried to universalize his story, the more special it appeared to be. But though he carried larger-sized luggage than he could fill and made *The Rope Dancers* rather fancily tragic, it was nowhere facilely sentimental, it nowhere stooped to conquer. However astigmatically, he had his own determined way of looking at things.

With *Look Homeward, Angel* the theatre's habit of making plays from serious novels found its best vindication in years. One of the few novels of any importance to be transferred to the stage without forfeiting an amplitude that is half their strength, or a personal accent that is half their essence, *Look Homeward, Angel* is with good reason an exception: in the Thomas Wolfe novel, amplitude is often sheer excess, accent mere rhetoric. What the book, with its unfortunate craving for size, its orgy of word-spending, its would-be philosophic shallowness, could pre-eminently bequeath to the stage was some notable characters. In adapting the novel, Ketti Frings largely took the people and let the purple go.

Her play did not, to be sure, purge Wolfe's novel of its faults while preserving all its fullness. Her play, in a sense, is not Wolfe's novel at all. It is something neater, smaller, simpler—a workable family play, set in the family boarding house and squeezed into a few weeks' span. The characters are no longer so revealingly lived with; a character like the mother, again, is not so symbolically large. The material, despite a tighter framework, has less true thematic value, is often simply episodic or picturesque. But these things confessed, *Look Homeward, Angel* is, on its own terms, almost always vivid and on occasion impressive. And unlike the book, it is not rampantly autobiographical, not literally self-centered. Eugene Gant is less the protagonist and more just part of a tribe; the property-mad, family-exploiting mother, the lusty ruin of a father, the snappish put-upon sister, the protective, early-dying brother Ben, all animate that tribe; and their tumultuous tribal strifes startle and sometimes rout the genteel, almost ghostly boarders.

What gives *Look Homeward, Angel* a certain vitality laced with truth is its sense of an actual family, at once riveted and riven— where, conversely, Eugene's love affair with a boarder does not seem a real love affair at all. The long-borne inner tensions snap when at last Eugene turns on his mother for the way she has used and fettered her children. In terms of Eugene himself, the play at its best conveys how, for almost every true writer, youth is a bursting of bonds and a simultaneous bondage to dreams; and how, for most men, the impact of their own flesh and blood can become at times a matter of blood and tears.

Soon after *Look Homeward, Angel* came, for most people, its closest rival among the season's American plays, William Inge's *The Dark at the Top of the Stairs*. In it Inge had gone back to the small-town world of his childhood, telling of a middle-class family in a rambling old house; of a life-speckled traveling salesman who loved but forever collided with his gently exasperating wife; of their unconfident, boy-frightened teen-age daughter; of their small son who can be hard and soft in the wrong places; and of the wife's sister and dentist brother-in-law. So life-sized, so recognizable, so frequently good for a laugh was it all that, despite bank balances and growing pains and matrimonial bumps, it somehow seemed comfortable and cozy.

But Mr. Inge had intended no mere sentimental journey, had indeed not so much traveled as tunneled back to the '20s. For all the gossip and shenanigans, the dress for the party and the dressing for the party, there were bogeys at the stairhead and phantoms outside the window. There were everywhere fears, doubts, deep-hidden voids; something gnaws at the chatterbox sister, drills against the dentist's heart, blows up in an adolescent Jew. And Inge often created his scene with apt and expressive detail; a moment was tense, a scene was touching, the general effect was very much the author's own. Yet the general effect, for all that, had a somewhat ploppy, India-rubberlike smack. Inge's most definitive quality—his feeling for human loneliness—became too insistent. It did not emerge from the characters; on the contrary, it shaped them. Nor did it, in the end, so much weave a mood as prescribe a method. One by one, each character was led up to the dark at the top of the stairs and revealed in his hair shirt. And each character's wound, however honestly representative, was dramatically a little commonplace. No mood enveloped the play because it kept reverting to parlor comedy and domestic vaudeville—things that instead of deepening the serious scenes emphasized them too much by contrast. Really deep chords never sounded, perhaps because a sort of plangent strumming never stopped; and the dark, though there, seemed less terrifying, and even less dark, from being so studiously spotlighted.

In *The Genius and the Goddess* Aldous Huxley, Beth Wendel and Alec Coppel dealt playfully, for an act and a half, with a wife's efforts to live with a genius. Just when the lady was all worn out from living with her self-centered physicist, the play turned serious —the genius got double pneumonia, the wife had now not to live with him but to keep him alive, and the solution was an affair with his assistant, which somehow re-invigorated the patient as well as herself. Generally wobbly and bloodless, the play was rather better when marking time with family-circle comedy than when moving forward with sex-triangle drama. But that it came to so little as a stage piece mattered less than that it smacked so little of Huxley; lacked all his old intellectual swordplay, his sudden satirical bite.

Sol Stein's *A Shadow of My Enemy* was a barely fictionized treatment of the Chambers-Hiss case. In large part following the public record, the play also used various devices to dramatize the narrative, to humanize it, and to editorialize about it. Though not without its real merits—the general fascination of the story, the vigorous and vibrant courtroom scenes—the play failed to seem impressive. The victim, to begin with, of a wooden production, the play fell awkwardly between a straight factual documentary and a rewoven imaginative drama; it was curiously oratorical; and unlike plays about Leopold and Loeb or the Scopes trial, it had to compete with the audience's own recent memories rather than re-arouse old ones. The impression, all in all, was of too little and too soon.

The Christmas season brought Shirley Booth to Broadway in a play with a theme that might make genius stumble. *Miss Isobel* offered an aging, white-haired heroine who becomes mentally ill and imagines that she is a young girl and that her embittered, put-upon old-maid daughter is her mother. For so ticklish a story the theatre, with its blunt visual effects, is far less suited than fiction would be; while the authors, Michael Plant and Dennis Webb, were not suited to it at all. After eyeing a grim but at least genuine theme—that the mother's pathos could complete the daughter's tragedy—they backed quickly away from it to trade in sticky pathos for pathos' sake. Even with Miss Booth's assistance, they could invoke no tears and only very occasional laughter; *Miss Isobel* was every bit as tedious as it was unpalatable.

William Gibson's *Two for the Seesaw*—which needed only two for the cast—offered Henry Fonda as an about-to-be-divorced Omaha lawyer who is downhearted and adrift in New York, and a remarkably appealing newcomer, Anne Bancroft, as a warmhearted racy-tongued Bronx-to-Bohemia floater whom Fonda meets at a party. All her life she has given too freely; he all his life has taken. The two, shuttling between their shabby little hole-in-the-walls, maintain a love affair in sickness and in health, in banter and in woe, managing to bridge a cultural and temperamental divide better than they can blot out the memory of his marriage.

Though spotty, the play was more than just another movie-soppy, movie-safe bit of lonelyhearts and flowers, or of split-level romance, or of double-dummy stage writing. It had its amusing and its touching scenes; it had nice dialogue, flashes of real theatre, moments of real feeling. But it mingled the capacities of an author with the mere commonplaces of a situation; and though it did not falsify its ending, it oversentimentalized it. And it had the peculiar drawbacks along with the peculiar enjoyments of a two-character play—wasted moments and overworked effects, more changes of scene than of

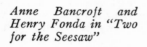

Anne Bancroft and Henry Fonda in "Two for the Seesaw"

story, and two telephones that almost constituted a liaison in themselves.

From Australia, by way of a triumphant London run, came Ray Lawler's *Summer of the 17th Doll,* a story of two field workers who for sixteen summers, during the long layoff period, have come to Melbourne for a fine home-style spree with two barmaids. But this seventeenth summer, with a new girl replacing one who had got married, and with strained relations between the two men, all the fun fizzles out. The two revelers, though one had been a Samson in the field and the other a Don Juan among women, by now are has-beens; their revels now are ended.

If the play—partly because of the production—failed of sufficient dramatic impact and verbal leverage, it preferred being prosaic and at times even dull to ever being false or flashy. It is a truthful play; nor, in treating understandably of believable human beings, is it merely drab; the Australian local color and working-class lingo alone would assure a certain piquancy. It has, besides, a soundly human theme: its last act vividly drives home with what deceiving colors and in what a dollhouse world these vacationers have staged their summer frisks; and how, even with the dollhouse in collapse, they struggle to hold on to their illusions. But though the demonstration rang true (and in the reading seems very touching) Mr. Lawler rather had to take the audience by the hand and lead it up to the truth; he could not quite illuminate his theme from within. In exhibiting the sad human arithmetic that twice two is four and that mankind wants to make it five, he was admirably clear; what was beyond him was the magical creative arithmetic that can raise a story to a higher power.

In *Sunrise at Campobello,* Dore Schary wrote of Franklin Delano Roosevelt from the August day in 1921 when he was stricken with polio to the day in June 1924 when he rose to nominate Al Smith for President. The interval between represented a catastrophe in F.D.R.'s life out of which he forged a triumph; and the play had, as a result, all the contours of the classically beleaguered stage hero. The play also offered the classic motif of external pressures with, on the one hand, F.D.R.'s imperious mother wanting her crippled son to retire and with, on the other, Louis Howe insisting that Roosevelt must still throw his hat in the ring. Thus the play had a self-contained narrative—the explicit record of a man's physical self-conquest which was in turn the measure of his inner adjustment and growth. Of F.D.R.'s relation to politics and public affairs there was hardly more in the play than the sounds of tuning up. In his relations to his family, he seemed all too conventionally gay, rationedly irritable, and distantly intimate. It was in his relations to himself that the play came off best. In Ralph Bellamy's extraordinarily effective impersonation of Roosevelt—in his coping with wheelchairs and crutches and braces, in his conversion of the humiliating into the heroic—there was no trace of either virtuosity or tear-jerking vaude-villism; there was a sense of characterization and indeed of character.

Mr. Schary's vivid portrait of Roosevelt vis-à-vis himself was his principal achievement. The play's limitations on other counts derive partly from the very nature of the undertaking. Mr. Schary was concerned with domestic rather than public matters, not least with home and mother, and he had plainly to approach such matters with sugar tongs. Some of the people in the play were not sufficiently made use of, others never came fully alive no doubt because they were actually alive: from considerations of taste the family side of *Sunrise at Campobello* was often lacking in flavor. And in places Mr. Schary's dialogue seemed fairly wooden or—when F.D.R. spoke —as though graven on stone. Whenever the play got beyond the family, whenever a Louis Howe or an Al Smith was around, things got notably livelier.

Winesburg, Ohio was, though for rather different reasons, almost as foredoomed to stage failure as *Miss Lonelyhearts*. The Sherwood Anderson book which Christopher Sergel adapted consists of a series of what can only marginally be called stories, most of them being character portrayals of the lost, the eccentric, the square-pegged, the defeated, some of them being incidents and encounters in small-town life. In a sense there is no mainland; each tale (whether or not each character) is an island. There is no real protagonist, for the aspiring young reporter and writer George Willard is essentially an ear for the townspeople's confidences. The peculiarly cumulative effect of what might almost be called Anderson's pathological lyri-cism, and of a small town that is really a kind of ghost town, would be hard to materialize on any stage; perhaps, indeed, it *ought* not to materialize.

In an effort to give it a hub, a unity, a stage center, Mr. Sergel really turned Anderson's book inside out, made the confidant of the book the protagonist of the play, made George Willard's longing to be a writer and his mother's attempts to set him free to become one, the general narrative. But a narrative has to be something more than simply a situation, and Mr. Sergel could only vary the same situation from one act to the next, while simultaneously either jetti-soning or greatly diminishing the other people in the book. Nor, by largely repeating a situation can one really vary it, as one cannot endow something with stage life by using dialogue that sounds more like prose. However sympathetic Mr. Sergel's intentions, he nowhere succeeded either on Anderson's terms or on his own.

John Osborne's *The Entertainer* greatly enforced the feeling, aroused by his *Look Back in Anger,* that he was by all odds England's most interesting new playwright in many years. This time he had no brilliantly disgruntled intellectual for a hero, but a flabbily disintegrating vaudevillian. On stage, Archie Rice is a cheapjack with rancid jokes and desperate jauntiness, whose very vulgarity lacks drive. Offstage, he is a shoddy, cynical family man, exploiting those who love him and embossing betrayal with abuse. Even with his back to the wall, he can somehow see the writing on it.

On stage *The Entertainer* seemed first of all Sir Laurence Olivier's evening: he had wonderfully caught Archie in all his rich, mangy detail—an out-at-elbows flop yammering that the world is out of joint; and really quite as notable was Brenda de Banzie as Archie's distraught, put-upon wife. But though requiring an expert production, *The Entertainer* can be—indeed, has been—much underestimated as a play. Alternating, as it does, home life with variety turns, it can misleadingly seem less a play than a stunt. The writing, again, necessarily lacks the brilliant crackle of *Look Back in Anger;* where Jimmy Porter has a superb talent for abuse, Archie Rice turns meanly abusive from having no real talent for anything. And where *Look Back in Anger* boasts a stingingly real attitude but has increasingly put-together situations, *The Entertainer* boasts a very genuine situation but too often strains for an attitude. Its least successful aspect is its attempt to enlarge its characters into blunt social symbols, to enfold its cheapjack in the Union Jack and convert a grubbily exact slice of life into contemporary England.

The truth is that, unlike *Look Back in Anger*—and doubtless in spite of its author—*The Entertainer* is concerned much less with society than with humanity. It is thus less topical; it is no snarling trumpet-call to inaction, but the whiny yet very affecting fiddling of a rather trite but a never bogus tune. And it is oddly unified: its stage scenes harmonize perfectly with its family ones. As against *Look Back in Anger,* where people swim flashingly about in a heavy surf of resentment, *The Entertainer's* is a drabber world in which people merely, and without very much showmanship, drown.

The Day the Money Stopped, which Maxwell Anderson and Brendan Gill adapted from Mr. Gill's novel, treated a classic stage theme: a fight over a will. It used classic combatants: the disinherited black sheep and his holier-than-thou brother. While the playboy with a rusting charm and the prig with a rankling virtue traded slurs, they were really laying siege to the holdings in the family vault by rattling

the skeletons in the family closet. Out, eventually, clattered illegiti-
macies and suicides and a crushed father image. And at the end
the disinherited playboy had wangled twenty grand only to spurn it.
The play also used a classic form: the brittle conversation piece.
In terms of insulting banter and the like, this had its good points;
but seldom were a classic action and a classic method so mismated.
Fights over a will make for melodrama, social drama, farce, comedy,
for banged fists, shaking fingers, skinny claws—but not for playfully
brandished rapiers. However often the brothers might pink each
other verbally, they used buttoned foils on synthetic flesh; nor was
there any more psychological probing than there was human drama.
    In *Blue Denim* James Leo Herlihy and William Noble embedded
a troubled teen-age sex comedy inside a sociological groundwork. At
fifteen Arthur Bartley takes refuge from his fond but unhelpful parents in a basement hideaway, to live in a world of beer and draw
poker with a pal, and of fledgling sex with a professor's daughter.
The girl becomes pregnant; Arthur vainly tries to signal to his
parents, then uses a forged check to pay for an abortion. In a sus-
penseful last act, everything suddenly comes out well—indeed, a
little too well. *Blue Denim* was twin-burner drama: Arthur's relations to his girl provided the plot; his relations to his family, the
basic problem. For though all too plainly Arthur and his girl had
better have stayed apart, the play in the final and family sense was
a lament for untogetherness. It dramatized the dangers in families
that lack a communications system; and what with the young
couple's agonizing jam, those dangers were vividly spotlighted and
the story line held. But there was not much at the end of the line,
and there was far more spotlight than illumination. Despite honest
details, good kid dialogue, and situations in which it was enough for
people just to be young or in trouble, too much of *Blue Denim* was
pat or false, was rigged up or spelt out. At the end, moreover, there
was more softness on the playwrights' part than perception on the
characters: truth, in *Blue Denim,* proved too fitful, put-togetherness
too frequent.
    Christopher Fry's *The Firstborn* was a stiffly earnest work, laid in
Egypt and centered in Moses. With the Pharaoh persecuting the
Jews, a Moses who was already estranged from the palace of his
upbringing turned wholly toward the people of his birth. In the
conflict, Pharaoh's young son Rameses sympathized with the oppressed; but when the firstborn in every Egyptian family was struck
down, the humane royal firstborn perished with the rest. The cry at
the end was the classic one over "the bewildering mesh of God," over
how the innocent must suffer with the guilty, and leaders must move

forward stricken with guilt. It was a searching enough theme to
build a play around; the trouble was that Fry provided almost nothing to build with—neither real dramatic bricks nor real psychological stones, only philosophic shards and ethical bits of glass. A story
that, told as vivid theatre, might have blazed with Biblical fire,
seemed utterly unwarmed. A story that, recounted as high drama,
might have seemed grandly severe, came off elaborately hollow. Very
likely this was no story for Mr. Fry to be treating: his literary con-
ceits and verbal arabesques suffocate anything truly alive. Half
don, half dandy, his forte is mannerism rather than substance, a
mocking wink rather than an observing eye. Whatever his intentions, the Egypt of *The Firstborn* was mummified.

Jane Eyre was always, as a novel, faintly absurd and decidedly
lurid; but to a story bordering on trash Charlotte Brontë brought
storytelling bordering on genius. As told by an uncoy, much buf-
feted Jane herself, the book advances, in a real rush of words, with
a beat of true emotion. Huntington Hartford's stage adaptation became *Jane Eyre* virtually without Jane, and chunks of story with no
hint of the storytelling. Everything stagiest about the book was
transferred to the stage; everything personally intense and imaginative vanished. For an act Eric Portman, playing Mr. Rochester
with jagged lure and rather like a masculine Tallulah Bankhead,
warded off collapse. But things more and more creaked till what
went up, melodramatically in smoke, seemed not so much Thornfield
Hall as a mass of theatrical deadwood.

The season's last play was also its most striking one. And like all
the season's most strikingly original plays—*Look Back in Anger,
The Entertainer, Summer of the 17th Doll*—Friedrich Duerrenmatt's *The Visit* was the work of a non-American. A Swiss play,
it brought the Lunts to Broadway in the first thing that has been
more than a romp or a vehicle for them in years; and their performances, coupled with Duerrenmatt's playwriting, made for a real
occasion. A theatre piece of fascinatingly acrid power, *The Visit*
begins misleadingly with light colors and a farce-comedy look, suddenly to darken the face of its canvas, to blacken the hearts of its
characters. A grisly fable of a woman's revengeful hate, it shows a
whole community succumbing to greed.

In the play, a high-handed, fabulously rich old woman, Claire
Zachanassian, returns to Gullen, the impoverished European town
of her birth to pour money into its lap—on one condition. Town
and townspeople can divide a billion marks if they will kill the man
who in Claire's youth denied that her child was his and made her
an outcast and prostitute. When the town rejects so outrageous an

Michael Wager, Mildred Natwick, Anthony Quayle, Torin Thatcher and Katharine Cornell in "The Firstborn"

offer, Claire does not argue; she can afford, she announces, to wait. She waits, and slowly the town capitulates to do her bidding. Something comparably cynical in tone, and in spots even similar in treatment, went into Mark Twain's *The Man That Corrupted Hadleyburg*. But Duerrenmatt's tale of the woman who corrupted Gullen is far more eerily sinister. In Madame Zachanassian with her entourage—pet panther, youthful eighth husband, blinded perjurers, American gangsters—are the all-too-obvious symbols of a ruthless, degenerate world. Moreover it was Claire herself who carefully reduced Gullen to poverty as a prelude to tempting it; and her revenge seems directed almost as much on the town that witnessed her shame as on the man who caused it. "The world," she cries, "made me into a whore. Now I make the world into a brothel."

Vividly lighted and staged, *The Visit* seemed as incredible and surrealist, yet as bluntly precise and compelling, as a dream. (Thus, right in the midst of her demands for his death, Claire had a touching, almost idyllic reunion with her betrayer.) The play's harsh power lies in just such incongruity, in its consistent theatricality,

LIBRARY
OF
MOUNT ST. MARY'S
COLLEGE
EMMITSBURG, MARYLAND

in its mingling batlike symbolic figures with small-town burghers and clods, in what it graphically evokes but never exactly defines. Was it simply Claire's betrayer, for example, that the townspeople finally killed, or was it their consciences? A more central question is how philosophically bleak is Duerrenmatt's own outlook—is his an outraged protest or an icy judgment; is he saying how sadly corruptible is man, or calling life itself corrupt? Not since Tennessee Williams' *Camino Real,* in any case, had a new Broadway play conveyed so fanged and carnivorous a world; but where Williams got mired in the very decadence and violence he seemed at war with, *The Visit* never got dramatically out of hand. Miss Fontanne played the monstrous Lady Bountiful with a fine enameled hardness, a high-styled fiendish poise, while Mr. Lunt, acting the betrayer in a quite different style, gave a vividly realistic picture of human fright faced with the inhumanly frightening.

Unimpressive in itself, the season's comedy seemed all the more so when set beside its drama. It offered nothing really distinguished; indeed it offered only one thing—*Time Remembered*—of even the most sporadic distinction. For the rest, there were two or three gag comedies that were fitfully amusing; two comedies from England whose actor-authors performed far more entertainingly than they wrote; and a good deal that was unattractive or inept.

Peter Ustinov's highly touted *Romanoff and Juliet* proved surprisingly thin. Laid in "the smallest country in Europe," it had the Soviet ambassador's son and the United States ambassador's daughter falling madly in love. With the two embassies in a tizzy over the romance, Mr. Ustinov bounced about as the head of the toy country, now issuing directives to his two-man army, now feeding the embassies secrets they already knew, now slily lending a hand to the love-making. With his spiels and shrugs and sallies, his messy air of heading a second-rate fraternal order rather than a nation, Mr. Ustinov the actor shone. But Mr. Ustinov the author did not. One reason was that *Romanoff and Juliet* should not have been a play; it should have been a musical comedy. Unorchestrated, its spoofing (of the U.S. and the U.S.S.R. alike) seemed mild and over-familiar; unvocalized, its romance consisted of lovers who did little but kiss when together and mope when apart. Had the lovers moped to music, had the ambassadors unbent in patter songs, had the public square swarmed and whirled with dancers, the show—and not just the star of it—might have been fun.

The other English author whose acting far surpassed his play-writing was Noel Coward. In *Nude with Violin* he wrote of a just-dead and extremely famous painter who, it turned out, had never painted a single one of his pictures. As the painter's cheeky, in-on-the-swindle valet, Coward buzzed about while the dead man's family tried to hush up a scandal and to cope with the various people who had done the actual painting. As an endlessly repeated joke—it could hardly be called a satire—about modern art and gullible art collectors, a never too diverting play turned more and more wearisome. *Nude with Violin* was, more accurately, Noel with just one string to his bow. As an actor, however, Coward was well placed for the goofy badinage, posh billingsgate and pecks that leave toothmarks which are his forte. But they were false-tooth marks at best, and not very many of those.

In *Nature's Way* Herman Wouk was also whacking modern art, but much else besides. A loud farce about a young musical-comedy composer and his wife, the play opened forte, with the wife six months pregnant. Next it revealed fortissimo that the two were four months married. Then arrived the composer's homosexual collaborator, to lure the husband to Venice as a better place to work. Other callers were a very modern and muddled obstetrician, a ruthless lady decorator, a second homosexual, and at length a batch of shoddy theatre folk. On the surface *Nature's Way* was just one more frantic farce that relied for its laughs on gamy subject-matter rather than witty treatment; but as the show proceeded it became clear that there was a message in Mr. Wouk's madness—that with every tasteless gag he was thwacking whatever repelled him as new-fangled or decadent in modern life. If the result proved generally deplorable, it was easy to see why. Had Mr. Wouk sought merely to amuse, his theme demanded not the ripe tomatoes of farce but the *sauce tartare* of a satiric comedy of manners. And if his concern was not just manners but morals, and his mood not amusement but anger, he should have wielded an honest whip. As it was, his exalting nature's way as opposed to society's waywardness seemed no gayer in approach than it seemed serious: it seemed, as a matter of fact, chiefly commercial.

Though not Jean Anouilh's only play with fairy-tale trimmings, *Time Remembered* was perhaps the first in which the bad fairy—far from triumphing or causing trouble—was not even allotted a role. At most, the ironist in Anouilh from time to time jabbed the romantic; nowhere did the cynic throttle him, and Anouilh awarded Cinderella her Prince Charming without any sudden rushing from ballrooms or bother of trying on shoes. A pretty-nothing about a young prince who is disconsolate over the death of a ballerina, the play tells how his lovably wacky aunt finds a young milliner who resembles the ballerina, and successfully schemes that her nephew shall fall in love anew.

There was something less moonlit than floodlighted about the play, which was most rewarding—in fact, very good fun—when it became a stylish theatre piece full of little acting doodads and knickknacks— a trio practicing orchid-eating, a wild snatch of *Swan Lake,* a quite mad hunting scene. Regarded as a story, as a sophisticated fairy tale, *Time Remembered* was sheer Molnar, without being sheer enough. To be sure, Anouilh had provided some good writing and elegant mannerisms. But the play lacked Molnar's élan, as well as any sustained sprightliness of its own. It often seemed merely thin where it should have been diaphanous, merely slight where it ought to have seemed airy. Perhaps it needed a born pastry-cook like Molnar, with his delicately browned and bite-sized ironies, his lightly philosophic macaroons. Or perhaps it needed the menacing side of a proper fairy tale—a wicked fairy, or a fuming stepsister, or a missing slipper. For all its undoubted graces, it fell short.

Sam Locke's *Fair Game* concerned a young, attractive, modest-budgeted divorcée who came to New York to study at City College, modeled size-tens in the garment center to help pay her bills, and soon had half the garment trade making improper proposals. One of Broadway's recurrently breezy, mass-aimed, gag-and-garter comedies, *Fair Game* had its quota of lively situations and bright broad lines. But bad hobbled after good, the crude latched onto the clever in a never-change-the-subject exploitation of the girl-who-cried-wolf theme. And *Fair Game* not only spelled out every word; it had a resolutely meager vocabulary.

Mass-aimed comedy reappeared in Norman Krasna's *Who Was That Lady I Saw You With?* Here a chemistry professor's wife caught him kissing a girl student and at once started packing for Reno. A pal of the culprit's, trying to be helpful, cooked up the explanation that the kiss was part of the professor's job as an FBI man. This had an out-of-the-frying-pan effect, for though the wife was mollified, the FBI got wind of the story; wheels began to turn, wires to cross, and the plot not only thickened but broadened and lengthened as well. For not quite half the evening, the play—though gagged to the windpipe—had its fair share of laughs. It had them, in part, just because the situation was so insanely silly; knowing he couldn't make his premise hold water, Mr. Krasna got a good deal of fun out of the way it leaked. But as the FBI got more and more involved, fun that was meant to snowball proceeded to melt. Silliness, instead of turning cartwheels, dragged a leg; acute FBItis set in, and at length came that death rattle for farce, when the play was

Ray Walston, Mary Healy and Peter Lind Hayes in "Who Was That Lady I Saw You With?"

in far worse trouble than the characters. For all its bounciness at the beginning, *Who Was That Lady I Saw You With?* eventually came to seem as long-drawn-out as its title, and pretty nearly as old hat.

Say, Darling, by Richard and Marian Bissell and Abe Burrows, proved a sort of part-time musical made out of a book that in turn had described how a big-time musical was made out of a book. In other words, *Say, Darling* the novel had chronicled how Mr. Bissell's earlier novel *7½¢* was converted into *The Pajama Game. Say, Darling* the novel took much harder pokes at show business than *Say, Darling* the play did; but as a mere monkeyshine on the making of musicals, and as the far-from-spiritual autobiography of a

fledgling librettist, the play bumped and bounced along fairly cheerfully.

The hep, sharp-tongued, Bissell-like fledgling of the novel had
far less individuality on the stage. On the stage *Say, Darling* came
off best as a kind of production trek—producers' offices, auditions,
rehearsals, hotel rooms, feuds. What with the high dudgeon and
the low language, the caricaturing of what was done and the making
wisecracks of what was said, even what failed to be authentic show
business made breezy vaudeville. Truly fresh and funny was a
young co-producer, a long-on-argot but short-on-savvy brat-about-
town, delightfully played by Robert Morse. For the rest, *Say
Darling* proved only passable entertainment, partly from a failure
of nerve—it offered many more clichés about show business than
genuine insights; and partly from a failure of high spirits—it needed
scenes where hilarity explodes and nonsense mounts. Above all, for
the show-within-the-show, it demanded of the composer, Jule Styne,
either far better music than he wrote, or far worse. If accuracy
was not to be the touchstone, then lunacy ought to have been.

It was—as has almost become standard—an extremely slim season
for revivals of the classics, even modern ones. Doubtless such luxuries are all very well for Off Broadway, but why should any name
producer of the richest city in the richest country in the world even
once in a season offer Shakespeare, let alone Sophocles or Molière
or Ibsen? Around Thanksgiving there was, however, a *Country
Wife* (in the most barn-like of all Broadway's theatres) and during
the spring there was a drastically cut *Back to Methuselah*. Despite
how much was wrong with it, *The Country Wife* was on the whole
enjoyable, thanks chiefly to Julie Harris in the title role—her
Margery Pinchwife was all gurgle and prance; and to Pamela Brown,
whose Lady Fidget was all polish and sneer. The two ladies played
rings around Laurence Harvey's too frilly Horner; in fact the whole
production was in a too foppish and falsely Restoration style.
Dancing pumps may suit Wycherley's masterpiece better than clogs,
but neither is ideal: the play needs vitality as well as manner. Full
though it is of both lust and lustiness, Wycherley did not write it
only to amuse: even as it leers, it looks people up and down; even
as it romps, it indicts. A panoramic view of sex, it saw in sex the
key to a whole faithless, dissolute, pleasure-loving society.

Back to Methuselah had not been seen on Broadway since the
original three-nights-long production in 1922. Cut to one night by
Arnold Moss, it still seemed sadly longwinded. With much help
from an unhappy production, Shaw's most ambitious stage work

Arthur Treacher, Tyrone Power, Faye Emerson, Arnold Moss and Valerie Bettis in "Back to Methuselah"

seemed also his most nearly solemn and most tediously absurd.   In the course of a narrative that begins in the Garden of Eden and clumps on to 31,958 A.D., Shaw cavepainted, blueprinted, skywrote his own memoir and futurama of mankind, insisting that man's present life-span is too short for the good life, and contending that if men but wish hard enough to live for centuries they can.   Here, as 20 years earlier in *Man and Superman,* Shaw exalted the Life Force; but like so many sequels, *Back to Methuselah* is inferior stuff.   Most vulnerable in the play is the mysticism that was the soft underbelly of Shaw's rationalism: his play is a coldly futuristic, inhumanly fleshless paean to pure essence.   Most repellent is the wet-fish asceticism that G.B.S. elevated from a personal trait into a philosophic ideal.   Where, in the brilliantly dialectical Hell Scene of *Man and Superman,* Shaw seemed a reverberant iconoclast, in *Back to Methu-*

selah he seemed a chilling crank. To be sure, in drastically cutting *Back to Methuselah,* Mr. Moss removed almost everything that cut two ways. Yet even what was left, if more medicinal than mischievous, was often fine and bracing prose—except that the cast, instead of making it crackle, intoned it with a depressingly cult-like fervor.

What stood out, several times very happily, during '57–'58 were certain special forms of theatre—readings, impersonations, and actual or essential one-man shows. Two of the best such occasions came early in the season. In *I Knock at the Door* Paul Shyre had made a very engaging reading version of the first volume of Sean O'Casey's autobiography. Six people, seated in front of lecterns, recounted a late-Victorian Dublin childhood that ends when a twelve-year-old boy has "learned poethry and kissed a girl." The boy who was to become O'Casey grew up, threatened with blindness, in a shabby and fiercely Protestant home watching his father die; while his already hard-beset mother was caught between doctor's orders to keep the child out of doors and the rector's insistence that he go to school and church. But the story had humor too, and small-boy adventuring, and a child's awareness that a world presented to him by Victorian grownups as square was for all that round. Being a reading version, *I Knock at the Door* very wisely put deft storytelling ahead of theatrical effect, and showed that if four walls and a passion are enough for a good play, almost as much can be achieved with six chairs and a prose style.

Even more notable was *A Boy Growing Up*—Emlyn Williams' reciting or interpreting or impersonating Dylan Thomas's tales of his "young dog" days. Eventually indeed, Williams and Thomas triumphantly became one. On a stage with a single chair, Williams expanded now into a lusty segment of Wales, now into a mad but exact re-living of childhood, now into a whole lurching animal-or-chestra of fun. He was Dylan Thomas, he was Dylan Thomas's characters, he was Dylan Thomas as a character; but as he dug into people, he dug equally into the prose, projecting every sharp-eyed cockeyed image, finding a broomstick for every airborne prank, split-seconding every doltish or schoolboy joke. If here and there the material had its weakish moments, or the performer his slightly too showy ones, the evening as a whole—which reached its peak in the marvelously demented *Adventures in the Skin Trade*—quite blotted them out.

There were a number of other special or hybrid offerings. *Simply Heavenly* was an Off-Broadway show that, having to move when its theatre was condemned, blithely moved to Broadway. With a book and lyrics by Langston Hughes and music by David Martin, it was scarcely a musical or a vaudeville and certainly not a play: a cheerful Harlem yarn with an unpressured sense of fun about it, it exhibited considerable clumsiness and an interminable love story. On Broadway, as it might not have done Off, it seemed inadequate. Though technically a revue, *Mask and Gown* was chiefly an evening with T. C. Jones, who had achieved overnight recognition, in *New Faces of '56,* as a female impersonator. When not mimicking Bette Davis, Louella Parsons, Judy Holliday or, most notably, Tallulah Bankhead, Jones gossiped and gamboled like a light comedienne. The comedienne gift is his truer one, though once the Man-Plays-Girl angle runs smooth, Jones is only as good as his material. The show, which included four other young people, ran much too long; and if the best of Jones added up to a sprightly act at a night club, the rest of Jones had all the fumbled jollity of a Club Night.

Though technically a variety show, *International Soiree* devoted its whole second half to France's famous blonde singer Patachou. Despite gamine bits and husky-voiced Parisian touches, Patachou proved a pure nightclub-personality girl, whose way with a song was merely part of her way with a crowd, and whose appeal—half physical and half fizz—had been worked out to the fifth decimal place. Lacking magic, she had decided know-how even when giving a much too long program in a much too large place.

Back on Broadway after some two years, England's Joyce Grenfell proved once again a gaily chirping mockingbird and impeccably well-bred ape. As a mimic and satirist, Miss Grenfell's range is not large, her lunges do not cut very deep, and half a loaf of her is, on the whole, better than all of one. But her art, if thin, is pure; and it is an art—the same that most richly flowered with Ruth Draper. In contrast to so well-bred an ape, the West Coast's Mort Sahl seemed a harangue-outang. Taking over the stage like a trained filibuster, Mr. Sahl ran on and on and on, a Beat-Generation Savonarola who cracked his whip up Pennsylvania Avenue one minute, down Madison Avenue the next. Ostentatiously irreverent, he was sometimes witty, oftener flip; sometimes sharp, oftener merely outspoken. In a theatre grown rather stuffy, he was a nice fresh breath of carbon monoxide; but besides talking far too long, he seemed too smug, too pleased with his manner and his mission. The danger, always, with anyone as much commentator as jokester is that the mocking will grow into the messianic; and already Sahl's audience have the air of followers rather than fans.

In a season when Off Broadway continued to spread and grow, so leading a playwright as Tennessee Williams chose to have his

Ken LeRoy, Chita Rivera, Larry Kert, Carol Lawrence an

double bill, *Garden District,* produced in an Off-Broadway house; and thanks to the second of the two plays, *Suddenly Last Summer,* achieved a striking success. The play, though lacking significance from an excess of sensationalism, was further proof that Williams, at his best, is unsurpassed in the American theatre at weaving dark spells, and unequaled at writing long, full-breathed dramatic arias. Similarly, two seasons after his *Waiting for Godot* had appeared on

Micky Calin in "West Side Story"

Broadway, Samuel Beckett's *Endgame* took place Off. The narrative of this pessimistic, not to say despairing work, is simply the last futile moves on an almost deserted chessboard, the last speculations and moans at the cemetery gates. As offered in a not well unified production, *Endgame* seemed less rewarding than when read; but whether or not the work of a real writer for the stage, it was clearly the work of a real writer. The Phoenix Theatre—roughly the point

where Broadway and Off Broadway meet—had one of its more interesting seasons. It opened with an adaptation of Schiller's *Mary
Stuart* which, as staged by Tyrone Guthrie, was good highbusted,
brass-throated, old-style theatre—all bravura and brag, and rushing
from one emotional exclamation point to another.   Guthrie next
staged Capek's *The Makropolous Secret,* which was chiefly notable
for Eileen Herlie's playing an opera-singer role to the richly
encrusted hilt.   Thereafter the Phoenix revived Cocteau's *The Infernal Machine,* a kind of revised and enlarged *Oedipus Rex* that,
starting off too much like a stunt and winding up too much like
Sophocles, seemed more interesting than successful.   In addition to
its revivals, the Phoenix offered a twin bill by Europe's well-known
avant-garde playwright, Eugene Ionesco, *The Chairs* and *The Lesson.*   *The Chairs,* thanks in large part to clever stagecraft and staging, proved effective; *The Lesson* on the whole did not.

Reckoning in the special revues and vaudevilles already mentioned, '57-'58 was a busy one in the musical field, with enough
on the good or passable side to excuse if not quite offset the bad.
For the bad was very bad, and there was very mediocre stuff to boot.
The musical season opened strong, with *West Side Story.*   This
proved an extremely popular re-telling, in terms of youthful gang
warfare, of *Romeo and Juliet.*   It also suggested that the salvation
of the serious musical (which in trying to blend text and music all
too often makes them collide) may lie at times in a third element,
dancing.
Certainly the impressive thing about *West Side Story* was the
dancing.   Jerome Robbins, as both director and choreographer of the
show, somehow made the feet that propelled the whole production
be equally the shoulders on which it rested.   As a master of patterned action, he expressed the tensions, the at once instinctive
hates and induced animosities, the juvenile-delinquent heroics and
brooding outcast rancors of Manhattan's rival gangs.   His switch-
blade rumblers jeered and snorted, crouched and slithered and
sprang; so that beyond vitalizing gang emotions and techniques,
Mr. Robbins managed to dance much of the documentary drabness
out of the story and most of the sociological shockingness into it.
Neither the music nor the book approached the choreography,
though Leonard Bernstein did better with his harsh, tingling music
for the dancers than with his lyrical duets and the like.   In terms
of story, Shakespeare's High-Renaissance ardors and angers do not
translate into Manhattan barbarism, and Arthur Laurents' fire-es-
cape balcony scenes and corner-drugstore Friar Lawrences were

tinged with bathos as well as corniness. And, quite aside from Shakespeare, wherever *West Side Story* turned away from what was savage, it proved far more sentimental than touching. Distinguished merit *West Side Story* quite lacked; but its distinguishing merit, its putting choreography foremost, may have been a milestone in musical-drama development.

Copper and Brass, a musical about New York's Finest in which Nancy Walker played a boneheaded cop, proved too much—or too little—for its engaging star. Left to her own devices—running amuck, as a plainclotheswoman, in a fur piece, or turning into a sort of basket case in the depths of a wildly modernistic chair—she could be fun. But everything about the show itself, whether spoken or danced or sung, had a police-shoes lightness and charm; indeed, *Copper and Brass* was almost everywhere lead.

Jamaica, boasting Lena Horne, had a good deal that was stylish and charming. To be sure, there was more atmosphere than action, and more grace than speed: even the humor was covert, and the book, frankly, had an idiot simplicity and almost insolent lack of purpose. But it was the sort of book that timidly shuffled around between tunes; and Harold Arlen's tunes had individuality and an island charm. They set off the beauty and elegant sexuality of Miss Horne twisting about in her tight-curving fishtail skirts. Indeed, the whole insouciantly strummed and strutted show achieved what something so frilly demanded—style. If *Jamaica* had almost no Broadway snap, it had even less Broadway brassiness. If it was a Jamaica with little ginger and no rum, those, after all, are largely its exports. From a musical-comedy standpoint, Lena Horne and gay colors and even a shiftless, lie-in-the-sun libretto represent its tourist attractions.

Rumple—which was the name of a newspaper-cartoon character in danger of extinction because his creator had lost the power to portray him—was predominantly a mess. The story clumped its senseless, longwinded way, broken in upon by unrewarding tunes and monotonously frenzied dances; in fact, the evening's only asset was that jaunty master of the soft shoe, the dead pan and the faraway smile, Eddie Foy. But even he could not move with the show; he could only draw attention away from it, like someone marching exuberantly out of step.

Christmastide brought *The Music Man*, with Meredith Willson— as librettist, composer and lyricist—creating an enormously popular one-man show. And it had, very palpably, a unified style, a sense of one-man showmanship. It had also a sustained swinging tempo: as his own triumvirate, Mr. Willson could escape all the Stop and

Go, all the Detour and Closed-for-Repairs signs, of musical-comedy collaboration. With Robert Preston, who had never danced or sung during twenty years in show business, becoming at a bound a brilliant song-and-dance man, Willson's 1912 yarn of a musical ignoramus who invades an Iowa town posing as a band-leader, had unrationed, old-fashioned, bring-the-whole-family high spirits.

All this, beautifully exploited in Morton da Costa's expert staging, gave *The Music Man* its contagious exuberance, and left only the more sour-pussed or critical-minded noticing that in theme the show was just one more sentimental-satiric bit of hoky poky, often even a sort of kids' show, that had also its sinking spells of wit and mild rashes of cuteness. Furthermore, the second half had an air of playing back much of the first and of lingering over a decidedly uninspired romance. Happily, *The Music Man* even walked backward and downhill with a certain élan; there was never any denying its bounce. Indeed, rather than seeming just sung or danced or chanted, its production numbers often seemed spieled or shilled, had often an infectious carnival air and ballyhoo rhythm. If *The Music Man* was not cream, but only nice fresh half-and-half, it did catch the jubilant old-time energy of a small-town jamboree.

With *The Body Beautiful* the musical season lapsed once more into the mediocre. A show about the fights world, *The Body Beautiful* was most sprightly when least pugilistic, as in a comedy scene in a steam room or with a bunch of small-fry warblers. But its bright spots were mere holidays in a lackluster year. The show's tunes seemed sold by the dozen, its gags came ready to serve, there was too much trite and tired business for even the tired businessman.

Derived from Alec Guinness's triumphant movie, *The Captain's Paradise, Oh Captain!* shimmered with musical-comedy possibilities and for a time aroused hopes. In addition to its amusing set-up of a Channel skipper who leads a wholesome domestic life in England while keeping a love nest in France, there were pleasant performers, here a nice tune or dance bit, there a nice dab of satire. Unhappily, as the plot thickened, the fun turned thin, and what should have had the naughty lure of Paris had only Broadway's routine hotcha. In time both the show and José Ferrer's staging of it not only lacked all taste of dry champagne, there was no longer even any gay popping of corks.

The last of the season's musicals should achieve a niche of sorts in Broadway history. *Portofino*—laid in Portofino during a *festa*—went back at least fifty years for what it wanted to do and to well before the Flood for how it did it. Perhaps once or twice, during a bit of dance routine, *Portofino* rose out of hopelessly vulgar amateurishness to almost professional banality.

THE SEASON IN CHICAGO

By Claudia Cassidy
Drama Critic, Chicago *Tribune*

COUNTING Marcel Marceau, which is a pleasure if perhaps not quite statistical cricket, ten shows played Chicago last season. Seven of them were shown to the 16,700 subscribers of the Theatre Guild-American Theatre Society, who got a refund because they had paid for eight. The best of the meager lot were *My Fair Lady* and *The Waltz of the Toreadors,* which were on subscription, and *Long Day's Journey into Night, Separate Tables* and Mr. Marceau himself, which were not.

Then why the refund? *Separate Tables* ran two and a half weeks, plainly not enough for the three-week subscription. Why not have rearranged the booking with the Guild's plump guarantee? Who knows the answer to that one? *Long Day's Journey into Night* played no matinees. Neither did the Guild's own O'Neill marathons, *Strange Interlude* and *Mourning Becomes Electra.* This time the lack of them was deemed an insuperable barrier. Subscription's most enticing plum, *My Fair Lady,* played three weeks of theatre parties before subscribers got a look at it. Perhaps its most surprising choice, *Compulsion,* was canceled after a queasy cat-and-mouse game with the Nathan Leopold parole.

Viewed from the New York point of vantage, just naming the Chicago shows is not enough. Even by overland journey they can suffer surprising sea change. These were our specimens of "living theatre" as the phrase goes in the realms of managerial council:

The Diary of Anne Frank, still with Joseph Schildkraut, but with an "actressy" Anne named Abigail Kellogg, and a shift in direction to underscore what probably was meant to be the light touch.

Middle of the Night, still with Edward G. Robinson, but with an inferior cast presumably directed with a crowbar. The playbill said "A Joshua Logan production . . . directed by Joshua Logan." A poster outside the theatre had a pasteover job reading "Directed by Joshua Logan . . . staged by Curt Conway." It was believed that Mr. Logan had taken a powder.

The Happiest Millionaire, still with Walter Pidgeon, and more

39

Summer exodus '57: the Broadway haywagon

bound for the straw-hat trail

happily still with George Grizzard, who cheered up a bleak joke perhaps private to Philadelphia.

The Most Happy Fella, still with Robert Weede and all the corn, but with a singularly unattractive cast apparently rehearsed in a boiler factory.

Visit to a Small Planet, still with Cyril Ritchard, who had at us with considerable archness, spurring a substitute cast to serious indiscretions.

On the other hand:

My Fair Lady came to town with more than $675,000 in the advance till, and six months later was still ahead of the game by half a million. Not just a stunning copy of a brilliant musical, but a beguiling show with a personality of its own. Anne Rogers, Brian Aherne, Charles Victor (a superior Doolittle) and Hugh Dempster headed a front rank company with a wonderfully spirited set of dancers. Everything off the top shelf, audiences enchanted, theatre as it should be. When Mr. Aherne quit at the end of June Michael Evans who had been playing the fake professor of phonetics, stepped blithely in. Mr. Evans was once the Gaston to Audrey Hepburn's Gigi, which gives you the idea.

Long Day's Journey into Night was another instance of what producers worth their salt can do. Nothing about the production was cheapened, nothing left undone. Careful casting brought us the Irish actor, Anew McMaster, with Fay Bainter, Roy Poole and Chet Leaming in a magnificent performance of a searing play. When Miss Bainter fell ill Ruth Nelson stepped in and turned out to be head and shoulders the finest of the three actresses who had played Mary Cavan Tyrone. She so dominated the part that for the first time I forgot to be haunted by the conviction that only the late Laurette Taylor really could have played it.

The Waltz of the Toreadors was less completely successful, but Melvyn Douglas and the Wagnerian Lili Darvas were the toast of the town for their scene of mortal combat in Anouilh's wittily bitter farce, and the mischievous casting of Paulette Goddard as Mlle. de Ste.-Euverte was its favorite topic of theatrical speculation.

Separate Tables, still with Eric Portman, Beryl Measor and William Podmore, had an interesting replacement in Geraldine Page. Everyone expected Miss Page to be good as the shambling wreck of the put-upon daughter, but she surprised us with the way she moved into the role of the fading beauty whose faint voice and ravaged eyes suggested the drugged fascination to which even a sensible man might become addicted.

If you wandered outside the loop you had the luck to find Emlyn

An out-of-town opening

Williams turning on the salt sea spigot of the Dylan Thomas *A Boy Growing Up,* and the misfortune to discover that Norman Corwin's pedestrian treatment of the Lincoln-Douglas debates (with Raymond Massey and Martin Gabel) missed the point the title, *The Rivalry,* understood.

With so little available in what by habit we call the season, some of what summer theatre offered was fresher, if makeshift. Burgess Meredith caught the drollery of *The Circus of Dr. Lao,* Buster Keaton had a fling at *Merton of the Movies,* and there were tryout glimpses of *Back to Methuselah* and *The Man in the Dog Suit.*

While theatre withered on the thinning vine the Chicago Symphony Orchestra flourished, Lyric Opera had its most prosperous season, and concerts and ballet had a busy winter. A wide screen cloud on the horizon is the leasing of the Civic Opera House to Cinemiracle for ten months of the year, leaving October and November open for the Lyric. This fences in opera and crowds out ballet. Committees immediately were formed to (a) restore the historic Auditorium, (b) build a theatre or two in the huge convention hall planned for the lakefront and (c) build a new theatre at an edge of the loop.

It would be nice to have them; nicer to have something to put in them.

Meanwhile, the record for 1957-58:

Shubert Theatre: *My Fair Lady,* 30 weeks, so far.

Erlanger Theatre: 22 weeks—*Cat on a Hot Tin Roof,* 6 held over, 11 in all; *The Diary of Anne Frank,* 10; *Long Day's Journey into Night,* 6.

Blackstone Theatre: 14½ weeks—*The Waltz of the Toreadors,* 5; *The Most Happy Fella,* 7; *Separate Tables,* 2½.

Harris Theatre: 10 weeks—*The Happiest Millionaire,* 6; *Visit to a Small Planet,* 4.

Great Northern Theatre: 6 weeks—*Middle of the Night,* 3; Marcel Marceau, 3.

THE SEASON IN LONDON

By Harold Hobson

Drama Critic, London *Sunday Times*

London Drama Critic, *The Christian Science Monitor*

MY FAIR LADY arrived at Drury Lane Theatre towards the end of the season and she was received royally. I do not mean by this merely that the Queen went to see the fifth performance on one of her rare visits to the theatre. What was particularly pleasurable to the cast, to Alan Jay Lerner, the author of the book and lyrics, to the composer, Frederick Loewe, and to those astute people who administer the Bernard Shaw estate, is that, after the tumult and the shouting which for weeks had preceded the arrival of the musical in London, there was no backwash of resentment, no latent protest against overpublicizing in the first night audience, such as caused *South Pacific* in the same theatre to be very nearly booed. *My Fair Lady* rode a hurricane of applause almost from the rise of the curtain; and this in spite of some disappointments.

The first and greatest of these was Julie Andrews as Eliza Doolittle. Miss Andrews left England a few years ago to play in the *The Boy Friend* in New York. She was then relatively unknown in Britain, except as a child prodigy. We understood that on Broadway she had made a great success, which she confirmed in *My Fair Lady*. We were ready to welcome her back in triumph, and, in our applause on the first night, did our best to do so. But we knew in our hearts that it was all pretense: that Miss Andrews' Cockney is not the real thing; and that, when she abandons dialect to show her love for Higgins in the Queen's English, her acting has nothing more than the laborious earnestness of a teacher of elocution. Some of us, too, were disappointed in the scenery, which seemed to be lavish, but without imagination. There was, however, one thing for which, in all the yelling and screaming that had gone on before *My Fair Lady* opened, we had not been adequately prepared; and it was this thing that made the show a triumph in London as it had been in New York. The Professor Higgins of Rex Harrison is the best Higgins anyone here has ever seen in *Pygmalion;* it is the best performance ever given on an English stage in a musical.

Other Higginses have got the Professor's tetchiness, his insolence,

The intermission t

London theatre

and his wit. What Harrison gives to the part that is unique in my experience is a conviction of devotion to phonetics; and this is something that would have afforded Shaw himself immense pleasure. It is the emotion which Harrison puts into his speech to Eliza about the glories of the English language, and his certainty that she will conquer them, that prepares the way for the triumph of the song, "The Rain in Spain." Harrison's is a wonderful performance, though one regrets that this personable actor now looks so thin, so emaciated, and so careworn. One would like to have seen him play the part a couple of wives ago.

The warmth of the reception of *My Fair Lady* was the more remarkable and the more welcome because the gallery at first nights has been gradually getting savager. Its attitude has now reached a point at which it seems genuinely delighted to give pain. There are moments when one thinks that it needs as much courage for an English company to present a new play as to face a firing squad. This situation began to develop into a fresh phase about eighteen months ago when the gallery at the Saville Theatre interrupted with boos and catcalls almost from the beginning of the second act a play by William Archibald called *The Crystal Heart*. The star was Gladys Cooper, and Miss Cooper is a woman of spirit. When she had to say to one of the characters "You ought to be dead," she turned on her heel and uttered the words to the gallery, which responded, "So ought you and the author." At the end there were cries and shouts of "Where is the author? Let's get at him," and Miss Cooper, with magnificent irony, swept to the howling mob one of the most tremendous curtsies ever seen on the stage.

This year five plays have been hooted; two of them, *Roseland* and John Cranko's off-beat musical, *Keep Your Hair On,* on successive nights: a record in the English theatre. One of the players in *Roseland*—Patrick Doonan, an actor of tough parts—committed suicide soon after its disastrous opening. What is it that causes these distressing scenes? Generally speaking, the first night gallery resents any criticism of Left wing forces and ideas; a play has to be very witty indeed that can criticize the Soviets without being punished for it at the end. It was this, combined with its stupidity, that brought about the downfall of *Bridal Suite,* in which the leading player was James Hayter, a cousin of Sir William Hayter, former British Ambassador in Moscow. Mr. Hayter is a chubby, good-humored man, and he lustily booed back at the gallery when it roared its disapproval of the play. Unlike Miss Cooper's curtsy, which was intended to mock and to hurt (as it rightly did), this lively action of Mr. Hayter's restored some measure of good temper all round, but the piece came off after five performances. To offset these failures, there is Agatha Christie's thriller, *The Mousetrap,* at the Ambassadors, where it has beaten *Chu Chin Chow's* record for the longest-running play on the British stage. It has totaled nearly 2,500 performances.

Altogether the season 1957-58 was highly successful. John Gielgud gave a curiously haunting and uncharacteristic performance in Graham Greene's *The Potting Shed;* Michael Redgrave, forsaking the interminable Shakespeare for a few weeks (after which he left the cast to play *Hamlet* at Stratford), sketched a most likable prig in N. C. Hunter's *A Touch of the Sun* at the Saville, which, in a gentle way, upheld the values of sensibility and art against those of commercial success; John Neville's Hamlet at the Old Vic, though no roof-raiser, was kind and affectingly vulnerable; Ruth Ford played Temple Drake for the English Stage Company in William Faulkner's *Requiem for a Nun* with a bitter, tight-lipped integrity and intensity that, aided by Zachary Scott's quiet, impeccable speaking of some of the author's most tranquil lines, made the play a memorable experience; and an early play of John Osborne's—*Epitaph for George Dillon*—which was written in collaboration with another actor, Anthony Creighton, showed that Mr. Osborne's talent is not a sporadic outburst, but has been developing for some time.

Almost throughout the entire season there has been rumbling discontent with the British censorship of the stage. It broke out into a positive explosion when the Lord Chamberlain refused to license for public performance at the Royal Court Theatre Samuel Beckett's *Endgame.* A year before this play had received a license for performance at the same theatre in French. It was in fact presented in French without interference from the censorship, and no particular deterioration in London's morals followed. It is understood that the Lord Chamberlain objected to one of the characters in the play referring, in a moment of distress, to the Deity as a "bastard." There are rumors that if Mr. Beckett would have changed the offending word to "swine," a compromise might have been reached; but Mr. Beckett stood on his rights as an author, and so far *Endgame* has not been publicly acted in England.

The last has not been heard of all this, for the Government is reported to be considering a new examination of the question of censorship. The present situation is paradoxical in that although plays which have been performed in most countries of Europe and in the United States cannot be publicly seen in London, nevertheless, under the system of club performances, London theatregoers can and do see plays which exceed in unconventionality of morals anything seen on Broadway or in Paris.

The most striking illustration of this is in connection with the subject of homosexuality. This word cannot be mentioned on the British public stage. A play like *Tea and Sympathy,* which recoils from homosexuality with horror, cannot receive a public license in Britain. So far as I know, all the plays about homosexuality which have been banned in Britain edge away from the subject with distress. Yet in a club theatre British theatregoers have this year seen a play, *Quaint Honor,* which deals with the seduction of a schoolboy by an older companion, who then defends with considerable mental agility the view that sexual relations between boys in boarding schools are beneficial and desirable. I do not know of any play in French or English which so unequivocally takes the line that in certain common circumstances homosexuality is to be commended; and it is ironic that it should have been seen by thousands of theatregoers, in a perfectly respectable club theatre, in a country which forbids homosexuality to be publicly mentioned on the stage, even if it is mentioned only to be denounced.

Although the censorship has been a great talking point both in the press and among the public, the most important theatrical development of the season has been the emergence of three new young authors of outstanding promise. For years now the British, when asked point-blank, "Who are your dramatists?", have shifted uneasily, and, with a brave smile replied, "Well, Terence Rattigan is a good craftsman." Twelve months ago Mr. Osborne gave us another name to add to our list, and now we have John Mortimer, Beverley Cross, and Robert Bolt. In background they have little in common except that they all have at some time or another been at a university, Mr. Bolt at Manchester, the others at Oxford or Cambridge. Professionally Mr. Mortimer is a divorce court lawyer, Mr. Bolt a schoolmaster in Somerset, and Mr. Cross, who has had a somewhat roving life, has been a seaman. They have each written fine and successful plays.

The first to make his mark was Mr. Bolt. His *Flowering Cherry* is a pitiless study of a bragging insurance official who maintains himself and his ego on an endless diet of poetic and picturesque spiritual lies. This Cherry was splayed at the Haymarket by Ralph Richardson with superb bravura. Mr. Bolt writes wittily, pungently, and at times with considerable flourishes of rhetoric; but he has a merciless eye for the weaknesses of human character. He is that very rare thing, a romantic realist.

Mr. Mortimer's success has been with two one-act plays, *The*

Dock Brief and *What Shall We Tell Caroline?* They too are studies in the perplexity of the human condition, and the problems it presents. Mr. Mortimer views these things through a peculiar personal fantasy that is very effective on the stage.

Mr. Cross's play, *One More River,* was presented by Sam Wanamaker in the splendid theatrical venture he has started in Liverpool in conjunction with Anna Deere Wiman. It is a play about a mutiny against a cruel and slave-driving captain. It is written in the fashionable vein of anger, and seems another attack on the directing classes. In the end it turns out to be something quite different, but it has a fine virility and vigor.

The arrival of these three young authors is, along with Mr. Osborne, the best sign we have of the vitality of British drama. They are each in an individual way a response to the discontent and challenge of the times, and they give to the English theatre a look of enterprise it has not had for a long while.

OFF BROADWAY

By GARRISON P. SHERWOOD

THE most important single statement in terms of the Off-Broadway theatre during 1957-58 is its further successful expansion. More than forty Off-Broadway theatres are now in use—the exact number is difficult to check accurately because of how quickly some of them come and go. During the season there was a staggering number of productions—over a hundred, in fact. Where in earlier days it was extremely difficult to obtain the services of an actor or actress with even the slightest Broadway reputation, today not only name players but even actual stars enjoy working Off Broadway. All this has given genuine stature and réclame to a number of Off-Broadway productions: indeed, some of them have surpassed the earlier Broadway ones. It will be recalled that when Tennessee Williams' *Summer and Smoke* was first produced on Broadway it had no particular success, but that when revived Off Broadway with Geraldine Page it proved an instant hit—more than that it was perhaps a kind of turning point in Off Broadway's fortunes. Thereafter came the success of other Off-Broadway productions of Broadway plays, notably O'Neill's *The Iceman Cometh*. During the past season the trend continued with Anouilh's *Ardéle* (done on Broadway as *Cry of the Peacock*), Edwin Justus Mayer's long-ago Broadway play *Children of Darkness,* and Arthur Miller's *The Crucible.*

So much success has created problems of its own, and could in fact become a kind of kiss of death. Everybody today wants in, wants a bigger slice of the Off-Broadway dollar. Costs have risen beyond all expectations. Rents in particular have skyrocketed. This is due in part to much better theatre facilities. Take the Cherry Lane as a case in point: five years ago the rental there was $125 a week; today it is $300. But a great deal of money has been spent on improving the Cherry Lane as a theatre. Many houses charge even higher rents, one indeed asking $800. Advertising budgets have perforce risen sharply, with a need of engaging professional press agents. Minimum salaries for stagehands are now about the same Off Broadway as on—$157.50 a week. Some theatres are also required to employ union company managers and treasurers, and in some of the larger houses porters and ushers must be hired. In the "old days" it was not unusual for a producer to do his own sweeping up; today Off Broadway is more and more taking on more and more of Broadway's set-up and personnel. To meet such rising costs, the price of tickets has had to go up and up, sometimes to around a $5 top.

To try to ward off doom, a number of the Off-Broadway producers have organized the League of Off-Broadway Theatres. They have asked the State Labor Board for a hearing in an effort to get Equity to recognize the League as a bargaining agent: the League wants in particular to have Equity amend some of its existing regulations. The whole situation is obviously not an easy one to adjust.

It is time to turn to some of the Off-Broadway productions of last season that have contributed to the situation. *Clerambard* by Marcel Aymé served to bring the French star, Claude Dauphin, to the Rooftop Theatre. So successful was this light comedy, not least because of Dauphin's ingratiating performance, that it had to extend its engagement again and again. *The Brothers Karamazov*, revived at the Gateway Theatre, played to crowded houses for several weeks. Downstairs in the same building is the Cricket Theatre which opened with *Palm Tree in a Rose Garden*, an interesting and provocative play, starring Vicki Cummings, that ran too short a time. At this same theatre during the spring appeared Anouilh's *Ardéle*, which in a new Lucienne Hill adaptation and with a charming set and a good production proved very entertaining. *Children of Darkness*, staged by José Quintero, proved a hit at the Circle-in-the-Square. Garcia Lorca's *Blood Wedding* received fine notices, as did a revival of *The Boy Friend* that should run for a year or more. In association with The City of New York, Joseph Papp offered some interesting revivals of Shakespeare that proved very popular.

Perhaps the most exciting and certainly the most talked-about production of the Off-Broadway season was Tennessee Williams' *Garden District*, consisting of two plays, *Something Unspoken* and *Suddenly Last Summer*. There were things in this double bill that represented Mr. Williams at both his best and his worst; in the far more effective *Suddenly Last Summer*, vividly directed by Herbert Machiz, Hortense Alden and Anne Meacham both scored by their acting (at this writing, Ann Harding has been lured out of retirement to replace Miss Alden). *The Crucible*, at the Martinique Theatre, proved in the opinion of many reviewers to be far better than was the original Broadway production; and Samuel Beckett's *Endgame* at the Cherry Lane, whatever its deficiencies, was a must for the more thoughtful theatregoer. The Shakespearewrights continued

*Musical comedy—
or musical serious?:
the dire occurrences,
awful agonies and
aberrations of the
new musicals are
pushing the old
song - and - dance
shows off the stage*

Tennessee Williams, author of "Garden District"

to please with their splendid revivals and the Equity Library Theatre
continued its activities.   Ben Hecht's *Winkelberg*, a play about the
poet Maxwell Bodenheim, had a disappointing run at the Renato
Theatre.   David Belasco's *Girl of the Golden West*, having Nancy
Wickwire as its greatest asset, was given an interesting but short-
lived revival at the Phyllis Anderson Theatre.   An unusual mood
drama in verse by Ettore Rella, *Sign of Winter*, had a month's run
at Theatre 74, and *Fools Are Passing Through* by Friedrich Duerrenmatt (author of *The Visit*) appeared briefly at the Jan Hus Auditorium.   *Dark of the Moon,* the perennially favored fantasy by
Howard Richardson and William Berney, enjoyed a successful stay
at the Carnegie Hall Playhouse.   Late in the season a farcical *Comic
Strip,* by George Panetta, opened at the Barbizon-Plaza Theatre and
looked promising for a healthy summer run.

   There were also a number of revivals of the classics, among them
Ben Jonson's *The Alchemist*, George Farquhar's *The Beaux Strata-
gem*, Christopher Marlowe's *Edward II*, Ibsen's *An Enemy of the
People*, Victor Hugo's *Gil Blas* and Synge's *The Playboy of the
Western World.*

The list of offerings could be much extended—almost interminably, indeed, if it was to include all Off Broadway's giddier efforts and foredoomed flops. What counts, however, is the increasingly large volume of its healthier activities. And oh, yes—*The Threepenny Opera* continues to run on and on at the Theatre de Lys.

TATTOO ON THE TIMPANI

By Richard Maney
Broadway Press Agent; Author of *Fanfare*

THE conviction that a resourceful press agent can redeem a play or musical that has numbed the reviewers and dismayed the customers, though widely accepted, is as false as the belief that warts will disappear if rubbed with bacon rind or that an enterprise initiated on Friday, the 13th, is doomed. Despite all saws to the contrary, the press agent is yet to be born who can fashion a silk purse from a sow's ear, or forge a goldbrick without compensating straws. Through guile or deception he may momentarily stay *rigor mortis* but he can only insure an audience for the condemned work through liberal use of writs and subpoenas and with promises of transportation to and from the shelter of the proscribed. The press agent for *The Ladder* (1926-28) couldn't trick vagrants into the Mansfield though admission was free and the seats comfortable.

Many stage offerings, to be sure, have prospered without critical blessing. Sufficiently charged with hokum and heroics, or blessed with a glittering star, an inferior work may have popular appeal though it flouts every standard employed from the day of Aeschylus to Tennessee Williams. Triumphs of mediocrity are not peculiar to the theatre. Consider the stamina of TV's Westerns and the literary reign of *Peyton Place.*

However potent their box-office appeal, however intoxicating their allure, stars are no insurance of success. Perhaps a dozen of Equity's elite can create a handsome advance sale and a plethora of theatre parties, but if the work they inhabit is thumbed down by press and public, their magic goes for naught. Even Tallulah's sorceries couldn't salvage *Eugenia,* any more than Ethel Merman, long rated an invincible, could cancel out the apathy loosed by *Happy Hunting.*

The press agent is an invention of the theatre. Up until the early 1900s he confined his activities to it because there was no demand for his services elsewhere. From the start he was identified as a harmless Munchausen, a confidence man given to gilding the lily. He prospered for more than half a century because white paper was

58

From Hollywood to Broadway: (top row) Anne Baxter, Robert Preston, Agnes Moorehead, Karl Malden and Shelley Winters; (bottom row) Joan Blondell, Dorothy McGuire, Lena Horne, Ricardo Montalban, Pat O'Brien and Teresa Wright

cheap, editors were tolerant, and he had little competition in his quest for free space. Another thing worked to his advantage. He could write passes.

The conditions under which he flourished from 1850 to 1915 no longer obtain. Today churches have press agents and so do chop suey parlors, industrial cartels and debutantes. Our political parties have publicists and propagandists and so do the Army, the Navy, the Marine Corps and the Air Force. An actor returning from a tour with a USO unit in the Pacific in 1943 told me the war with Japan was a minor issue. "The hot war is between the press departments of the four branches of our armed services." The struggle for recognition and esteem—even notoriety—is all-consuming. Kings in exile have press agents and so do hamburger heavens, dictators on the lam, Miami Beach and Sun Valley. Many of these would rather be libeled than ignored. Forty percent of the text of the average newspaper is press agent-inspired. What was once a fringe activity suggestive of thimble-rigging or smuggling is now big business or, worse yet, the spokesman for big business.

As currently practiced in the theatre, press agentry is fraught with peril, confusion and mischance. It boils with intangibles, imponderables and, to maim a metaphor, boomerangs. A publicity coup schemed for *The New York Times* may blossom in the *Taxi Age*. Though press agents are often frustrated—modern editors have built-in radars that enable them to detect the bearer of spurious tidings at fifty feet—they are often credited with triumphs of which they wot not. When the Notre Dame band played the entire score of *My Fair Lady* between the halves of the Army-Irish game last October to the delight of 100,000 spectators and 20,000,000 vidiots, the ignorant hailed me as a blend of Aladdin and P. T. Barnum.

Flattered as I was by this tribute, I had to confess that the concert had been pulled off behind my back. I had no more to do with it than I had with the rendition of "I Could Have Danced All Night" and "On the Street Where You Live" at the national political conventions in Chicago and San Francisco in 1956, two séances seen and heard by other millions.

The press agent's product is publicity. Publicity has been defined as "information, with a news value, designed to advance the interests of a place, person, cause or institution, usually appearing in public print." This verdict is cribbed from a work obviously printed before radio and television started to throw their voltage around, before sponsors of floor waxes and deodorants became the arbiters of our cultural fare. The press agent who seeks to dazzle or subdue his prey through these media has one advantage—a captive audience.

In theory the press agent is dedicated to extending the line at the box-office. His degree of success depends upon the skill and insistency with which he can cry the assets of his charge and smother its flaws. A vivacious unknown may rescue a play with structural flaws and plot deficiency. Examples? Audrey Hepburn in *Gigi* and June Lockhart in *For Love or Money*. Thanks to the fascinating conduct of these hoydens both plays prospered beyond their worth.

There's another definition for publicity that will not be found in any dictionary. It's what the average actor seeks, nay demands, and without which he fumes and smolders, regardless of his rank or import. Because of the player's thirst for recognition producers often are able to temper their salary demands with promises of publicity. Called upon to implement these promises, the press agent may find himself defying his own canons, i.e., beating the drum for a drab who in no way enhances the operation. The press agent's life is full of such contradictions. He devotes much of his time to salving

Members of Hollywood's exclusive Comedians' Club, enjoying a quiet Sunday breakfast at the Beverly Hills Country Club, include: (clockwise) Groucho Marx, George Burns, Jack Benny, Danny Kaye, George Jessel, Lou Holtz, the Ritz Brothers, Chico Marx and Harpo Marx

ruffled egos, to arbitrating mutinies, to cajoling the aggrieved and hinting at coups so dark and obscure that he cannot reveal their nature, a tactic coined by Quintus Fabius Maximus in his scuffles with Hannibal.

A minor player in *Twentieth Century* badgered George Abbott and Philip Dunning so persistently that they finally urged me to placate him in some fashion. This mime's talents, it developed, were scant. When I pressed him for a peg on which to hang a short essay, he boasted that, equipped with a magnifying glass and a delicate pen, he could and did inscribe the President's annual State of the Union speech on the face of a postcard. Though stunned by this confession, I fashioned a report on it which appeared on the drama page of an evening paper—this was 1933, when paper was cheap, drama standards low, competition slack. On the publication of this salute, my opponent exulted. He didn't exult for long. A landlady in the Bronx to whom the fugitive was in arrears appeared in the lobby of the Morosco flourishing a notice of garnishment. Moral: It's sometimes better to leave your light under a bushel.

Although most producers feign modesty, even suggest that their significance be soft-pedaled that their colleagues may profit, many of them are as publicity-crazed as any ingénue or prima donna. Indeed Billy Rose's thirst for acclaim surpassed that of any of the llama trainers, leading men or strip teasers over whom he presided in his adventures in and out of doors. It was best capsuled by Richard Rodgers who cornered me in a restaurant to ask, "Has anyone told you that Larry Hart and I are writing the lyrics and music for Mr. Rose's *Jumbo?*"

Desire for publicity, in the case of producers, ebbs with experience. The more service he has seen the less he is impressed by applause. Repetition of a sensation once enjoyed can never approximate the glow born of his first victory. This dictum is to be ignored in the case of acrobats, adagio dancers, character actors, juveniles and soubrettes.

Not all actors are dedicated to the publicity-at-any-cost gambit. Few of them will go to the extravagant lengths or breadths of Jayne Mansfield and other sirens of similar design. Sir Laurence Olivier shrinks from publicity as he would from a *cobra de capello*. He would rather submit to the water drip than face a reporter. "No one ever won an interview!" That's the Olivier slogan. Alec Guinness is indifferent to public testimonials. Given cover treatment by one of our great news weeklies, he brushed it off as balderdash and tommyrot. In common with all players on either side of the ocean, both Guinness and Olivier are inevitably misquoted in interviews.

That's their story. The truth is that, lulled into a sense of well-being by a flattering questioner, actors sometimes blurt out the truth about their associates and employers. On seeing their verdicts in print they are appalled. The vast range between their private and public prejudices and preferences is governed by thoughts of retribution, the potential of unemployment, penalties of ill will and other considerations.

The theatrical press agent prospers who has the respect, if not the affection, of his opponents, the editors and other supervisors of print, sight and sound. He would be well advised not to try to put over a swindle, unless the foe acquiesce in it. Quality has higher rewards than quantity. A paragraph in the *Times* has more impact on the box-office than a column in a tout sheet. Truth is a powerful weapon. It is encountered so rarely that it's often accepted as heresy. The less brazen a bulletin or communiqué, the more effective it is. The publicity potential is increased by the attractiveness and style of its presentation. Insinuation is more to be desired than boasting. Deftness is more profitable than delirium. Scrutinize and study the armor of the opposition. The chinks are there and they can be probed.

The text for this discourse is taken from Ecclesiastes, I, 2: "Vanity of vanities—all is vanity."

THE TEN BEST PLAYS

LOOK BACK IN ANGER

A Play in Three Acts

By John Osborne

[JOHN OSBORNE *was born and brought up in London's Chelsea. He was educated at Oxford, where he was president of the Oxford University Dramatic Society. He started writing for trade magazines, then switched to acting. He was an actor-manager in provincial repertory before joining the English Stage Company. He acted in "Don Juan," "The Death of Satan," "The Making of Moo" and "Cards of Destiny." His "Look Back in Anger" and "The Entertainer" have been produced in leading playhouses throughout Europe. He has directed television for the B.B.C.*]

For the cast listing, see page 288.

EVERYTHING, including the kitchen stove, is gathered under the slanting roof of this one-room attic flat deep in the English Midlands. It is furnished with a double bed, a couple of sagging, seedy armchairs, a so-called dressing table, a dining-room table with chairs, an ironing board and a bookshelf.

On this dreary Sunday afternoon Jimmy and Cliff are sprawled in the armchairs, behind the Sunday papers they are reading. "Why," Jimmy asks, "do I do this every Sunday? Even the book reviews seem the same as last week's. Different books—same reviews. Have you finished that one yet?" Cliff has not. "I've just read," says Jimmy, "three whole columns on the English Novel. Half of it's in French. . . ."

At the ironing board Alison, beautiful and silent, goes about her week's ironing. Her expensive skirt is topped by one of Jimmy's shirts. She looks as sloppy as the men. To make an aimless Sunday pass, Jimmy launches an attack on Alison and on the British upper classes to which she belongs, or belonged. Cliff, either to get on with his reading or to help Alison, tells Jimmy to leave her alone. Jimmy's

"Look Back in Anger": By John Osborne. Copyright © 1957 by Criterion Books, Inc. Published by Criterion Books, Inc. Reprinted by permission of Criterion Books, Inc., New York, N. Y.

decision that he's now hungry brings groans and comments from both of the others. He then retorts that he likes to eat, and likes to live, and wants to read the Sunday papers he's paid his own money for. Cliff, while handing over the paper to Jimmy, catches Alison's eye. Advising her to take it easy, he reaches for her hand. His admiring looks and words draw a smile from her. "Give her finger back, and don't be so sickening," says Jimmy. "What's the Bishop of Bromley say?"

CLIFF (*letting go of* ALISON)—Oh, it says here that he makes a very moving appeal to all Christians to do all they can to assist in the manufacture of the H-bomb.

JIMMY—Yes, well, that's quite moving, I suppose. (*To* ALISON.) Are you moved, my darling?

ALISON—Well, naturally.

JIMMY—There you are: even my wife is moved. I ought to send the Bishop a subscription. Let's see. What else does he say. Dumdidumdidumdidum. Ah yes. He's upset because someone has suggested that he supports the rich against the poor. He says he denies the difference of class distinctions. "This idea has been persistently and wickedly fostered by—the working classes!" Well! (*He looks up at both of them for reaction, but* CLIFF *is reading and* ALISON *is intent on her ironing.*)

Jimmy has lost their attention, yet knowing this, tries only the harder. He suggests that the Bishop of Bromley is merely the nom de plume of Alison's Daddy. Cliff tells Alison to ignore these offensive remarks. Quickly Jimmy asks: "Did you read about the woman who went to the mass meeting of a certain American evangelist at Earl's Court? She went forward, to declare herself for love or whatever it is, and, in the rush of converts to get to the front, she broke four ribs and got kicked in the head. She was yelling her head off in agony, but with 50,000 people putting all they'd got into 'Onward Christian Soldiers,' nobody even knew she was there." Jimmy is ignored. He cries for tea, then decides that's not what he wants. He explodes: "God, how I hate Sundays! It's always so depressing, always the same. We never seem to get any further, do we? Always the same ritual. Reading the papers, drinking tea, ironing. A few more hours, and another week gone. Our youth is slipping away." But he's not going to let it go quietly. To Cliff's suggestion that they go to the movies, Jimmy barks an irritated No. What he wants at this moment is just some ordinary human enthusiasm.

Next, Jimmy turns critical of the way Cliff is slopping around in his new trousers. He even wonders what Cliff would do without him. Alison asks if she can press the trousers. Cliff, after emptying the pockets, takes off his pants and hands them to Alison, while Jimmy grabs at Cliff's matches to light his pipe. This time Cliff objects, and tries to get Alison to protest against the smelly pipe. Alison answers: "I don't mind it. I've got used to it." "She's a great one for getting used to things," says Jimmy. "If she were to die and wake up in paradise—after the first five minutes she'd have got used to it."

Cliff wants a cigarette: Jimmy reminds him of doctor's orders. Told to shut up, he doesn't: "All right," Jimmy says virtuously, "they're your ulcers. Go ahead and have a bellyache if that's what you want. I give up. I give up. I'm sick of doing things for people. And all for what? Nobody thinks, nobody cares. No beliefs, no convictions and no enthusiasm. Just another Sunday evening . . ."

To while away the time, Jimmy now decides to turn on a radio concert. He discovers that it's to be an all-Vaughan-Williams program. "Well, that's something, anyway," he snorts. "Something strong, something simple, something English . . ." Announcing that people like himself are not supposed to be very patriotic, he still can understand how Alison's Daddy must have felt when he came back, with Edwardian memories, from a lifetime in India.

Even Jimmy regrets the passing of that brief and tempting period: "If you've no world of your own, it's rather pleasant to regret the passing of someone else's. I must be getting sentimental. But I must say it's pretty dreary living in the American Age—unless you're an American, of course. Perhaps all our children will be Americans. That's a thought, isn't it?"

This thought falls on deaf ears. Cliff is once more reading. Jimmy turns his attention to Alison and to the only friend of hers that he can bear—the only one who speaks his language, though in a different dialect. When this friend—Webster—comes to see them (Jimmy hopes he won't come tonight), he gets something which he's had from nobody since Madeline. Cliff rouses himself sufficiently to ask who's that. Alison answers: "Oh, wake up, dear! You've heard of Madeline enough times. She was his mistress. Remember? When he was fourteen. Or was it thirteen?" "Eighteen," Jimmy says. Cliff gets mixed up about all Jimmy's women, but wonders if she was the one so many years older than he. "Ten years," says Jimmy. "Proper little Marchbanks, you are!" Cliff says.

Thinking of Monday, and of having to work behind their sweet-stall, Cliff is depressed. Jimmy, his thoughts on Madeline, launches another attack on Alison. Cliff, wanting his trousers, tells Jimmy to dry up. Even Alison begs him not to go on. Jimmy muses: "I don't

think I could provoke her. Nothing I could do would provoke her.
Not even if I were to drop dead." Short of this, Jimmy does his best.
With Alison's Mummy and Daddy as motive power, he makes verbal
dashes in all directions.   He includes a full-bodied description of
Alison's public-school brother, Nigel—"the Platitude from Outer
Space."

Cliff, during this tirade, stares at the floor.   Alison, eyes fixed on
her work, manages to keep on ironing.   Cheated of a response and
determined to draw blood, Jimmy tosses out: "Yes, that's the little
woman's family.   You know Mummy and Daddy, of course.   And
don't let the Marquis-of-Queensberry manner fool you.   They'll kick
you in the groin while you're handing your hat to the maid.   As for
Nigel and Alison"—Jimmy continues in reverent tones—"they're
what they sound like: sycophantic, phlegmatic and pusillanimous."

Cliff wants to turn on the concert, but Jimmy now attacks harder
than ever.   Cliff is troubled.   Alison, leaning against the ironing
board, closes her eyes.   On Jimmy marches.   "God help me," cries
Alison, "if he doesn't stop, I'll go out of my mind in a minute."
That's just fine with Jimmy: he is waiting for her to break.   Managing to control herself, Alison carries on with her ironing, forcing
Jimmy to retreat momentarily and listen to the concert.

As Cliff gets back his pressed trousers with a smile from Alison, he
thanks her with a kiss and an embrace.   They have a cigarette together; then Cliff returns to his newspapers and Alison to her ironing.
Jimmy simultaneously returns to the barricades.   Noticing that Alison's ironing causes static, he takes the noise that women make for
his text.   In the midst of his speech, church bells chime.   Refusing
to be muffled or drowned out by bells, Jimmy dashes for the window
and yowls: "Wrap it up, will you?   Stop ringing those bells!   There's
somebody going crazy in here!   I don't want to hear them!"   "Stop
shouting!" Alison cries.   "You'll have Miss Drury up here."   Jimmy
doesn't give a damn about Miss Drury.   "That mild old gentle-
woman," he growls, "doesn't fool me, even if she takes in you two.
She's an old robber.   She gets more than enough out of us for this
place every week.   Anyway," he finishes her off, "she's probably in
church swinging on those bloody bells!"

After several efforts to divert Jimmy, Cliff starts roughhousing with
him.   They fall on the floor and struggle close to the ironing board.
In due time, Jimmy hurls Cliff deliberately at the board.   It collapses,
and Alison is burnt.   Refusing any apology, she screams at Jimmy
to get out.

Cliff, alone with her, takes her to a chair and helps her as best
he can.   He comforts her, finds bandages, and in a roundabout way

offers her his love. She wants nothing more to do with love. She has had enough.

ALISON—I keep looking back, as far as I remember, and I can't think what it was to feel young, really young. Jimmy said the same thing to me the other day. I pretended not to be listening—because I knew that could hurt him, I suppose. And—of course—he got savage, like tonight. But I knew just what he meant. I suppose it would have been easy to say, "Yes, darling, I know just what you mean. I know what you're feeling." (*Shrugs.*) It's those easy things that seem to be so impossible with us. (CLIFF *stands—holding the bandage, his back to her.*)

CLIFF—I'm wondering how much longer I can go on watching you two tearing the insides out of each other. It looks pretty ugly sometimes.

ALISON—You wouldn't seriously think of leaving us, would you?

CLIFF—I suppose not.

ALISON—I think I'm frightened. If only I knew what was going to happen.

CLIFF (*kneeling on the arm of her chair*)—Give it here. (*She holds out her arm.*) Yell out if I hurt you. (*He bandages it for her.*)

Hesitantly, Alison tells him that she's pregnant. "After three years of married life, I have to get caught out now." It had always been out of the question for them, Alison says—"What with this place, and no money, and oh—everything. He's resented it, I know. . . ." She has no idea what she will do if it's too late. Cliff asks why she doesn't tell Jimmy. "After all," Cliff says, "he does love you. You don't need me to tell you that." "Can't you see?" Alison cries, "he'll suspect my motives at once. He never stops telling himself that I know how vulnerable he is. Tonight it might be all right—we'd make love. But later, we'd both lie awake, watching for the light to come through that little window and dreading it. In the morning, he'd feel hoaxed, as if I were trying to kill him in the worst way of all. He'd watch me growing bigger every day, and I wouldn't dare to look at him." "You may have to face it, lovely," says Cliff.

ALISON—Jimmy's got his own private morality, as you know. What my mother calls "loose." It's pretty free, of course, but it's very harsh, too. You know, it's funny, but we never slept together before we were married.

CLIFF—It certainly is—knowing him!

ALISON—We knew each other such a short time, everything moved at such a pace, we didn't have much opportunity. And afterwards, he actually taunted me with my virginity. He was quite angry about it, as if I had deceived him in some strange way. He seemed to think an untouched woman would defile him.

CLIFF—I've never heard you talking like this about him. He'd be quite pleased.

ALISON—Yes, he would. (*She gets up, the clothes folded over her arm.*) Do you think he's right?

CLIFF—What about?

ALISON—Oh—everything.

CLIFF—Well, I suppose he and I think the same about a lot of things, because we're alike in some ways. We both come from working people, if you like. Oh, I know some of his mother's relatives are pretty posh, but he hates them as much as he hates yours. Don't quite know why. Anyway, he gets on with me because I'm common. (*Grins.*) Common as dirt, that's me. (*She puts her hand on his head and strokes it thoughtfully.*)

With a kiss, Cliff advises Alison to tell Jimmy that she is pregnant. Jimmy enters at this point and merely glances at the two of them embracing. Then, without really looking at Alison, he inquires how her arm is. Cliff says: "She's beautiful, isn't she?" After more of this, Jimmy remarks: "Why don't you both get into bed and have done with it?" Cliff maintains that Alison is beautiful and that Jimmy's too much a pig to say so. "You're just a sexy little Welsh-man, and you know it!" Jimmy answers. "Mummy and Daddy turn pale, and face the east every time they remember she's married to me. But if they saw all this going on, they'd collapse."

Trying to re-establish himself, Jimmy is friendly and pleasant. As Alison, disengaging herself from Cliff, looks for a cigarette, Jimmy remarks that Cliff is getting to look more like a randy little mouse every day. Mouselike, Cliff capers about, then leaves to buy some cigarettes. By this time Jimmy wants to apologize, and Alison wants to forgive. "There's hardly a moment when I'm not watching and wanting you," Jimmy says. "I've got to hit out somehow. Nearly four years of being in the same room with you, night and day, and I still can't stop my sweat breaking out when I see you doing—something as ordinary as leaning over an ironing board." They make up with a passionate kiss. Jimmy knows what he would like to do right now. Alison reminds him that Cliff will be back in a minute. "What did he mean by 'don't forget'?" Jimmy asks.

ALISON—Something I've been meaning to tell you.

JIMMY (*kissing her again*)—You're fond of him, aren't you?
ALISON—Yes, I am.
JIMMY—He's the only friend I seem to have left now. People go away. You never see them again. I can remember lots of names—men and women. When I was at school—Watson, Roberts, Davies. Jenny, Madeline, Hugh . . . (*Pause.*) And there's Hugh's mum, of course. I'd almost forgotten her. She's been a good friend to us, if you like. She's even letting me buy the sweet-stall off her in my own time. She only bought it for us, anyway. She's so fond of you. I can never understand why you're so—distant with her.

Alarmed at this different mood, Alison pleads: "Jimmy—please no!" He says she is so very beautiful, "a beautiful, great-eyed squirrel." Delighted, relieved, Alison imitates a squirrel; then, her arms around his neck, calls Jimmy a "jolly super bear" . . . a really sooooooooooooooooper, marvelous bear." Jimmy agrees that bears and squirrels *are* marvelous. Alison dances as squirrels do when they are happy. "What makes you think you're happy?" Jimmy asks. "Everything just seems all right suddenly. That's all. Jimmy—" she says, ready to tell him her news. But Cliff, having gone only to the front door, comes back. Someone is on the phone for Alison.
The second that Alison's friend Helena is mentioned, the affectionate mood is shattered. As Alison leaves, Jimmy demands: "What does she want? What would make her ring up? It can't be for anything pleasant. Oh, well, we shall soon know."

JIMMY (*settling on the table*)—Few minutes ago things didn't seem so bad either. I've just about had enough of this "expense of spirit" lark, as far as women are concerned. Honestly, it's enough to make you become a scoutmaster or something, isn't it? Sometimes I almost envy old Gide and the Greek Chorus boys. Oh, I'm not saying that it mustn't be hell for them a lot of the time. But, at least, they do seem to have a cause—not a particularly good one, it's true. But plenty of them do seem to have a revolutionary fire about them, which is more than you can say for the rest of us.

Talking for the sake of talking, and only half listening to what he says, Jimmy picks up Alison's bag and starts rummaging through it. Going on and on about the "Michelangelo Brigade," he suspiciously looks through his wife's bag hoping to find himself in letters from her mother. He finds nothing. No one even mentions him. As Alison returns, Jimmy spews out: "She writes long letters back to Mummy, and never mentions me at all, because I'm just a dirty word to her too." He throws the letter at Alison's feet, his anger boiling over. "Well," says he, "what did your friend want?"

ALISON—She's at the station. She's—coming over.

JIMMY—I see. She said, "Can I come over?" And you said, "My husband, Jimmy—if you'll forgive me using such a dirty word—will be delighted to see you. He'll kick your face in!"

ALISON (*quietly*)—She's playing with the company at the Hippodrome this week, and she's got no digs. She can't find anywhere to stay—

JIMMY—That I don't believe!

ALISON—So I said she could come here until she fixes something else. Miss Drury's got a spare room downstairs.

JIMMY—Why not have her in here? Did you tell her to bring her armor? Because she's going to need it!

ALISON (*vehemently*)—Oh, why don't you shut up, please!

JIMMY— Oh, my dear wife, you've got so much to learn. I only hope you learn it one day. If only something—something would happen to you, and wake you out of your beauty sleep! (*Coming in close to her.*) If you could have a child, and it would die. Let it grow, let a recognizable human face emerge from that little mass of indiarubber and wrinkles. (*She retreats away from him.*) Please —if only I could watch you face that. I wonder if you might even become a recognizable human being yourself. But I doubt it. (*She moves away, stunned, and leans on the gas stove. He stands rather helplessly on his own.*) Do you know I have never known the great pleasure of lovemaking when I didn't desire it myself? Oh, it's not that she hasn't her own kind of passion. She has the passion of a python. She just devours me whole every time, as if I were some overlarge rabbit. That's me. That bulge around her navel—if you're wondering what it is—it's me. Me, buried alive down there, and going mad, smothered in that peaceful-looking coil. Not a sound, not a flicker from her—she doesn't even rumble a little. You'd think that this indigestible mess would stir up some kind of tremor in those distended, overfed tripes—but not her! (*Crosses up to the door.*) She'll go on sleeping and devouring until there's nothing left of me. (*He exits.* ALISON's *head goes back as if she were about to make some sound. But her mouth remains open and trembling, as* CLIFF *looks on.*)

ACT II

Alison's friend, Helena Charles, is still in the house two weeks later. This Sunday afternoon Helena, in her expensive clothes, exudes authority, but the strain is beginning to tell. She makes the salad for supper, while Jimmy in the next room wails away on his trumpet and Alison, limp from the heat, wishes Jimmy would lose that damned instrument.

HELENA (*pondering*)—It's almost as if he wanted to kill someone with it. And me in particular. I've never seen such hatred in someone's eyes before. It's slightly horrifying. Horrifying—(*she crosses to food cupboard*)—and oddly exciting. (ALISON *faces her dressing mirror and brushes her hair.*)

ALISON—He had his own jazz band once. That was when he was still a student, before I knew him. I rather think he'd like to start another and give up the stall altogether.

HELENA—Is Cliff in love with you?

ALISON—No . . . I don't think so.

HELENA—And what about you? You look as though I've asked you a rather peculiar question. The way things are, you might as well be frank with me. I only want to help. After all, your behavior together is a little strange—by most people's standards, to say the least.

ALISON—You mean you've seen us embracing each other?

HELENA—Well, it doesn't seem to go on as much as it did, I admit. Perhaps he finds my presence inhibiting—even if Jimmy's isn't.

Trying to define her relationship to Cliff, Alison decides: "It's like being warm in bed. You're too comfortable to bother about moving for the sake of some other pleasure." Finding this hard to believe, Helena asks for Jimmy's reaction. Alison thinks that for Jimmy it would be a question of allegiances: ". . . and he expects you to be pretty literal about them. Not only about himself and all the things he believes in, his present and his future, but in his past as well."

On her harrowing honeymoon, Alison had a look at this past. Directly after her wedding, Jimmy took her to his best friend's warehouse flat, where she was at once cut off from all the people she had ever known. It was a nightmare, and having fought with her family, she couldn't ask them to rescue her.

LIBRARY
OF
MOUNT ST. MARY'S
COLLEGE
EMMITSBURG, MARYLAND

Using her as a sort of hostage, Jimmy and his warehouse friend Hugh started inviting themselves in Alison's name to the houses of all her friends, where they would wolf food, cadge drinks, help themselves to cigars and go in for blackmail. People would do anything to be rid of them.

Hearing all this, Helena is incredulous. She can't understand why Alison married Jimmy at all. Alison says that she had no single reason, but many different vague ones. She tries to explain to Helena how unsettled things were when her family came home from India; how strained were her relations with her father. She felt lifeless, and then Jimmy, looking so frail and yet so full of fire, burst upon the scene. Her family's sense of outrage at the very sight of Jimmy settled the matter. Jimmy made up his mind to marry her, and there never seemed any choice for Alison.

Helena wants to know what happened to Hugh. Alison describes Hugh's feelings about the England of the moment and how he decided he must go abroad—to China, or some other God-forsaken place. "He said," Alison recalls, "that England was finished for us, anyway. All the old gang was back—Dame Alison's Mob, as he used to call it. . . ." Jimmy refused to go with him, and accused Hugh of giving up: "He thought it was wrong of him to go off forever, and leave his mother all on her own. He was upset by the whole idea. They quarreled for days over it. I almost wished they'd both go, and leave me behind. Anyway, they broke up. A few months later we came up here, and Hugh went off to find the New Millennium on his own. Sometimes I think Hugh's mother blames me for it all. Jimmy too, in a way, although he's never said so. He never mentions it. But whenever that woman looks at me, I can feel her thinking 'If it hadn't been for you, everything would have been all right. We'd have all been happy.' Not that I dislike her—I don't. She's very sweet, in fact. Jimmy seems to adore her principally because she's been poor almost all her life, and she's frankly ignorant. I'm quite aware how snobbish that sounds but it happens to be the truth."

Helena thinks it high time for Alison either to tell Jimmy about the baby or to get out of this madhouse. She's convinced that Jimmy doesn't know what the word "love" means. Pointing to the toy squirrel and bear on the dresser, Alison tries to explain their game of love as little furry creatures with little furry brains, full of dumb, uncomplicated affection for each other—"a silly symphony for people who couldn't bear the pain of being human beings any longer. And now, even *they* are dead, poor little silly animals. They were all love, and no brains."

Cliff, arriving for tea, is surprised to see Helena all dressed up and Alison obviously fixing to go out. He is even more surprised that they are on their way to church. Jimmy, having put down his trumpet in order to eat, is halfway through his tea before he discovers that Helena's influence is at work—that Alison is going to church. Jimmy, though surprised, is not silenced. He launches a fiendish attack on Alison's mother and ignores Cliff's urgent plea for peace.

Capturing Helena's horrified attention, Jimmy rips into her as well. To him, she is a saint in Dior's clothing, a cow, and a sacred cow at that. When Helena coolly offers to slap his face, Jimmy reminds her that, being no gentleman, he wouldn't hesitate to lay her out. Then, for further effect, Jimmy foists his memories of his father's death on Helena. As a boy of ten he had been with this dying veteran of the Spanish Loyalists. He had learnt of his father's bitterness and despair and of his mother's embarrassment at his father's being on the wrong side. "You see," Jimmy tells Helena, "I learnt at an early age what it was to be angry—angry and helpless. And I can never forget it. I knew more about—love . . . betrayal . . . and death, when I was ten years old than you will probably ever know all your life." Helena, in answer, reminds Alison that it is time to leave, and goes for her things.

In impotent rage, Jimmy cries out that someday Alison may want to come back. "I shall wait for that day," he cries. "I want to stand up in your tears, and splash about in them, and sing. I want to be there when you grovel. I want to be there, I want to watch it, I want the front seat."

Returning with two prayer books, Helena ruins his final effect. "There's a telephone call for you," she says. Certain that it's bad news, Jimmy goes out. Then Helena berates Cliff for allowing this to happen. "I'm not the District Commissioner, you know," Cliff answers. "Listen, Helena—I don't feel like Jimmy does about you, but I'm not exactly on your side either. And since you've been here, everything's certainly been worse than it's ever been. This has always been a battlefield, but I'm pretty certain that if I hadn't been here, everything would have been over between these two long ago. I've been a—a no-man's land between them. Sometimes, it's been still and peaceful, no incidents, and we've all been reasonably happy. But most of the time, it's simply a very narrow strip of plain hell. But where I come from we're used to brawling and excitement. Perhaps I even enjoy being in the thick of it. I love these two people very much. . . . And I pity all of us." He leaves.

Left in full command, Helena carefully outlines the plans she has made. She has wired Alison's father to come and fetch her; when he arrives the next afternoon, Alison is to go home with him. Alison numbly thanks Helena and agrees to go.

Jimmy returns with his unhappy news—that Hugh's mother is very sick. Alison refuses to go with him to see her. Though Jimmy, actually begging, insists that he needs her, Alison turns away; with the church bells ringing, she picks up her prayer book and goes off with Helena.

SCENE II

The following evening, Alison's Colonel father, sitting in one of the battered chairs, watches his daughter pack. It's all beyond him; but though Jimmy speaks a different language, the Colonel regrets now that he and his wife had attempted to interfere. He feels that they were all to blame in one way or another; he even says that perhaps Alison and himself were the guiltiest. At least his wife and Jimmy acted in good faith.

The Colonel thinks that he and Alison find it more comfortable to sit on the fence. "Sitting on the fence!" cries Alison, "I married him, didn't I?" "Oh, yes, you did," the Colonel murmurs. "In spite of all the humiliating scenes and threats!" continues Alison. "What did you say to me at the time? Wasn't I letting you down, turning against you, how could I do this to you, etcetera?" Hedging, the Colonel admits that he is confused, which does not help Alison's own state of confusion. "Why did you ever have to meet this young man?" he asks.

ALISON—Oh, Daddy, please don't put me on trial now. I've been on trial every day and night of my life for nearly four years.

COLONEL—But why should he have married you, feeling as he did about everything?

ALISON—That is the famous American question—you know, the sixty-four dollar one! Perhaps it was revenge. Oh, yes. Some people do actually marry for revenge. People like Jimmy, anyway. Or perhaps he should have been another Shelley, and can't understand now why I'm not another Mary, and you're not William Godwin. He thinks he's got a sort of genius for love and friendship —on his own terms. Well, for twenty years, I'd lived a happy, uncomplicated life, and suddenly this—this spiritual barbarian—throws down the gauntlet at me. Perhaps only another woman could understand what a challenge like that means—although I think Helena was as mystified as you are.

COLONEL—I am mystified. (*He rises and crosses to window.*)
Your husband has obviously taught you a great deal, whether you
realize it or not. What any of it means, I don't know. I always
believed that people married each other because they were in love.
That always seemed a good enough reason to me. But apparently
that's too simple for young people nowadays. They have to talk
about challenges and revenge. I just can't believe that love between
men and women is really like that.

ALISON—Only some men and women.

COLONEL—But why you? My daughter . . . No. Perhaps
Jimmy is right. Perhaps I am a—what was it? an old plant left
over from the Edwardian Wilderness. And I can't understand why
the sun isn't shining any more. You can see what he means, can't
you? It was March, 1914, when I left England, and, apart from
leaves every ten years or so, I didn't see much of my own country
until we all came back in '47. Oh, I knew things had changed, of
course. People told you all the time the way it was going—going to
the dogs, as the Blimps are supposed to say. But it seemed very
unreal to me, out there. The England I remembered was the one
I left in 1914, and I was happy to go on remembering it that way.
Besides, I had the Maharajah's army to command—that was my
world, and I loved it, all of it. At the time, it looked like going on
forever. When I think of it now, it seems like a dream. If only
it could have gone on forever. Those long, cool evenings up in the
hills, everything purple and golden. Your mother and I were so
happy then. It seemed as though we had everything we could ever
want. I think the last day the sun shone was when that dirty little
train steamed out of that crowded, suffocating Indian station, and
the battalion band playing for all it was worth. I knew in my heart
it was all over then. Everything.

ALISON—You're hurt because everything is changed. Jimmy
is hurt because everything is the same. And neither of you can
face it. Something's gone wrong somewhere, hasn't it?

COLONEL—It looks like it, my dear.

When Helena comes in, she finds Alison weeping on her father's
shoulder. The Colonel, with great courtesy, thanks Helena for her
kindness and offers to carry her suitcase for her. But Helena has
other plans. It looks as if she will stay tonight because of a job
appointment the next day in Birmingham.

Cliff, coming in, hears this. He urges Alison to wait for Jimmy
but she refuses. "Who's going to tell him?" Cliff asks. "I can tell

him," says Helena. "That is, if I'm here when he comes back."
"You'll be here," Cliff says quietly.

Having left a letter for Jimmy, Alison leaves with her father.
Cliff has no intention of waiting. "I've had a hard day," he tells
Helena, "and I don't think I want to see anyone hurt until I've had
something to eat first, and perhaps a few drinks as well. I think
I might pick up some nice, pleasant little tart in a milk bar, and
sneak her in past old mother Drury. Here!" Tossing the letter
at Helena, Cliff says: "He's all yours. And I hope he rams it up
your nostrils!"

Alone, Helena aimlessly picks up the teddy bear, sits on the bed,
then leaning back against the pillow, looks at the toy she is holding.

Jimmy arrives in a rage—among other things he was almost run
over by the Colonel's car. He takes Alison's letter, reads it with
angry sneers and warns Helena to stay out of his way if she doesn't
want her head kicked in.

Helena calmly announces that Alison is going to have a baby.
Jimmy is taken aback, not so much by the news as by her.

JIMMY—All right—yes. I am surprised. I give you that. But
tell me: Did you honestly expect me to go soggy at the knees and
collapse with remorse? (*Leaning nearer.*) Listen, if you'll stop
breathing your female wisdom all over me, I'll tell you something:
I don't care. (*Beginning quietly.*) I don't care if she's going to
have a baby. I don't care if it has two heads! (*He knows her
fingers are itching.*) Do I disgust you? Well, go on—slap my
face. But remember what I told you before, will you? For eleven
hours I have been watching someone I love very much going through
the sordid process of dying. She was alone, and I was the only
one with her. And when I have to walk behind that coffin on
Thursday, I'll be on my own again. Because that bitch won't even
send her a bunch of flowers—I know! She made the great mistake
of all her kind. She thought that because Hugh's mother was a
deprived and ignorant old woman, who said all the wrong things
in all the wrong places, she couldn't be taken seriously. And you
think I should be overcome with awe because that cruel, stupid
girl is going to have a baby! (*Anguish in his voice.*) I can't believe it! I can't. (*Grabbing her shoulder.*) Well, the performance
is over. Now leave me alone and get out, you evil-minded little
virgin. (*She slaps his face savagely. An expression of horror and
disbelief floods his face. But it drains away, and all that is left
is pain. His hand goes up to his head, and a muffled cry of despair*

escapes him. HELENA *tears his hand away, and kisses him passionately, drawing him down beside her.*)

ACT III

On a Sunday evening several months later, Jimmy and Cliff are sprawled in their respective armchairs, immersed in the Sunday newspapers. At the ironing board, doing the week's work, stands Helena. The identity of the girl at the ironing board has changed, but life goes on much as usual, though Helena has changed, too: her hair is now down.

Jimmy conducts his usual running commentary on the oddities in the news. Helena, an attentive and participating audience, is only beginning to get used to him. She never used to be sure when he was or wasn't being serious. Cliff advises: "When in doubt, just mark it down as an insult."

Wanting to know their plans for tonight, Jimmy asks if Helena will be going to church. Taken aback, Helena says she doesn't think so. "Do I detect a growing satanic glint in her eyes lately?" asks Jimmy. "Do you think it's living in sin with me that does it? Do you feel very sinful, my dear? Well—do you?" After a lengthy attack on Helena's religion—which has replaced his attacks on Alison's family—he has Helena on the defensive, but not cowed. With Cliff backing her up, she requests that they have just one day without "tumbling over religion or politics." "Yes," says Cliff, "change the record, old boy, or pipe down." Obliging, Jimmy gets up and remarks: "Thought of the title for a new song today. It's called 'My mother's in the madhouse—that's why I'm in love with you.'" Perhaps, Jimmy adds, he could work it into their act. Equally obliging, Cliff joins Jimmy in their familiar music-hall routine, with Helena adding her feed lines from the ironing board.

Afterwards, Jimmy feels he has had enough gagging, and pushes Cliff away. The Sunday roughhousing starts. This time Cliff's only clean shirt gets dirty, and Helena takes it out to the bathroom to wash it. Cliff, Jimmy remarks, doesn't care for Helena. "You didn't seem so very keen yourself once," Cliff replies.

For Cliff, things are no longer the same. He's ready to try something different. For Jimmy, it seems as if he spends his life saying good-bye, but he is willing to let this good, loyal friend go. "And," he adds, "all because of something I want from that girl downstairs —something I know in my heart she's incapable of giving. You're worth a half a dozen Helenas to me or to anyone."

After Cliff gets his shirt from Helena and retires to dry it over the fire in his room, Jimmy says to Helena: "Get yourself glammed up, and we'll hit the town—"

Helena comes to Jimmy, puts out her hand and runs it over his head. "Right from that first night," Jimmy remarks, "you have always to put out your hand to me first. As if you expected nothing, or worse than nothing, and didn't care. You made a good enemy, didn't you? What they call a worthy opponent . . ." Jimmy is almost ready to believe Helena's protestation of love. He's ready, if she'll help him, to close down the sweet-stall and start out from scratch. Helena thinks that's a wonderful idea, as she thinks his next idea—of their going out to a pub and then coming home to make love—equally wonderful.

Kissing Jimmy's hand, Helena moves away to fold the ironing board and get dressed. Jimmy, in turn, starts to hurry up Cliff. Before he can get to the door, it has opened and Alison enters. She wears a raincoat, her hair is untidy, and she looks rather ill. There is a stunned pause.

ALISON (*quietly*)—Hullo.

JIMMY (*to* HELENA, *after a moment*)—Friend of yours to see you. (*He goes out quickly, and the two women are left looking at each other.*)

SCENE II

As Jimmy, in the next room, blows loudly on his trumpet, Alison accepts a cup of tea from Helena. Obviously sick and broken, she does all the apologizing for intruding. When Helena says she has every right to be here, Alison wants no book of rules. She asserts that even before she met Jimmy, she had given up believing in the divine rights of marriage.

This to Helena sounds more and more like Jimmy. Becoming increasingly ashamed, and more like her old "correct" self, she says fiercely: "You talk as if he were a book or something you pass around to anyone who happens to want it for five minutes. What's the matter with you? You sound as though you were quoting him all the time. I thought you told me once you couldn't bring yourself to believe in him." "I don't think I ever believed in your way either," Alison answers. "At least," Helena justifies herself, "I still believe in right and wrong! Not even the months in this madhouse have stopped me doing that. Even though everything I have done is wrong, at least I have known it was wrong." But, as she had written to Alison, she did love Jimmy.

The girls sit talking about him as if he were a character in a novel. They agree that he is futile, that he was born out of his time, and they realize they said all this before Helena had taken Alison's place.

With her sense of good and evil momentarily to the fore, Helena now insists that she is leaving Jimmy. "Oh," she says, "I'm not stepping aside to let you come back. You can do what you like. Frankly, I think you'd be a fool . . . but that's your own business. I think I've given you enough advice."

ALISON—But he—he'll have no one.

HELENA—Oh, my dear, he'll find somebody. He'll probably hold court here like one of the Renaissance popes. Oh, I know I'm throwing the book of rules at you, as you call it, but, believe me, you're never going to be happy without it. I tried throwing it away all these months, but I know now it just doesn't work. When you came in at that door, ill and tired and hurt, it was all over for me. You see—I didn't know about the baby. It was such a shock. It's like a judgment on us.

ALISON—You saw me, and I had to tell you what had happened. I lost the child. It's a simple fact. There is no judgment, there's no blame—

Over the noise of the blaring trumpet, Helena yowls for Jimmy to stop it, for God's sake. She wants to speak to him. "Is your friend still with you?" he calls back, but then enters.

Even Jimmy thinks that Alison looks ghastly and suggests that she'd better sit down. He can see without a diagram what's happened to her. "And doesn't it mean anything to you?" Helena asks. "I don't exactly relish the idea of anyone being ill, or in pain," Jimmy says. "It was my child, too, you know. But it isn't my first loss." "It was mine," says Alison.

Claiming it is none of Alison's doing, Helena tells Jimmy that she is ready to dash for the London train. She sees suddenly, tonight, what she has really known all along: "That you can't be happy when what you're doing is wrong, or is hurting someone else. I suppose it could never have worked, anyway, but I do love you, Jimmy. I shall never love anyone as I have loved you. But I can't go on." Sincerely, passionately, she says: "I can't take part—in all this suffering. I can't!" Jimmy's voice stops her at the door: "They all want to escape from the pain of being alive. And, most of all, from love. I always knew something like this would turn up—some problem, like an ill wife—and it would be too much for those delicate, hot-house feelings of yours." Giving Helena her toiletries and clothes, Jimmy continues: "It's no good trying to fool yourself about love. You can't fall into it like a soft job, without dirtying your hands. It takes muscles and guts. And if you can't bear the thought of messing up your nice, clean soul, you'd better give up the whole idea of life, and become a saint. Because you'll never make it as a human being. It's either this world or the next." Helena goes out quickly.

The church bells' ringing upsets Jimmy further. Again apologizing, and again offering to leave, Alison hears Jimmy say that she denied him the comfort of a small bunch of flowers at the funeral. "The injustice of it is almost perfect!" he cries. "The wrong people going hungry, the wrong people being loved, the wrong people dying." He works on her: "I may be a lost cause," Jimmy says, "but I thought if you loved me, it needn't matter." Alison cries silently.

ALISON—It doesn't matter! I was wrong, I was wrong! I don't want to be neutral, I don't want to be a saint. I want to be a lost cause. I want to be corrupt and futile. (*All* JIMMY *can do is watch her helplessly.*) Don't you understand? It's gone! It's gone! That—that helpless human being inside my body. I thought it was so safe and secure there. Nothing could take it from me. It was mine, my responsibility. But it's lost. (*She slides down against the leg of the table to the floor.*) All I wanted was to die. I never knew what it was like. I didn't know it could be like that! I was in pain, and all I could think of was you, and what I'd lost. I thought: if only—if only he could see me now, so stupid and ugly and ridiculous. This is what he's been longing for me to feel. This is what he wants to splash about in! I'm in the fire, and I'm burning, and all I want is to die! It's cost him his child, and any others I might have had! But what does it matter—this is what he wanted from me! (*She raises her face to him.*) Don't you see! I'm in the mud at last! I'm groveling! I'm crawling! Oh, God— (*She collapses at his feet. He stands, frozen for a moment, then he bends down and takes her shaking body in his arms.*)

JIMMY (*shaking his head and whispering*)—Don't. Please don't . . . I can't— You're all right. You're all right now. Please, I—I . . . Not any more . . . (*She relaxes suddenly. He looks down at her, full of fatigue, and says with a kind of mocking tender irony*)— We'll be together in our bear's cave, and our squirrel's drey, and we'll live on honey and nuts—lots and lots of nuts. And we'll sing songs about ourselves—about warm trees and snug caves, and lying in the sun. And you'll keep those big eyes on my fur, and help me keep my claws in order, because I'm a bit of a soppy, scruffy sort of a bear. And I'll see that you keep that sleek bushy tail glistening as it should, because you're a very beautiful squirrel, but you're none too bright either, so we've got to be careful. There are cruel steel traps lying about everywhere, just waiting for rather mad, slightly satanic, and very timid little animals. Right? (ALISON *nods*.) Poor squirrels!

ALISON (*with the same comic emphasis*)—Poor bears! (*She laughs a little. Then looks at him very tenderly, and adds very, very softly*.) Oh, poor, poor bears! (*She slides her arms around him*.)

UNDER MILK WOOD

A Play in Two Acts

By Dylan Thomas

[DYLAN THOMAS *became one of the best-known and most admired poets of his generation. Born in Carnarthenshire, Wales, he was educated at the Swansea Grammar School. He practiced journalism for a year and did free-lance writing and at the age of 17 had a poem published in a magazine. At 20 he had his first book issued. He gained notice in the United States in 1938 by winning Poetry Magazine's Oscar Blumenthal Prize. In 1939 he turned to prose and wrote a group of stories entitled "The Map of Love." Later came his principal works: "New Poems," "Deaths and Entrances" and "In Country Sleep" in verse, and "Portrait of the Artist as a Young Dog" in prose. Aside from his play "Under Milk Wood," he wrote several radio scripts and a few film scenarios. While on a lecture tour in this country he died in New York, November 10, 1953, at the age of 39.*]

For the cast listing, see page 291.

ON a moonless Spring night in Llareggub, South Wales, "starless and bible-black," one can hear the hushed town breathing . . .

FIRST VOICE—Listen. It is night moving in the streets, the processional salt slow musical wind in Coronation Street and Cockle Row, it is the grass growing on Llareggub Hill, dewfall, starfall, the sleep of birds in Milk Wood. . . .

Behind the eyes of the sleepers, one can hear their dreams. . . . Captain Cat, the retired blind seacaptain, asleep in his bunk in the seashelled ship-in-bottled, shipshape best cabin of Schooner House dreams of

SECOND VOICE—never such seas as any that swamped the decks of his S.S. *Kidwelly* bellying over the bedclothes and jellyfish-

"Under Milk Wood": By Dylan Thomas. Copyright 1954 by New Directions. Reprinted by permission of New Directions, New York, N. Y.

Photo by LIFE Photographer Yale Joel, © *TIME, Inc.*

Peter Ustinov, Gerald Sarracini and Elizabeth Allen in
"Romanoff and Juliet"

SIG ARNO
as The Headwaiter
in "Time Remembered"

EMLYN WILLIAMS
as Dylan Thomas
in "A Boy Growing Up"

RAY WALSTON
as Michael Haney
in "Who Was That Lady
I Saw You With?"

JULIE HARRIS
as Mrs. Margery Pinch
wife in
"The Country Wife"

LAURENCE OLIVIER
and
BRENDA DE BANZIE
as Archie and Phoebe Rice
in "The Entertainer"

JO VAN FLEET
as Eliza Gant
in "Look Homeward,
Angel"

ANNE BANCROFT
as Gittel Mosca
in "Two for the Seesaw"

ROBERT PRESTON
as Harold Hill
in "The Music Man"

PAMELA BROWN
as Lady Fidget
in "The Country Wife"

PETER USTINOV
as The General
in "Romanoff and Juliet"

KENNETH HAIGH
as Jimmy Porter
in "Look Back in Anger"

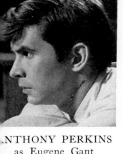

ANTHONY PERKINS
as Eugene Gant
in "Look Homeward,
Angel"

ALFRED LUNT
as Anton Schill,
LYNN FONTANNE
as Claire Zachanassian
in "The Visit"

RALPH BELLAMY
as FDR
in "Sunrise at
Campobello"

Photo by Friedman-Abeles

Lena Horne, Josephine Premice and Ossie Davis in "Jamaica"

Photo by LIFE Photographer Gordon Parks, © *TIME, Inc.*

Charles Saari, Pat Hingle and Teresa Wright in "The Dark
at the Top of the Stairs"

"West Side Story" costume designs by Irene Sharaff

Model by Oliver Smith for a set in "West Side Story"

Set design by Howard Bay for "The Music Man"

"The Music Man" costume designs by Raoul Pene du Bois

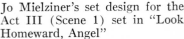

Jo Mielziner's set design for the
Act III (Scene 1) set in "Look
Homeward, Angel"

© by Jo Mielziner

Set design by Ralph Alswang for
"Sunrise at Campobello"

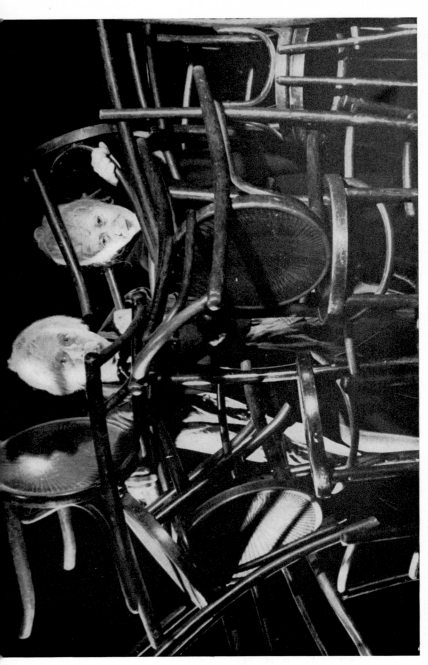

Eli Wallach and Joan Plowright in "The Chairs"

Photo by Friedman-Abeles

Laurence Olivier in "The Entertainer"

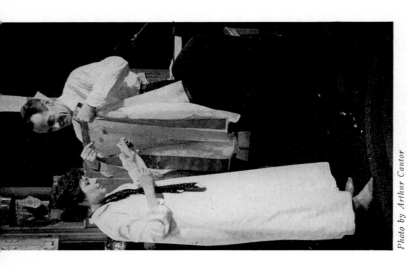

Photo by Arthur Cantor

Anne Bancroft and Henry Fonda in "Two for the Seesaw"

"Infernal Machine" costume designs by Alvin Colt

Costume designs by Miles White for "Jamaica"

Set design by Ben Edwards for "Jane Eyre"

Sketch by William and Jean Eckart
for a set in "The Body Beautiful"

Photo by Fred Fehl

"Rumble" scene from "West Side Story"

Photo by Friedman-Abeles

Kenneth Kakos, Ralph Bellamy and Perry Skaar in "Sunrise at Campobello"

Photo by Vandamm

Scene from "Time Remembered";
set design by Oliver Smith

Oliver Smith's set design for "Winesburg, Ohio"

Photo by Friedman-Abeles

Hugh Griffith, Anthony Perkins and Jo Van Fleet
in "Look Homeward, Angel"

slippery sucking him down salt deep into the Davy dark where the fish come biting out and nibble him down to his wishbone, and the long drowned nuzzle up to him.

FIRST DROWNED—Remember me, Captain?

CAPTAIN CAT—You're Dancing Williams!

FIRST DROWNED—I lost my step in Nantucket.

SECOND DROWNED—Do you see me, Captain? the white bone talking? I'm Tom-Fred the donkeyman . . . we shared the same girl once . . . her name was Mrs. Probert . . .

WOMAN'S VOICE—Rosie Probert, thirty-three Duck Lane. Come on up, boys, I'm dead.

THIRD DROWNED—Hold me, Captain, I'm Jonah Jarvis, come to a bad end, very enjoyable.

FOURTH DROWNED—Alfred Pomeroy Jones, sea lawyer, born in Mumbles, sung like a linnet, crowned you with a flagon, tattooed with mermaids, thirst like a dredger, died of blisters.

FIRST DROWNED—This skull at your earhole is

FIFTH DROWNED—Curly Bevan. Tell my auntie it was me that pawned the ormolu clock.

Wanting to know how it is "above," the drowned ask questions ranging from "Is there rum and lavabread?" . . . "Bosoms and robins?" to "Who milks the cows in Maesgwyn?" . . . "When she smiles, is there dimples?" and "What's the smell of parsley?" Captain Cat answers them all: "Oh, my dead dears!"

In Cockle Row, dressmaker and sweetshop-keeper Miss Price dreams of her lover—"tall as the town clock tower, Samson-syrup-gold-maned, whacking thighed and piping hot, thunderbolt-bass'd and barnacle-breasted"—as Mr. Mog Edwards, the draper, enters her dream to take her to his Emporium on the hill. "Throw away your little bedsocks and your Welsh wool knitted jacket, I will warm the sheets like an electric toaster," he promises; "I will lie by your side like the Sunday roast." Clasping his hands, Miss Price replies: "I will knit you a wallet of forget-me-not blue, for the money to be comfy. I will warm your heart by the fire so that you can slip it in under your vest when the shop is closed." Kneeling, Mr. Edwards begs: "Myfanwy, Myfanwy, before the mice gnaw at your bottom drawer will you say—" "Yes, Mog, yes, Mog, yes, yes, yes," she says. "And," says Mog, "all the bells of the tills of the town shall ring for our wedding."

Up in his attic, Jack Black, the cobbler, dreams of chasing naughty couples, flogging tosspots and "driving out the bare bold girls from the sixpenny hopes of his nightmares."

Laughing in his sleep, Evans, the undertaker, dreams of childish pranks of long ago.

FIRST VOICE—And in the little pink-eyed cottage next to the undertaker's, lie, alone, the seventeen snoring gentle stone of Mister Waldo, rabbitcatcher, barber, herbalist, catdoctor, quack, his fat pink hands, palms up, over the edge of the patchwork quilt, his black boots neat and tidy in the washing-basin, his bowler on a nail above the bed, a milk stout and a slice of cold bread pudding under the pillow; and, dripping in the dark, he dreams of

MOTHER—
This little piggy went to market
This little piggy stayed at home
This little piggy had roast beef
This little piggy had none
And this little piggy went
wee wee wee wee wee
all the way home to

WIFE (screaming)—Waldo! Wal-do!

MR. WALDO (rising)—Yes, Blodwen love?

WIFE—Oh, what'll the neighbours say, what'll the neighbours . . .

FIRST NEIGHBOUR—Poor Mrs. Waldo

SECOND NEIGHBOUR—What she puts up with

FIRST NEIGHBOUR—Never should of married

SECOND NEIGHBOUR—If she didn't had to

FIRST NEIGHBOUR—Same as her mother

SECOND NEIGHBOUR—There's a husband for you

FIRST NEIGHBOUR—Bad as his father

SECOND NEIGHBOUR—And you know where he ended

FIRST NEIGHBOUR—Up in the asylum

SECOND NEIGHBOUR—Crying for his ma

FIRST NEIGHBOUR—Every Saturday

SECOND NEIGHBOUR—He hasn't got a leg

FIRST NEIGHBOUR—And carrying on

SECOND NEIGHBOUR—With that Mrs. Beattie Morris

FIRST NEIGHBOUR—Up in the quarry

SECOND NEIGHBOUR—And seen her baby

FIRST NEIGHBOUR—It's got his nose . . .

Wondering what he'll do for drink now that he's sold the pianola and the sewing machine, the neighbours cry, "Poor Mrs. Waldo," and his wife cries, "Oh, Waldo, Waldo!" Turning his back on her, Waldo solves it: "Hush, love, hush. I'm *widower* Waldo now. . . ."

In her dust-defying bedroom in her house for paying guests at the top of the town, Mrs. Ogmore-Pritchard, widow—twice—of—"Mr. Ogmore, linoleum, retired, and Mr. Pritchard, failed bookmaker, who maddened by besoming, swabbing and scrubbing, the voice of the vacuum-cleaner and the fume of polish, ironically swallowed disinfectant, fidgets in her rinsed sleep, wakes in a dream, and nudges in the ribs dead Mr. Ogmore, dead Mr. Pritchard, ghostly on either side. . . ." She demands that each of the gentlemen recite his hygienic tasks for the day, with the final reminder: "And before you let the sun in, mind it wipes its shoes."

Butcher Beynon's daughter, schoolteacher Gossamer, deep in sleep, is not at all surprised to find what she's looking for—Sinbad the bartender. While Organ Morgan, the town organist, hearing cacophonous sounds in his dreams, cries "Help" at the sea-end of town, Mr. and Mrs. Floyd, the cocklers, are sleeping side by side, "like two old kippers in a box." High on the hill, farmer Utah Watkins all night long counts wife-faced sheep; while Willy Nilly, the postman, dreams of walking all night as he does all day. Lily Smalls, dreaming of royalty and happily caught in the wash-house by a mogul, squeals appreciatively, "Ooh, you old mogul!" as she is dragged off.

SECOND VOICE—Mrs. Rose Cottage's eldest, Mae, peels off her pink-and-white skin in a furnace in a tower in a cave in a waterfall in a wood and waits there raw as an onion for Mister Right to leap up the burning tall hollow splashes of leaves like a brilliantined trout.

MAE ROSE COTTAGE (*very close and softly*)—
    Call me Dolores
    Like they do in the stories.

FIRST VOICE—Alone until she dies, Bessie Bighead, hired help, born in the workhouse, smelling of the cowshed, snores bass and gruff on a couch of straw in a loft in Salt Lake Farm and picks a posy of daisies in Sunday Meadow to put on the grave of Gomer Owen who kissed her once by the pigsty when she wasn't looking and never kissed her again although she was looking all the time.

Mary Ann Sailors has dreams of a domesticated Garden of Eden. Up in Donkey Street, just before dawn, Dai Bread dreams of Harems; Polly Garter dreams of Babies; Nogood Boyo dreams of Nothing; and Lord Cut-Glass dreams of Tick tock tick tock tick tock tick tock.

Time passes; dawn inches up; a voice from a guide-book tells us:

"Less than five hundred souls inhabit the three quaint streets and
the few narrow by-lanes and scattered farmsteads that constitute
this small, decaying watering-place which may, indeed, be called a
'backwater of life' without disrespect to its natives who possess, to
this day, a salty individuality of their own. . . ."

The first to rise is Reverend Eli Jenkins, who fails to wash in his
rush to greet the day in verse. Lily Smalls, Mrs. Beynon's treasure,
coming downstairs from a dream of uninterrupted larking, puts the
kettle on and shudders at her reflection in the shaving mirror.
Jolted from thoughts of Nogood Boyo by Mrs. Beynon's shouting
"Lily!", she gets Mrs. Beynon's tea. At the schoolhouse opposite
Mr. Pugh, cup and saucer in hand, goes upstairs to his wife, whispering:

> "Here's your arsenic, dear.
> And your weedkiller biscuit.
> I've throttled your parakeet.
> I've spat in the vases.
> I've put cheese in the mouseholes.
> Here's your . . . (*Gives tea to Mrs. Pugh*)
> nice tea, dear."

Mrs. Pugh says it isn't. Ascertaining that Reverend Jenkins has re-
cited his morning poem to empty Coronation Street, Mrs. Pugh
demands her glasses—*not* her reading ones, but the glasses to look
out, to see the village start the day.

Mrs. Pugh checks on Lily Smalls' washing of Mrs. Beynon's
stoop: "She's tucked her dress in her bloomers . . . oh, the bag-
gage!" Seeing Policeman Attila Rees stomping forth, Mrs. Pugh
trusts that he is off to arrest Polly Garter "for having babies." She
sees Mary Ann Sailors open her bedroom window above the tap-
room and inform the heavens: "I'm eighty-five years three months
and a day!" "I will say this for her," says Mrs. Pugh, "she never
makes a mistake."

Dai Bread, the baker, hurries grumbling to the bakery as Mrs.
Dai Bread I borrows a loaf of bread from a neighbour, and Mrs. Dai
Bread II, in her gypsy finery, lolls at her doorway. Lord Cut-Glass,
in hand-me-down clothes, hurries out to empty slops, then hurries
back in again to his clocks. Nogood Boyo is, as he says, up to no
good in the wash-house. And Polly Garter, hanging up the wash in
her garden that grows nothing else, gives her breast to her latest
baby.

Now Llareggub has breakfast. Miss Price in her print housecoat
—considering herself "natty as a jenny-wren"—pit-pats to her

breakfast egg at the same time that Mr. and Mrs. Cherry Owen, sitting down to last night's forgotten supper, post-mortem last night's binge.

Mrs. Cherry Owen—See that smudge on the wall by the picture of Auntie Blossom? That's where you threw the sago. (Cherry Owen *laughs with delight.*) You only missed me by a inch.

Cherry Owen—I always miss Auntie Blossom too.

Mrs. Cherry Owen (*ladles soup into bowls*)—Remember last night? In you reeled, my boy, as drunk as a deacon with a big wet bucket and a fish-pail full of stout and you looked at me and you said (*raises arms*) "God has come home!" you said, and then over the bucket you went, sprawling and bawling, and the floor was all flagons and eels.

Cherry Owen—Was I wounded?

Mrs. Cherry Owen—And then you took off your trousers and you said, "Does anybody want a fight!" Oh, you old baboon. (*She pushes his face.*)

Cherry Owen—Give me a kiss.

As Mr. and Mrs. Cherry Owen laugh delightedly together, Mr. and Mrs. Butcher Beynon, waited on by Lily, "enjoy, between bites, their every morning hullabaloo." Today Mr. Beynon, assuring Mrs. Beynon that the liver she is eating really is her favourite cat, gets her all upset as intended.

All over town babies and old men are cleaned. Blind Captain Cat, hearing the sound of the school bell and of children's feet, and the muffled knocking on a door, is aware that Willy Nilly the postman has started his morning rounds at the kid-glove-covered knocker on Mrs. Ogmore-Pritchard's door. "Careful now," Captain Cat says to himself, "she swabs the front glassy. Every step's like a bar of soap. Mind your size twelveses. That old Bessie would beeswax the lawn to make the birds slip."

Mrs. Willy Nilly's kettles having steamed open every piece of mail, Willy Nilly is able to recite the contents of her letter from Builth Wells to Mrs. Ogmore-Pritchard. Indeed, Willy Nilly pleads for the vegetarian gentleman birdwatcher correspondent who desires a room and bath in Mrs. Ogmore-Pritchard's guest house. Mrs. Ogmore-Pritchard, not wanting anyone even to breathe on her furniture, gives a flat no. Mr. Willy Nilly's heavy feet then proceed to Mrs. Rose Cottage with news of her sister's twins, and from there to the schoolhouse, where Mrs. Pugh demands that Willy Nilly surrender the package intended for Mr. Pugh's hands alone.

"Never you mind," orders Mrs. Pugh, "what's inside it?" "A book called *Lives of the Great Poisoners*," Willy Nilly says. At Mog Edwards' shop, Willy Nilly, delivering Miss Price's daily love letter, tells the day's news: "Very small news," he says. "Mrs. Ogmore-Pritchard won't have birds in the house, and Mr. Pugh's bought a book now on how to do in Mrs. Pugh." "Have you got a letter from her?" Mog Edwards begs. "Miss Price," says Willy Nilly, waving the lavender-scented envelope, "loves you with all her heart. . . ." He recites the letter that's more a shop inventory than a declaration of passion, though it ends with twenty-one X's. Mog, in turn, giving his love missive to Willy Nilly, urges that it be delivered in all haste.

Hearing Mr. Waldo on his way to a morning pick-up at the Sailors Arms, Captain Cat murmurs that he's about to receive a letter. "It's another paternity suit, Mr. Waldo," Willy Nilly proclaims. Taking a bundle of similar papers from his pocket, Mr. Waldo adds this latest to his collection and proceeds as before to the pub. Now, as all the townswomen gather round the pump for a good gossip, Captain Cat—conscious of a sudden hush—knows that Polly Garter has appeared. "Hullo, Polly, my love," Captain Cat says softly, "can you hear the dumb-goose hiss of the wives as they huddle and peck or flounce at a waddle away? Who cuddled you when? Which of their gandering hubbies moaned in Milk Wood for your naughty mothering arms and body like a wardrobe, love? Scrub the floors of the Welfare Hall for the Mothers' Union Social Dance, you're one mother won't wriggle her roly poly bum or pat her fat little buttery feet in that wedding-ringed holy tonight, though the waltzing breadwinners snatched from the cozy smoke of the Sailors Arms will grizzle and mope." A cock crows. "Too late, cock, too late," says Captain Cat. The town's morning is half over.

At Mrs. Organ Morgan's general shop, the women babble on. The day's news has passed through so many mouths that it is by now only faintly recognizable.

FIRST WOMAN—Mrs. Ogmore-Pritchard
SECOND WOMAN—La di da
FIRST WOMAN—got a man in Builth Wells
THIRD WOMAN—and he got a little telescope to look at birds
SECOND WOMAN—Willy Nilly said.
THIRD WOMAN—Remember her first husband? He didn't need a telescope
FIRST WOMAN—he looked at them undressing through the keyhole

THIRD WOMAN—and he used to shout Tallyho

SECOND WOMAN—but Mr. Ogmore was a proper gentleman

FIRST WOMAN—even though he hanged his collie.

THIRD WOMAN—Seen Mrs. Butcher Beynon?

SECOND WOMAN—she said Butcher Beynon put dogs in the mincer

FIRST WOMAN—go on, he's pulling her leg

THIRD WOMAN—now don't you dare tell her that, there's a dear

SECOND WOMAN—or she'll think he's trying to pull it off and eat it.

FOURTH WOMAN—There's a nasty lot live here when you come to think.

FIRST WOMAN—Look at that Nogood Boyo now

SECOND WOMAN—too lazy to wipe his snout

THIRD WOMAN—and going out fishing every day and all he ever brought back was a Mrs. Samuels

FIRST WOMAN—been in the water a week.

SECOND WOMAN—And look at Ocky Milkman's wife that nobody's ever seen

FIRST WOMAN—he keeps her in the cupboard with the empties

THIRD WOMAN—and think of Dai Bread with two wives

SECOND WOMAN—one for the daytime one for the night.

FOURTH WOMAN—Men are brutes on the quiet.

THIRD WOMAN—And how's Organ Morgan, Mrs. Morgan?

FIRST WOMAN—You look dead beat

MRS. ORGAN MORGAN—it's organ organ all the time with him

THIRD WOMAN—up every night until midnight playing the organ.

MRS. ORGAN MORGAN—Oh, I'm a martyr to music.

The day advances with the old people dreaming in the sun while the young dream over their work; and Mrs. Willy Nilly with her battery of steaming kettles, steaming open the latest love dispatch from Miss Price to Mog, reads it aloud to her attentive husband. At the shore, fishermen, looking at the smooth blue sea that hasn't a ripple on it, decide that it's much too rough for fishing and head straight for the Sailors Arms. Children, having their recess, play and sing.

FIRST VOICE—The music of the spheres is heard distinctly over Milk Wood. It is "The Rustle of Spring. . . ."

ACT II

Passing the time of day with Mrs. Dai Bread II, Mrs. Dai Bread I consults the former's crystal ball. "Cross my palm with silver," says Mrs. Dai Bread II, "out of our housekeeping money." Mrs. Dai Bread II sees in her crystal a featherbed, three pillows, and along with these, a little hairy man. Mrs. Dai Bread I is all agog as she recognizes Dai Bread. As Mrs. Dai Bread II describes the little man undressing, beating his hairy chest, getting into bed, and putting his arms around one of the women, her crystal clouds over: she can't see which one of the women receives the honour.

Polly Garter, sweeping and scrubbing Welfare Hall, sings about the man she loved best, as Reverend Jenkins, busy at his morning calls, stops outside the hall to listen.

POLLY GARTER—
    Now men from every parish around
    Run after me and roll me on the ground
    But whenever I love another man back
    Johnnie from the Hill or Sailing Jack
    I always think as they do what they please
    Of Tom Dick and Harry who were tall as trees
    And most I think when I'm by their side
    Of little Willy Wee who drowned and died.

    Of Tom Dick and Harry were three fine men
    And I'll never have such loving again
    But little Willy Wee who took me on his knee
    Little Willy Weazel is the man for me.

REV. ELI JENKINS—Praise the Lord! We are a musical nation.

Mr. Waldo, drinking his late morning stout, has to listen to Sinbad's outpouring of love for Gossamer Beynon: "She's a lady all over," Sinbad says. Thinking of a woman "soft as Eve and sharp as sciatica to share his bread-pudding bed," Mr. Waldo answers—

MR. WALDO—No lady that I know is.
SINBAD—And if only grandma'd die, cross my heart I'd go down on my knees Mr. Waldo and I'd say Miss Gossamer I'd say
CHILDREN'S VOICES—
    When birds do sing hey ding a ding a ding
    Sweet lovers love the Spring . . .

SECOND VOICE—Polly Garter sings, still on her knees,
POLLY GARTER—
  Tom Dick and Harry were three fine men
  And I'll never have such
CHILDREN—ding a ding
POLLY GARTER—again.

The morning has gone; school is over; and Captain Cat, at his porthole, hears the children's playing and teasing and the resulting sobs of one of their number. As these little tormentors run off to spend their sticky pennies at Miss Price's shop—

SECOND VOICE—Gossamer Beynon high-heels out of school. The sun hums down through the cotton flowers of her dress into the bell of her heart and buzzes in the honey there and couches and kisses, lazy-loving and boozed, in her red-berried breast. Eyes run from the trees and windows of the street, steaming "Gossamer," and strip her to the nipples and the bees. She blazes naked past the Sailor Arms, the only woman on the Dai-Adamed earth . . .

Aware of Sinbad at every step, Gossamer, not caring in her deepest self that he's common, would just like to gobble him up. But to all outward appearances she remains the demure, crisp school-marm, knowing nothing of Sinbad's existence, on her way home to lunch.
  In the dusty, dark dining room of the schoolhouse, Mr. and Mrs. Pugh are eating silently their cold grey meal. Mr. Pugh, as he forks in "shroud meat," reads, underlines certain passages in his new book and smiles in secret. "Persons with manners," says Mrs. Pugh, "do not read at table." Allowing that some people were, of course, brought up in pigsties, Mrs. Pugh asks Mr. Pugh what is the book by his "trough." "It's a theological work, my dear," Mr. Pugh answers. *"Lives of the Great Saints."* Mrs. Pugh smiles. ("An icicle forms in the cold air of the dining vault.") "I saw you talking to a saint this morning," she says. "Saint Polly Garter. She was martyred again last night. Mrs. Organ Morgan saw her with Mr. Waldo. . . ."
  At lunch with her husband, Mrs. Organ Morgan tries to interest him in Polly Garter's latest. Thinking of all Polly's babies, begot because she can't even say no to midgets, Mrs. Organ Morgan asks her husband which of Polly's boys he likes best. "Oh, Bach without any doubt. Bach every time for me," Organ Morgan answers.
  "Lord Cut-Glass, in his kitchen full of time, squats down alone

to a dogdish, marked Fido, of peppery fish-scraps and listens to the voices of his sixty-six clocks (one for each year of his loony age) and watches, with love, their black-and-white moony loudlipped faces tocking the earth away . . ." Spring has no more meaning than Time for Lord Cut-Glass in his shack at the bottom of the town that has fallen "heads over bells in love."

As Polly Garter hums her song and longs for loving, Mr. Pugh dreams of ghastly murderous concoctions to administer to Mrs. Pugh, and Captain Cat, slumbering at his window in the sun and dreaming of his past, "weeps as he sleeps and sails."

Sailing in his dinghy Nogood Boyo, catching nothing as usual, dreams of Mrs. Dai Bread II, but—as usual even in his dreams—without success. This lazy afternoon finds Mae Rose Cottage lazing in a field, blowing hopefully on a puff ball: "He loves me, he loves me not, he loves me . . ." And in his cool dark parlour, Reverend Eli Jenkins writes lovingly of the facts and figures that make his life work: the White Book of Llareggub. He is surrounded by the heavy portraits of poets and preachers, and faint ladylike watercolours of pale green Milk Wood and a picture of his mother.

FIRST VOICE—There is no known likeness of his father Esau, who—undogcollared because of his little weakness—was scythed to the bone one harvest by mistake when sleeping with his weakness in the corn. He lost all ambition and died, with one leg.

REV. ELI JENKINS—Poor Dad,
SECOND VOICE—grieves the Reverend Eli,
REV. ELI JENKINS—to die of drink and agriculture.

Up at Utah Watkins' farm, the end of this Spring day is reflected in the great eyes of the cows that Bessie Bighead greets by name—and milks—as "the dusk showers slowly down over byre, sea and town."

With the first sign of dusk, Mrs. Ogmore-Pritchard draws her germ-free blinds and, sitting on a highbacked hygienic chair, wills herself to quick sleep and to visions of Mr. Ogmore and Mr. Pritchard. She orders the reluctant ghosts to tell her their tasks in the proper order. "We must take our pyjamas from the drawer marked pyjamas," say Mr. Ogmore and Mr. Pritchard. "And then," says Mrs. Ogmore-Pritchard, "you must take them off."

Still lying in clover Mae Rose Cottage, buttoning her blouse, determined to be fast, tells the sneering goats that she'll sin till she blows up! And, as he does each evening, Reverend Eli Jenkins recites to Llareggub Hill his sunset poem:

"We are not wholly bad or good
Who live our lives under Milk Wood,
And Thou, I know, wilt be the first
To see our best side, not our worst.

"O let us see another day!
Bless us this night, I pray
And to the sun we all will bow
And say, good-bye—but just for now!"

As night comes on, once again Jack Black, the cobbler, with torch and bible, goes out to meet Satan in the Wood. He blinds Mae Rose Cottage with his light and chases the screaming girl home. Once again Lily Smalls and Nogood Boyo are in the wash-house, and Cherry Owen and Mr. Waldo are in Sailors Arms, where suffering Sinbad serves them and longs for Gossamer.

It is no longer dusk. It is night, and all over the town "babies and old men are bribed and lullabied to sleep." At the same moment young girls at their mirrors prepare for the dance, and the drinkers in the Sailors Arms drink to its failure. "Down with the waltzing and the skipping," says Cherry Owen. "Dancing isn't natural." He has just had seventeen pints of flat, warm, thin, Welsh, bitter beer.

While Reverend Eli Jenkins writes about Llareggub Hill, Captain Cat dreams once again in his bunk of the drowned dead.

FIRST VOICE—Organ Morgan goes to chapel to play the organ. He sees Bach lying on a tombstone.
ORGAN MORGAN—Johann Sebastian!
CHERRY OWEN (*drunkenly*)—Who?
ORGAN MORGAN (*kneels*)—Johann Sebastian mighty Bach. Oh, Bach, fach.
CHERRY OWEN—To hell with you.

Neatly and happily apart, little islands of contentment, as they appear in the warm White Book of Llareggub, Mog Edwards and Myfanwy Price write their nightly letters of love.

FIRST VOICE—And Mr. Waldo, drunk in the dusky wood, hugs his lovely Polly Garter under the eyes and rattling tongues of the neighbours and the birds, and he does not care. He smacks his live red lips.

But it is not *his* name that Polly Garter whispers as she lies

under the oak and loves him back. Six feet deep that name sings
in the cold earth.

POLLY GARTER (*sings*)—
    But I always think as we tumble into bed
    Of little Willy Wee who is dead, dead, dead.
FIRST VOICE—The thin night thickens. A breeze from the
creased water sighs the streets close under Milk waking Wood.
The Wood, whose every tree-foot's cloven in the black glad sight
of the hunters of lovers, that is a God-built garden to Mary Ann
Sailors who knows there is Heaven on earth and the chosen people
of His kind fire in Llareggub's land, that is the fair day farmhands'
wantoning ignorant chapel of bridesbeds, and, to the Reverend Eli
Jenkins, a greenleaved sermon on the innocence of men, the suddenly wind-shaken wood springs awake for the second dark time
this one Spring day.

TIME REMEMBERED

A Comedy in Two Acts

By Jean Anouilh

Adapted by Patricia Moyes

[Jean Anouilh *was born in Bordeaux in 1910 and has been an increasingly prominent figure since the success of his first play "L'Hermine" in 1932. A year later he wrote "Mandarine." This was followed by, among others, "Eurydice" (done here as "Legend of Lovers"), "Antigone," "Cry of the Peacock" (done Off Broadway this season as "Ardéle"), "Ring Round the Moon," "Mademoiselle Colombe," "The Lark" and "The Waltz of the Toreadors."*]

[Patricia Moyes *was asked by B.B.C. to make an English version of Jean Anouilh's "Léocadia," and "Time Remembered" was the result. Mrs. Moyes apprenticed for the theatre as general assistant to British playwright-actor Peter Ustinov. A play of her own, "A Fiddle at the Wedding," was produced in London in 1953. She is assistant editor of British "Vogue" Magazine.*]

For the cast listing, see page 301.

LATE one afternoon, a young girl named Amanda, her cheap suitcase at her feet, sits, fidgets and waits amid the splendor of the Duchess's sitting room.

Suddenly a door opens, and the tiny Duchess, preceded by her lorgnette, bursts into the room. Bearing down on Amanda, examin-

"Time Remembered": By Jean Anouilh, English version by Patricia Moyes. Reprinted by permission of Coward-McCann, Inc., New York, N. Y. "Time Remembered" is the sole property of the authors and is fully protected by copyright. It may not be acted either by professionals or by amateurs without written consent. Public readings and radio or television broadcasts are likewise forbidden. All inquiries concerning rights except stock and amateur rights should be addressed to the author's agent, Dr. Jan van Loewen, International Copyright Agency, 81-83 Shaftesbury Ave., London, W. 1. All inquiries concerning stock and amateur rights should be addressed to Samuel French, Inc., 25 W. 45th St., New York 36, N. Y.

ing her from head to toe and finding her absurdly small, the Duchess
wonders aloud how she does it. Utterly bewildered, Amanda murmurs that she does her best. "Not good enough," the Duchess rattles on. "You must make a serious effort. My child, I am sixty.
I have improved upon nature all my life, and intend to go on doing
so." In the next breath she orders Amanda to wear high heels, and
in the one after that asks Amanda to guess how tall she herself is
in bare feet, and is nettled when Amanda guesses correctly.

DUCHESS (*annoyed*)—Not a bad guess. I am five foot one and
three-quarters. However, it is of no consequence, as you will never
see me in bare feet. I am glad to say nobody has ever seen me in
bare feet, except the dear Duke, of course. But he was as blind as
a bat. (AMANDA *extends her hand in an attempt to interrupt. The*
DUCHESS *seizes it.*) Good. You have pretty hands. As I thought.
They may be accustomed to making hats, but they have a certain
air about them. In any case, who doesn't make hats these days?
I don't, of course. But then I belong to a different world altogether. Now, I trust that the telegram explained quite clearly why
I want you here.

AMANDA—I gathered you had a situation here in the household,
madame.

The Duchess thereupon asks of the Duke, who has been dead and
buried a good fifteen years, if he doesn't find Amanda delicious.
Naturally confused to find no Duke in sight, Amanda next becomes
angry to hear that the Duchess had her fired from her milliner's job
two days ago. "Well, of all the cheek!" Amanda cries. The
Duchess merely asks the Duke if he doesn't find Amanda adorable,
and sweeps out of the room.

Grabbing her suitcase in a state verging on tears, Amanda finds
herself blocked by a bowing butler. Angry and bewildered, she refuses his offer of a cold collation. His only reply is: "I beg mademoiselle's pardon, but my enquiry was purely rhetorical. Her Grace
has given orders that the cold collation will be served." To the accompaniment of lilting music, footmen stream into the room, bearing dish after elaborate dish. Not soothed by the music and insisting
that she is not hungry, Amanda passes up all the silver dishes and
takes a tangerine. As she begins to peel it the Duchess, now accompanied by tweedy Lord Hector, streaks back and snatches the tangerine out of her hand. "No tangerines, no oranges or lemons," the
Duchess orders. "They make you thin and you cannot afford to lose
a single ounce. . . ." The Duchess instructs her butler to remove
the collation and to bring an egg.

At the breaking point, Amanda shouts "No, madame!" She is not hungry; she does not like eggs. The Duchess merely passes this off with an "Adorable" to Lord Hector. Hector answers: "Adorable." The two then disappear.

Demanding to be told why she is here, Amanda again grabs the suitcase. The butler, without answering her question, leaves the room. Stamping her foot, the furious, frustrated Amanda cries: "Crud, crud, crud!" "What a hideously inelegant word!" comments the Duchess, suddenly bouncing in through a secret door. "Say *merde*, my dear, it's so much more explicit. Crud is not only ugly, it is inexact."

On this appearance, the Duchess at least apologizes to Amanda for keeping her shut up and supplies the barest hint of a reason: she does not wish to have a certain person, about to return from his walk, see Amanda. This time Amanda will not let her go. "Not let me go? Did you hear that, Gaston?" says the Duchess to the dead Duke. "We are prisoners in our own home . . . just as we were under Francis the First." Assuring her that she has no intention of keeping the Duchess a prisoner, Amanda wishes only that—if she is to be of no use to the Duchess—she be allowed to catch the 6:19, the last train back to Paris. That train, the Duchess answers, may appear on the timetables, but does not run. "You stopped it running so that I couldn't get away," Amanda cries. "A hundred and fifty years ago, my dear," the Duchess replies, "I would most certainly have done so. Unfortunately since 1789 my family has lost much of its influence over the administration. No, it was not I who canceled the train. It was the Freemasons. . . ." The Duchess describes their dark plot to prevent the public from visiting her basilica, and her means to outwit them by motor coaches. Amanda is more confused and despairing than ever. The Duchess is not reassuring when she says to Amanda: "You must take my word for it that the reason I have been popping in and out of this room like a jack-in-the-box for the last ten minutes is simply that I cannot summon up the courage to tell you the truth of why I made you come here." And out she goes again.

Declaring that they're all mad, stark staring mad, Amanda is determined to get to Paris even if she has to walk. This time, when she picks up her suitcase, she escapes through the French doors into the garden.

Scene II

In the park of the château, Amanda comes upon an antiquated, ivy-covered taxi and an ice-cream cart. Crying with relief, she asks to be driven to the station. Hopping happily into the cab, she as quickly hops out again. "There are rabbits in your taxi!" she tells the driver indignantly. Picking up his most distressed rabbit, the equally indignant driver asks if he isn't entitled to keep rabbits just because he is paid thirty thousand francs a month to do nothing. Retreating rapidly, Amanda trips. "Oh," she says reassured, "it's only a bit of ivy." The driver finds the ivy easy to cultivate; Amanda thinks it must be awkward to take with him when he drives. The driver calls to the ice-cream man: "Hey! Joseph! D'you know what she just said? Asked me if the ivy follows me around! She's a character, she is. Can't you just see me taking it out for a walk every day to make wee wee on the Boulevard. . . ." Noticing that there are creepers all over the cab, Amanda says the taxi obviously can't go at all. She is wrong. The livid driver rushes to the car, starts the motor and challenges Amanda to say that it won't go. She feels that she is the one who is going mad. And when the ice-cream man has no ice-cream to sell her, she is not in the least surprised. She simply gives him a pin and asks that he stick her. The pinprick at least makes her feel alive.

The Duchess and Lord Hector, arriving at a canter, collide with Amanda. Only when Amanda starts to cry does the Duchess start to explain. After many false starts and incredible meanderings, the Duchess and Hector piece together some of the reasons for Amanda's being brought here. Hector hesitantly leads off: "Well, mademoiselle, some years ago my cousin, the Prince Albert, visited Dinard, where he met a young woman who—"

Duchess (*interrupting*)—No, no, no! Be quiet, Hector. You manage to invest the story of this exquisite romance with such flat-footed platitudinous boredom that I prefer to make the sacrifice and tell it myself. Two years ago, mademoiselle, my beloved Albert became deliriously enamored of a lady of incomparable beauty and impeccable aristocracy . . . a lady of whom you will certainly have heard. I will tell you her name. Léocadia Gardi.

Amanda—The ballerina?

Duchess—Yes, child. The great and glorious ballerina. The divine Gardi, as they called her. Ah, the exquisite, ethereal grace of that first entry of hers in *Swan Lake.* (*Carried away by the memory of it, she runs into the wood and returns dancing the entrance.* HECTOR, *as the Prince in* Swan Lake, *joins and they dance a few measures.*) Unhappily I am no dancer. When I was a girl I was as light as thistledown on my feet—but thirty years of waltzing with the dear Duke proved too much for my delicate talent . . . a pity, but there it is. Where was I?

HECTOR—In *Swan Lake.*

DUCHESS—Oh, yes . . . Léocadia. Dear Léocadia. You say you knew her well. That will be the greatest help to us.

AMANDA—Oh, no. I didn't know her at all. I just read about her death in the newspapers.

DUCHESS—Alas, yes! You know how she died?

AMANDA—An accident, I think.

DUCHESS—Yes. The poor darling always wore a scarf of immense length; she had a different one for every costume she possessed . . . very becoming they were, too . . . they became quite a legend, Léocadia's scarves. As she said good-bye to you, she would fling her scarf around her lovely neck and knot it in her own inimitable way. . . . Well, one evening, leaving the house of some friends, she was knotting the scarf with the grandest, most extravagant gesture of her career. Alas, she realized too late that the knot was in the wrong place . . . but art was stronger than nature. . . . She could not bring herself to spoil that incomparable gesture. She flung out her arm . . . uttered a single cry . . . a strangled one, of course . . . and fell . . . dead. (*She sniffs.*) Finish it, Hector. I can't go on.

HECTOR (*merely repeats*)—Dead . . .

DUCHESS—It was only three days before this tragedy that poor Albert fell in love with her. He has never recovered from those three days. Now do you begin to understand?

AMANDA—No.

The Duchess, wound-up, cannot stop explaining. She describes Albert's determination to take his own life, and her own decision to save him by taking him on an enthralling cruise one and a half times around the world. But the hundred and twenty days spent on board consisted of Albert seated in his cabin gazing at a photograph of his dear departed, while the Duchess in her cabin gazed at Albert through the intervening keyhole.

Amanda, though still at sea, begins at least to take an interest in the story. The Duchess describes their return to France and Albert's return to Dinard, where her spies reported that he spent his days chatting with a taxi-driver, an ice-cream merchant and sometimes the landlord of a little inn called the *Chime of Bells*. His nights he spent at a certain Viennese nightclub, where he always sat at the same table, waited on by the same waiter.

When the Duchess found this out, she bought the taxi and the ice-cream cart; and thankful that Albert and Léocadia had not visited the Eiffel Tower, she had the inn and the Viennese nightclub rebuilt, stone by stone, in the park.

Having done all this for love of her nephew, the Duchess still lacks the courage to tell Amanda why she was brought here too. She hopes that Hector will help her out, that they can break the news to Amanda in unison. But the Duchess cannot come to the point until darkness has fallen. Then, when Amanda cannot witness her embarrassment, she manages to begin. "Tell me then, child," asks the Duchess, "have you had many lovers?" That being a bit abrupt, the Duchess changes it to "flirtations." After a pause, Amanda says softly: "Yes, madame. I have had flirtations, but I have never been in love." The Duchess fears for the melancholy Prince unless she can bring Léocadia back to life for him. "My dear," she says, "I am a very influential old woman, even in these democratic days, and ludicrously rich. I have done everything in my power for him—but I have failed. And now I cannot lift a finger to save his life . . . unless you will help me."

AMANDA—But how, madame? I dare not think that you mean . . . well, in any case, why me? I'm not very pretty, and even if I was, how could anybody come between him and his memories?

DUCHESS—Nobody could . . . except you.

AMANDA (*amazed*)—Me?

DUCHESS—The first time I saw you in Madame Rensada's shop, child—I wept. Because, to anyone who knew her as she really was, you are the living image of Léocadia. (*Silence. The park is vibrant with rustling leaves and chasing shadows.*)

AMANDA (*very soft*)—Even so, I'm afraid I can't do it, madame. I may be poor and insignificant, but at least my flirtations have been my own. . . .

DUCHESS (*soft and very sad*)—Of course. I beg your pardon.

There is a sound of a bicycle bell. Trembling and throwing pride to the wind, the Duchess begs Amanda to take pity on her. She reasons: "My dear, he is handsome, he is charming. Why shouldn't he be one of your very own flirtations—for a moment?" In a whisper, Amanda asks what she should say to the Prince. Embracing her, the Duchess says: "Just say, 'Excuse me, can you tell me the way to the sea?' "

As Amanda addresses him, the Prince stops, gets off his bicycle and catches sight of her. "Yes, mademoiselle?" "Can you tell me the way to the sea?" Amanda asks. "The second turning on the left, mademoiselle," the Prince replies and, with a bow, remounts and cycles off. "He didn't recognize me," Amanda says; but, looking after the Prince, she agrees to change her mind and stay for that night, at least.

SCENE III

The next morning, seated at a table in the living room, the butler —as paymaster for the Duchess—gives the ice-cream man and the taxi-driver their weekly wages. They leave, but when the nightclub headwaiter is paid, he remains. "Her Grace," he informs the butler, "requested me to wait upon her here at nine o'clock, in order to discuss certain details relating to the entirely imaginary Viennese nightclub which I run in the park." Asking him stiffly to be seated, the butler can't help blurting out, in a reserved sort of way, what has been bothering him. He has been unable to detect in this headwaiter's case any of the slackness he invariably finds in those who serve "customers" rather than "masters."

HEADWAITER (*inscrutable*)—I fear I cannot follow your train of thought.

BUTLER—I will elucidate. I have failed, to my great astonishment, to observe in you any signs of this degeneracy. I understand you used to work in Dinard, in a short-lived establishment which, if I may say so, could not in the nature of things have been . . . shall we say . . . five star?

HEADWAITER (*pale*)—It was an excellent restaurant of its kind . . . excellent . . . but five star, no. Three, say. But not five.

BUTLER—As I thought. So I would like to put a question to you. Did you not spend long years of service in a private household before—

HEADWAITER (*bowing his head, with a stifled sob*)—Yes, you are right. I did. I did . . . before . . . but then one day—

Silencing him with a gesture, the butler confesses that he merely wished to "verify his contention" that a butler worthy of the name can always be distinguished by a sense of form that no come-down can eradicate. With renewed dignity, the headwaiter thanks him, and the butler, brushing it aside in his superior way as nothing at all, goes to inform the Duchess of the headwaiter's presence.

Entering in her usual whirl, this time followed by Lord Hector and a flamboyant, Léocadesque Amanda, the Duchess is immensely gratified by the headwaiter's shocked "Aah!" of recognition. He considers Amanda's appearance, in a word he picked up from the newspapers, "phantasmagoric." Determined that the Prince shall be equally thunderstruck, the Duchess dashes out to order sheaves of orchids that Léocadia, who used to nibble them ceaselessly, was never without.

Left with the headwaiter, Amanda asks, with an embarrassed smile, how long he's been playing at being a memory. He has been at it, he answers, for two years, for very good pay, though it embarrasses him to mention the money.

AMANDA—I only saw him for a moment last night—and it was very dark. What's he like? Is he nice?

HEADWAITER—He's neither nice nor not nice. He just doesn't seem to be there at all, if you know what I mean.

AMANDA—What does he do when he comes into your restaurant?

HEADWAITER—He sits down at a table—always the same one— the table they had that night. Then he orders what they ordered then—a bottle of Pommery. I bring the champagne and two glasses. Then he sits and stares at the empty chair opposite him, without saying a word. Sometimes for five minutes. Sometimes all night. And then he goes away.

AMANDA (*dreamy*)—Poor fellow.

HEADWAITER—And we drink the champagne.

And that's not much fun any more, for it is beginning to affect the headwaiter's liver. Amanda wants to know if the two were lovers. After a moment, the headwaiter says haughtily: "That I can't say, mademoiselle. They certainly didn't spend the night together in my establishment. . . . The people who run the *Chime of Bells*—they've been brought here too, you know—they maintain . . . but then I have reason to believe that they circulate the story to try to look important themselves." Amanda thinks aloud: "And even if they were lovers . . . they had so little time together . . . just one night." There is an urgent note in her voice as she asks whether the headwaiter thinks the Prince is *really* heartbroken. "How can one presume," the headwaiter answers loftily, "to analyze the grief of the aristocracy, mademoiselle?"

Having ordered two hundred orchids and posted the butler as a sentry to warn of the Prince's approach, the Duchess is ready to stage-manage Léocadia's entrance into the *Blue Danube* restaurant. She instructs Amanda to screw up her eyes and duck her head à la Léocadia, has the headwaiter and Lord Hector push the furniture around, then orders the headwaiter to give his instinctive impression of the divine Léocadia. The headwaiter confesses that his first impression was one of shock.

HEADWAITER—A shock. First of all, Mademoiselle Léocadia was beautiful—very beautiful indeed. But she had a most disturbing way of looking you straight in the eyes, walking right up to you, and then looking away at the very moment when you expected her to speak to you. She did it with an air of arrogance, of distinction . . . which reminded me more than anything of . . . may I speak frankly, Your Grace?
DUCHESS—Please do.
HEADWAITER—A dog! A mad dog! A demented Borzoi!
DUCHESS (*enthusiastic*)—A demented Borzoi! (*To* AMANDA.) Remember all that. It is surprisingly accurate. This fellow has a rare and courageous gift of observation. It's quite true—the whole of Léocadia's character was revealed in that particular and inimitable manner of walking. (*She demonstrates.*) Holding your eyes with hers until your noses were in imminent danger of collision, and then—suddenly—losing interest and passing you by without another glance. There is her whole personality in a nutshell. (*She bumps into* HECTOR.) I am quite different, of course. With my height, I have to stand on tiptoe to look anybody in the eyes. It's very provoking.

The Duchess now thinks that only the headwaiter can demonstrate Léocadia's manner. Dying to perform, the headwaiter needs no coaxing: "When Mademoiselle Léocadia came in, the orchestra had just started to play, by special request, a tango which was very popular that year—'The Chains of Love.'" The Duchess orders Lord Hector to contribute the music, since he drove everyone mad two years ago by whistling the tune.
Hector attacks "The Chains of Love"—and the headwaiter makes his entrance in dead seriousness, apparently performing the steps of some outlandish tango. The Duchess is rapturous; she orders Amanda to walk behind him and copy everything he does. Hector plays the music again; the headwaiter performs again, with Amanda following suit while bursting with laughter. Finishing his promenade, the headwaiter watches his pupil enthusiastically. "Bravo,

mademoiselle," he cries. "Just like that! Now, come right up to me—look me in the eye! Be arrogant! Be haughty! I'm only a headwaiter! I'm lower than mud! You don't even see me any more!" She doesn't. Covered with confusion, Amanda stops dead as Prince Albert, pushing the horrified butler aside, demands to know the meaning of this masquerade.

After a proper show of aristocratic temper, during which every-one except the Duchess takes cover, the Prince asks to speak to the young lady alone. Not the least intimidated, the Duchess—making last frantic signals to Amanda—departs.

Acknowledging that his aunt has placed her in an embarrassing position, the Prince assumes that Amanda must have been desperate for employment of some sort. Hearing Amanda's tale of his aunt's firing and hiring, he is amused: "She's an amazing woman." "Amaz-ing is right," Amanda says somewhat bitterly. "But since yester-day I've got to the point where nothing amazes me any more."

Amanda reminds the Prince that she spoke to him last night in the dark. He apologizes for not recognizing her, but wonders why she asked him the way to the sea. "Apparently that was the par-ticular phrase of which you had to be reminded," Amanda says. Thunderstruck, the Prince repeats: "Excuse me, can you tell me the way to the sea?" He sits in a chair seemingly in an endless trance. Clearing her throat with no effect, Amanda starts to tiptoe out, but is stopped by his sudden cry: "Don't go! Come back, where I can see you! You are plain. You walk badly. You are not in the least like her. You never could be like her. You're just a common little milliner, with no mystery, no aura—"

AMANDA—What's that?

PRINCE (*surprised*)—What?

AMANDA—An aura?

PRINCE—If you imagine that I'm going to give you lessons in your own language into the bargain—!

AMANDA—I only wanted to know if it's an insult.

PRINCE (*looking at her, he cannot repress a little smile*)—No, it is not an insult.

Amanda is glad, because if it had been, she would have told him just what she thought of him. The very weary Prince is not in the least interested. Sitting in his huge chair, he suddenly tries out the phrase: "Excuse me, can you tell me—" in different tones. Ex-hausted and defeated, he stops. Out of pity, Amanda speaks as she

did in the park. "Who taught you to imitate that voice?" asks the
Prince almost humbly. "Nobody," Amanda replies. "It's my own
voice." Having her repeat it again, to Amanda's complete bewilder-
ment the Prince relives the conversation of two years ago. She can't
understand that when she had said the identical thing the night
before, the Prince hadn't even noticed.

The Prince begs Amanda to accept his aunt's proposition to stay
—for a little while, say three days. His sudden kindness wins
Amanda's sympathy. He confesses that the only reason he has sub-
mitted to his aunt's lunatic whims and her rebuilding mania is the
hope that all this will help him in his terrible struggle. He begs
Amanda not to laugh. "I agreed to all this," confesses the Prince,
"because I am on the verge of . . . forgetting." A whole town has
been built in this park to preserve the memory of his love for
Léocadia, and he can't even remember the color of her eyes or the
first words she spoke to him. "Stay here for three days," he asks
Amanda, "and let me watch you moving through those memory-
ridden haunts where I seek for her in vain. Try—forgive me for
saying this—but please try to be not yourself, but her—just for
three days." Amanda promises to try, but as the Prince, bounding
back to life, demands Amanda's help with one detail or another,
she weakens, decides she can't be of use. The Prince wills her to
be Léocadia, orders her to be Léocadia: "You *are* her. . . ."
Slightly scared, Amanda says: "I'm not. I'm Amanda." Looking
at her as if in a dream, then walking towards her, the Prince talks
to the real Léocadia.

ACT II

In the empty, plush, gilt and crystal-lit atmosphere of the *Blue
Danube*, the neglected gypsy fiddlers ply their violins assiduously,
the tenor sings an overzealous "Chains of Love," while the headwaiter, his underlings and the frilly cloakroom attendant stand and
wait.

When the Prince and Amanda arrive, the staff leaps into action.
As the somber Prince stands by, Amanda does her show-stopping
version of Léocadia: she drops her furs into the hands of the overjoyed attendant, slithers into the room and tosses her chewed-up
orchid to the singer.

The headwaiter, solicitously hovering about as they are seated,
takes the Prince's usual order: "The same as last night." Suddenly
jarring everyone's sensibilities, Amanda—thinking only that she is
thirsty—orders gin and lime with lots of water. The headwaiter is

stunned. Realizing too late what she has done, Amanda takes it all back. Finding water enough for this one drink creates an uproar, but when that is done, and the elaborate ritual involving a large number of people is completed, the headwaiter, however greatly pained, serves Amanda her gin and lime with water. Under the icy glances of the Prince and the headwaiter, Amanda, instead of enjoying a relaxed drink, gulps it down to get rid of it.

The gin out of the way, the Prince concedes stiffly that despite her plebeian limitations, Amanda has done very well up to now. Though her language is not laden, like Léocadia's, with slang, her silences and orchid-nibbling have been properly reminiscent. Idling on the sunlit river that afternoon, the Prince had found Amanda's evocation of Léocadia's spirit nearly faultless. "Yes," the Prince continues, "you were quite perfect. A touch livelier than she perhaps . . . a little too much flesh and blood. . . ." "It's very difficult to be anything else when one is alive," says Amanda. "But I'll do better this evening! I feel so light, as if I'm hardly weighing on my chair at all . . . but that's no wonder, considering the meals we've been having." "Léocadia," the Prince replies, "always laid her glove on her plate." Finding herself lucky to have so many gloves, Amanda even thinks that one day she might eat one since she has been subsisting solely on orchids and champagne.

Unconsciously, the Prince and Amanda have drawn close to each other. The Prince relives the turning point of his and Léocadia's lives: that second evening . . .

PRINCE—We talked of nothing but ourselves . . .

AMANDA—Did you do the talking, or did she?

PRINCE—Well . . . both of us . . . perhaps she more than I . . . why do you ask me that?

AMANDA—No reason . . . just that it seemed to me . . . if I had fallen in love with you after that long sunny afternoon on the river, I'd have wanted to sit quite still, feeling the smooth satin of my dress against my sunburnt skin and the icy stem of my glass between my fingers . . . and just looked at you without saying a word.

By nature Amanda is a chatterbox, but wanting to do the best possible job these three days, she has decided that since she can't talk as well as Léocadia, she at least can ape her method of keeping silent. "How," she inquires, "did she say nothing to you?"

PRINCE—She spoke a little less loudly.

AMANDA (*stupified*)—But she went on speaking?

PRINCE—Oh, yes. She would always answer her own questions, or else finish your reply for you. At other times, she just murmured words at random—in Rumanian, as a rule—that was her mother-tongue. That uninterrupted monologue was one of her greatest charms. She would punctuate her talk with deep, fascinating ripples of throaty laughter, thrown into the conversation at the moment when they were least expected, and dying away into what was almost a sob.

AMANDA—I must seem very dull beside her.

PRINCE—No, no. You have done very well, mademoiselle, to present me with such an accurate and precious picture of her rare moments of silence. (*He has taken her hand quite naturally—now he suddenly drops it.*) I beg your pardon.

AMANDA (*looking at her hand*)—For what?

PRINCE—I took your hand. She hated anybody to touch her.

AMANDA—Even you?

PRINCE—Especially me. She used to say that I had coarse peasant hands—hands made to hurt and destroy.

AMANDA (*taking his hand quickly and looking at it*)—Peasant hands?

PRINCE (*a little embarrassed*)—The skin is hard, I know. But what with yachting and tennis . . . and then, I don't know if you agree with me, but I simply cannot play golf in gloves. . . .

AMANDA (*still looking at his hand*)—How funny. You're a gentleman of leisure, and yet your hand does look like a peasant's. Hold out your arm so I can see it properly. (*She shuts her eyes and, after a pause, murmurs—*) No. They are hard, but they would never do anybody any harm.

The Prince, staring at his hand, thinks that if Léocadia had said that, he would have been wild with joy. But it now comes out that she never, even on that second night with all her endless talking, said simply "I love you." At night now, when he sits at this table by himself, he has difficulty conjuring up her presence opposite him; he only dares take the liberty of having her call him by the name "Albert," which she never would do. He has never dared have her say she loved him.

Amanda, almost tenderly, orders him to look at her, to watch her lips and remember how they look as she says repeatedly, "I love you, Albert." The Prince, taking his agitation out on the headwaiter and the orchestra, cries that he does not wish to hear the music that is being played. The headwaiter, in a fit of trembling, shakes the champagne so that the cork explodes. As he goes in cringing embarrassment for another bottle, Amanda orders another gin and lime. Through clenched teeth the Prince would like to know the meaning of this gratuitous insolence. Amanda has merely decided to put up no longer with his bad temper, and to be herself for a while.

A lovers' quarrel shapes up. The Prince, accusing Amanda of only thinking of herself these last two days, asks why she hurt him by saying the words she knew Léocadia had never said. "I hoped they would help you," Amanda says. "You're lying," retorts the Prince. "Yes, I'm lying," answers Amanda, rising to her feet. "Please," she continues, "forgive me what I'm going to say. But it seems to me that a love affair is too precious and beautiful a thing to play around with like this. I know you'll be furious with me, and probably drive me away—but I'll go back to Paris happier if I've told you what I think. She never loved you. But that isn't really important, because you can give all your heart to someone and get nothing in return—and anyway, I'm certain you know already, deep down, that she didn't love you. But there's worse to come, and I must say it before I go. You're young and rich and handsome and charming and your hands aren't really hard . . . just strong and useful . . . you ought to try to live, and be happy and forget the past—because I'm absolutely positive that you didn't love her either." Through the hushed, horrified, breathless atmosphere of the *Blue Danube,* the Prince, calling her stupid and insolent as well, orders the headwaiter to get Amanda's wrap and have someone else see her back to the house. He will have her paid off in the morning. Retorting that he is only hurting himself by bringing money into the picture, Amanda announces to the shivering headwaiter, who brings her the fur cloak: "You can take it back to the house yourself. Me, *I* don't wear furs in the summer. *I'm* quite warm enough, thank you."

Suddenly calling her back, the Prince dismisses the staff and explains to Amanda: "Mademoiselle. I belong to a class which is invariably represented in humorous fiction as consisting entirely of effete young half-wits and dithering dotards. I suppose it's only to be expected that you should think me an imbecile." Over her protests, the Prince insists that it is just as difficult for him to convince people that he is not a blockhead as it would be for the scion of a long line of village idiots.

Deciding that they must explain themselves to each other once and for all, the Prince orders Amanda to sit down. "Why?" she asks. "Because," says the Prince, "I am about to embark on an extremely long speech." And indeed he does.

Life is wonderful to talk about or to read about, says the Prince, but terrible to have to live. Finding that each day brought at least twelve waking hours to be filled, the Prince hadn't cared to find happiness through drugs or drinks, or the determined brightness of the Boy Scout who fills every second with some efficiently performed useless task, or to live the clean life doing Swedish exercises and thinking along lines of M. Coué. Consequently, he was bored. Having no artistic talent, no great gift of scholarship, he got caught up in the "terrible roundabout of fashionable seasons—and believe me," he says, "it's a dog's life. If the professional classes put half the imagination and tenacity into their businesses that the idle rich do into being bored to tears in exactly the right place on exactly the right date all over Europe, they would soon make their fortunes. I haven't even any vices. Vices are wonderfully strong, simple things. But I haven't even one." As the awful truth of this penetrates his mind, he pauses. Amanda says softly: "Have you finished?" The Prince has almost finished. He wishes to tell how the brilliant, preposterous orchid-eater had dispersed this fog of boredom for three days. Though a madwoman with ridiculous affectations, she was intelligent and outrageously witty and had made life worth living. She not only had taught him the value of his world, but had also taught him the value of Amanda's world of uncomplicated happiness. He stops, then after another pause, suddenly cries out: "I do not love you, mademoiselle! You are beautiful—even more beautiful than she—you are desirable, you are gay and tender and compact of all manner of delights—youth, nature, life . . . and even common sense into the bargain. But I do not love you!" Tears streaming down her face, Amanda hopes that he has quite finished. "Yes," says the Prince, "I have finished." "Well," says Amanda, mustering all her dignity, "personally, you leave me cold." She goes.

Alone, the Prince makes his pathetic appeal to the headwaiter: "You've never doubted that I loved her more than all the world, did you, Ferdinand?" Ever obsequious as he pours Prince Albert's champagne, the headwaiter answers: "Oh, sir! How can you ask such a thing! You worshiped her. We all remarked on it, amongst ourselves. Such great love was unforgettable, sir—even to us, who only stand and wait." "Thank you, Ferdinand," says the Prince.

Scene II

In another section of the park, Amanda, exhausted from grief and a night of wandering, has sunk to the ground in uneasy, tear-stained sleep. As the rosy dawn creeps into the sky, the Duchess and Hector, with their ghilly, reluctantly out shooting only because the calendar says it is a shooting day, argue over who was responsible for bringing down a white bird. The bird turns out to be Amanda, who, on waking, wants to get away as fast as she can. Léocadia has proved too strong for her. "She is very strong, child," the Duchess agrees, "but she is no stronger than you. Remember she has one enormous disadvantage for any young woman. She is dead—" In spite of Léocadia's hold on the Prince, the Duchess points out that nobody this morning is stronger than Amanda, twenty years old, alive and in love. Léocadia had the witchery of the night on her side, but Amanda has, on hers, all the strength of the morning.

As the Duchess discreetly disappears, and the sun rises triumphantly, Amanda stretches her arms and laughs up into the sunshine. A little inn, chimney smoking, trees in tubs and tables on the terrace, appears at a distance. Amanda goes to it.

Approaching the landlord of the *Chime of Bells,* Amanda has one of her Alice-in-Wonderland conversations that only occur with transplanted taxi-drivers and ice-cream men. By bribing him to drink his own liquor, she finds out that the Prince and Léocadia's meeting at the *Chime of Bells* is something the landlord knows only at secondhand.

AMANDA—What d'you mean? Can't you remember?

LANDLORD (*embarking on the second drink*)—No, I can't, and I'll tell you why. When they told the proprietors of this inn they wanted to knock it down and rebuild it here, brick by brick—well, they'd been there seventeen years, see? They were planning to retire—got a little cottage by the sea. So they put me in to run the place.

AMANDA—But what happens when the Prince comes? Suppose he asks you questions?

LANDLORD—Oh, they briefed me good and proper, don't you worry. I've got it all pat—how they arrived in a taxi, how they ordered lemonade . . . every detail. I couldn't tell it better if I'd been there and seen them for myself—and if ever I'm stuck, I make it up. But he never notices. Sometimes I wonder if he was there himself!

Amanda, liking the landlord, says he will never know how much he has done for her. Bursting with youthful confidence, she takes charge as soon as the shivering and unhappy Prince arrives. Ordering him to sit in the sunshine, she countermands his order for lemonade and orders two coffees: "Big cups," she says, "with rolls and butter." Past surprise, the landlord takes the order as the Prince, observing this vital new Amanda, expresses concern. He finds her quite terrifying. As Amanda piles into her breakfast, the Prince asks who she is. "Just a girl in a white dress buttering a roll in the sunshine," she says offhandedly. When the Prince gives a miserable cry that this is the last day, Amanda says calmly: "The last? What do you mean? It's the third day—and it's only just the beginning." Over the Prince's feeble protests, Amanda tells him to wake up from his horrible dream: "You've known me for three days just as you knew her . . . and you're in love with me."

PRINCE—I do not love you!

AMANDA—If you didn't love me you wouldn't deny it so vehemently. (*Going to him.*) Touch me—please touch me. Everything will suddenly be so simple . . .

PRINCE—If I touched you, Amanda, I think I would love you . . . (*He crosses back to the safety of the inn.*) I don't want to love you . . .

AMANDA—If you don't love me, I shall have to go away. But when I have gone, you will remember me, even more than you remember her. (*Going to him.*) Your hands and your heart will remember me.

PRINCE (*calling in spite of himself*)—Léocadia . . .

AMANDA (*implacable*)—You will remember me . . .

PRINCE (*finally, softly*)—Yes, I will remember you . . .

AMANDA—Put your two hands on my shoulders . . .

PRINCE—Amanda . . .

AMANDA (*softly*)—My darling, Albert.

PRINCE—Amanda . . . (*Suddenly he puts his hands on her shoulders, and stands quite still.*)

AMANDA (*whispering*)—Why don't you say anything? Now *I* am afraid.

PRINCE (*a strange, wondering voice*)—But it is so simple . . . and so real . . . and so safe . . . (*He embraces her passionately.*)

The LANDLORD *discovers them and closes the blinds of the little terrace tactfully on them.*)

From the distance, the Duchess and Hector still argue over the shooting of a bird. "You're such a clumsy oaf," she says. "I knew you'd have to go and kill a bird sooner or later." According to the ghilly, it's not a heron nor even a flamingo: "It's an outlandish sort of bird you don't often see in these parts. Funny sort of creature. Its feathers are much too long, they get caught up in the branches when it tries to fly, and its feet are so arched it can't perch anywhere. You can see it miles away, with that tuft of bright-colored feathers on its head . . . and as for the noise it makes . . . well, you heard that ridiculous squawk when Your Grace fired that shot—" Telling the ghilly to go and take the bird with him, the Duchess orders him to bury it. Picking up a feather that has fallen from the bird, the Duchess eulogizes: "Léocadia. Poor Léocadia. She bid for immortality by strangling herself with her own scarf. And now we have killed her again, and in a way that would have hurt her most . . . we have killed her memory."

THE ROPE DANCERS

A Play in Three Acts

BY MORTON WISHENGRAD

[MORTON WISHENGRAD *is a native New Yorker. Since 1943 he has written many radio scripts, among them those for "Lands of the Free," "The Eternal Light" series, "The Jeffersonian Heritage" and "Cavalcade of America." On television he was most recently represented by his adaptation of Robert E. Sherwood's "There Shall Be No Night." He has also done many adaptations for the Theatre Guild of the Air.*]

For the cast listing, see page 302.

IT IS moving day in a New York tenement at the turn of the century. Margaret Hyland and her daughter Lizzie are moving their few belongings into two fifth-floor rooms. The kitchen, with its window facing the street, shows a few scattered bundles and a half-empty barrel, while the little bedroom (with its view of the airshaft and of a fire ladder to the roof) has a mattress and spring not yet put together, and a small bookcase. Margaret Hyland goes into the hall for her tailor's dummy as Lizzie starts putting away books.

Bringing in the last load, the moving man collides with Margaret's bad temper. Cringing at her mother's acid tone, Lizzie tries to make amends by offering the man her little sandwich lunch. About to refuse, he looks at the frail little girl, then wolfs down the peace offering. As he starts putting the bed together, Margaret asks unpleasantly from the kitchen why he is so long in the bedroom: "I asked you to move us from Lispenard Street and that's all. Don't think I'm going to pay you for doing something I didn't ask and that I can do myself." "All right, lady," the man answers. "I'm done . . . pay me." Since getting the money out of several purses—and hiding places—is a complicated procedure, the moving man's contempt increases. He takes his pay without counting it, says

"The Rope Dancers": By Morton Wishengrad. © 1958 by Morton Wishengrad. Reprinted by permission of Crown Publishers, Inc., New York.

good-bye to Lizzie and starts for the door. Margaret then hands him a dime tip. "Five flights up!" he exclaims. Ignoring Margaret, he drops the dime into Lizzie's pocket and leaves.

Though her left hand still remains in the pocket, Lizzie extracts the dime with her right, and gives it to Margaret. "You're another fool," Margaret says. "You aren't," Lizzie answers; "you have the ten cents." Margaret starts putting the coin back in the purse but on second thought leaves it on the table.

Going to the window, Lizzie cranes her neck to see children wading in the horse trough. "If they were my children," says Margaret, "I'd find something for them to do with their time." This remark leaves Lizzie unresponsive. Since she can't even enjoy the children at a distance, she asks for her jump-rope, but Margaret has more important things to unpack first. Never stopping for a moment's rest, she holds out dishes to Lizzie which the child takes with both her right and her mittened left hand. Lizzie is about to put them in the cupboard when Margaret tells her she knows better than that: "Put them on the sink."

LIZZIE—You washed them before we moved . . . in scalding water.

MARGARET—I'm going to wash them again. And then I'm going to wash the cupboard again. I'm going to scrub this flat from top to bottom. I don't live in other people's dirt.

LIZZIE (*responding with the mechanical flattery expected of her*) —You're clean, Ma. You're the cleanest thing I ever saw.

MARGARET (*pleased*)—I'm going to make you a nice new dress, just as soon as I finish the shirtwaist for Mrs. Bernard and the velvet coat for the lady near Washington Square.

LIZZIE—You work too hard.

MARGARET—To work is to pray.

Asserting that she's no complainer in spite of what James Hyland said, Margaret tells Lizzie that if her father had been a man like other men, she wouldn't have to take in sewing. Infuriated by the look of misery on Lizzie's face, Margaret's tongue turns venomous. She finally hears herself, and stops: "The evil tongue in my face . . . I swear I'll bite it off with my own teeth." Lizzie runs now to comfort her. "You're a good mother," Lizzie says, as with her mittened hand she strokes Margaret's cheek.

There is a knock on the door and the sound of a cheery voice. Their fourth-floor neighbors have come to call. As Margaret shakes her head violently, Lizzie pleads with her: "Yes, Ma. We're in a new house. You promised!" Making a real effort, Margaret unchains and unlocks the door.

Breezy, good-natured, sloppy Mrs. Farrow and her dirty-faced daughter Clementine, bearing a nasty-looking cake, have come calling. Shoving Clementine into the room, Mrs. Farrow says: "Put the cake on the table and say hello to the new kid. When you want them to shut up, they jabber." Having sized up an afraid-looking Lizzie, Clementine remarks while picking her nose: "The moving man was cursing from halfway down the fifth to the landing of the first. On account of her mother only offered him ten cents for a tip."

FARROW—Don't say "her mother" . . . it ain't ladylike. (*Craftily.*) Her mother's name is . . .

MARGARET (*grudging it*)—Mrs. Hyland.

FARROW (*triumphant*)—We're pleased to make your acquaintance and you'll find this a friendly tenement. People take an interest.

MARGARET—I would ask you to come in but we're not fixed up yet.

FARROW (*a merry laugh*)—I've had four children born here and I'm still not fixed up. (*She walks in.*) It's true the back is sunnier, but the front has a window on the street. You couldn't give me the back for no rent and a dollar besides. (*Goes to the window.*) I could sit in the window from my first cup of coffee until bedtime. It's my pleasure. Anytime you want to talk to me just open the window and yell Farrow or sparrow and I'll answer. (*Suddenly—*) She's shy, ain't she?

MARGARET—What did you say?

FARROW—Young girl. She's shy and she's pale. Instead of that pretty Sunday dress and a bow in her hair, she ought to be out in the horse trough with my kids. Oats all over the cobblestones and the cool running water. It's just like the country. Clementine, you take her down.

With rising anger, Margaret says: "No." Mystified, Mrs. Farrow says they'd better go before her supper burns, but Clementine will be glad to pick Lizzie up for her first day of school. Again she runs into a "No." Margaret says Lizzie isn't going to school: she didn't go to public school where they lived before and there's no reason for her to go here. "There sure is," Mrs. Farrow retorts, "there's the truant officer." Liking the idea of Lizzie's not going to school,

Clementine thinks there's no reason why she should go either. "There's two reasons," says Mrs. Farrow. "First, it's the law, and second, I ain't havin' you around the house; and third—" she swats Clementine on the behind—"you put that dime back on the table. March! You have to watch them all the time or they'll steal your birthmarks. I've got a big pot of potato soup on the stove. I'll bring you some." "That's good of you, Mrs. Farrow," Margaret thanks her coolly, "but we don't need anything." "You must be lucky," answers Mrs. Farrow. Then with a pleasant greeting to Lizzie, and a yank at Clementine, Mrs. Farrow leaves.

The minute they have gone Margaret apologizes to Lizzie for not being more neighborly. Deliberately ignoring her mother, Lizzie, to get back at her, does everything irritating she can think of. In desperation, Margaret—untying the pots and pans—holds out the jump-rope. With a rapturous expression Lizzie starts to skip. Deaf to everything but the rhymes she composes while skipping, Lizzie ignores Margaret's admonition that she stop before she tires.

Having nothing in the house to eat, Margaret knows that she could make Lizzie happy by accepting the Farrow soup, but she puts off visiting the fourth floor with fantasies of how friendly she will be with Mrs. Farrow tomorrow. Stopping her rope-jumping, Lizzie asks her to go now—Mrs. Farrow may not be home tomorrow. "She's always home—sitting in the window—she said so," says Margaret. "Why can't you do it now?" Lizzie begs. Margaret bursts out: "Because she's a slob!" And ordering Lizzie to bolt and chain the door after she has gone out, Margaret goes out for groceries.

Realizing that her mother has forgotten her purse, Lizzie shrugs and goes back to her rope, this time skipping faster and faster till the rope becomes a blur. A tap at the bedroom window brings her up short. Rushing into the room and catching sight of her father on the ladder outside, Lizzie joyously opens the window and her arms.

James Hyland, who had been biding his time till Margaret went out, laughs with his daughter and does a little jig. Now noticing that Margaret still dresses Lizzie in flawless white, now quoting a snatch of poetry, now observing that their new home has a window on the street, James next asks Lizzie if she does any reading. "The mark of the cultured individual . . . wherever one goes . . . one reads." Lizzie says she was going to send him their new address. "I believe you," says James. "A remarkable specimen of womanhood your mother! Let her inhabit a place but for an hour and it is invested with that exquisite perfume which is next to godliness . . . soap. There are some, though, who prefer the smell of human-

ity; and who shall say which of us is right and which wrong?" Not
having seen her father for such a long time, Lizzie asks where he
has been. Gaily evasive, James cries: "Elsewhere!"

Obviously jobless and hungry, James quickly tires as he tries to
play a game with Lizzie. Not wanting to worry the child, he tells
her that *she* must go up on the roof where he was, and sit in the
sun as much as she can to get color into her cheeks. He advises her
to eat nutritious eggs, too. But what she wants to know is: did
James bring her a book? "It is your nature," she says. As James
gazes at this child of his, Mrs. Farrow enters with some potato soup.

Smelling the soup, James comes to life and with a gallant bow
introduces himself as Lizzie's father. Mrs. Farrow could have sworn
that Margaret was a widow. "I am an agreeable man in most
things," says James, "but in that I could not oblige her." Not
being able to resist the soup, James becomes downright eloquent
over its merits. As Mrs. Farrow listens with pleasure to this high-
flown spiel, she sighs: "And there I was fretting I wasn't going to
like my new neighbors on the fifth." She sees that she has said
something wrong.

JAMES—No . . . but I must tell you that for the time being Mrs.
Hyland and I maintain separate establishments. To put the matter
briefly, I occupy another domicile. Are you sure you cannot stay?

FARROW—Oh, I must go. (*Watching him eat.*) You're hungry.

JAMES (*shaking his head*)—Not at all. But this is ambrosia never
dreamt by Discorides.

FARROW—I wish Mr. Farrow thought so.

JAMES—There *is* a Mr. Farrow?

FARROW—And five little sparrows.

JAMES—You destroy me.

FARROW—Tell me, Mr. Hyland . . . (*Giggles.*) What line of
business do you follow?

JAMES (*a sweeping gesture*)—The curvature of the earth.

As fascinated as Mrs. Farrow by James's easy talk, Lizzie nevertheless posts herself at the window so that she can warn them of
Margaret's return. Enjoying herself hugely, Mrs. Farrow sits down.
"A woman," she says, "has no greater pleasure . . . than to feed
a man." Warmed by the soup, James unreels a longish story filled
with classical references and the mention of a supposedly famous
doctor. Mrs. Farrow, who could listen forever, says admiringly,
"You have a story for everything, don't you?" and laughs con-
tentedly at all James says. "My dear," James says, as he rises and

goes to her, "you have that rarest, that most blessed, most precious quality which our Maker can bestow upon womankind." He takes her hand in his own. "You listen. This afternoon you have reminded me of something I had forgotten. . . ." "Yes, Mr. Hyland?" says Mrs. Farrow. "That I'm a man," James answers.

Returning for the purse she had left behind, Margaret finds them looking into each other's eyes. Ignoring Mrs. Farrow and her potato soup, Margaret says: "Well, James, you have words for every one else . . . have you no word for me?" Mrs. Farrow beats a bewildered retreat to the fourth floor.

Ordered to her bedroom that her mother and father may talk alone, Lizzie drags her leg very noticeably. Despairing that Margaret will send James away again and blinded by tears, Lizzie tries to concentrate on her books; but she can hear all that passes between her parents.

First of all, Margaret orders James to take off his jacket, then she sets to work deftly at sewing on a missing button. That finished, Margaret begins to mend a small tear in the cloth. James marvels that she can't resist the mending. "I can resist anything," Margaret says. "Don't be too sure," James warns her. "The ancients had a saying: 'More than the calf needs to suckle does the cow need to give suck. . . .' "

James has come home because he needs his family. Margaret tells him to go back to that woman or to the others. "There have been no others in some years," he says. "I have been making my own circuitous approach to monogamy. Margaret, I came back because occasional visits with Lizzie no longer satisfy my need. I crave to be with her. Not just for a few hours each week the way it used to be, but all the time. Constantly." "We have no marriage," Margaret maintains. "We can make a family," James pleads, "even if we have no marriage. Let me stay. I can sleep in the kitchen again. Someone has to teach her." But Margaret, who earns her living by sewing, says she can hire a teacher and that of all the people in the world, James would be the last one she would hire—because, she explains, their daughter loves him. As Lizzie gives a start in the bedroom, James wants to know what he has done that is so terrible and beyond forgiveness. "The mark that is on her flesh," Margaret answers.

Accusing James of being a weakling, Margaret deliberately humiliates him in front of Lizzie. Sure that he hasn't even the money for a night's lodging, she offers him a coin to amuse her as he did Mrs. Farrow. "Make me smile, James," she taunts him. "Tell me

one of your stories, so that I can laugh." "Well," she shouts, "did
you spend all your talk on Mrs. Farrow? Is there nothing left for
me?" She goes to him, and standing very close, demands: "Where
are all the words?" "You choke me, Margaret," James answers.
"I'll tell you what you do to me," she lashes back, "my fastidious
James Hyland who never kept a job more than a month, but who
always had to carry two clean handkerchiefs . . . you choke *me*."
As he reaches up to touch her lips, her arm comes down hard. "I
am no rag doll for your fingers to touch," she cries. "You can't
come back and make a plaything of my life. I am five flights above
the street. These are my four walls. My rent is paid in advance.
So you go! And let me shut the door after you! And turn the key!
And draw the chain across!"

Despising himself for saying even a word, James tells Lizzie that
he has brought her *The Lady of the Lake* as a defense against
truant officers. Lizzie, assuming Margaret's tone, says: "I don't
want anything from you. Nothing. Not a thing." Triumphant,
Margaret now allows James to leave the book, and go. "He will be
all right," Margaret tells Lizzie. "Don't worry about him. He
heals. He will walk downstairs broken-hearted, but on a corner a
man will say, 'Sir, can you tell me the hour?' and he will deliver a
talk on time . . . so full of quotations . . . he'll be invited into the
nearest tavern for a glass of sherry from Spain." Margaret insists,
over James's protests, on letting Lizzie know what a liar he has been
to the whole world. James pleads that she let Lizzie love him a
little, but Lizzie is by now as hard as her mother. As James opens
the door, he discovers Clementine listening to their every word.

Unperturbed, Clementine announces that two men, one a policeman, are looking on the next block for an Elizabeth Ursula Hyland.
Calling her a "snotnose," Margaret orders her away. Clementine
repeats that the men will be coming here. Margaret now screams:
"Don't you ever wash your face? Don't you ever comb your hair?
You sneak, you thief . . . you slob's daughter . . ." Hurt, Clementine takes her revenge. Looking at Lizzie, she asks: "Why does
she wear a glove on that hand?" As Lizzie trembles violently, Margaret shouts at Clementine: "I hope you die."

ACT II

Disdaining James's offer of help, Margaret hastily puts the bed
together and makes it up while James comforts Lizzie in his arms.
Drawn to James, aware of his love for her, Lizzie asks why he

never speaks up for himself or makes any effort to answer Margaret. "What is there to say?" James murmurs. "You're my father," Lizzie cries passionately. "I'm a bag of wind," he says. Throwing her arms about him, Lizzie pleads: "Take me away . . . anywhere, any place. Wherever you go. Take me. Take me." Saying that she would starve, that he is incapable of earning a dollar, James makes plain that Lizzie never could depend on him. Abruptly pushing herself out of his arms, acting exactly like her mother, Lizzie offers James the dime from the table. He is crushed. He asks her not to despise him. Now terribly sorry, Lizzie kisses him; he in turn takes her mittened hand and kisses it gallantly back. Margaret says wearily that the truant officers will find Lizzie up and about if she doesn't hurry. James holds onto her hand. "But darling," he says, "what if they do?" Frightened, Lizzie tries to pull away.

JAMES—You can go to school like other children.

LIZZIE—I mustn't.

JAMES—Margaret, let her go to school with other children.

LIZZIE—No. (*As she pulls her hand from* JAMES's *grasp, she leaves the mitten in his hand. As* LIZZIE *screams,* MARGARET *seizes the exposed hand and, like some wild creature, with its maimed young, she plunges it into her mouth.*)

JAMES (*struggling against the nausea that has risen into his own mouth*)—Don't do that! Don't do that! (MARGARET *for once is bewildered. She withdraws the hand and covers it with the mitten.*)

MARGARET (*bemused*)—Come, Lizzie, your bed is made.

LIZZIE—I know, Mama. (*She drags her leg through the room, gets into bed . . . covers herself.*)

MARGARET—You uncovered her.

JAMES—It was an accident.

MARGARET—You shouldn't have uncovered her. It was wrong.

JAMES—How long will you do this to her?

MARGARET—You did it to her.

JAMES—All right. I did it to her. (*He starts for the door and she stops him.*)

MARGARET—They will meet you on the stairs. You'll talk. You can't help talking.

JAMES—And would that be such a terrible thing?

MARGARET—Never as long as you live!

JAMES—It is nothing, Margaret. It's a trivial thing she has.

MARGARET—God's punishment, James Hyland, is never a trivial thing.

JAMES—What is it? A little girl was born with six fingers on her left . . .

As Margaret covers his mouth with her hand, they hear footsteps approaching. When a knock comes, Margaret sits down and asks James to be seated. When knocks are repeated, Margaret unlocks the door but leaves it chained. Refusing to honor either the Board of Education's credentials or a court order that are successively thrust through the opening, Margaret finally yields to the Policeman's threat to break down the door. She opens up.

Lameschnik, the truant officer, who has come to see that Lizzie goes to school, is extremely skeptical about her illness. "Yeah," he says, "I have the record. In Canal Street when a representative of the Board of Education called, she was sick. And she was sick in Hudson Street, and she was sick when you moved to Lispenard Street. For a sick kid you certainly travel her around, don't you?" Having looked into the bedroom and seen Lizzie in bed, the Policeman reports that the child *is* sick. Old hand Lameschnik merely asks him to check her feet; and cursing, the Policeman discovers under the quilt that Lizzie still has her shoes on.

Lameschnik orders Margaret to dress the child at once, and when she refuses, he prepares to do the job himself. James intervenes. Silent till now, he bowls over Lameschnik with an intricately pretentious way of asking: What is the meaning of the compulsory education law? Since Lameschnik is lost after the first phrase, James answers his question himself. "Why," says he, "is there a civil statute, and criminal penalties if the statute is disobeyed, to compel the education of the young? Why? To guarantee that whatever is latent within the child will be kindled and encouraged. Educate. Education. *Educatus . . . educo. E,* meaning *out,* and *duco,* lead . . . Educate . . . to lead out . . . therefore, to draw out what is already there. Let us see what is there, and what has been drawn out. Lizzie, come." Horrified, Margaret orders Lizzie to stay where she is, but James insists on putting his daughter through her paces.

James asks Lizzie a question in Latin, and another in French; he asks her to identify quotations from Landor, Blake and Pope. He asks her who wrote *The Spirit of the Laws,* and the distance between New York and London. She answers enthusiastically and correctly. James submits that to this date the education of Elizabeth Hyland has been accomplished in her home and not at all to the detriment of the state or herself. Impressed though he is, Lameschnik never strays from the path of duty. With the law behind him, he tells them to dress Lizzie and come with him. If Lizzie is really sick, Lameschnik will take her to Bellevue. Trembling, Lizzie wheels about with her dragging leg and goes back to bed. Whereupon Margaret appeals to Lameschnik in his own children's name. "You said you had children of your own." "Two boys and two girls," Lameschnik answers. "And the four of them put together—and they're my own kids—don't know half as much as she's got in her little finger. For God's sake! A girl like that! What are you afraid of sending her to school for! What? Why?" Saying she's no different than anybody else's kid, it suddenly dawns on Lameschnik. "Tell me," he says, "why does she keep one hand in . . ." Margaret furiously tells him to shut up. Having had enough, Lameschnik orders the Policeman to go in and get Lizzie, and if need be, carry her.

As the Policeman starts for the bedroom, Margaret starts for the window. Stepping out onto the ledge, she says that if they do not leave her house, she will jump. Amid screams from below, James Hyland says that Margaret means what she says, she *always* means what she says. The Policeman blows his whistle crazily. The whistle brings Lizzie, nightgown and all, forgetful of her dragging leg, into the kitchen. Trying to prevent her from seeing what is going on, James puts his arms around her. As Mrs. Farrow can be heard calling out to Margaret, Lizzie forces herself from James's restraining hands and cries: "Mama. No, Mama." She tries to say more, but something awful has happened suddenly to her arms. They shake in an uncontrollable, demented fashion. As the whistle blows again, Margaret, telling Lizzie to stop it, comes into the house.

SCENE II

Despite all that Margaret has said to her and to Clementine, Mrs. Farrow, risking insult, has brought whiskey to tide James and Margaret over this bad hour. She has also sent Clementine for the doctor. Margaret will have nothing to do with spirits or doctor: she wants no stranger in her house. "Mrs. Hyland," Mrs. Farrow tells her, "you be decent with Dr. Jacobson; he saved my little Tommy from the milk fever." "You said you were going to bring me a cup of coffee," Margaret answers. "If you intend to bring it . . . bring it." "I'll spit in the cup to sweeten it. Can't you take a kindness from no one?" "No one," says Margaret.

As James in the bedroom sings to Lizzie, Mrs. Farrow, returning with the coffee, listens. "A man like that!" she sighs . . .

FARROW—Farrow's a hard-working man but if James Hyland asked me I'd go away with him in an hour.

MARGARET—You kept your word . . . you spit in my coffee.

FARROW—Sure, you would say that. (MARGARET *pours the coffee down the sink; rinses the cup and returns it to* MRS. FARROW.)

MARGARET—Shall I dry it for you? (MRS. FARROW *spits in* MARGARET'S *face.*)

JAMES (*from doorway of bedroom*)—Mrs. Farrow!

MARGARET—Don't raise your voice to her. She is a person who knows how to hit back. I have respect for her.

Having had enough, Mrs. Farrow departs as quickly as she can.

Dr. Jacobson arrives. Not wanting to disturb Lizzie more than he has to, he simply listens to her heart, gives her a sedative, and tells her that he'll return when she awakes.

As James tentatively holds the whiskey Mrs. Farrow left for him, Dr. Jacobson asks for information about the child. As one colleague to another, James delivers a classical medical description of the onset of a disease. Winning Dr. Jacobson's admiration, James, about to embark on a learned discourse, suddenly checks himself. He confesses that he is a fraud who believes in his own lies. "We all do," says Jacobson and is curious to know what profession James really follows. "I am a man," says James, "who starves by his own wits." Whereupon he pours the whiskey back into the bottle and corks it.

Though it is still too early to diagnose Lizzie's illness, Dr. Jacobson does not rule out the possibility of St. Vitus's dance. Promising the Hylands that they will not be further disturbed by policemen or Mr. Lameschnik, and that he will come back later, Dr. Jacobson leaves.

When Margaret orders him to leave, James offers to do an errand, wait for Lizzie to wake up, kiss her and then leave. Margaret accepts this condition of his scornfully. "Tell me, Margaret," James says, "what is it that made you so strong and me such a weakling?" "Thirteen years of the same marriage," she answers.

Reluctant to leave, James remembers that there was love once; that Margaret loved him those two years before Lizzie was born. Margaret only recalls how he wrote and she worked. She recalls too that he never finished anything. "There are times when it doesn't come," James protests. "What does a writer do when it doesn't come?" "He struggles," Margaret answers. "The neighbor children going out to the factories and a grown man sleeping in the afternoons. And then going out . . . to taverns." James begs that, whatever happened when Lizzie was conceived, Margaret not deny the memory of the good years. Having pawned those memories with her wedding ring, Margaret lets James do the weeping for their lost love.

Scene III

Lizzie still sleeps, while Margaret in the fading light sews. Returning with the needed groceries, James stores them away in the cupboard.

JAMES (*watching her sew for a moment*)—I used to read to you when you sewed. Shall I read to you now?

MARGARET—Since you must either talk or die, you might as well read.

JAMES (*angry though he is*)—"When Zarathustra came into the next city, which lay beside the forest, he found in that place many people gathered together in the market; for they had been called that they should see a rope dancer."

MARGARET—A rope dancer!

JAMES—A tightrope. "And Zarathustra spoke thus unto the people: 'Man is a cord above an abyss. A perilous arriving, a perilous traveling, a perilous looking backward, a perilous trembling and standing still. What is great in man is that he is a bridge and no goal . . . I love them that are great in scorn . . . (*saying the words by heart as he looks up from the page*) . . . for these are they that are great in reverence, and arrows of longing toward the other shore.'" (*She looks up at him, and he rises unbidden and brings her the opened page and holds it for her to see for herself. Her body tenses at his nearness.*)

MARGARET—I have sewing to do.

JAMES—So have I, so have I. (*Finding his place—*) "What is the greatest thing ye can experience? It is the hour of great contempt. The hour when you say, 'What good is my virtue? And yet it hath not made me passionate?'"

MARGARET—You think I have no passion?

JAMES—Only the passion to deny passion. (*He taps the open page insistently.*) "It is not your sin . . . it is your self-satisfaction that cries unto heaven. Your very sparingness in sin cries unto heaven. Where is the lightning to lick you with its tongue? Where is the frenzy with which you should be inoculated?"

Reading no more, James somehow breaks through Margaret's reserve. Recapturing something of their feeling for one another, he touches her hair with his fingers, lifts her from her chair, and turns her to him. She does not move away as he strokes her neck. "I loathe you, Margaret," James says. "I detest you; but let me only see you, and my mouth is filled with desire. I look at you. I look.

Such a penalty to pay for eyes!" Bending, he kisses her breast, as the door behind them opens.

Dr. Jacobson announces himself. As he inquires about Lizzie, Margaret is stabbed by guilt: in these last minutes she had forgotten the child. Lizzie, however, is awake and calm, and hearing that the Doctor wants to examine her, says: "All right, Ma, don't worry." But when Dr. Jacobson wants to take the child's pulse, she will only thrust forth her right hand, and its frightened heartbeat shocks him.

Going out of the room, Dr. Jacobson asks casually about Lizzie's terrible fright. He gets nowhere. Wishing to pay him off, Margaret dismisses him. "Lizzie will be all right . . . after you are gone," she says. "Quite apart from the St. Vitus's dance, your daughter requires medical care," Dr. Jacobson persists. "Mrs. Hyland, I'll go now, because I do not wish to excite her. But I will come again and you must allow it." She refuses. Coming from Lizzie's room, James is startled to see Dr. Jacobson leaving once more, but he too refuses to tell about Lizzie. The Doctor remarks that the parents are united in silence. "We are hardly united," says Margaret. "Mr. Hyland is going, as a matter of fact." Overhearing this, and taking this last chance to keep her father in the house, Lizzie reveals her trouble to the Doctor.

She drags herself into the room and performs for him. With calculated gestures, and repeating some of her jump-rope rhymes, Lizzie claps her hands so that Dr. Jacobson can't fail to see the mitten. "That's enough!" cries Margaret.

LIZZIE—But I have to tell him why I don't go to school. Then the truant officer won't come back.

MARGARET (*frantically*)—Stop it.

LIZZIE—I don't go because I'm unnatural.

MARGARET—Stop it!

LIZZIE (*over-riding* MARGARET'S *panic with her own rising hysteria*)—I wear a mitten to cover my left hand. Look! (*She raises her hand.*) Not even a glove . . . a glove has five fingers. Look. A mitten.

MARGARET—Oh, no. No.

LIZZIE—Look . . . (*She pulls her mitten off and extends the fist to* DR. JACOBSON. . . . *He goes slowly toward her and gently takes her fist in his own hands.*)

JACOBSON—Your hand is warm from the glove.

LIZZIE—Not a glove. A mitten. Count them, Dr. Jacobson. Count them! (*Shrieks.*) Why don't you count them? One . . . two . . . three . . . four . . . five . . . six.

JACOBSON—Is that all? Now let's go in and lie down.

LIZZIE—You didn't listen! (*Wildly.*) I have six fingers.

JACOBSON—All right. That's not so terrible.

LIZZIE (*weeping with hopelessness*)—He's a stupid doctor. He's dumb. Pa, make him understand that my name is Elizabeth Pamela Ursula Hyland and I have six fingers.

JACOBSON—My name is Isaac Jacobson. I have a stomach ulcer.

MARGARET (*whispering*)—No, Dr. Jacobson, not the same thing.

JAMES (*bitterly*)—She has covered Lizzie's hand for eleven years.

JACOBSON—What a waste of life! We all wear a glove over something. You should see them in my office. The people who are ashamed. The ones who have no teeth, or too much hair. The short ones, the fat ones, the disappointed ones. They don't talk about it. I have to guess. It's hard for us to go into the presence of another and stand naked. Child, you have nothing to be ashamed of.

MARGARET—Evil is on her hand.

JACOBSON (*picks up* LIZZIE's *hand and looks at it*)—Evil is in the mind.

As Margaret instinctively hides the hand in hers, Dr. Jacobson says: "No. Not any more."

Lizzie's brave effort has cost her another convulsive attack. Her parents and the doctor have difficulty getting her to bed. Using the jump-rope as sole means to hold her down, Margaret and James restrain Lizzie. To relax her body, Dr. Jacobson administers chloroform.

When the child is still, Margaret asks what the cure is for this illness. "You mean," Dr. Jacobson answers, "what is it that makes her mind so afraid her body tries to run away? You can answer that, Mrs. Hyland."

Though no one has discovered whether St. Vitus's dance comes from an infection, or what microbe carries it, the possibility remains that it could be "fright." While she is so deeply anesthetized, while she cannot feel any pain, Jacobson suggests that they remove the finger. James urges Margaret to agree: "You have had her finger for eleven years. You've had it long enough. Let Dr. Jacobson have it."

Margaret recalls the Doctor saying that even without St. Vitus's dance so poorly developed a child as Lizzie would require medical care. Lizzie, Margaret contends, has no blood to spare. Dr. Jacobson accuses her of insisting on her daughter's illness. "Is that what

I do?" Margaret asks. "Then you mustn't ask me any more. He's the father. Ask him." "Take it off," says James.

Remembering that Mrs. Farrow has a long table of the sort that he will need, Dr. Jacobson asks James to help him carry it upstairs.

When the men leave, Margaret discovers the jump-rope still in her hand. Smiling strangely, she tries a few skips. Then as the rope comes high, she snaps it viciously against her neck, twists it, forces her arms out wide and beseeches the "Jehovah of her judgment" to "Pull it tight for me—I have no more strength."

ACT III

Two hours later, neither Margaret nor James is looking after the sick child. In the dark bedroom, Mrs. Farrow watches at Lizzie's bedside, and deals with Clementine who has been sent to bring her mother home.

FARROW—You tell your father I'll come down when I get there. The woman out of the window half the day and the child operated . . . and all Peter Farrow can think of is his own belly. Tell him to read your brothers a story.

CLEMENTINE (*her jaw falls open*)—What?

FARROW—What do you mean what? You tell your father to stop snapping his suspenders and to read the kids a story.

CLEMENTINE—How?

FARROW—Out of a book, that's how. Other men do it. Plenty of other men. You tell him I said so.

CLEMENTINE—He'd kill me.

FARROW—Peter Farrow won't kill nobody and it'll give him something to think about till I get down. (*She hears* LIZZIE *stirring*.) Look what we've done! We woke her up! Go down to your father, Clementine. Go on, before I cut off your head and put on a button.

Awakening, Lizzie remembers that her father is never coming back. "You had a foolish dream," Mrs. Farrow says. "It's a dream," Lizzie feels, "only when he comes back. She won't let him." Washing the child and making her comfortable, Mrs. Farrow gives Margaret as much credit as possible—a good and conscientious worker who has gone to deliver a shirtwaist. Lizzie only wants to talk of her father. "Mrs. Farrow," she says, "do you know that James Hyland is one of the finest unpublished poets in America?"

Putting Lizzie's head against her bosom, Mrs. Farrow combs her

hair and gives her a few sips of water. Lizzie thanks her. Lowering
the child into bed and covering her, Mrs. Farrow sighs: "Your body
is so thin." Lying back, Lizzie says: "You have a soft bosom."
"Child, child," Mrs. Farrow cries, "you're starved!"

A moment later, minus jacket, watch and chain, but in high good
humor, James prances into the room. Not finding Margaret, he says
bitterly: "So she left her alone." "So did you, Mr. Hyland," answers
Mrs. Farrow.

Informing Mrs. Farrow that this is an occasion for rejoicing and
singing hosannas, James brings forth a parrot. "You went from the
child for that?" Mrs. Farrow says coldly. He has also brought a
ring for Lizzie's finger, which he displays happily. "It's brass," says
Mrs. Farrow. "A gimcrack ring for five cents!"

As Margaret comes wearily back into the house and looks in on
Lizzie, Mrs. Farrow says: "She took a little water." Margaret is
grateful. Leaving James to sit near Lizzie, Margaret stays with
Mrs. Farrow in the kitchen. Knowing that her table has been
needed by the Doctor, Mrs. Farrow would like to know just what he
did to Lizzie.

MARGARET—She was born with six fingers and I hid it in a mitten.
No one to play with, so she skipped rope. (*She sits holding her
things.*) Made up little songs. Dancing with a rope, on a rope,
without any rope at all. Her whole body dancing. Today she had
fits and they call it St. Vitus's dance. James and I, we gave her
what we didn't give each other, and maybe she didn't need that.
She has always been torn between us, and we are always running
from each other; and who is left and always caught? It is always
the child. (MRS. FARROW *impulsively holds out her hand, and*
MARGARET *takes it.*) Oh, Mrs. Farrow! We strong ones, we have
no chance against the James Hylands of the world. We are always
right and they are always loved.

FARROW—Call down if you need me. Any time.

MARGARET—I will. (JAMES *comes out of the bedroom and sees
them.*)

FARROW (*coldly*)—Good evening, Mr. Hyland.

As Margaret sets wearily to work, James returns to Lizzie and sits
by her bed till she wakes up. Lizzie is rapturous that he has come
back, and he now announces that this is the glorious day of her
birth. He explains what Dr. Jacobson did while Lizzie slept. "Only
five fingers!" Lizzie marvels. "Now," James says, "you are like
everyone else." There being nothing to hide any more, James is all

Art Carney and Siobhan McKenna in "The Rope Dancers"

for ripping off the pockets from Lizzie's dresses. "I need my pockets," Lizzie says desperately. "I've got to have my pockets." Yielding, James kisses her. "I'm tired, Daddy," Lizzie says, "let me sleep again."

Rejoining Margaret, James says that this one time, today, it would not kill her to kiss her daughter. Margaret answers that she has tried many times. "But," she says, "you were always there before me. You held her so tight you squeezed me dry." James dreams: "Lizzie and I will walk in the street now. She won't be timid with the world. She will wear her ring and we will walk. You won't stop it now. Lizzie and I. Hand in hand. I'm a worthless husband but I can be father—enough to teach her to laugh. I feel very good tonight. And I never thought I would." Picking up Mrs. Farrow's bottle of whiskey, Margaret says: "Celebrate. And then I will put you next to Lizzie and when Dr. Jacobson returns, he will find you together." "There is a vileness in you," James shouts.

Holding the whiskey without any intention of drinking it, James is sure that Margaret wishes him drunk so that when they stand in front of the magistrate with the child between them, she can be the irreproachable mother and he the drunken braggart. But no more. Mrs. Farrow can have her whiskey. "Margaret," he pleads, "let me be the only thing I am. A father is more than a husband. A mother is more than a wife! Even if we have no love, for the sake of the child. We can still do it, Margaret, even now. Please." "Don't beg," says Margaret.

James angrily tells her to shut up and listen to him. "Not even when you die will you be more beautiful than when you carried Lizzie," he says. Why did she shun him then, why did she cease being a woman the instant her body became a mother? "The night Lizzie was conceived," Margaret answers, "you were drunk! . . . Drunk, James Hyland, you got drunk in the afternoon, and in the evening you went to a whore. And then you came to me—still wet with the whore—and fathered your child—and you bragged! You gentle man, you family man—you bragged." James cries. "Cry. Yes, cry, cry, James Hyland, be ashamed and wash yourself clean with tears. But I cannot cry and I have the outcome of it. 'When lust hath conceived, it bringeth forth sin; and sin when it is finished, bringeth forth death.' " She knows they are judged and they are punished. "I went to the whore; what did you do?" James says. "I played the whore. I lusted for you," Margaret confesses. "And I reveled in my own lust. Two years."

Incredulously James realizes that all these years it wasn't he that she was punishing, but herself. God is her sixth finger, he says. Even more incredulously, Margaret now plays the whore again. Turning the key in the door and chaining it, Margaret savagely kisses James. Like an animal, she kisses him again. Holding her hand over his mouth, she starts pulling down her dress. Realizing that this is a creature he doesn't know at all, he cries: "Why did you wait until this moment to show me?" "Because," she answers, "of what happened today. Because even though you promise and promise to go away, I know now you'll never go . . . unless I show you the kind of woman I am. Stop talking. Let us be animal and animal with each other . . . let me disgust you. The last illusion of James Hyland." She lets her dress fall and stamps on it.

Hearing the carriage below, trying to shake Margaret back to her senses, James orders her to put on her dress. Only through pouring whiskey down her throat can he stop her hysterical abandon. She is amused to find that whiskey makes her sober, but then she agrees with James: it isn't funny at all, it is sad. "Everything must be opposite with me," Margaret says. "Contrary! I make sin out of everything I want, everything I need." She promises that she will be good.

Carrying a cloth and a bowl of water to Lizzie, Margaret busies herself in the room. As she shuts the bedroom window, James opens the door—it is Mrs. Farrow, not the Doctor. By the time the Doctor arrives, Margaret has discovered that Lizzie is not asleep, but dead.

As the grief-stricken parents hover over the child, Dr. Jacobson makes his examination. Stricken, he prays: *"Boruch dayan emes . . . Blessed be the righteous Judge."*

"It was only a minor operation," James repeats inanely. "My dear," Dr. Jacobson says to Margaret, and to himself, "we don't know anything." Left alone with Lizzie, Margaret kisses her at last. "I always kiss you after you've fallen asleep. Don't I, Lizzie?" she says. "Tell your father." And putting her hands together, she prays: "Pity, God, pity. Pity for the living who destroy their own."

James brings the saddened Doctor some whiskey. "There was no medical reason," sighs Dr. Jacobson, "but your wife . . . she knew. There was too much haste. Mr. Hyland, you cannot take eleven years of deformity and suddenly cut it off with a knife. To be whole . . . it requires preparation."

All strength having ebbed from her, Margaret asks Mrs. Farrow to do her one more favor and bathe Lizzie. And turning to her husband, she says: "I no longer have the strength of my sickness. Help me, James." She asks him not to go away. "I won't," he assures her. "We will still be a family."

LOOK HOMEWARD, ANGEL

A Play in Three Acts

By KETTI FRINGS

(Based on the novel by Thomas Wolfe)

[KETTI FRINGS *was born in Columbus, Ohio. By the age of 13 she had lived in about as many towns, from Brooklyn, N. Y. to Portland, Ore. Her first book, "Hold Back the Dawn," was filmed by Paramount. She wrote a novel, "God's Front Porch," as well as stories for leading magazines. Her first play, "Mr. Sycamore," was produced by the Theatre Guild, and she has adapted for the screen such plays as "Come Back, Little Sheba" and "The Shrike."*]

[THOMAS WOLFE *first studied playwriting under Frederick H. Koch at the University of North Carolina. There young Wolfe wrote and acted in several plays. After graduation he went to Harvard and for three years continued to study under George Pierce Baker in the famous 47 Workshop. Here he wrote several plays, among them "Mannerhouse," which had a long run when produced in Germany and "Welcome to Our City," which the Theatre Guild considered producing in 1923. He is best known for his tetralogy— "Look Homeward, Angel," "Of Time and the River," "The Web and the Rock" and "You Can't Go Home Again." He died September 15, 1938, at the age of 37.*]

For the cast listing, see page 303.

IN the year 1916, in the town of Altamont, North Carolina, Eliza Gant runs a boarding house. The rambling, draughty, flimsy, fifteen-room frame building has an electric sign over its door: DIXIELAND. Along the front and side of the house runs a typically Southern verandah where, in the warm evenings, the boarders rock and gossip.

"Look Homeward, Angel": By Ketti Frings. © 1958 by Edward C. Aswell as Administrator, C.T.A. of the Estate of Thomas Wolfe and/or Fred W. Wolfe and Ketti Frings. Reprinted by permission of Charles Scribner's Sons, New York, N. Y.

136

Behind the shell of Dixieland the boarders' rooms, and those left over for the Gant family, have a depressingly worn and shabby look. In his own book-scattered cell, the youngest of the Gants, seventeen-year-old Eugene, is trying to capture and write down what his brother Ben is like; outside, on the verandah, Ben passes the time of day with pleasant, boozy Mrs. "Fatty" Pert.

What worries Ben is getting away from this "burg" and doing his bit to drive the Huns from the sky. Mrs. Pert can't help exclaiming: "You're twenty pounds underweight! I never saw anyone like you for not eating." "Maguire gave me a thorough check-up this spring," Ben answers. "How would your family feel if you went?" asks Mrs. Pert. "What family?" says Ben. "The batty boarders? Apologies, Fatty. I never associate you with them. Except for Gene, nobody'd know I was gone. . . ." Ben is obsessed with the dream of flying.

Ben's overworked sister Helen has no time for dreams as, followed by her helpful husband Hugh, she brings out the cups for the boarders' after-dinner coffee. Discovering Mrs. Pert, she cries out that dinner is almost finished. Tempted by the "charlotte russe," Fatty drops her knitting and heads for the dining room. Helen has hardly time to complain that her mother has left her to slave for a crowd of "old cheap boarders," before that crowd, ringing the service bell, yells "Helen!" She dashes in, leaving her nice quiet husband to wish she had more time to take care of him. His dream is of a house of their own. Ben, knowing this well, very much hopes that Hugh will soon save enough money to move away.

Eliza Gant, interested in housing solely as an investment, arrives home from a stimulating business foray with her real-estate broker brother, Will Pentland. She is now intent on selling her husband's marble yard right from under him. Pointing with her index finger, she stresses the fact that she's going to get after Mr. Gant this very day concerning the bank's offer for his shop. Her brother leaves and Eliza, seeing Ben on the porch, stops short. She wonders that he should be home at this time of the day. "I'm working afternoons this week," says Ben. "You always sound so short with me, Ben. Why is that?" his mother asks. "You don't even look at me. You know I can't stand not being looked at by the person I'm talking to. Don't you feel well?" "I feel good," he says.

Hearing the whistle of the noonday train, Eliza calls for her other son, Eugene, noticing at the same time Mrs. Pert's knitting. "Ben," she says, "I hope you haven't been lying around here wasting time with that Mrs. Pert again." "Listen to her!" says Ben. "It's the nicest time I spend." "I tell you what," Eliza continues, "it doesn't look right, Ben. What must the other boarders think? A woman her age . . . a drinking woman . . . married. Can't you find some-one young and pretty and free to be with? I don't understand it. You're the best-looking boy I've got." To keep things pleasant, Ben promises to look around, but the next moment, as Eliza orders Eugene to distribute Dixieland advertising cards at the depot, Ben becomes abruptly unpleasant.

Eugene hates drumming up trade. The great, hulking seventeen-year-old finds it deceptive and degrading.

ELIZA—Oh, my . . . my! Dreamer Eugene Gant, what do you think the world is all about? We are all . . . all of us . . . selling something. Now you get over to the depot right this minute. And for heaven's sake, boy, spruce up, shoulders back! Look like you *are* somebody. (EUGENE *starts off.*) And smile! Look pleasant! (EUGENE *grins, maniacally.*)

BEN (*suddenly, as he watches* EUGENE *limping*)—Gene! What are you walking like that for?

EUGENE—Like what?

BEN (*rises*)—What are you limping for? My God, those are my shoes you've got on! I threw them out yesterday!

ELIZA—They're practically brand new.

BEN—They're too small for *me*, they must be killing him.

EUGENE—Ben, please!

ELIZA—Maybe you can afford to throw out brand new shoes.

BEN—Mama, for God's sake, you ask him to walk straight, how can he? His toes must be like pretzels!

EUGENE—They're all right. I'll get used to them.

BEN (*throwing down his paper*)—My God, it's a damned dis-grace, sending him out on the streets like a hired man . . . Gene should be *on* that train, going to college!

ELIZA—That's enough—that's just enough of that! You haven't a family to provide for like I have, Ben Gant. Now I don't want to hear another word about it! Gene will go to college when we can afford it. This year he can help his Papa at the shop.

BEN—I thought you were going to *warm up* Papa, so he'll sell the shop.

ELIZA—Ben Gant, that wasn't intended for your ears. I'd ap-preciate it if you wouldn't mention it to Mr. Gant until I have. Hurry off now, son, get us a customer!

EUGENE—Why should Papa sell his shop?

ELIZA—Now you're too young to worry about my business. You tend to yours.

EUGENE—What business do I have to attend to, Mama?

ELIZA—Well, get busy, get busy! Help your Papa at the shop.

EUGENE—I don't want to be a stonecutter.

ELIZA—Well, go back to delivering newspapers. Work for Uncle Will in his real-estate office. But keep the ball rolling, child. Now hurry on or you'll be late! (EUGENE *exits.*)

HELEN (*entering*)—Mama, dinner's practically over! I'm no slave!

ELIZA—I'll be right in, Helen. (HELEN *exits, slamming door.* ELIZA *sighs.*) What's the matter with him, Ben? What's wrong with that boy? What's the matter with all of you? I certainly don't know. I tell you what, sometimes I get frightened. Seems as if every one of you's at the end of something, dissatisfied, and wants something else. But it just can't be. A house divided against itself cannot stand. I'll vow, I don't know what we're all coming to. (*Approaches side door and pauses.*) If you like, this once, as long as you're home, why don't you eat here? I'm sure there's plenty left over.

Ben turns down the "good hot meal" of the boarders' leftovers. As he starts off downtown, Eliza says lamely: "Well, have a nice day at the paper, son."

Onto the verandah, stuffed with Eliza's food, troop an assortment of boarders for their after-dinner coffee. Ranging from the new boarder, Mr. Farrel, a sixty-year-old ex-dancing master, to Florry Mangle, a humorless, ever-hopeful spinster, they pursue their usual after-dinner activities. They take possession of special chairs, criticize the quality of Mrs. Gant's coffee and the size of the dessert portions. Coarse, elderly Mrs. Clatt remarks to her equally unattractive son: "I'm told the best boarding house food in town is down the street at Mrs. Haskell's." Her son says he's heard the same thing. "Then move into Mrs. Haskell's!" cries Hugh. "Hugh!" cries Helen, giving him a shove as she goes into the house.

Miss Mangle prefers the "informal and entertaining" atmosphere of Mrs. Gant's place. Mrs. Clatt's son says that it hasn't been that way lately: "It's been over a month since Mrs. Gant had to have Mr. Molasses Edward and his two Dixie Ramblers evicted for not paying their rent. She certainly loves to see the police swarm around!"

At the very moment that Eliza Gant is welcoming a new boarder, a young woman so superior and attractive that she can't believe her luck, Eugene, the advance courier of bad news, races home. Drawing Eliza aside, he bursts out: "Mama, Papa's been at Laughran's again."

Dr. Maguire is trying to steer him home now." Eliza cries: "The doctor? Is he sick or is he drunk?" "He's rip roaring!" shouts Eugene. "He's awful. He kicked Uncle Will again!"

A small riot can be heard in the distance. Eliza, with a fine new young lady boarder all but won, doesn't think that she can stand what's coming. Eugene tries his consoling best: "At least it's been a month this time."

The whirlwind, shouting vituperation, approaches. "My God," Jake Clatt says, "Mr. Gant's on the loose again!" Eugene tries to herd the boarders into the parlor until Mr. Gant is safely upstairs. "Come along, Mr. Farrel," says boarder Miss Brown; "let's clear the deck for the old geezer."

In his wild, untrammeled state, bearded, disheveled, coatless W. O. Gant needs room in which to flail his arms and bellow his insults. Accompanied by Dr. Maguire and a disreputable drinking crony, W. O. clatters up the back verandah steps, scattering people before him as he advances. Deliberately driving a frightened Mrs. Clatt into the house, Mr. Gant at the same time can hear Eliza speaking to him. "I am not sick, Madame," he replies. "I am in a wild, blind fury." And, by raising a chair and threatening her, he proceeds to show it.

Gant insists that he doesn't live here, that he lives at *92 Woodson Street*. "That was some years ago," Dr. Maguire says; "this is your home now, Gant." "This barn?" Gant shouts. "This damnable, this awful, this murderous and bloody barn—home! Holy hell, what a travesty on nature!" Will Pentland, putting in his two cents, enrages Gant further. "Pentland—now that's a name for you." Gant searches for Will. "Where are you, Will Pentland?" Seeing him, he staggers in his direction: "You're a Mountain Grill! Your father was a Mountain Grill and a horse thief, and he was hanged in the public square." Offered some coffee, Gant kicks the cup and yells: "Hah! Some of Mrs. Gant's *good* coffee?" What *he* could use is some good bourbon. Maguire thinks hopefully it might knock him out.

A witness of the scene, the young lady boarder, Laura James, offers the small vial of whiskey that she carries in case of accidents. Maguire, accepting it from her, remarks: "Good God, this won't fill one of his teeth." But he tries it as bait to get Gant onto the porch.

Coming out to her father, Helen saves the day. He leans against her and complains of a pain in his guts, and she, all sympathy, answers: "Come with me now. I'll put you to bed, and bring you some soup." Gant has to sit down. He pats a space beside him, saying: "Sit down, Helen, you and me. Sit and talk. Would you like to hear some Keats . . . beautiful Keats?" This is more than Eliza can bear. "He's got his audience now," she says, "that's all he wants." She suggests that he go into the house. Instead, he starts some drunken singing in which his crony joins him. Eliza promptly removes the drunken friend from the premises.

HELEN—Dr. Maguire's here to give you something for your pain, Papa.

GANT—Doctors! Thieves and bloodsuckers! "The paths of glory lead but to the grave."—Grey's Elegy. Only four cents a letter on any tombstone you choose, by the master carver— Any orders? (*He groans with pain.*) It's the Devil's own pitchfork. Don't let them put me under the knife—promise me, daughter. Promise me! (HELEN *nods. With a giant effort,* GANT *pulls himself up.*) "Over the stones, rattle his bones! He's only a beggar that nobody owns."

MAGUIRE—Good God, he's on his feet again.

EUGENE—Hugh, let's get him in the house.

GANT (*throwing off* HUGH *and* EUGENE)—I see it! I see it! Do you see the Dark Man's shadow? There! There he stands—the Grim Reaper—as I always knew he would. So you've come at last to take the old man home? Jesus, have mercy on my soul! (GANT *falls to the ground. There is an agonized silence.* EUGENE, *the doctor, and* HUGH *rush to him.*)

ELIZA—Dr. Maguire.

DR. MAGUIRE (*feels* GANT'S *heart*)—He's just passed out, Mrs. Gant. Men, let's carry him up!

Pulling herself together, Eliza seizes Laura's suitcase. "I think you'll enjoy it here," she says, "it's quiet and peaceful—oh, nobody pays any mind to Mr. Gant. I'll tell you what: we don't have occurrences like this every day." Laura is plainly doubtful. Seeing this, Eliza quickly reduces her rates. The minute Laura yields, Eliza, poking out her hand, adds: "That's in advance, that is."

As the deal with Laura is sealed with dollar bills, shattered Mr. Farrel appears, suitcase in hand, trying to get past Eliza unnoticed. "Mr. Farrel!" Eliza cries. "Where are you going? Mr. Farrel, you've paid for a week in advance." Without a word, Mr. Farrel disappears. "Well," says Eliza cheerfully, "they come and they go—" and takes Laura in the house to her room.

Ben, having heard the news, dashes home. Finding that his father

is safe upstairs, he relaxes with a cup of coffee and a cigarette, waits
for Maguire, and takes on Eugene's disturbed questions.

EUGENE—What's it all about? It doesn't make sense. Can you
figure it out, Ben? Why does he do it?

BEN—How should I know? (*Drinks his coffee.*) Is Maguire
almost through?

EUGENE (*hurt, not understanding* BEN's *preoccupation*)—Ben, remember in the morning when we used to walk together and you were
teaching me the paper route? We talked a lot then.

BEN—Listen to him! We're talking.

EUGENE—If he hates it so much here, why does he stay?

BEN—You stupid little fool, it's like being caught in a photograph.
Your face is there, and no matter how hard you try, how are you
going to step out of a photograph? (DOCTOR MAGUIRE *enters.*)
Shut up now, will you? Hello, Doc.

DR. MAGUIRE—Your sister sure can handle that old goat like a
lamb! The funny thing though is that people like him. He's a good
man, when sober.

Ben, wanting to enlist in the Canadian air force, asks Maguire to
okay him. "In Christ's name, Maguire," he cries out tensely, "you'll
recommend me, won't you? You examined me just a couple of
months ago." Taking his time, Maguire sets down his bag and asks
Ben to stick out his chest. Posing a few decoy questions, Maguire
unexpectedly prods Ben's solar plexus with a strong finger. Ben's
distended chest collapses. "They'll have to save this world without
you, Ben," Maguire says. Grabbing the doctor, Ben cries: "What do
you mean?" He insists on knowing whether he is all right. "Yes,
Ben," Maguire says quietly, "you're all right. Why, you're one of
the most all right people I know." Carefully feeling Ben's arm,
Maguire continues: "You're a little run down, that's all. You need
some meat on those bones." As Ben breaks away, Maguire reminds
him: "You can't exist with a cup of coffee in one hand and a cigarette
in the other. Besides, the Altamont air is good for you. Stick
around. Big breaths, Ben, big breaths." "Thanks," Ben says; "as
a doctor, you're a fine first baseman." "Take it easy; try not to
care too much," Maguire advises.

Eugene, when the doctor has left, wants very much to comfort
Ben, who will have none of it. Gathering himself together, pulling
out some money, Ben orders Eugene to get his much-too-long hair
cut and to buy some new shoes. Eugene doesn't want to be always
on the receiving end. Ben roughhouses playfully with him over the

giving and taking of the bills, but in another moment becomes as tense as before. He orders Eugene to get out of town, to go to college and be all the things he can be. He cries out passionately that Eugene must get the money from the family, or beg it, take it, steal it, but get it somehow: "Get it and get away from them. To hell with them all!" A spell of coughing overtakes Ben. He continues in a pegged-out way: "Neither Luke, nor Stevie, nor I made it. But you can, Gene. I let her hold on until it was too late. Don't let that happen to you. And, Gene, don't try to please everyone. Please yourself—"

Noticing Laura James' hat on the bench, Ben changes the subject. He says that he dreams of these elegant women. Eugene is confused. Why then does Ben choose such company? "Mrs. Pert?" Ben asks. "Fatty's a happy woman. There's no pain in her she feels she has to unload onto someone else. . . ."

And as he sets off for work, Ben carefully dismisses his whole idea of going to Canada: "I have to bring you up first, don't I?"

Pacing back and forth while looking up at Laura's window, Eugene awkwardly avoids the advances of lady boarder Brown. Not content with coy remarks, Miss Brown sings and dances sensuously in front of Eugene, causing him to back away so fast that he stumbles over a table. Singing "Pony Boy" and dangling her parasol, Miss Brown swishes off. Eugene, sitting down, takes off his shoes and rubs his aching toes.

Returning for her hat, Laura smiles at Eugene. All he can do is hide his shoeless feet in embarrassment, for which he is rewarded with another smile.

Scene II

In the warm Southern evening, Dixieland boarders amuse themselves as best they can, while the rest of the world pairs off, or wishes to. Ben and Fatty drink beer together; Eugene sits yearning on the side steps.

Fatty wonders who Ben is always talking to with that upward glance of his. "Who, him?" says Ben; "that's Grove, my twin. It was a habit I got into, while he was still alive." Fatty wishes that Ben had known her when she was young and "some different." "I bet you weren't half as nice and warm and round as you are now," Ben answers. Hoping his mother never hears him talk like that, Mrs. Pert says: "Dear, I only hope when the right girl comes along, you won't be sorry for the affection you've lavished on me." Ben wants nothing to do with that "right girl."

Against a background of boarders' talk and Jake Clatt's ukulele, Ben tells Fatty that when he's with her, he's comfortable. "People don't understand," he says. "Jelly roll isn't everything, is it?" Fatty warns him that his little brother Eugene is taking in everything he says. "Gene knows all about jelly roll—don't you?" Ben calls to him. "Where do you think he's been all his life—in Mama's front parlor?"

What Eugene has been waiting for happens: Laura seeks him out and asks to sit next to him. Flustered and delighted, Eugene introduces himself awkwardly. Laura had noticed him on her arrival. "I was coming from the station. You know where the train crosses the street," she says; "you were just standing there staring at it. I walked right by you and smiled at you. I never got such a snub in my whole life. My, you must be crazy about trains." Eugene is overcome by the notion of Laura's standing beside him and his not knowing it. Discovering that she comes from Richmond, Eugene bursts with questions about that big city, and before she can answer them all, pours out, almanac-style, some facts that he's picked up. He knows the number of books in the Richmond Library; he wonders how long it would take to read a hundred thousand books—about twenty years, he figures. He knows that Virginia's William and Mary is the second oldest college in the country. "Is it?" says Laura. "What's the oldest?" "Harvard!" exclaims Eugene. "I'd like to study there! First Chapel Hill. That's our state university. Then Harvard. I'd like to study all over the world, learn all its languages. I love words, don't you?" Laura's smiling reaction to Eugene's eagerness makes him wonder if she's laughing at him.

LAURA—I'm smiling because I'm enjoying myself. I like talking to you.

EUGENE—I like talking to you, too. I always talk better with older people.

LAURA—Oh!

EUGENE—They know so much more.

LAURA—Like me?

EUGENE—Yes. You're very interesting.

LAURA—Am I?

EUGENE—Oh, yes! You're very interesting!

When Jake Clatt, leaving Florry Mangle, tries to persuade Laura to take a stroll, Laura murmurs: "It feels to me like it's going to rain." Jake Clatt doesn't think so. Eugene gets to his feet and says firmly: "It's going to rain, all right." The best Jake can manage is a cutting: "Good night, sonny." It hits home.

A train's whistle brings Eugene to one of his favorite subjects: trains.

EUGENE—Mama took us on one to St. Louis to the Fair, when I was only five. Have you ever touched one?

LAURA—What?

EUGENE—A locomotive. Have you put your hand on one? You have to feel things to fully understand them.

LAURA—Aren't they rather hot?

EUGENE—Even a cold one, standing in a station yard. You know what you feel? You feel the shining steel rails under it . . . and the rails send a message right into your hand . . . a message of all the mountains that engine ever passed—all the flowing rivers, the forests, the towns, all the houses, the people, the washlines flapping in the fresh cool breeze—the beauty of the people in the way they live and the way they work—a farmer waving from his field, a kid from the school yard—the faraway places it roars through at night, places you don't even know, can hardly imagine. Do you believe it? You feel the rhythm of a whole life, a whole country clicking through your hand.

LAURA (*impressed*)—I'm not sure we all would. I believe *you* do.

Eugene and Laura are now very conscious of one another. They interrupt each other with questions, but it mostly boils down to how long Laura is staying, how old Eugene is, and how old Laura is. Laura gets to the point but Eugene gets there first. "How old are you?" he asks. Laura says that she is twenty-one; Eugene says that he is nineteen.

EUGENE—You're only twenty-one?

LAURA—How old did you think I was?

EUGENE—Oh, about that. About twenty-one, I'd say. That's not old at all!

LAURA (*laughs*)—I don't feel it is!

EUGENE—I was afraid you might think I was too young for you to waste time with like this!

LAURA—I don't think nineteen is young at all!

EUGENE—It isn't, really, is it?

LAURA—Gene, if we keep rushing together like this, we're going to have a collision.

Laura gets up and Eugene follows her to the side step, where they collide further in whispers. Fatty and Ben laugh together; inside

the house, Eliza, pitcher and glass in hand, enters Mr. Gant's bedroom. She is not welcomed.

In bed, he keeps his back turned and his words sharp. Even talking as he does, she wishes he would face her. She reminds him that
they've been married thirty-one years. This is enough to make Gant
groan. She recalls how they met: "I can remember like it was yesterday," says Eliza. "I'd just come down from Cousin Sally's and I
passed by your shop and there you were. I'll vow you looked as big
as one of your tombstones—and as dusty—with a wild and dangerous
look in your eye. You were romantic in those days—like the fellow
says, a regular courtin' fool— 'Miss Pentland,' you said, 'you have
come into this hot and grubby shop like a cooling summer shower—
like a cooling summer shower.' That's just what you said!"

GANT—And you've been a wet blanket ever since.

ELIZA—I forgive you your little jokes, Mr. Gant. I forgive your
little jokes. (*Sits beside him, finds needle and thread under her
collar, mends his dressing gown.*)

GANT—Do you? (*Slowly turns towards her and looks at her
finally.*) Do you ever forgive me, Eliza? If I could make you
understand something. I was such a strong man. I was dozing just
now, dreaming of the past. The far past. The people and the place
I came from. Those great barns of Pennsylvania. The order, the
thrift, the plenty. It all started out so right, there. There I was a
man who set out to get order and position in life. And what have I
come to? Only rioting and confusion, searching and wandering.
There was so much before, so much. Now it's all closing in. My
God, Eliza, where has it all gone? Why am I here, now, at the rag
end of my life? The years are all blotted and blurred—my youth a
red waste—I've gotten old, an old man. But why here? Why here?

ELIZA—You belong here, Mr. Gant, that's why! You belong here.
(*She touches his hand.*)

GANT (*throws her hand away*)—And as I get weaker and weaker,
you get stronger and stronger!

Eliza feels the moment propitious to have W. O. accept the bank
offer. "Well, I'll tell you what," she says, "twenty thousand dollars
is a lot of money! Like the fellow says, it ain't hay!" "And my
angel, my Carrara angel? You were going to sell her too?" Gant
asks. Eliza is tired of hearing about that angel. "You always have
been," Gant says. "Money dribbled from your honeyed lips. But
never a word about my angel. I've started twenty pieces of marble
trying to capture her. But my life's work doesn't interest you."

Eliza suggests that perhaps his gift as a stonecutter is limited, and having made the point, urges him to sell the shop. Gant, in his fury, all but leaps out of bed, and having vented his anger, gets in a bit of his own: "At least my first wife understood what it meant to me." And sentimentally feeling for the plump pillow, he says: "Cynthia, Cynthia . . ." He gets a rise out of Eliza. After a long silence, she says: "Mr. Gant, I guess I never will understand you. I guess that's just the way it is. Good night. Try to get some sleep." She gets up and tucks the bed clothes about him. "I reckon it's like the fellow says," Eliza finishes. "Some people never get to understand each other—not in this life."

Outside his room Eliza tries to calm herself, but out on the verandah she breaks loose. She lands into Mrs. Pert on every count she can think of and when Ben, having had enough, tells Fatty to come for a walk, Eliza lashes out at Mrs. Pert: "I don't want any butt-ins from you, do you understand? You're just a paying boarder here. That's all. You're not a member of my family, and never will be, no matter what low methods you try!"

Eugene, leaving Laura, tries miserably to stop his mother. "I'm only trying to keep decency and order here," she cries, "and this is the thanks I get! You should all get down on your knees and be grateful to me!" That word sets Ben off. What are they to be grateful for?—selling the house Gant built with his own hands—moving them into this barn to share everything with boarders so that Eliza can be Queen Bee? For putting Eugene on the street at eight to do anything to bring in a penny? "Gene is old enough to earn his keep," snaps Eliza. "Then," Ben yells, "he's old enough for you to let go of him! But no, you'd rather hang on to him like a piece of property! Maybe he'll grow in value, you can turn a quick trade on him, make a profit on him. He isn't a son, he's an investment! You're so penny mad that—" Eliza slaps Ben. They stare at each other, then Ben says: "Come on, Fatty," and leaves. Eugene is miserable. All Eliza's grievances well up in her. Eugene does his best to comfort her as she remembers how close she and Ben used to be. His thoughts on Laura, Eugene says gently: "It's late. You're tired."

With one of her marked switches, Eliza puts all this out of her mind: "Well, like the fellow says, it's no use crying over *that* spilt milk. I have all those napkins and towels to iron for tomorrow." In another moment she's the vigorous real-estate operator, proud of her reputation for being the smartest trader in town. Her glee even makes Eugene laugh with her. His mind still on Laura, Eugene promises to go to bed in a little while. "Don't forget to turn off the sign," Eliza says. "Good night, son." With a kiss, she advises him not to neglect his health, to see to it that he gets plenty of sleep. "Don't work too late," says Eugene, heading for the side door. But Eliza is now wound up; real-estate schemes and dreams pour from her. "Now for God's sake," Eugene cries, "go and finish your work so you can get some sleep!"

When his mother finally goes into the house, Eugene with desperate softness calls for Laura. He gives up; but Laura, coming out of the side door and brushing aside his apologies for the family fight, accepts his invitation to go for a walk. Hand in hand the two of them set off. A moment later Eliza, her mind still on one particular piece of property, returns to show Eugene the map she has drawn of it. Finding the sign still lighted and no son in sight, she calls up to his room, then turns off the sign herself. After that she comes out into the warm night and calls off in the darkness: "Ben? Ben?"

ACT II

A week later, at his father's marble yard and shop, Eugene is working at an emery wheel. Wearing one of his father's aprons, he pedals away under the benign smile of a lustrous, white Carrara angel. When his mother comes looking for Gant, Eugene observes out of the corner of his eye that she is dressed for action in her "dealing and bargaining" costume. Doesn't she look all right? Eliza exclaims. "Heaven knows," says she, "I always try to look neatly respectable."

EUGENE—Come on, Mama.

ELIZA—What! I declare! I might have a better dress than this, but law's sake, there's some places it don't pay to advertise it! Oh, Gene, you're smart, smart, I tell you! You've got a future ahead of you, child.

EUGENE—Mama, what kind of a future have I got if I can't get an education?

ELIZA—Pshaw, boy, you'll get an education if my plans work out! I'll tell you what though—in the meantime, it wouldn't hurt you to work in Uncle Will's office, would it?

EUGENE—I don't know anything about real estate, Mama.

ELIZA—What do you have to know? Buying and selling is an instinct, and you've got it. You've got my eye for looking and seeing and remembering, and that's what's important. Why, there isn't a vital statistic about a soul in Altamont I don't carry right in my head. What they make, what they owe—what they're hiding, what they show! (*She laughs, enjoying her cleverness.*) You see, Eugene, I'm a poet, too—"A poet and I don't know it, but my feet show it— they're longfellows!"

Eugene wants to get on with the job his father is paying him for. "Paying you?" Eliza cries. "How did you manage that?" She refuses to understand that Eugene needs more than free room and board. As always, she disapproves of his wanting new clothes that he will quickly outgrow. Eliza also points out that if Eugene wants the clothes to impress someone as mature as Miss James, he's decidedly too young. "I don't think you realize how young you are," she argues, "just because you're tall and read a lot of books." Luckily, deciding to wait no longer for Gant but to catch him unawares later on, Eliza bustles off to big deals with her brother.

Alone, Eugene quietly approaches the white, smiling angel and cups his hand tentatively over the statue's breast. Gant, sneaking back to the yard, watches with a smile. As Eugene gives a guilty start, Gant says: "I've done that myself many a time, son, many a time."

Gant, having seen Eliza from Laughran's neighboring saloon, wants to know if she'll be back. "I have a mind what she's up to," he says. "She'll be back with freshly drawn up papers tucked in her bosom. Yes, when you touch the breast of Miss Eliza, you feel the sharp crackle of bills of sale, not like the bosom of this angel." Eugene, seating himself below the angel, asks Gant to tell him about his first marriage, to Cynthia.

EUGENE—You loved her, didn't you, Papa?

GANT—She had a real glowing beauty. Sweet, noble, proud, and yet soft, soft—she died in her bloom.

EUGENE—She was older than you, wasn't she?

GANT—Yes. Ten years.

EUGENE—Ten years! But it didn't make any difference, did it?

GANT (*confidingly*)—She was a skinny, mean, tubercular old hag who nearly drove me out of my mind!

EUGENE (*shocked*)—Then why do you talk about her the way you do? To Mama?

GANT—Because I'm a bastard, Gene. I'm a bastard!

When Laura, picnic basket in hand, comes to the yard, Gant is courtly and charming, but fairly quick in leaving the young couple alone. Laura is upset: Helen, who packed this lunch for them, knows about Eugene and Laura and now Laura can see that W. O. knows about them, too. "Gene," she cries in shame, "I lied to you—I'm twenty-three years old." "Is that all?" Eugene says. "You're not nineteen, either," Laura says, "you're seventeen." With his arms about her, Eugene settles it: "I'm a thousand years old, all the love I've stored up for you." In her role of "older woman," Laura insists that there be rules. Eugene is equally insistent that rules are made by jealous people who have no talent for love, and with his arms reassuringly around her, says that nothing has changed between them.

Mme. Elizabeth, Altamont's prosperous madam, comes into the yard for Mr. Gant. As she goes to the office, Laura and Eugene escape to a distant corner. Gant, by now changed into decent clothes, comes out and greets Mme. Elizabeth fulsomely. She looks him over and sentimentally recalls the six whole years in which they have not seen each other—except to nod to.

Gant, dusting off a stone bench, asks Madame to be seated. "Oh, W. O.," she sighs, "you and your gallant manners. But I'm no chicken any more, and no one knows it better than I do. If you only knew how often we talk about you up on Eagle Crescent. What a man you were! Wild! Bacchus himself . . ." She wonders if Gant remembers the song he sang when sufficiently liquored up. Imitating him, Mme. Elizabeth sings: "Up in *that* back room, boys!" and Gant, laughing, joins in. Giving her an affectionate slap on the fanny, he confesses: "The loss of all that, that's the worst, Elizabeth." "Oh, W. O., W. O.! We do miss you," croons Mme. Elizabeth. Joining her on the bench, Gant asks after the girls. Suddenly distressed, Mme. Elizabeth remembers the reason for her visit: one of her favorite girls had suddenly died. Gant wonders sympathetically if it was anyone he knew.

MME. ELIZABETH—Since your time, W. O. We called her Lily.
GANT—Tch . . . tch . . . tch. Lily.
MME. ELIZABETH—I couldn't have loved her more if she had been my own daughter. Twenty-two. A child, a mere child. And not a relative who would do anything for her. Her mother died when she was thirteen, and her father is a mean old bastard who wouldn't even come to her deathbed.
GANT—He will be punished.
MME. ELIZABETH—As sure as there's a God in heaven—the old bastard! I hope he rots! Such a fine girl, such a bright future for her. She had more opportunities than I ever had—and you know what I've done here. I'm a rich woman today, W. O. Why, not even your wife owns more property than I do. I beg your pardon—I hope you don't mind my speaking of her— (GANT *gestures to go right*

ahead.)   Mrs. Gant and I both understand that property is what makes a person hold one's head up!   And Lily could have had all that too.   Poor Lily!   No one knows how much I'll miss her.   (*A moment's quiet.   GANT is respecting her grief.*)

GANT—I suppose you'll be wanting something for her grave?   (*As MME. ELIZABETH nods, he rises.*)   Here's a sweet lamb . . . *couchant* lamb, it's called.   *Couchant* means lying-down in French.   That should be appropriate.

But Mme. Elizabeth has already made up her mind.   She wants the Angel, and no matter how Gant tries to divert her, she will settle for nothing less.   Increasingly upset, Gant shouts: "It's not for sale! Anything you like . . . *everything* you like . . . I'll give it to you . . . I'll make you a present, for old time's sake.   But not my angel!" Showing her accustomed business manner, Mme. Elizabeth merely demands: "How much, W. O.?"   Unable to control himself any longer, Gant yells: "She's Carrara marble from Italy, and too good for any whore!"   He calls for Eugene to help him out and, retreating to his office, leaves Eugene to placate Madame.

"I've heard the trouble your mother has with the old terror—" says Mme. Elizabeth.   "Now I believe it!   All I'm asking is that he sells me that angel—for one of my dear girls who's gone—a dear, young girl in the flower of life—" indicating Laura—"like this young girl here."   Eugene says tactfully that he believes his father is saving the angel for his own grave, and Madame, once more mawkish in her feelings for poor W. O., is in a receptive mood to purchase whatever Eugene suggests.   With the further help of a standard volume of memorial poems, Eugene sells her the couchant lamb; and Madame, hoping that Eugene never loses someone he loves, retires with tearful, majestic dignity.

Determined to make a sale of her own, Eliza, accompanied by brother Will, appears back at the yard.   Decreeing a family conference, Eliza at least temporarily gets rid of Laura.   Eugene must attend; Ben under orders straggles in, and W. O., all spruced up, is trapped as he comes out of his office.

Eliza starts off by announcing that Gant knows the doctor wants him to retire and that Eugene, with his plans for college, needs money. "Oh, for God's sake, get to the point, Miss Eliza," says Gant.   "Have you got the papers from the bank?"   Eliza plays dumb.   "You know what I mean," says Gant; "fish for them, woman!"   Pointing to her bosom, Gant repeats, *"Go ahead,* fish for them!"   While Gant roars with laughter and Eugene echoes him, Eliza fishes out a large envelope.   Oddly enough, Gant doesn't need much persuasion.   He looks over the $20,000 bank check, and is seemingly ready to sell. Eugene, doing his best on his father's behalf, praises him as an artist: "There isn't a cemetery in the state that isn't filled with his work— you can always recognize it. Clean, and pure, and beautiful. Why should he give it up?" Gant perversely signs the document; then, slyly refusing to endorse the check over to Eliza, he puts it in his pocket and announces his plans.

GANT—This is my check, isn't it? I'm the one who had the fore-sight to buy this little pie-cornered lot thirty-one years ago for four hundred dollars . . . money from the estate of Cynthia L. Gant, deceased. I guess I'm entitled to the profit.

ELIZA—Now, Mr. Gant, if you're thinking to get my dander up . . .

GANT (*picks up his hat, puts it on*)—Miss Eliza, I've been wanting to get away from here for a long time. I'm taking Gene with me. I'm going to put him in that college there at Chapel Hill.

Hearing a few more of her husband's plans, Eliza springs into action, leaps at him, seizes the check from his pocket, tears it up and then flings the pieces to the ground. Crying that she will get an injunction against him, Eliza swears she will go to court and have him declared mad. She promises to fight him tooth and nail until she wins. "All the things you've said about me are true, Eliza," says Gant. "I've only brought you pain. Why don't you let me go?" "Because you're my husband, Mr. Gant! You're my husband. Thirty-one years together and we'll go on—we must go on. A house divided against itself cannot stand. We must try to understand and love each other. We must try . . ."

As Will sees Eliza home, Gant, sinking into a chair, begs Eugene to get him a bottle from Laughran's. Though weak and feverish, Ben tells Gant to leave Gene alone: "If you want to get sick, do it yourself." "Ungrateful sons!" intones Gant. "Oh, the sad waste of years, the red wound of all our mistakes." He goes on his own.

Looking at his father as he goes, Ben says that he might have suc-ceeded if he hadn't tried to take Eugene with him: "He could still make it, but he won't try again." Eugene is horrified that his parents' love could have turned into this torture. "They're strangers," Ben says; "they don't know each other. No one ever really comes to know anyone." Eugene protests that he knows Ben and that he knows Laura. "Listen to him!" says Ben. "No matter what arms may clasp us, what heart may warm us, what mouth may kiss us, we remain strangers. We never escape it. Never, never, never."

As Ben leans back and closes his eyes, Eugene worriedly leans down and feels his brother's face. Trying to lift him to his feet, Eugene cries: "Why didn't you tell somebody you're sick, you crazy idiot!" He tries again to lift him. "To hell with them, Gene," says Ben, "to hell with them all. Don't give a damn for anything. Nothing gives a damn for you. There are a lot of bad days, there are a lot of good ones— That's all there is . . . a lot of days . . . My God, is there no freedom on this earth?"

As Eugene tries frantically to get Dr. Maguire on the phone, Ben, looking up in anguish at the Carrara angel, cries: "And still you smile . . ."

Scene II

The next night, a painful tension grips Dixieland. In Ben's room, Dr. Maguire and Helen hover over his still body. At the hall telephone, W. O. tries frantically to trace Sailor Luke Gant who had been summoned home and has failed to arrive. Alone and motionless on the porch waits Mrs. Pert, as Laura and Eugene do too, side by side on the bench in the yard.

Steeling herself, Eliza enters Ben's room just as Maguire orders: "With both of you in here soaking up oxygen, leave that door open." Weak as he is, Ben rebuffs his mother and asks for Fatty. Over Helen's angry protests, he gathers his dwindling strength and calls: "Fatty! Fatty!"

Not interested in anyone's feelings but Ben's, Dr. Maguire summarily sees to it that Mrs. Pert is allowed in the room and that Eliza and Helen go out of it.

BEN—Fatty, stay by me. Sing to me. "A Baby's Prayer at Twilight" . . .

FATTY (*sitting beside him*)—Sh-h-h, Ben. Be quiet, dear. Save yourself.

BEN—Hold my hand, Fatty.

Eugene, outside, hears Fatty singing and looks up at Ben's room. When his mother, with Helen comforting her, comes out on the verandah, Eugene asks: "How does he seem, Mama?" "He couldn't stand to see me worrying," Eliza tells herself; "that's what it was, you know. He couldn't stand to see me worrying about him."

To prevent possible explosions as each member of the family relieves his distraught feelings on another, Maguire says that Ben is a little better. In an aside to Eugene, however, he tells the truth: "It's both lungs now. I can't tell them. But see to it that they stay around. I'm going next door and phone for some oxygen. It may ease it a little for him. It won't be long."

Turned gay and noisy with relief, the family welcomes Luke home. From the sidelines, tragically burdened, Eugene forces himself to join in the welcoming. As Luke, over plates of ice cream, remembers vividly what it was like to be young in Dixieland, and comes to the time when Ben and Gene and Luke took their paper routes together, Eugene bursts into tears. Jumping to her feet, Eliza cries: "Eugene. Child, what is it? What is it?" And a moment later, as Mrs. Pert calls out for her, she knows.

Eugene rushes off after Maguire, as Gant, coming out to greet Luke, hears that Ben is not doing so well. "Jesus, have mercy," Gant cries, "that I should have to bear this in my old age. Not another one. First Grover, now Ben . . ." Luke admonishes him: "For God's sake, Papa, try to behave decently, for Ben's sake."

Hurried back by Eugene, Maguire pushes past the crowd in the bedroom. "You women," he says, "step back, give him air."

BEN—It's one way—to step out of—the photograph—isn't it, Fatty?

FATTY—Hush, Ben, don't say that!

HELEN (*to the doctor*)—There must be something you can do!

MAGUIRE (*straightens up*)—Not all the king's horses, not all the doctors in the world can help him now.

HELEN—Have you tried everything? Everything?

MAGUIRE—My dear girl! He's drowning! Drowning!

ELIZA (*in deep pain*)—Mrs. Pert, you're standing in my place . . . (MRS. PERT *moves away.* ELIZA *steps close to* BEN, *sits.*) Ben—son. (*She reaches to touch him. His head turns toward her, drops. There is a last rattling, drowning sound.* BEN *dies.*)

MAGUIRE (*checks* BEN'S *heart*)—It's over. It's all over.

When Maguire comes out with his bag, Eugene begs to be told if Ben said anything at the end. "If he found what he was looking for?" answers Maguire. "I doubt that, Gene. At least he didn't say anything." Eugene goes to Ben's room, as Luke approaches Maguire.

LUKE—How long have you known, Doc?

MAGUIRE—For two days—from the beginning. Since I first saw him at three in the morning in the Uneeda Lunch with a cup of coffee in one hand and a cigarette in the other.

GANT—Was there nothing to be done?

MAGUIRE—My dear, dear Gant, we can't turn back the days that have gone. We can't turn back to the hours when our lungs were sound, our blood hot, our bodies young. We are a flash of fire—a brain, a heart, a spirit. And we are three cents' worth of lime and iron—which we cannot get back. (*He shakes his head.*) We can believe in the nothingness of life. We can believe in the nothingness of death, and of a life after death. But who can believe in the nothingness of Ben?

HELEN—Come on, Papa, there's nothing more to sit up for. Let me put you to bed. Come along.

Helen leads the old man into the house as the doctor goes; her husband and brother follow her. Only Laura remains on the yard seat.

Eugene goes to his mother and begs her to leave Ben. "He doesn't turn away from me any more," Eliza says. "Mama, you've got to let go," Eugene tells her. But Eliza, her rough clasp tightening on Ben's hand, shakes her head.

Eugene leaves the room, and coming onto the verandah, sinks to his knees. As Laura watches, Eugene prays: "Whoever You are, be good to Ben tonight. Whoever You are, be good to Ben tonight . . . Whoever You are . . . be good to Ben tonight . . . be good to Ben tonight . . ."

ACT III

Two weeks later, at dawn, Eugene stands putting on his shirt at the window of Laura's room. Knowing this is Laura's last morning at Dixieland, Eugene is loathe to leave her. From her bed, Laura begs him not to go so soon. Sitting beside her, and once more taking her in his arms, Eugene says: "Oh, Laura, I love you so. When I'm close to you like this, it's so natural. Are all men like me? Tell me." "I've told you. I've never known anyone like you," Laura replies.

As Laura has feared, Eugene decides that they must marry immediately. With the money Ben left him, Eugene wants to take Laura today to her parents in Richmond and then, after their marriage, go to work for his Uncle Will. Leaving Laura to go pack his bag, Eugene looks back for the last time: "I'll never have to sneak out of this room again."

Ready for her daily visit to Ben's grave, Eliza, while taking flowers from a pail of water, overhears Eugene talking on the phone. She is surprised and pleased to hear him accept her brother Will's offer, but horrified at what she hears next. Eugene breaks the news to his uncle that he's marrying Miss James and going to Richmond with her on the noon train. Eliza freezes in pain, then, as Eugene starts to go upstairs, calls out to him. All Eugene says is: "Well, now—with your second sense, I thought you would have guessed it, Mama." Nothing Eliza says about Miss James will change Eugene's mind. Desperately changing her tactics, Eliza talks of her plans for him. "Mama," Eugene cries, "I don't want your plans, I've got my own life to live!" Eliza races on: "But you don't know! Gene, listen, you know that Stumptown property of mine? I sold it just yesterday so you could go to Chapel Hill—you know, child, you can have it." "It's too late, Mama," Eugene answers, "it's too late." "Why law, child," says Eliza, "it's never too late for anything! It's what Ben wanted, you know." Giving her a quick kiss, Eugene goes into the house to pack.

Eliza hurriedly phones Will to sell that Stumptown property this very morning. He's not to argue; she'll explain later. As Eliza hangs up, Helen, coming into the hall, observes: "Well, it's never too early in the morning to turn a trade, is it? What are you selling?" Eliza merely says: "Some property I own." "Maybe," says Helen, "you can put a little of that money into getting somebody else to help you at that altar of yours, the kitchen stove." Her mother tells her to get breakfast started and hold Eugene; she'll be in later. "Oh, all right," Helen snaps. "You let me know when I can let him out!"

This much accomplished, Eliza moves in on Laura, who has been expecting her all along. Over Eliza's accusations, the truth comes out. Laura has no intention of marrying Eugene; she is engaged to a young man in Richmond. "Mrs. Gant, this isn't easy," Laura says. "I should have told Gene long ago . . . but I didn't. A girl about to get married suddenly finds herself facing responsibilities. I never liked responsibilities. Gene knows how I am. I like music, I like to walk in the woods, I like . . . to dream. I know I'm older than Gene, but in many ways I'm younger. The thought of marriage frightened me. I told my fiancé I needed time to think it over. I fell in love with Eugene. I found the romance I'd never known before, but I also found that it isn't the answer. Gene is a wonderful boy, Mrs. Gant. He must go to college. He must have room to expand and grow, to find himself. He mustn't be tied down at this point in his life. He needs the whole world to wander in—and I know now that I need a home, I need children—I need a husband. For people like me there are rules, very good rules for marriage and for happiness —and I've broken enough of them. I telephoned Philip last night. He's arriving at the depot on that early train. We're going on to Charleston together, and we'll be married there. He loves me, and

I will love him too after a while. . . ." Taking a note from the desk,
Laura asks Eliza to give it to Eugene, and to say good-bye to Mr.
Gant and the others, especially Helen, who works so hard. Saying
good-bye to Eliza, Laura warns her that someday she too will have
to let Eugene go.

The rest of the family is getting up as Eugene, suitcase in hand,
enters Laura's room. Only his mother is there. Without the least
delicacy, Eliza says right off: "She just walked out on you, child.
Just walked out on you . . ." Sure that Eliza has sent Laura away,
Eugene dashes wildly out of the house, and is on his way to the station
when Eliza stops him with Laura's letter.

As Eugene reads the letter, the train can be heard pulling out of
the station. Now, when he needs arms to comfort him, Eugene gets
kidding from Helen, and Eliza's salesmanlike pep talk. He begs to
be left alone.

ELIZA—Why, I'd be ashamed to let any girl get my goat like that.
When you get older, you'll just look back on this and laugh. You'll
see. You'll be going to college next year, and you won't remember a
thing about it. (EUGENE *turns, looks at her.*) I told you I'd sold
that Stumptown property, and I have. This year's term has started
already but next year . . .

EUGENE—Mama, *now! Now!* I've wasted enough time!

ELIZA—What are you talking about? Why, you're a child yet,
there's plenty of time yet . . .

EUGENE (*rises, walks about her, imploringly*)—Mama, Mama,
what is it? What more do you want from me? Do you want to
strangle and drown me completely? Do you want more string? Do
you want me to collect more bottles? Tell me what you want? Do
you want more property? Do you want the town? Is that it?

ELIZA—Why, I don't know what you're talking about, boy. If I
hadn't tried to accumulate a little something, none of you would have
had a roof to call your own.

EUGENE—A roof to call our own? Good God, I never had a bed
to call my own! I never had a room to call my own! I never had a
quilt to call my own that wasn't taken from me to warm the mob that
rocks on that porch and grumbles.

ELIZA (*rises, looking for an escape*)—Now you may sneer at the
boarders if you like . . .

EUGENE—No, I can't. There's not breath or strength enough in
me to sneer at them all I like. Ever since I was this high, and you
sent me to the store for the groceries, I used to think, "This food is
not for us—it's for them!" Mama, making us wait until they've

eaten, all these years—feeding us on their leftovers—do you know what it does to us—when it's you we wanted for us, *you* we needed for us. Why? Why?

ELIZA (*trembling*)—They don't hurt me like the rest of you do— they wouldn't talk to me like you are, for one thing. (*Starts toward side door.*)

EUGENE—Because they don't care—they're strangers. They don't give a damn about you! They'll talk like this about you behind your back—I've heard them do that plenty!

ELIZA (*turns*)—What? What? What kind of things do they say about me?

EUGENE—What does it matter what they say—*they* say! Doesn't it matter to you what I say? (*Takes her in his arms, holds her.*)

ELIZA (*beginning to weep*)—I don't understand.

EUGENE (*releases her, moves away*)—Oh, it's easy to cry now, Mama, but it won't do you any good! I've done as much work for my wages as you deserve. I've given you fair value for your money, I thank you for nothing. (*Crosses up to verandah.*)

ELIZA—What's that? What are you saying!

EUGENE—I said I thank you for nothing, but I take that back. Yes, I have a great deal to be thankful for. I give thanks for every hour of loneliness I've had here, for every dirty cell you ever gave me to sleep in, for the ten million hours of indifference, and for these two minutes of cheap advice.

ELIZA—You will be punished if there's a just God in Heaven.

EUGENE—Oh, there is! I'm sure there is! Because I have been punished. By God, I shall spend the rest of my life getting my heart back, healing and forgetting every scar you put upon me when I was a child. The first move I ever made after the cradle was to crawl for the door. And every move I ever made since has been an effort to escape. And now, at last I am free from all of you. And I shall get me some order out of this chaos. I shall find my way out of it yet, though it takes me twenty years more—alone.

ELIZA—Gene! Gene, you're not leaving?

EUGENE—Ah, you were not looking, were you? I've already gone.

Eliza, sitting on the verandah edge, stunned, doesn't answer Gant when he comes out and complains of no food to warm him. Going for firewood, Gant says some day he's going to tear down and burn up Dixieland. Eliza wishes that he *would* burn up this barn, and not to wait till he's drunk to tear it down. She's prepared to do it right now. Jumping up, she starts by shaking the newel post with demoniacal strength. "I'll tear you down!" she cries. "I'll kill you, house,

Hugh Griffith in "Look Homeward, Angel"

kill you! I'll shake you to pieces!" She picks up Mrs. Pert's rocker and sends it crashing. Gant gleefully enters into the spirit of the thing: "Let me help you, Mrs. Gant!" Starting to tear down the other post, Gant says: "God-damned barn! Thief! Travesty on nature!" "God-damned barn!" cries Eliza, kicking in the lattice panels under the verandah.

Helen yells for Hugh. Will, arriving, gasps: "My God, what are they doing?" Gant screams at the house: "Clatt—Mangle—Brown —come out of there, you rats, all of you—come out, come out, wherever you are!" With the boarders beginning to yell and squeal inside the house, Eliza echoes hysterically: "Come out, come out, wherever you are!"

Hugh, asked to hand Gant the axe from the wood box, is happy and willing to take part in this orgy of destruction. As the boarders flee Dixieland, Gant, chasing them, axe in hand, yells: "Squeal, you croaking bastards. Croak and run! Run for your lives!" Eliza, throwing a flower pot after them, screams: "Go to Mrs. Haskell's!" Helen restrains Eliza as she is about to hurl a chair. Gant crows: "Look at 'em run! Oh, Miss Eliza, what a woman you are!" About to embrace her, Gant sees Eliza's shocked face. The reaction has set in. "Mr. Gant, Mr. Gant, what have you done?" she cries. "What have you done?" "What have I done?" Gant says. "What have I—Merciful God, woman!" Helen doesn't know what got into her father. Will never saw such an exhibition. Eliza now sends Will and Helen with her apologies as peace emissaries to the boarders, and asks Hugh to help her clean up the mess. "Let them go, Miss Eliza," Gant begs. *"Let the boarders go!"* "I just don't know what came over me," Eliza says.

In the wake of battle, Eugene comes out of the house with his suitcase. Hearing that he's off to Chapel Hill to study with the money Eliza has promised him from her Stumptown property, Gant says: "Oh? By God, maybe it isn't going to be such a God-damned miserable day, after all! Got any money, son?" Thanking his father, Eugene says he has Ben's money. Tucking some bills in Eugene's pocket, Gant says good-bye: "You're going to bust loose, boy. You're going to bust loose, all over this dreary planet!"

Knowing full well that she has been defeated, Eliza, while promising to deposit money for him in the Chapel Hill Bank, makes one last feeble effort to keep Eugene with her. Getting nowhere, she changes her tune: talks cockily of picking up and lighting out herself. Soon her ebullient manner deserts her; her talk drifts off. Pulling herself together for one final effort, after a long silence Eliza says: "I hate to see you go, son." "Good-bye, Mama," Eugene says. Eliza, turning with unsteady steps to the house, answers: "Try to be happy, child, try to be a little more happy—" The dam breaks. Eugene, dropping his bag, catches Eliza's hands in his: "GOOD-BYE . . . GOOD-BYE . . . GOOD-BYE . . . MAMA . . ."

ELIZA (*holding him*)—Poor child . . . poor child . . . poor child. (*Huskily, faintly.*) We must try to love one another. (*Finally* EUGENE *moves from* ELIZA, *picks up the valise, as the lights start dimming, holding a spot on her.* ELIZA *seems to recede in the distance as into his memory.*) Now for heaven's sake, spruce up, boy, spruce up! Throw your shoulders back! And smile, look pleasant! Let them know up there that you *are* somebody!

On his way, wanting to find the world, the memory of Ben's voice reminds Eugene: "The world is nowhere, no one, Gene. *You* are your world."

THE DARK AT THE TOP OF THE STAIRS

A Play in Three Acts

By William Inge

[WILLIAM INGE *was born in Independence, Kansas in 1913, and educated at the University of Kansas and Peabody College. He taught with Maude Adams at Stephens College, Columbia, Missouri, and once conducted a playwriting class at Washington University in St. Louis. He was drama, film and music editor for the St. Louis "Star-Times." The Broadway production of his "Come Back, Little Sheba" in 1950 immediately placed him in the category of the "most promising" playwrights. "Picnic," produced in 1953, advanced his standing, winning for him both the Drama Critics Circle Award and the Pulitzer Prize. "Bus Stop" in 1955 made him one of Broadway's leading dramatists.*]

For the cast listing, see page 305.

IN the early 1920's, in a small Oklahoma town near Oklahoma City, Rubin Flood—a harness salesman—and his wife and two children live comfortably enough in the kind of sprawling frame house that earlier in the century signified solid respectability.

Following Rubin downstairs from the dark hall above, Rubin's wife Cora tries her best to keep him from going off on the road till the following morning. Getting together his harness paraphernalia from its place in a living-room cupboard, Rubin repeats: "I gotta make a livin'." "Other men," Cora persists, "make a living without traveling all over the country selling harness."

RUBIN—The way other men make a livin' is *their* business. I gotta make mine the best way I know how. I can't be no schoolmaster like your old man when he brung you all out here from Pennsylvania. I can't be no dentist like your brother-in-law Morris. I was raised on a ranch and thought I'd spend my life on it. Sellin' harness is

"The Dark at the Top of the Stairs": By William Inge. Copyright © 1958 by William Inge. Reprinted by permission of Random House, Inc., New York, N. Y.

Judith Robinson, Charles Saari, Teresa Wright and

Pat Hingle in "The Dark at the Top of the Stairs"

about all I'm prepared for . . . as long as there's any harness to sell.

CORA—I envy women who have their husbands with them all the time. I never have anyone to take me any place. I live like a widow.

RUBIN—What do you want me to do? Give up my job and stay home here to pleasure you every day?

Cora maintains it's the children she worries about: their shy, six-teen-year-old daughter, Reenie, and their ten-year-old Sonny, who is constantly taunted by the neighborhood boys. They need their father. "You din allus talk like that," Rubin argues. "God almighty, when those kids was born, you hugged 'em so close to ya, ya made me think they was your own personal property, and I din have nothin' to do with 'em at all." He compares her to an old mare they used to have on the ranch. Cora would like to change not just his way of living, but his language too. Rubin tells her to stop picking on him: after seventeen years of marriage, she should either accept him the way he is or look for a new man. Cora says she wants no new man.

Kissing Rubin good-bye, Cora brings up the question of the money she will need while he's away. She asks for twenty-five dollars but settles for the twenty he offers her. As she helps him with some last minute button-sewing, she tells him of the dance at the country club to which the Ralstons have invited Reenie.

RUBIN—The country club, huh? By God, I'd die in the poor-house 'fore I'd ever do what Harry Ralston done.

CORA—Now, Rubin . . .

RUBIN—I mean it. He shot himself in the foot to collect enough insurance money to make his first investment in oil.

CORA—Do you believe all those stories?

RUBIN—Hell, yes, I believe it. I know it for a fact. He shot himself in the foot. He oughta be in jail now. Instead he's a social leader, givin' parties out at the country club. And I'm supposed to feel real proud he invited my daughter. . . .

To Rubin, the town is oil-boom crazy. Working to support his family, he wants no part of the speculating. Trying to agree with him, Cora can't help feeling left out of things.

Sonny's arrival, announced by the yells and taunts of the neigh-borhood, causes Cora to leap into action. Running out on the porch, in spite of Rubin's telling her not to, she threatens to call the boys' mothers. Wanting Sonny to fight his own battles, Rubin does his best to stop her. "If they touch one hair of that boy's head I'll destroy them," she answers. Having rid Sonny of his oppressors merely by kidding with them, Rubin addresses himself to Sonny.

RUBIN—Want me to teach you how to put up a good fight?
SONNY—No.
RUBIN—What else can I do? Buy him a shotgun?
CORA—There should be *something* we can do. *Something* . . .
RUBIN—Everybody's gotta figure out his own way of handling things, Cora. Whether he fights or whether he runs.

Told to say good-bye to his father, Sonny gives such an indifferent "G'by" that Rubin just plain gives up and leaves.

"Most boys your age worship their fathers," Cora puzzles. Although Sonny admits to liking Rubin "all right," he likes his collection of movie stars more. Changing the subject, Sonny comments: "Mom, it just makes it worse when you come out and tell those boys you're going to call their mothers." Watching him get his scrapbook, Cora says: "That's all the friends you have. Not real friends at all. Just pictures of all the lovely friends you'd like to have. There's a mighty big difference between pictures of people and the way people really are."

Wishing she could understand her little son better, Cora waxes emotional and says she loves him more than anything else in the world. Showing no emotion in return, Sonny finds the moment ripe to ask to go to the movies after supper. When he fails on the first try, he starts begging. Getting nowhere, he argues that he's done all his homework. In the midst of his endeavors, Reenie and her flapperish friend Flirt bring home the dress Cora had bought for her to wear to the Ralston dance.

"Is Dad going to be awfully mad, Mom?" Reenie asks worriedly. "I told you he's not going to know anything about it for a while, Reenie," Cora answers. "He gave me some money before he left, enough for me to make a small down payment. My, I bet Flirt thinks we're terrible plotting this way." "Shucks, no," Flirt says, "Mama and I do the same thing." Except they do it on a grander scale, in Oklahoma City.

Attracted by the stars on Reenie's new dress and venturing to touch them, Sonny precipitates a violent brother-sister fight. Cora stops their shouting at each other and, as Reenie disappears into the parlor to try on the dress, talks to Flirt. Flirt starts a non-stop flow of gossip about the Ralstons: how by shooting himself Mr. Ralston got his money to invest in oil; how the country-club women didn't want Mrs. Ralston, a former store clerk, in the club, and how Flirt is positive Mary Jane Ralston peroxides her hair. Cora stops this, too. "Isn't it terrible for me to say all these things when I'm going to her birthday party?" Flirt giggles. "But I don't care. She just invited me because she had to. Because my Daddy's her Daddy's lawyer."

Appearing in her new dress, which Cora raves over, Reenie is all the same worried. The boy who has been assigned to escort her to the party is a Jew, and she worries if it's all right going out with a Jew. Cora doesn't see why not if he's nice. Flirt has just found out his name is Sammy Goldenbaum; ". . . and he comes from Hollywood, California, and his mother's a moving picture actress." As Sonny perks up for the first time, Flirt disillusions him quickly: "She just plays itsy-bitsy parts in pictures. . . ." Still disturbed, Reenie wonders what a Jew is like. Flirt has heard that some of them can be awful fast with girls.

CORA—I'm sure they're just like anyone else . . .
FLIRT—They don't believe in Christianity.
CORA—Most of them don't.
REENIE—But do they act different?
CORA—Well . . .
FLIRT—My Daddy says they always try to get the best of you in business.
CORA—There are lots of very nice Jewish people, Reenie.
FLIRT—Oh, sure! Gee whiz, of course.
REENIE—I don't know what to expect.
FLIRT—Kid, he's a boy. That's all you have to know.

Reenie is still scared to go out with anyone so different. Flirt, who would date a Jewish boy if she had no other way to get to the dance, says Reenie is crazy. But she is not too crazy for Flirt to ask her help in studying before she goes.

With a Hershey bar as bait, Sonny is shooed off to get the groceries for supper. Reenie now decides that the only reason Flirt likes her is for help she gives her in school work. This, and buying the dress behind her father's back, and going to the dance with a Jew, all contribute to Reenie's upset state. "Daughter, you're just look- ing for excuses," Cora says. "You just don't want to go, do you? Reenie, don't you want to have friends?" "Yes, but . . ." Reenie manages. "You're not going to make friends just staying home playing the piano, or going to the library studying your lessons. I'm glad," Cora says, "you're studious and talented, but those things aren't enough just in themselves." Not being able to talk, Reenie retreats to her piano.

Cora is phoning her sister in Oklahoma City to invite her to dinner before Reenie's dance, when Rubin storms back into the house. He has found out about the dress.

REENIE (*pokes her head into room*)—I told you he'd be mad, Mom. Let's take the dress back, Mom. I don't want to go to the party anyhow.

CORA—Get back in that parlor, Reenie, and don't come in here until I tell you to. (*Shuts sliding parlor doors.*)

RUBIN—See there! That girl don't even want the dress. It's *you,* puttin' all these high-falutin' ideas in her head about parties, and dresses and nonsense.

CORA—Rubin, of course Reenie doesn't want to go to the party. She never wants to go any place. All she wants to do is lock herself in the parlor and practice at the piano, or go to the library and hide her nose in a book. After all, she's going to want to get married one of these days, isn't she? And where's she going to look for a husband? In the public library?

RUBIN—I bought her a fine dress . . . just a little while back.

It turns out that the dress he remembers buying is three years old and has long since been cut up and dyed black. Even so, Rubin insists that he hasn't the money right now to throw away on party clothes. Cora says angrily that he can always find the money for a bottle of bootleg whiskey and a few other things that she won't mention. She knows what goes on when he is out on the road.

CORA—Maybe you don't have money to buy your daughter a new dress, but it seems you have money to take Mavis Pruitt to dinner whenever you're over there, and to a movie afterwards, and give her presents.

RUBIN—I've known Mavis . . . Pruitt ever since I was a boy! What harm is there if I take her to a movie?

CORA—You're always too tired to take me to a movie when you come home.

RUBIN—Life's different out on the road.

Cora refuses to drop the subject: she has heard about various presents that Rubin has given. She wishes that people would not tell her these things. She can't help hearing. She assumes that there's a woman in every town he visits, which is the reason he wants to get away: ". . . to go frisking over the country like a young stallion."

RUBIN—You just hush your mouth. The daughter'll hear you.

CORA—A lot you care about your daughter. A lot you care about any of us.

RUBIN—You don't think I care for ya unless I set ya on my knee and nuzzle ya.

CORA—What you need for a wife is a squaw. Why didn't you marry one of those Indian women out on the reservation? Yes. She'd make you rich now, too, wouldn't she? And you wouldn't have to pay any attention to her at all. (SONNY *is seen coming onto porch.*)

RUBIN—All right. Maybe that's what I *shoulda* done.

CORA—Oh. So you want to throw it up to me!

With Cora arguing that Rubin never wanted to marry her, and Rubin insisting that what they were arguing over was the dress, the fight comes to a head when he orders her to take the dress back.

CORA—I won't.

RUBIN—Ya will.

CORA—Reenie's going to wear her new dress to the party, or you'll have to bury me.

RUBIN—You'll take that dress back to Loren Delman, all $19.75 of it, or I'm leavin' this house for good and never comin' back.

CORA—Go on. You're only home half the time as it is. We can get along without you for good.

RUBIN—Then that's what you're gonna do. There'll be ice-cream parlors in hell before I come back to this place and listen to your jaw. You take this back!

CORA—Get out! Get out and go to Ponca City. Mavis Pruitt is waiting. She's probably getting lonesome without you. (SONNY *enters quietly from dining room and watches.*)

RUBIN—By God, Cora, it's all I can do to keep from hittin' you when you talk like that.

CORA—Go on and hit me! You wouldn't dare! (*He does, as* REENIE *watches from parlor.*)

RUBIN—I'll go to Ponca City, and drink booze and take Mavis

to the movies, and raise every kind of hell I can think of. T'hell
with you! (RUBIN *exits . . . the car drives off.*)

Reflecting on the fine points of the fight, Sonny concludes that
this was just about the worst one his parents ever had. Two things
stand out for him: why hadn't his father wanted to marry his mother,
and, when he hit her, had he hurt her? Reenie, in a state over her
father's departure, is infuriated by Sonny's indifference. "I hate
you!" she cries. Sonny returns the compliment. Loving her father,
Reenie hates her dress as the cause of all this trouble. But as Cora
orders, she goes to hang it up carefully. That done, Reenie, ignoring her mother, retreats to her piano for solace. Needing sympathy,
craving love, Cora appeals to Sonny. His one-track mind on the
movies, Sonny pays no attention. "If the world was falling to
pieces all about you, you'd still want to go to the movies, wouldn't
you?" Cora says. Sonny doesn't see why not. Cora asks him if
it doesn't mean anything to him that she's unhappy. He answers
half-heartedly that he's sorry. "Sonny," Cora pleads, "I want you
kids near me tonight. Can't you understand? Oh, God, wouldn't
it be nice if life were as sweet as music! Come, help me set the
table, Sonny."

ACT II

Cora's sister, Lottie, and her dentist-husband, Morris, having come
over from Oklahoma City, are amusing themselves after dinner. At
the piano, Lottie sings a loud duet of "Smiles" with Sonny, while
Morris, in Rubin's armchair, works patiently at a puzzle. Having
sent Reenie upstairs to bathe and dress for her party, Cora, over
the din of "Smiles," corrals Sonny for kitchen duty. "I have to do
everything around here," says old-lady Sonny. "I know it," Lottie
sympathizes. "I know," Sonny echoes.

Hardly waiting for Cora and Sonny to disappear, Lottie spills
everything that she has picked up to Morris: Rubin has fought
with Cora and left. "What about this time?" Morris asks with no
show of interest. "About a new dress she bought for Reenie," Lottie
says. "But what difference does that make? They could fight
about anything. Only this time he hit her."

MORRIS—He did?
LOTTIE—Don't tell her I told you. Poor Cora. I guess she has
a hard time with Rubin.

Morris—Has Rubin walked out again?

Lottie—You guessed it. Do you know what she wants to do now, honey? She wants to bring the kids over to Oklahoma City to live *with us.*

Morris—Oh!

Lottie carefully instructs Morris not to agree with Cora and to leave things to her. Knowing he can't bear to hurt people, including his patients, she begs him not to go soft-hearted at the last minute. "They'd drive me crazy. You, too. You know they would," she says.

That taken care of, Lottie gets back to Rubin's playing around with Mavis Pruitt. Unwilling to be involved in this sort of talk, Morris murmurs: "Well, whatever Rubin does . . . like that . . . is his business."

Lottie—My! Don't we sound righteous all of a sudden! Well, I bet anything he still sees her.

Morris—Well, don't let on to Cora.

Lottie—I won't. Did I ever tell you about the first time she met Rubin?

Morris—Yes, honey.

Lottie—I did not! Well—anyway, Cora and I were coming out of the five-and-dime. She'd wanted to buy a little lace to put on a dress. And here comes Rubin, like a picture of Sin, riding down the street on a shiny black horse. My God, he was handsome. Neither of us knew who he was. But he looked at Cora and smiled, and Cora began to get all nervous and fluttery. And do you know what, he came by the house that night and wanted to see her. Mama and Papa didn't know what to do. But Cora went out riding with him. He'd brought a buggy with him. And six weeks later they were married. Mama and Papa were worried sick. Rubin's people were all right, but they were ranchers. Kind of wild. And Cora only seventeen, not out of high school. I think that's the reason Papa had his stroke, don't you, Morris?

Morris—Maybe . . .

Lottie—I do. They just felt like Cora might as well be dead as married to a man like Rubin. But Cora was always a determined creature. Mama and Papa were no match for her when she wanted her own way.

Morris—Well, I like Rubin.

Lottie—I do too, honey. I'm not saying anything against him.

And he's made a lot better husband than I ever thought he would. But I'm glad I'm not married to him. I'd be worried to death all the time. I'm glad I'm married to a nice man I can trust. Trust. Trust.

As the time of the party approaches Reenie, feeling sick and pan-icky, comes down to appeal to Lottie. Lottie doesn't hesitate to tell Cora that the child should stay home. Saying that Reenie gets this way before every party, Cora maintains stubbornly that it's something she must get over; she's got a date and a dress and if Reenie doesn't go now, the Ralston girl will never again invite her. Suddenly Lottie has a brilliant idea. She sends Morris out to the car for the prized bottle of Coty's *L'Origan* she bought at a drugstore anniver-sary sale. She's sure this will make Reenie feel good. "You'll have her smelling like a fancy woman," Morris says. "How do *you* know what a fancy woman smells like?" Lottie retorts. "I can make a joke, can't I?" Morris says.

Choosing the moment that Lottie is upstairs with Reenie, Cora broaches the subject of visiting Oklahoma City to Morris, only for Lottie to clatter down again intent on breaking up the conversation. When Cora retires once more to the kitchen, Sonny fills the breach with his movie star collection. "Every time we come over here," Lottie says, "we've got to look at his movie stars."

MORRIS—Got any of Norma Talmadge?

SONNY—Sure.

LOTTIE—Norma Talmadge, Norma Talmadge! All you ever think about is Norma Talmadge. I don't know what you see in her. Besides, she's a Catholic.

MORRIS—Honey, you've just got a bug about the Catholics.

LOTTIE—Oh, I do, do I! Maybe you'd like to marry Norma Talmadge some day and then let the Pope tell you what to do the rest of your life, making you swear to leave all your money to the Church, and bring up all your children Catholic, and then join the Knights of Columbus and take an oath to go out and kill all the nice Protestant women when the day comes for the Catholics to take over the world. (CORA *crosses to sideboard*—)

MORRIS—Honey, where do you pick up these stories?

LOTTIE—Well, it's the truth. Marietta Flaymyer told me. Cora, Marietta has this very close friend who used to be a Catholic but isn't any more. She even joined a convent, but she ran away because she found out all those things and wouldn't stand for them. This friend told Marietta that the Catholics keep the basements of their churches filled with guns and all kinds of ammunition . . .

CORA—Lottie! (*She exits.*)

LOTTIE— . . . because some day they plan to rise and take over the world, and kill off all the rest of us who don't want to be Catholics. I believe every word of it, too.

MORRIS—Well . . . I still like Norma Talmadge. Got any Bebe Daniels?

Denying that Rudolph Valentino is one of her favorites, asserting that she saw *The Sheik* four times only to keep friend Marietta company, assuring them that Valentino is not a Catholic (Marietta's friend had a book listing all the Hollywood people who are Catholic), Lottie still admits to the shivers each time she looks at him.

When the coast is once more clear, and Lottie has taken on the curling of Reenie's hair, Cora pleads with Morris to let her bring the children to stay with him. Promising to get a job, to cook for them, to straighten up after them, Cora asks helplessly if they would be too much in the way. Unable to say no, Morris is saved by the simultaneous arrival of Flirt under military escort, and the news that Reenie has vomited all over the bathroom. Leaving Sonny and Morris to do the honors, Cora rushes to Reenie.

Seeing that there is to be a delay, Flirt has the uniformed boys come in. She introduces her gangling cadet, Punky Givens, and Sammy Goldenbaum introduces himself. Morris receives them pleasantly. When Lottie rattles down the steps, talking sociably a mile a minute, Sammy again introduces himself. Unflagging in her efforts to fill the conversational void, Lottie inquires after Sammy's actress mother, and remembers that Cora told her how prominent Punky's parents are.

After Reenie appears, only to rush back upstairs again, a bored Flirt asks Sonny for player-piano rolls so they can at least dance. Lottie continues to make conversation: when she and Morris went to California for a Shriners' Convention she found it so wonderful that she would think that Sammy would prefer going home for his spring vacation.

SAMMY—Well, I . . . I guess I don't really have a home . . . Mrs. Lacey.

LOTTIE—Did you tell me your mother lived out there?

SAMMY—Yes, but you see, she's pretty busy in moving pictures, and . . . Oh, she feels awfully bad that she doesn't have more time for me. Really she does. But she doesn't have a place where I could stay right now . . . and . . . But it's not her fault.

LOTTIE—Where's your father?

SAMMY—Oh, I never knew him.

LOTTIE—You never knew your father?

SAMMY—No, you see he died before I was born. My mother has been married . . . a few times since then. But I never met any of her husbands . . . although they were all very fine gentlemen.

LOTTIE—Well—I just never knew anyone who didn't have a home. Do you spend your whole life in military academies?

SAMMY—Just about. I bet I've been to almost every military academy in the whole country. Well, I take that back. There's some I didn't go to. I mean . . . there's some that wouldn't take me.

SONNY—My mother says you're a Jew.

LOTTIE—Sonny!

SAMMY—Well . . . yes, Sonny. I guess I am.

LOTTIE—That's perfectly all right. Why, we don't think a thing about a person's being Jewish, do we, Morris?

MORRIS—No. Of course not.

Sammy tells how his father, whom he takes after, was Jewish, while his mother isn't. Sonny, told to apologize, doesn't know what he's done, and Sammy says it's all right: "It doesn't bother me that I'm Jewish. Not any more. I guess it used to a little . . . Yes, it did used to a little." Lottie rushes in with a solution: Sammy should turn Christian Scientist. A Jewish woman that she knows did this and has been happy ever since. Still bewildered, Sonny apologizes.

As Flirt hauls Punky into the parlor to dance to "The Sheik of Araby," Sammy first asks Lottie in a flattering manner to dance, then—when she refuses—takes it upon himself to amuse Sonny with a pig-a-back ride. After a while, the dancing in the parlor has turned into necking, and the ride in the living room into playing with Sammy's sword. After Sonny has made some wild lunges, Sammy sees to it that the sword is sheathed, and asks: "What'll we do now, Sonny? Are there any games you want to play? Do you want to fight the Indians? Or set bear traps? Or go flying over volcanoes? Or climb the Alps?" Sonny gives a delirious "Yes" to all of these things. Sammy would love to do them too, but they can't tonight. Sonny offers to show his movie stars, but Sammy has had enough of movie stars. Then Sonny offers to speak a piece. Treating this as news of great importance, Sammy orders the music stopped and says: "Where do you want to stand, sir?" He ushers everyone into the parlor, where there is a little platform which Sonny uses when he practices. As Sonny recites "To be or not to be" to his captive audience, Cora, with Reenie in tow, descends the stairs.

After the applause for Sonny has died down, Cora greets Sammy. He in turn compliments a shyly grateful Reenie and is happy to find her quite unlike Flirt. He confesses that he hasn't been to many parties and that when he goes, he is apt to worry that the world is against him. "See, I've spent most of my whole life in military academies," he tells Reenie. "My mother doesn't have a place for me where she lives. She . . . she just doesn't know what else to do with me. But you mustn't misunderstand my mother. She's really a very lovely person. I guess every boy thinks his mother is very beautiful, but my mother really is. She tells me in every letter she writes how sorry she is that we can't be together more, but she has to think of her work. One time we were together, though. She met me in San Francisco once, and we were together for two whole days. She let me take her to dinner and to a show and to dance. Just like we were sweethearts. It was the most wonderful time I ever had." As Punky yawns, Sammy apologizes for boring everybody. "Oh, no," they all chorus back.

After good nights have been said, Sammy suddenly has the idea of including Sonny in the party, but is quickly talked out of it. Sonny promptly throws a tantrum. "Now we'll never get there," says Flirt. To everyone's amazement, Sammy stops the tantrum, then promises to bring Sonny all the party favors. Declaring that they're buddies forever, Sonny throws his arms around Sammy in a great hug. "Gee! I love kids," Sammy says.

In a kind of triumphant leavetaking, the praise of the grown-ups ringing in his ears, and with a rosy, approving Reenie at his side, Sammy goes to the car. The ladies think Sammy is just about the nicest young man they have ever met; but Morris, not wishing to go into it, finds him a very unhappy boy. "Morris," says Lottie, "I think you make these things up. Ever since you went to the psychologist you've gone around imagining everyone's unhappy. Where are you going, Morris?" "Thought I'd go out for a little walk, honey," Morris answers.

Lottie wastes no time in advising Cora, after shocking her with some fairly rough talk, to get Rubin back at all costs. She further tells Cora that if she and the children came to live in Oklahoma City, it might mean the end of her marriage to Morris. Cora isn't the only one who has problems; Lottie reveals that Morris hasn't come near her in over three years. This is more shocking to Cora than Lottie's off-color stories. "Did you notice the way Morris got up out of his chair suddenly and just walked away with no explanation at all?" Lottie asks. "Well, something inside Morris did the same thing several years ago. Something inside him just got up and went for a walk, and never came back." At least, says Cora, Morris never hit Lottie. Lottie wishes he would. She wishes that someone would love her enough to hit her. "Morris and I go around always being so sweet to each other that sometimes I wonder maybe he'd like to kill me."

Lottie remembers being petrified at the thought of giving in to a man; and so was Cora, she adds, until Rubin came along and practically raped her. Over Cora's warning not to let Sonny hear this kind of talk, Lottie lets the dam burst. She points out stridently that Rubin had Cora pregnant inside of two weeks after they met, and that it probably killed their father. Cora won't have Rubin blamed: "I was crazy in love with him. He just swept me off my feet and made all my objections seem kinda silly. He even made Mama and Papa seem silly."

LOTTIE—Maybe I shoulda married a man like that. I don't know. Maybe it was as much my fault as Morris's. Maybe I didn't . . . respond right from the very first.

CORA—What do you mean, Lottie?

LOTTIE—Cora, I'll tell you something. Something I've never told another living soul. I never did enjoy it the way some women . . . say they do.

CORA—Lottie! You!

LOTTIE—Why? Because I talk kinda dirty at times? But that's all it is, is talk. I talk all the time to convince myself that I'm alive. And I stuff myself with food to feel that I've got something inside me. And I'm full of all kinds of crazy curiosity about . . . all the things in life I seem to have missed out on. Now I'm telling you the truth, Cora. Nothing ever really happened to me while it was going on.

CORA—Lottie . . .

LOTTIE—That first night Morris and I were together, right after we were married, when we were in bed together for the first time, after it was all over, and he had fallen asleep, I lay there in bed wondering what in the world all the cautioning had been about. Nothing had happened to me at all, and I thought Mama and Papa musta been makin' things up.

CORA—Oh, Lottie!

LOTTIE—So, don't come to me for sympathy, Cora. I'm not the person to give it to you.

As Morris, back from his walk, urges that they start home before the rain, Lottie with a final gesture of abandon rips off her corset in front of everyone so she can ride home in comfort. Then, between "thank-you's" and last minute gossip, Lottie casually tells Cora to bring the kids to Oklahoma City. They'll manage somehow, even if someone has to sleep in the bathtub. But by now Cora has changed her mind, too.

In the quiet wake of Lottie's departure, Sonny urges Cora to move them to California, but, going to the phone, Cora calls long distance. "I bet he isn't there," Sonny offers. "I bet anything—" Sonny is right. Rubin hasn't been in Blackwell all week. Telling Sonny to run along to bed, Cora, as she disappears into the kitchen, bursts into tears.

After a few tentative steps upwards, Sonny calls, "Mom!"

CORA (*re-enters*)—Sonny, I thought I told you to go to bed— go on. Sonny, why are you so afraid of the dark?

SONNY—'cause you can't see what's in front of you. I'm not afraid if someone's with me.

CORA—Sonny—you mustn't be so afraid of the dark, you're the man of the house now. Come on, Sonny. We'll go up together.

ACT III

Late the next day—it is raining out—Reenie mopes over her humiliation at the party, and Cora, wanting Rubin home on any terms, now feels that it was her fault he hit her. What is more, Cora suspects that her pampering the children may have done them more harm than Rubin's negligence.

Reenie says miserably that Sammy went off and left her: "He went out to the cars at intermission time with some other girl." She tells her mother that Sammy had kissed her on their way to the club, but he must not have found her "hot stuff." Cora is disappointed in Sammy; she had found him such a nice boy. Reenie, too, had liked him very much.

In her present shattered state, Reenie decides that if married life consists of fighting, she would prefer to stay single and live alone. "Weren't you happy last night when Sammy kissed you?" Cora asks. "I guess," Reenie answers, "you can't count on happiness like that." Hating to have a child of hers miss the experience of love, Cora is doing her best to advise Reenie when a car drives up outside. It is Sonny, arriving home in a chauffeur-driven limousine from an old lady's where he had been invited to recite.

Flushed with success, brandishing five dollars given him for speaking his piece, glutted with cocoa and ice cream and cake, Sonny is ready to pass up supper and blow his money in an orgy of movies and chocolate-marshmallow sundaes. Cora puts her foot down: "Now wait a minute, Sonny. This is the first money you've ever earned in your life, and I think you should save it." When he sees that Cora means what she says, Sonny cries furiously: "Look what you've done. I hate you! I wanta see the movie. I've just gotta see the movie. If I can't see the movie, I'll just kill myself." Getting hold of the party noisemakers, Sonny cuts loose. Ordering him to stop the racket, Cora says: "The young man was very thoughtful to have sent you the favors. I wish he had been as thoughtful in other ways." Sonny is delighted to learn that Reenie didn't have a good time. "Serves her right," he says vindictively. "Serves her right."

Having had enough of this, Cora finds the time ripe to clear up some matters with Sonny.

SONNY—Have I done something bad?

CORA—Well, I don't know if you have or if I have. Anyway, we've got to talk about it. Sonny, you mustn't come crawling into my bed any more. I let you do it last night, but I shouldn't have. It was wrong.

SONNY—I was scared.

CORA—Just the same, that's not to happen again, Sonny. It's not the same when a boy your age comes crawling into bed with his mother. You can't expect me to mean as much to you as when you were a baby. Can you understand, Sonny? I think you're older in your feelings than I ever realized. You're a funny mixture, Sonny. In some ways shy as your sister. In other ways, bold as a pirate.

SONNY—I don't like you any more at all.

Cora can see now what she has done by keeping him too close. Saying that she still loves him, telling him to run along to the store, she stops the conversation. Good and mad, Sonny is about to leave when Flirt arrives.

Thoroughly distraught and wanting to see Reenie, Flirt has *awful* news for all of them. "Sammy Goldenbaum . . . has killed himself," she says. The hotel where Sammy jumped from the fourteenth floor has just notified Mrs. Given.

FLIRT—Oh . . . it's really the most terrible thing that ever happened to me. I never did know anyone who killed himself before.

CORA—Does anyone have any idea what made him do it?

FLIRT—No! Punky says that he used to get kind of moody at times, but Punky never expected him to do anything like *this*.

CORA—Why did he go to Oklahoma City in the middle of the night?

FLIRT—No one knows that either . . . for sure. But one thing did happen at the party. He was dancing with Mary Jane Ralston . . . that cow . . . just before intermission . . . And Mrs. Ralston . . . she'd had too much to drink . . . comes out in the middle of the floor and stops them.

CORA—What for?

FLIRT—Well, you know how Mrs. Ralston is. No one takes her very serious even if she does have money. Anyway she came right out in the middle of the floor and gave Sammy a bawling out.

CORA—A bawling out? Why?

FLIRT—She said she wasn't giving this party for Jews, and she didn't intend for her daughter to dance with a Jew, and besides, Jews weren't allowed in the Country Club anyway. And that's not so. They are too allowed in the Country Club. Maybe they're not permitted to be members but they're certainly allowed as guests. Everyone knows that. Where were you when it all happened?

REENIE—I . . . I . . .

CORA—Reenie wasn't feeling well. She left the party and came home.

FLIRT—The other kids told me Sammy was looking for you everywhere. He was going around asking everyone, "Where's Reenie?"

Flirt has all the details, although she doesn't understand them. Sammy's mother cried when she was notified, but asked them to have the funeral in Oklahoma City. She would pay for everything, but she wouldn't come herself because she was working. Through her tears Sammy's mother had also asked that it be kept out of the papers because it wasn't generally known that she had a son.

After saying that the Givens would drive them all—Sammy's soul mourners—to the funeral, Flirt runs home. The minute she has gone, Cora turns on Reenie. Where, she asks, was Reenie when Sammy went off? "I was up in the girls' room," Reenie confesses. When no one had cut in on them, Reenie had left Sammy with Mary Jane Ralston while she fled to nurse her embarrassment out of sight. "You ran off and hid," Cora accuses her, "when an ounce of thoughtfulness, one or two kind words might have saved him."

CORA—A nice young man like that, bright and pleasant, handsome as a prince, caught out here in this sandy soil without a friend to his name and no one to turn to when some thoughtless fool attacks him and he takes it to heart. (REENIE *sobs uncontrollably.*) Tears aren't going to do any good now, Reenie. Now you listen to me. I've heard all I intend to listen to about being so shy and sensitive and afraid of people. I can't respect those feelings any more. They're based on nothing but selfishness. (REENIE *starts to run out of the room.*) Reenie! It's a fine thing when we have so little confidence in ourselves we can't stop to think of the other person.

Sonny's reaction to Sammy's tragedy is to "hate people." Lecturing him on tolerance, Cora sends him off to the store. Aware of the waiting barrage of boys' taunts, Cora does not go to Sonny's aid. She closes the door firmly behind him.

Entering silently through the dining-room doors, Rubin drops his bags. Cora, frightened, cries: "My God!" Rubin hadn't meant to startle her, but because his boots were muddy, had come in the back way. When almost at once Cora wants to know why he wasn't in Blackwell the night before, Rubin says: "I lost my job."

CORA—Rubin! You've always sold more harness for the company than any of the other salesmen.

RUBIN—Yah. The oney trouble is, *no* one's selling much harness today because no one's buyin' it. People are buyin' automobiles. Harness salesmen are . . . things of the past.

CORA—Do you mean . . . your company's going out of business?

RUBIN—That's it! You won the kewpie doll.

Conscience-stricken, Cora apologizes, but when she hears that Rubin was in Tulsa to see about selling oil-field equipment, she resumes her former attitude about traveling jobs. She says flatly that he is to go downtown for a store job that he could get in a minute. "God damn!" shouts Rubin, "I come home here t'apologize to you for hittin' ya. I been feelin' all week like the meanest critter alive because I took a sock at a woman. My wife, at that. I walked in here ready to *beg* ya to forgive me. Now, I feel like doin' it all over again. Don't you realize you can't talk to a man like that? Don't you realize that every time you talk that way, I just gotta go out and raise more hell, just to prove to myself I'm a free man? Don't you know that when you talk to a man like that, you're not givin' him credit for havin' any brains, or any guts, or a spine, or . . . or a few other body parts that are pretty important, too? All these years we been married, you never once really admitted to yourself what kinda man I am. No, ya keep talkin' to me like I was the kinda man you think I *oughta* be. Look at me. Don't you know who I am? Don't you know who I am?" Rubin is determined to take that "good-paying" Tulsa job if he can get it.

Insisting that she no longer cares about money, Cora asks only that Rubin give the children something of himself. Suddenly all his self-doubts rise to the surface. Bewildered, a stranger in the land where he was born and where he found it easier to pioneer than settle down, Rubin confesses to feeling he has nothing to offer his children. He is just doing the best he can. "The new job is work I've never done," says Rubin. "Work I never even thought of doin'. Learnin' about all that God damn machinery and how to get out there and demonstrate it. Working with different kindsa men that's smarter than I am, that think fast and talk sharp and mean all business. Men I can't sit around and chew tobacco with an' joke with like I did m' old customers. I . . . I don't like 'em. I don't know if I'm gonna like them." "But you said you wanted the job," Cora answers. "I don't like them, but I'm gonna join them. There's nothing else for me to do," Rubin says. "I'm scared. I don't know how I'll make out . . . I . . . I'm scared." Cora, with new understanding, knows that he is doing his very best.

They now apologize earnestly to each other: Rubin again for hitting her; Cora for provoking him; Rubin for making a fuss about buying Reenie the new dress; Cora for buying it. They love each other and admit they need each other.

RUBIN—You're clean and dainty. Give a man a feeling of decency and order . . . and respect.

CORA—Thank you, Rubin.

RUBIN—Just don't get the idea you can rearrange *me* like ya do the house, whenever ya wanta put it in order.

CORA—I'll remember. When you have fears about things, please tell me, Rubin.

RUBIN—It's hard for a man t'admit his fears, even to hisself.

CORA—Why? Why not?

RUBIN—He's always afraid of endin' up like . . . like your brother-in-law Morris.

Rubin asks Cora if there is any chance of their being alone awhile that night. "I think Reenie plans to go to the library," she says. "If you give Sonny a dime, I'm sure he'll go to the movies." This is a very satisfactory deal for Rubin.

When Reenie, hearing Rubin, comes down to greet him joyously,

Pat Hingle in "The Dark at the Top of the Stairs"

he feels so good that Sonny's subsequent cold refusal of his offer of a movie doesn't irritate him. "Go on," Cora answers. "I'll be up in a minute, Rubin." "I'm goin' upstairs now," Rubin announces, "and have my bath."

Left together and suddenly bound together by their memory of Sammy, Reenie and Sonny become friends. Sonny offers Reenie the party favors to keep for good. Reenie wonders: "You never were thoughtful like this . . . before." Coming from the dining room, Cora overhears Sonny inviting Reenie to be his guest at the movie tonight. "Sonny!" Reenie warns him, "Mother told you you had to save that money." In open rebellion, Sonny smashes his piggy bank at the fireplace. "I don't care," he cries, "she's not going to boss me for the rest of my life. It's my money, and I've got a right to spend it."

Proud to be treated by her little brother, Reenie leaves with him. As they go out the door, Cora tries to embrace Sonny. "Don't, Mom," he says. Cora now understands. "Cora, come on, honey," Rubin calls down the stairs. "I'll be up in a minute, Rubin," she answers. "Good-bye, Sonny." As the children leave, Rubin calls again. "I'm coming, Rubin," calls Cora as she starts upstairs. "I'm coming . . . I'm coming."

SUMMER OF THE 17TH DOLL

A Play in Three Acts

By Ray Lawler

[Ray Lawler *was born in Footscary, a suburb of Melbourne and at the age of 13 went to work as a factory hand. After 11 years he broke away and decided to devote himself to the theatre. "Summer of the 17th Doll" was his tenth full-length play; one of his earlier works, "Cradle of Thunder" in 1952 won an Australian competition. "Summer of the 17th Doll" was a success in both Australia and London; on Broadway it was Lawler's debut as both playwright and actor.*]

For the cast listing, see page 310.

THE scene is Carlton, a once fashionable but now scruffy suburb of Melbourne, where in a two-storied brick cottage lives old Emma with her barmaid daughter Olive. Their frowsy living room is decorated on all sides with kewpie dolls, pieces of coral, and brilliantly plumaged birds and butterflies.

While Bubba Ryan, a twenty-two-year-old neighbor, seems to be further decorating things with be-ribboned candy canes, another barmaid sits haughtily by. In her "good black" and string of pearls, Pearl Cunningham, a big, well-corseted woman with dyed red hair, looks at a magazine and listens suspiciously to Bubba's remarks about a wedding that she attended but Olive stayed away from. "She wouldn't believe," Bubba says, "even up till the Saturday afternoon that Nance'd ever go through with it." "If you ask me," Pearl says, "I'd say this Nancy had her head screwed on the right way." "She got tired of waiting, I think," Bubba decides. "Olive doesn't mind it, she just looks forward to the next time, but it used to get on Nance's nerves a bit. 'N', of course, she reads a lot, and this feller, this Harry Allaway—he works in a book shop, and he'd bring books into the pub for her. I s'pose that's how he got around her, really. I don't reckon Barney's ever read a book in his life." "Mmmmm,"

"Summer of the 17th Doll": By Ray Lawler. Copyright © 1957 by Ray Lawler. Reprinted by permission of Random House, Inc., New York, N. Y.

broods Pearl, adding: "I'm fond of a good book myself now and then." With a tolerant smile, Bubba explains: "You won't need any till after April. Even Nancy, she only used to read in the winter. . . ."

Pearl takes exception to Bubba's "nasty talk" and particularly to that line about no reading till after April.

When Olive enters, all dressed up in her new summer clothes, Bubba says she looks lovely. Pearl, on the other hand, does not find the dress to her taste. The minute Bubba goes to the kitchen for beer, Pearl takes exception to the way Bubba acts . . . just as if she owns the place.

OLIVE—Well, whaddya expect? She's been runnin' in and out ever since she was old enough to walk. Roo and Barney she treats as if they were uncles . . . (*She laughs suddenly.*) God, you're a wag. Talk about Cautious Kate!

PEARL—Why?

OLIVE—Look at them suitcases by the stairs! You'd think someone was gettin' ready for a moonlight flit.

PEARL (*firmly*)—That's different. I've taken my overnighter up, and I'm not taking anythin' else till I'm certain.

OLIVE—Don't be silly. I told yer, he's all right.

PEARL—Yes. Well, I find that out for meself, if you don't mind.

OLIVE—Oh, nobody's tryin' to talk you into anythin'. Just don't take too long to decide, that's all.

Next, sniffing at a group snapshot that Olive shows her, Pearl remarks that she finds the whole thing a "bit intimate." "Listen, luvvie," Olive answers, "you better make up your mind. These are a coupla sugarcane cutters fresh from the tropics—not two professors from the university."

Bubba brings out the bottles of cold beer. As they set them around the table, Olive persuades Bubba to tell Pearl the reason for the candy walking sticks. Telling a longish story of how till she was fifteen Barney and Roo brought her walking sticks, after which she in turn gave *them* canes, Bubba senses how unimpressed Pearl is. Anxious to escape, and promising to greet the men after tea, Bubba leaves through the French windows.

Waiting in the growing dark, wondering where her mother went after the community sing, Olive surmises that her shrewd old mother met Barney and Roo at the terminal and touched them for money even before they could get a taxi. Pearl is outraged that Olive would talk of her mother so. "Listen," says Olive, "a fiver's nothin'. She shakes them down for all they're worth the whole time they're here. 'Course they're a wake up, but they don't seem to mind. 'Fact, I think Roo likes it. Good old Roo," Olive says, looking at the photograph. "I reckon he's got the best-lookin' mouth in the world."

The waiting has increased Pearl's determination to avoid any "ghastly mess." Since her daughter Vera is almost grown up, Pearl talks virtuously of setting her a good example. Riled, Olive would like things understood now, right from the start: "Now look, that's one thing I'm not gunna stand for."

PEARL—What?

OLIVE—You know what! That respectable mother stunt. Don't you try and put that over on me.

PEARL—I didn't say a word.

OLIVE—You said wrong, didn't yer? 'N' nasty mess? That's enough. I've told you over 'n' over again what this lay-off is, yet every time you open your mouth you make it sound like somethin'— low and dirty. Well, if that's the way you look at it, you don't have to stay, y'know—nobody's forcin' you to make any decisions about it—you can get your bags from the hall and clear out before they get here.

PEARL (*defensively*)—Just because I don't think it's altogether proper.

OLIVE—Yeh. Just because of that.

PEARL—Nobody would say it was a decent way of livin'.

OLIVE—Wouldn't they? I would! I've knocked about with all sorts from the time I was fourteen, and I've never come across any- thin' more decent in my life. Decency is—it depends on the people. And don't you say it doesn't!

PEARL—I meant decent like marriage. That's different, you said yourself it was.

OLIVE (*with a slight shudder*)—It's different all right. Compared to all the marriages I know, what I got is—(*she gropes for depth of expression*)—is five months of heaven every year. And it's the same for them. Seven months they spend up there killin' themselves in the cane season, and then they come down here to live a little. That's what the lay-off is. Not just playin' around and spendin' a lot of money, but a time for livin'. You think I haven't sized that up against what other women have? I laugh at them every time they try to tell me. Even waitin' for Roo to come back is more excitin' than anythin' they've got. So you make up your mind right now— you either gunna be polite to them and hang on until you get to know Barney well enough to decide, or you're gunna get out of here right now.

Uncapping a bottle of beer, and pouring two drinks, Olive explains how different these men are from city men who roll home to their wives every night. With defiant pride she tells Pearl: "Nancy used to say it was how they'd walk into the pub as if they owned it— even just in the way they walked you could spot it. All round would be the regulars—soft city blokes havin' their drinks and their little arguments, and then in would come Roo and Barney. They wouldn't say anythin'—they wouldn't have to—there'd just be the two of them walkin' in, then a kind of wait for a second or two, and quiet. After that, without a word, the regulars'd stand aside to let 'em through, just as if they was a—coupla kings. She always reckoned they made the rest of the mob look like a bunch of skinned rabbits. Poor old Nancy." Pearl says: "She got what she wanted." Upset, Olive finds Pearl sounding like her mother. "She's fond of Roo, y'know," Olive says, "but every time he's away and we have a row, Emma throws him up at me like a dirty dishcloth." For the first time, Pearl is sympathetic: "I know. Aunt of mine was like that. Used to store everythin' up and let go at family funerals." "Oh, chronic!" Olive agrees. "Doesn't it make you mad?"

When the taxi finally draws up, the women, hastily hiding the opened beer under the table, pop peppermints into their mouths.

With old Emma slung over his shoulder, Barney strides with ease up the veranda, and after a slap on Emma's rear, dumps her down in the house. As Olive moves happily into Roo's arms, Pearl, who has been watching Barney apprehensively, limply accepts his hand and introduction. "I'm Missus Cunningham. How d'yer do," she stammers. "I'm pretty good," Barney grins, "how's yerself?" The cocky, sunburned, slightly pot-bellied little man forces Pearl to meet his eyes. Embarrassed, she says: "O'y'know—a bit hot."

When Olive inquires how things are coming, Barney says: "Well, we've got as far as Barney and Missus Cunningham." Under big Roo's smile, Pearl finally relaxes a bit, but not for long. As the men rush to the veranda and yowl for Bubba, Pearl needs more soothing. "Hey, cut it out, you two," Olive calls after them, "it's Sunday. Come inside, you'll see her after." Hearing that Pearl works in the same pub as Olive, Barney now shouts "Whacko!" and as he goes to sit beside her, remarks that it's going to be just like old times.

Emma makes plain that it's not like old times: if she hadn't been at the terminal to meet the men, they never would have come near

Olive's house. Covering up quickly, Barney, kidding Emma, distracts Olive, and Emma marches off huffily to the kitchen.

As Roo takes his bags upstairs, Olive sends Pearl off to the kitchen and gives Barney a telegram from Nancy. He's to stay away from her, Olive warns him. "What'd you bet I couldn't get her back?" Barney asks.

OLIVE—It wouldn't do you a scrap of good. Not in this place, anyway. The day she got married I swore I'd never have the two of you here together again no matter what happened. Pearl's the one you've got to concentrate on.

BARNEY—Ah, Pearl'll be all right.

OLIVE—Will she? Don't be too sure of that. 'Fact, she's got her bags piled up by the stairs, 'n' if she doesn't take to you by tomorrow mornin' she's shiftin' out.

BARNEY—Why? What's the matter?

OLIVE—She's not too shook on the whole thing. Doesn't understand it, for one thing; then she's got a daughter, kid of eighteen. Livin' with relations at present, but it makes Pearl nervous, she's scared of puttin' her foot wrong. Then when I wised her up about your handful of errors, that made her more nervous still.

By now Barney is disgusted. Olive warns him that if he passes up Pearl he is not going to bring any of his painted crows to live in her house. When he cockily agrees to take Pearl on, Olive warns him further that it's not going to be such a push-over. It is now Barney's turn to tell her a few things. Olive isn't going to have such a push-over, either. Emma had been right when she said that Roo was going to North Melbourne. Not that he's mad at Olive, but he's broke.

As Barney tells Olive that it was the worst season they ever had, he has to prevent her from running up to Roo. He thinks it best that she should get the details from him.

BARNEY—Well, first set off, Roo, the silly cow, strains his back. . . . There's no need to throw a fit, nothin' serious, nearly better. But it slowed him down all through the season, see. (*Frankly putting cards on the table.*) Roo's a pretty hard man, y'know, on the job. Got no use for anyone can't pull their weight; and bein' able to pick and choose almost, 'coz everyone knows he's one of the best gangers there is, gen'rally he gets a champion bunch together. But he's gotta be hard doin' it sometimes. (*Facing her.*) This year he got the boys to turn off Tony Moreno. You must've heard us talk

of Tony, real character, everyone likes him, but anyway Roo thought
he was gettin' too slow. Instead he takes on a big young bloke we'd
heard a lot about, name of Johnnie Dowd. Cracked up to be as fast
as lightnin'.
OLIVE—Was he?
BARNEY—Yeh. Not as good as Roo, when he's fit, mind yer, but
he could run rings round the best of us. And this time he even made
Roo look a bit sick.

When the boys kidded Roo over Dowd's outstripping him, Roo,
in spite of his bad back, made a running fight of it. ". . . And with
a busted back—how the hell could he win?" Olive cries. With a
shrug, Barney reckons that Roo figures he's twice as good as anyone
else. Two months ago, on a flaming hot day, Roo and Dowd had a
"blue." "Bad?" Olive asks. "Pretty bad. I was right on the spot
when it happened," Barney says. "Started off over nothin'. They
was workin' side by side, and when Dowdie finishes the strip he looks
back to see how far behind Roo was. Well, right at that moment
Roo's knees went. Never seen anythin' like it, they just buckled
under him and there he was, down on the ground. This strikes
Dowd as bein' funny, see, and he starts to laugh. Well, that did it.
Roo went him and it was on, cane knives and the lot. Took six of
us to separate 'em; could've been murder, I reckon. 'Course the
boys all blamed Roo for it, so he did his block again, packed up his
gear and walked off. (*There is an uncomfortable pause.*) I didn't
see him after that till I picked him up in Brisbane a week ago."
Olive stares accusingly at Barney when she grasps that he did not
go along with Roo. Barney alibis uncomfortably, then somehow
his sneaking admiration for Dowd slips out: "Of course I had to put
me foot in it all over again by tellin' him how they made Dowdie
ganger in his place, and what a bottlin' job he done." Unperceived
by Olive or Barney, Roo, coming downstairs, overhears this. "Well,
you gotta give him credit," Barney says; "for a kid he made a very
smart fist of it. . . ." "Yeh," says Roo, "and have you told her
'bout the big booze-up he threw when yez all got back to Cairns?"
"Being sarcastic won't get you anywhere," Barney answers. "Blab-
ber-gutsin' doesn't take you far, either," Roo retorts.
Intervening, taking the blame on herself for asking, Olive tells
Barney to take his bags upstairs—to the little back room for tonight.
Once again cocky, Barney goes upstairs. Olive and Roo stand together in embarrassed silence. Olive insists on knowing why he was
going to North Melbourne instead of to her. As he blurts out angrily
that he's flat broke, she becomes furious. "Yeh," she shrills, "and

I'd care a lot for that, wouldn't I?   That's how I've always met you, standin' on the front veranda with a cash register, lookin' a-like a bloody—"   As she bursts into tears, Roo takes her into his arms. He tries to explain that he doesn't want to sponge.   "I won't bludge on you," he maintains stubbornly.   He will get a job, but they aren't going to think about it any more tonight.   Saying his tongue is hanging out after that long plane ride, what he wants is his beer, Roo changes Olive's mood.   Fishing out the bottle she hid as the men arrived, and rushing over to the stairs, she yells: "Up there, Cazaly— come on down—the party's on—"

When Barney comes down loaded wtih presents, he hands Roo, behind his back, a doll.   As Pearl and Emma come from the kitchen with the supper salad, Roo suddenly holds high his gift. "Here you are—" he says to an overjoyed Olive—"the seventeenth doll!"

SCENE II

The remains of last night's party are everywhere evident: food on the table, glasses and bottles all around, and paper scattered over the floor.   Feeling a change of weather in her old bones, Emma brings in the milk and the morning newspaper, while Roo, hungover and disapproving, brings in from the veranda beer bottles that Barney had drunkenly thrown there at the height of the party.

All dressed for work and cheerfully munching a piece of toast, Olive hovers over Roo.   She wishes he would have let her give him breakfast in bed.   Roo, stolidly reading the paper, says she knows he doesn't like eating in bed.   "Just for a change," says Olive, massaging his shoulder.   "How's your back?   Barney told me how you strained it—at least, he didn't say how you did it, just about how it slowed you down so much."   "Trust Barney," Roo answers.   Changing the subject, picking up the seventeenth doll from a chair, Olive finds it prettier than ever.   She thinks someone went to special trouble when this was made.   "Other times they've been pretty," she says, "but this one's beautiful."   Holding it in her arms almost as if it were a baby, Olive asks Roo: "You know why I like the dolls more than anythin' else you've brought down?   Well, the birds and coral and—butterflies and stuff—all that you got me 'coz I wanted to know what it was like up there.   But the dolls—they're somethin' you thought of by yourself. . . . So they're special!"   Though he grunts in embarrassment, Roo is touched.

When Olive next broaches the possibility of his coming to the pub today, or of booking seats for shows she's been waiting to see, Roo avoids a direct answer.   As Olive goes out to call the others to breakfast in the kitchen, Emma, who has overheard this last, accuses Roo of having a bit of cheek to turn up flat broke. Taking anything she has to say in his stride, Roo asks her calmly where the Lyman Paint Company is, that's advertising for help. "Around the corner, 'bout three blocks down," Emma says. "Ah," Roo grunts.

EMMA—That Barney—is 'e broke too?

Roo—Don't reckon so. He oughta have pretty near his usual packet.

EMMA—Just as well. I wouldn't think of helpin' him out.

Roo (*twinkling*)—Was you think' of helpin' me?

EMMA—I might. (*Hastily.*) Only a loan, mind yer. I'd want it back again.

Roo—How much—a fiver?

EMMA (*coolly*)—Smart Alec, ain't yer? What d'yer say to fifty?

Roo—Quid? You got fifty quid?

EMMA (*triumphantly*)—I got more, I got nearly—well, never mind. And don't you let on to anyone I even got fifty. But that's what I could let you have, if you want it.

Roo (*admiringly*)—You beaut! Who'd you pinch it from—Olive?

EMMA—Her? What I git from her hardly pays for me community. No, I got me own way of earnin' a few bob.

Roo—I'll bet you have. Keepin' nit for the S. P. bookies, eh— drummin' up trade for the sly grogs— (BUBBA, *dressed for the street, enters on side veranda.*)

EMMA—Ask no questions, you get told no lies. (*She catches sight of* BUBBA.) Well, you're an early bird—don't tell me you've come to help me clean up?

BUBBA—I'm off to work, I only dropped in for a minute. . . .

EMMA—Thought it was too good to be true. Same as usual— everythin' left to the old girl.

Thinking it awful that Nancy and Barney should have messed things up, Bubba has something very much on her mind: "Roo, can I ask you somethin'?" "What?" says Roo, smiling at her. "About the lay-off . . . it's going to be just the same, isn't it? I mean, it's still goin' to be Selby at Christmas time, and . . . and all the rest. You won't alter anythin'?" Roo reassures her as he would a child. Confessing, with a tremulous smile, that with Nancy gone she was afraid it would be different, Bubba gives Roo a hug and leaves.

Emma comes back to remind Roo of her offer; he reckons he'd better not. "Start takin' oscar from wimmen," Roo says, "and don't know where you'll end." Not given to compliments, Emma tells Roo she considered him from the very start a packet of trouble but honest. If he won't take her money, what will he do? Roo asks if she would be surprised to hear he was out for a job in town. Whether it is because he is going to get a job, or because of the effect this is going to have on the rest of the household, Emma, at any event, is pleased.

The next one to hear the news from Roo is Barney. He is horrified. He offers his money to Roo.

Roo—I don't want your money, I can still earn my own. (*Bitterly.*) Even if I have got a busted back.

Barney (*stung*)—You pig-headed mug. What about all those times you've carried me—every year when I've run dry down here you've kicked me on. . . .

Roo—Yeh, well, this time you'd better hang on to what you've got for as long as you can. That won't be happenin'.

Barney—It's all that lousy rotten pride of yours, ain't it? You're crook on me because I stayed up there with Dowdie and didn't walk out with you.

Roo—I'm not crook on anythin'.

Barney—Oh, yes, you are. You got a snout on that kid the first day you saw him workin'.

Roo (*intensely*)—Cut it out. . . .

Barney—I watched yer! The morning after you turned poor old Tony Moreno off . . .

Roo (*furiously*)—Cut it out or I'll bash your face in!

Barney—Righto. You go and get yourself a job. See if I care. I'll find some way of amusin' meself.

For the moment, Barney's heart isn't in enjoying the lay-off. When Olive wants to have all arrangements with Pearl straightened out before they go to work, Barney tells her sullenly about Roo's getting a job. Olive is as appalled as he is and rushes upstairs to dissuade Roo from taking such a disastrous step. Barney now has a quiet talk with a suddenly nervous Pearl.

Though mechanical and somewhat absent-minded in his courting, Barney doesn't do too badly. Preserving her righteous manner as Barney explains away his "errors," Pearl hangs on to his every word.

Barney—Ever since I was a kid, whenever I've met a good-lookin' woman, I've always felt like an excited eel in a fishbasket.

Pearl—Don't make jokes about it.

BARNEY—I'm not. I know it's nothin' to be proud of—but I'm not gunna apologize for it, either.

PEARL (*outraged*)—And that's that! Just sayin' you're weak gives you the right to run around and have kids wherever you want to—

BARNEY—No, it doesn't. But the ordinary bloke's got a way out, he can get married. There's always been a sorta reason why I never could . . .

PEARL (*incredulously*)—With children in three states? I'd like to hear of any reason that big!

BARNEY (*bluntly*)—Righto then—you listen. My eldest boys, the two of 'em, are both about the same age.

PEARL—Well?

BARNEY—Well, use your nut, don't you see what it means? Their mothers was in trouble at the same time. Oh, I'm to blame for that, and I'm not sayin' I ain't, but I was only a silly kid when it happened. Eighteen, I was.

PEARL—Old enough to face up to your responsibilities.

BARNEY—Maybe it is, but it's hardly old enough to face up to a big decision like—which of the two was I s'posed to marry? You just think of it—two good decent girls, and you can only make it right for one of them. I nearly went mad. Whichever one of them I married, I thought it'd be a rotten insult to the other. And it would have been. Both of them said so.

Barney's done everything for them, though. He paid all their bills right through, and after that he started paying maintenance. But he left it up to them which one he should marry. "You decide," Barney had said. "Well," he says with relish, "they're sittin' up there in that little one-horse town in New South Wales still arguin' about it! And I'm as far off marriage as ever I was—'coz if there's one thing I do believe in, it's first come, first served!"

As Barney puts the finishing touches to his picture of the special woman who would understand a bloke like him, Pearl is so confused she is ready to tumble. "She's got to have experience, f'rinstance, so she can spot this kind of bloke from the mob. Then she's got to be able to take him for what he is, not try to tie him down. . . ." Olive's appearance interrupts Barney's clincher. Seeing Olive, he says airily that he'll tell Pearl this last quality some other time. Disappointed, Pearl goes for her things.

As Barney faces the prospect of passing the day by himself, his cockiness deserts him. Roo plans on job-hunting as soon as he puts the girls on the tram for town. Emma doesn't want Barney lolling

around her house. Suddenly the picture brightens. As Pearl goes out
the door, she casually remarks that Barney might take her bags upstairs, then quickly adds: "Don't come to any conclusions, there's
nothin' settled yet!"

ACT II

On a blazing hot New Year's Eve, after Roo's hard day's work at
the paint factory, the foursome has settled for a dull evening at home.
Olive plays cards with Roo; Pearl knits away for one of Barney's
"errors," while Barney champs furiously at the bit. They turn down
every suggestion he makes. When he starts reminiscing about gay
holidays in the past, the others tell him to shut up.

Entering in evening dress through the French windows, on her way
to a dance that she doesn't want to go to, Bubba—surveying the
group—asks: "Aren't you goin' out anywhere at all?" "Naah," says
Barney as he looks at Pearl untangling wool, "we're havin' one of
those sensational at-home parties." On an impulse, Bubba suggests
that they would be welcome at the Morrises. Barney's game to go,
but no one else is. In a kindly fashion, Roo tells Bubba that she'll
be late for her dance. She departs, amid the kisses and New Year's
greetings, only to have Pearl ask suspiciously, the minute she's gone,
about the Morrises and why they aren't going this year? Olive explodes: " 'Cause the Morrises are cousins of Nancy's, that's why!"

A little while later, Pearl maliciously remembers that Olive had
once compared Roo and Barney to two birds of paradise flying down
out of the sun, coming south every year for the mating season.
Winding her wool, she rocks with laughter at this image, as the
others, stony-faced, are not amused.

PEARL—It was how you talked all the time. Look what you said
about them Sunday-night boat trips up the river. Beautiful, you
said.

OLIVE—Well, was it my fault it rained?

PEARL—No, but even if it hadn't—that terrible old boat—

OLIVE—You didn't give it a fair go.

PEARL (*on her mettle*)—All right then, what about Christmas at
that week-end place in Selby? You can't say I didn't give that a
fair go.

BARNEY (*staring*)—And what was wrong with Selby?

PEARL—Oh, it wasn't bad, but the way she cracked it up, I expected a palace . . .

Roo (*truculently*)—You wouldn't find a better little place than that this side of Sydney.

PEARL—Oh, get away with you. It hasn't even got electricity.

Angry, sick of cards, thinking now it's just plain silly to wait up for midnight, Olive starts for bed. Galvanized into action, Barney suggests getting Emma in to conduct a sing-song. "She wouldn't play," Roo says. "You know what she said last time." "She'll play," Barney assures him. "Emma," he calls out to the veranda, "what you doin' out there?" "Gettin' a sea breeze off the gutter," she snaps.

Tempted by a quid, and allowed her choice of tunes, Emma agrees reluctantly: "Righto. Get yourselves organized, and no muckin' about."

Having removed her ring rather grandly and placed it on top of the piano, Emma plays the accompaniment very seriously until she hears a flatted note. She asks them to try it again. Next time around, it's still wrong. Livid with irritation, Emma turns on Pearl. Barney bursts out: "Look, we're not after a singin' lesson, Emma; all we want's a bit of fun. . . ." Emma accuses them of being muckers who don't care if it's right or not. Wrathfully proclaiming that *she* never sang a bad note in her life, she rises to Barney's bait. The "community" and Mr. Munro would vouch for that.

BARNEY—And what would he know about it?

EMMA—He's the conductor, ain't he? D'yer reckon he'd get me to sing a solo every year for me birthday if I sung it flat?

OLIVE—Does it for a laugh, p'bably.

EMMA—That's a flamin' lie and you know it. I'll bring him 'round here.

Roo—You silly old rabbit, they're only pullin' your leg.

EMMA—Oh, so that's what you got me in for, is it—to poke mullock?

BARNEY (*hitting a note*)—You was asked in to play the pianner—

EMMA—Yeh—for a single fiddlie! (*She bangs the flap down, puts her ring back on, and charges out angrily, throwing over her shoulder.*) Well, I wouldn't listen to what youse call singin' for all the tea in China. Bunch of croakin' amachers! (*She stumps across veranda.*)

PEARL—Well, I suppose you could say that's one of the shortest community singin' sessions on record.

OLIVE (*disgustedly*)—Aah, she gets worse all the time.

Roo—You shouldn't have said that, 'bout them only gettin' her to sing for a joke.

Olive—Well, who does she think she is—Nellie Melba?

Roo—No, but her singin', that's one thing she's proud of.

Olive—Look, she treads on my corns and she doesn't say she's sorry. Emma's got to learn to knuckle down a bit.

Roo (*angrily*)—Righto. Forget it!

Barney now suggests opening up a few bottles. With a what-the-hell attitude, the girls go into the kitchen for food and beer. Paying no attention to the marked coolness Roo shows for him, Barney cagily slips in the fact that he was surprised to run into their gang at the pub today. Not putting anything past Barney, Roo says he probably arranged the meeting. Barney assures Roo that everyone, including Dowd, wanted to see him. Roo doesn't want to see Dowd. "Well," says Barney, "that puts me in a fine spot, doesn't it?" "How the hell does it affect you? You wanta go, you go," Roo answers.

Barney (*fiercely*)—You know I wouldn't without you. Righto —so I didn't walk out with you up north. But that was the only time I ever slipped. I've stood by you other times, haven't I?

Roo—I didn't need you other times. That was once I did.

Barney—All right, I was in the wrong. But give me a chance to make it up, won't yer? Twenty years of knockin' around to-gether, I oughta deserve that much.

Roo (*softening*)—What is it you want to do?

Barney (*eagerly*)—Help you to get back on top with the boys.

Barney proposes that as long as Roo is working in that dump, and his money is running out, they should join the boys and go up the Murray with them for the grape harvest. "You selfish little bas-tard!" Roo yells. "You listen to me—we come down here for the lay-off, five months of the year, December to April. That leaves another seven months still hangin'—what d'yer reckon Olive does in that time? Knocks around with other blokes, goes out on the loose every week? No, she doesn't, she just waits for us to come back again—'coz she thinks our five months is worth all the rest of the year put together! It's knowin' that that brought me down this time, broke and—and when I would have given anythin' to have stopped up there. But I couldn't let her down—and if I hear you mention either grapes or the Murray to her now, I'll kick you so far they'll have to feed you with a shanghai." Told to get himself a job when his money runs out, Barney considers this the final insult: "Like in a paint factory? Pigs I will!"

Returning, the girls pour the last drinks of the old year. Coming to sit beside Roo, Olive apologizes softly for all the moaning she's done. As rockets go off sporadically, she says now she is glad that they didn't go out. Half gay, half defiant, Barney echoes this with a toast: "Happy days 'n' glamorous nights!" Almost choking on her beer, Pearl gasps that Barney shouldn't say things like that.

OLIVE—What?
PEARL—D-didn't you hear him?
BARNEY—All I said was . . .
PEARL—Glamorous nights! I mean—look at us!

Olive's resolve breaks; she crumples. Roo, crouching by her, tries to comfort her while Barney stares shamefacedly into his beer, as New Year's bells and cheering can be heard.

SCENE II

Rolling drunk, Barney, accompanied by young Dowd, comes home from a day's drinking. They catch Roo, still in his dirty work clothes, sprawled sound asleep in the living room. With no chance of escape, Roo reluctantly accepts Dowd's apology, and to Barney's delight even shakes hands with Dowd. Over Olive's well-meaning objections, Roo even agrees to go with the boys to the races the following afternoon. "Whatever you like," he tells Dowd. "You fix it up with Barney. I—I got to get off these clothes 'n' have a shower." "Sure," says Dowd, "looks like we caught you right home from work." Hurt, Roo answers stiffly: "Yeh." He goes upstairs.

Barney, the fixer, is elated. Buttering up Dowd, Barney suddenly decides on a switch of plans: not the gang, but just the three of them. "The sheilas then, Pearl 'n' Olive, we'll take them, too. That'll break the ice." "And where do I come in?" Dowd asks. "Oh, that's all right, we'll fix you up with one as well," Barney says. "Not anythin' as old as them, you won't," Dowd protests. "I still got me own teeth, remember."

These plans misfire badly. Pearl does not care to get her own daughter for Dowd. In fact, she's furious. Unaware of what he's done, Barney lopes out on the back veranda after Bubba. Bewildered, Dowd wonders where Barney's off to now. As for Pearl, she doesn't know and he can go to hell for all she cares. Almost in tears over Barney's pimping for her daughter, Pearl pulls herself together and as she leaves the room says: "Tarred with the same brush, the lot of yer."

As Barney, very pleased with himself, returns with Bubba in tow, Dowd greets him: "Hey, that woman you left here, that Pearl, she's gone all snaky." "Ah, forget 'bout her," Barney says, "here's the one I want you to meet, Bubba Ryan." "You see this feller?" he tells Bubba. "Know where he comes from? Way up north where the sugar grows. And you want to know somethin' else? He's one of the best cutters and . . ." As Bubba's face lights up with interest, Dowd in a manly way takes over. He insists on talking to Bubba alone. He wants to give her a chance to get out of the date, since he had noticed that when Barney was rushing her into it, she had looked as if she hadn't wanted to go.

Bubba admits to being surprised that Barney should have brought someone from up north back to the house. Dowd understands: "They've sat pretty tight on this joint, haven't they? D'you live here?" Bubba says she's from next door. "Oh. That makes it bigger hide than ever, then," says Dowd. Looking disparagingly around the room that had become something of a legend up north, Dowd hurts Bubba by his frank disappointment at the tawdry decorations. Realizing what he's done, he exclaims: "What's the matter then? I've hurt you some way."

BUBBA (*turning on him*)—You shouldn't have said that about the dolls. They mean somethin' to Olive and Roo, it's—it's hard to explain. You wouldn't understand it.

DOWD—Tell me somethin', will yer? Why is it every time I come across anythin' connected with Roo, I'm supposed to act like I was too young to live up to it?

BUBBA—I don't know. Maybe it's like the walkin' sticks . . .

DOWD—The what?

BUBBA—The lolly walkin' sticks. They're a sort of present—a joke we have every year when they come down.

That beats Dowd, but he now only cares that Bubba, for all the cracks he has made, is willing to come with him. He has one last thing to clear up: Bubba's name sounds as if they've been keeping her in the cradle, too. Gratefully, she tells him her real name and when Dowd, smiling, decides that she's "Kathie" to him, they have reached an understanding.

Dowd gone, Roo's reaction to Barney's change of plans is one of seething anger. He now understands why Barney brought Dowd

back here. He wanted to show him how low Roo had sunk. Roo
shouts they're going to have it "fair dinkum" for once. Without
realizing how far he's gone until it's too late, Barney says that others
beside himself had seen how blind jealous Roo is of young Dowd.

BARNEY—The boys. They weren't too pleased when you walked
out on them up there, y'know. They weren't pleased at all. And
I'm drummin' yer, you don't pull your socks up pretty quick, you're
gunna find next season that our mob have got a new ganger for keeps.
    ROO—Dowd?
    BARNEY—Yeh, Dowd!
    ROO (*deceptively quiet*)—And that's why you brought him here,
eh? So's I could make it up with him and get back on top with
the boys?
    BARNEY—'Course it is.
    ROO (*springing the trap*)—Maybe you thought I could turn the
trick at the races tomorrer, on a little party cooked up between you
and Dowd—with Bubba as a bait!
    BARNEY (*quickly*)—Oh, that. I—I was makin' a switch. . . .
    ROO (*explosively*)—You was makin' a switch right enough! Your
money's runnin' out, you know you can't put the bite on me any
more, and so here's the new champion, all loaded and ready. And
it wasn't enough to chase after him up north after I walked out on
the gang, now you're aimin' to get him in here for the lay-off as well.
    BARNEY (*dangerously*)—You reckon I'd work a point like that?
    ROO—You'd do that and worse. 'Coz you're a slimy little leech
that won't drop off even when it's got its belly full.

The men lunge at one another, and the fight is on. They fight
their way onto the back veranda, where the women try to break it
up. "Any more of that," shouts Olive, "and the two of you will
sleep out in the gutter for the night. Men your age, you oughta have
more sense. What do you think you're up to, anyway?" Roo tells
her it's none of her business, whereupon Olive begins to lose her
temper. "Oh, isn't it? I'm s'posed to sit out in the back while you
kick one another to pieces, I s'pose? And why? All because you
had one rotten season up north." "It ain't that at all," Roo says.
Swaying to his feet, Barney contradicts him: "It is. Why don't you
be a man and admit it?" Over Olive's protests, Roo forces Barney
(since it had been his lie) to tell the truth: Roo never had a bad
back. "Did you hear that?" Roo asks all of them. "No strain,
nothin'. Dowd did a better job than me because he's a better man
than I am. That's what he wanted you to know!" As he shoves

Barney from him, Barney cries out that he never would have told on Roo. Roo thinks it high time that the women know they're dealing with a couple of no-hopers, and, to make this clear, and to take his revenge on Barney, he brings to light that this ladies' man no longer has a way with the ladies. Barney has been turned down right and left, and Roo has the names of the women who said no and laughed at him. Barney croaks that they all lied. "Yeh?" Roo taunts him. "And I s'pose Mrs. Kelly lied when she had you thrown out of the Royal pub? 'N' the cook at Adam's, she was lyin', and the little New Australian woman, and Skinny Linton's missus? All of them lyin', and you're still the best there is—like hell you are!" "That's enough, Roo," Barney blazes. "And Nancy—after seventeen years, you couldn't even hold Nancy!" Roo finishes. "You dirty rotten swine!" Barney cries and seizing the nearest thing—the vase containing the seventeenth doll—swings angrily at Roo's head. Roo pulls it out of Barney's hand and throws it away, smashing vase and doll. Olive, sinking to her knees, picks the doll up.

ACT III

The following morning Pearl, dressed in her respectable black and with her suitcase close by, is ready to clear out. The living room, where she says her unemotional good-byes to Olive, has been cleared of all its souvenirs. After Olive late at night had cleaned up after the brawl, not a sign of dolls or decoration remained.

In her farewell piece, Pearl again asks Olive to take stock of what she really has: "Look at this place now you've pulled down the decorations—what's so wonderful about it? Nothin'. It's just an ordinary little room that's a hell of a lot the worse for wear. And if you'd only come out of your day-dream long enough to take a grown-up look at the lay-off, that's what you'd find with the rest of it." In steely tones, Olive repeats that everything she ever said about Roo and Barney and the time they spent here was Gospel true. It is Pearl's fault that she is not Nancy.

As Barney, unmoved by her departure, offers to help with the bags, Pearl can't resist asking him: "That first mornin'—you said there was three things a woman needed to have. You never told me what the third was." Barney answers coolly: "Don't you think it's a bit late for that now? And you haven't got it anyway— Oh, don't let it worry you. I've only met one woman who had." "Nancy," Pearl says. "Yeh," Barney answers. "And even she didn't have enough to keep the two of us together. . . . I'll carry your bag out."

Coming downstairs as Barney goes with Pearl to her taxi, Roo runs into trouble with Olive over last night's fight. He tries, inarticulately, to explain how he felt about shaking hands with Dowd. "Righto," Olive snaps, "so it means a lot to all of you up north. But why the hell couldn't you leave it up there? It's got nothin' to do with our time down here, has it? Did you have to smash that up as well?" Catching a glimpse of Emma nearby, Olive—almost in tears as she goes upstairs—accuses her of eavesdropping. "Course I was," Emma tells Roo. "I told you, it's the only way I can find out anythin'. And a mornin' like this, wouldn't miss it for all the tea in China. This is what I call interestin'. The lot of yez squabbling at last 'stead of all that playin' around went on other times. Only thing I'm sorry for is Nancy ain't here. She knew which way the wind was blowin', that one." Roo appeals to Emma.

Roo—C'mon, Emma, you're supposed to know the lot. Whose fault do you reckon it was—mine or Barney's?

EMMA—What fault?

Roo—Oh, I don't just mean the blue last night—who's to blame for messin' up the whole thing?

EMMA—You're kiddin', aren't yer?

Roo—No, fair dinkum, I want to know.

EMMA—Well, I'll be blowed! How long did you think these lay-off seasons were gunna last—forever? They're not for keeps, you know; these are just—seasons.

Roo—I know, but whose fault was it we come a cropper?

EMMA—Nobody's fault, yer melon!

Roo—Don't be silly, it must be somebody's . . .

EMMA (exasperated)—Why must it? All that's happened is you've gone as far as you can go. You 'n' Barney 'n' Olive, you're too old for it any more.

Roo—Old?

EMMA—That's it—old! Take a look in the mirror.

Roo—Nobody tells me I'm old. I'm as good a man now as ever I was.

EMMA—Are yer? Then who the hell was that bloke Barney brought here last night? a mirage or somethin'?

Roo—I ain't old! Old is—what you are, and—and—Tony Moreno. (This is a shock.)

EMMA—I didn't mean you was up for the pensions. But you ain't seventeen any more either. Look, sit down a minute. . . . Strikes me you don't know what's hit you, do you?

Roo—All I know is somethin' went wrong, and I reckon it was Barney.

Emma—Well, maybe Barney had a bit more to do with it than you did, but he's been slippin' longer than you have, don't forget that . . .

Roo—I ain't slipped. Never you say that. What I had was one lousy season.

Emma—So far. That's the first.

Roo—You think there could be another bad as that?

Emma—Lots of them. Don't you?

Emma puts it on the line: there is a time for sowing and a time for reaping, and now it's reaping time. Emma has made Roo understand; she knows, however, that Olive, still crying over dolls, is another matter.

It is Bubba's turn to be upset over last night. Coming in with Barney, she won't believe that the day at the races has been called off. "He asked me!" Bubba keeps repeating. And no matter how Barney and Roo speak to her, she is determined to keep her date. She is sure she knows what she wants.

Roo—We've spoilt it for you, ain't we? A long time.

Bubba—Not spoilt—it's—it's just that nothin' else is any good, that's all.

Roo—Even after what you saw last night?

Bubba—That won't happen to me.

Roo—How can you be sure, Bub?

Bubba—Because I won't let it! Dolls and breakin' things, and—and arguments about who was best—what do they all matter? That wasn't the lay-off.

Roo—It's what it came to.

Bubba—Well, it won't for me. I'll have what you had—the real part of it—but I'll have it differently. Some way I can have it safe and know that it's goin' to last.

Hoping that she's outgrown the lot of them, Barney gives Bubba Dowd's address; and Roo, not wanting her to cheapen herself in front of all the other workers, asks her to phone Dowd. Taking their fatherly warnings to heart, Bubba promises that they don't have to worry about her. As she darts out the back way, Roo answers: "Yeh, we know—Kathie."

Barney is off, too. He's going up the Murray with Dowd and the boys. Roo simply doesn't care. "That fixes that, then," Barney says defiantly. "And I tell yer, it's not just that me money's runnin' out, either. Last night was the finish for my books. We're poison to each other now. I reckon the only way out for both of us is to split up for a while." Roo agrees with one difference: they won't be meeting back north. Roo isn't going. Barney is horrified and says that's crazy. "It won't be so bad," Roo says. "Bad, me foot. You're talkin' about winter, remember," Barney answers. Roo has lived all his life in the sun and admits the sun's great, but now it appears to him that he's had too much of a good thing.

Finding the men together, a curt and constrained Olive is surprised that they're talking after last night. They've been working out the damage, Barney reports; and now because he's leaving Monday, he has to go and pack.

Olive—Monday! Oh, no wonder you were lookin' over the damage. . . .

Roo—Olive, I wanna talk to you. . . .

Olive—I'll bet. Settlin'-up-time already, is it? Well, make me an offer—vase decorations, and everythin' else you've smashed—how much?

Roo—Now, just a minute. . . .

Olive—This is where I collect, ain't it? In cold hard cash, Roo—seventeen summers—what are they worth?

Roo—Will you stop your bitchin' long enough for me to tell you somethin'? Barney's the one that's goin' on Monday, not me. I'm stayin' right here. Talkin' money that way! It's rotten!

Making up over Olive's tears, Roo announces his intention of staying here always. "Look," he says, taking her hand, "I know this is seventeen years too late, and what I'm offerin's not much chop, but I want to marry you, Ol." He unleashes a tropical storm.

Turning into a distraught and screaming creature, Olive cries that he has to go back to the fields. Terrified that he could even think she'll let all this end up in marriage and every day work in a paint factory, Olive pounds Roo's chest, demanding that he give her back what he has taken. Grabbing her wrists, Roo cries: "Olive, it's gone. Can't you understand? Every last little scrap of it—gone!" As she falls to the floor, like an animal in her feeling of loss, she cries: "I won't let you—I'll kill you first!" "Kill me, then," Roo yells. "But there's no more flyin' down out of the sun—no more birds of paradise. . . ." Squatting beside her, Roo bangs his hand on the floor: "This is the dust we're in and we're gunna walk through it like everyone else for the rest of our lives!"

Doubling over in pain, Olive won't accept any help from Emma. Barney is witness, too, as Olive gets to her feet and pushes her mother aside. Lurching forth drunkenly, Olive—bag in hand—staggers out the door across the veranda and out of sight down the street. Turning on the men grimly, Emma says: "There's nothin' you can do for her now—except to clear out and never come back. The lay-offs in this house are finished—for all of you."

Reaching a decision, Barney says to hell with Dowd and the boys. He won't even get in touch with them. He and Roo will go off on their own, to places they've never been. As Roo looks at the seventeenth doll, Barney continues: "There's all the West. We can hit Perth, then work our way right through up to Broome there." Watching Roo pick up the doll, he goes on desperately in rising tones: "That Rum Jungle you hear so much about! There's a packet in it, they reckon. I bet fellers like us could really clean up there—and we wouldn't have to give a Continental for—" He has failed. Roo, picking up the doll, in baffled insensate rage smashes it and tears at it, until there is nothing left. Slowly collapsing on the piano stool, Roo buries his head in his hands. "Come on, Roo. Come on, boy," Barney says. Taking Roo's coat, he drapes it over his shoulders. Acknowledging to one another by a single look all that they have lost, Barney makes a move toward the door, and Roo starts to follow.

SUNRISE AT CAMPOBELLO

A Play in Three Acts

BY DORE SCHARY

[DORE SCHARY *was born in Newark, N. J., in 1905. After finishing high school in Newark he did publicity and newspaper work before beginning a long career in Hollywood. There he did some 35 screen plays for Columbia, Paramount and Warner Brothers before joining Metro-Goldwyn-Mayer in 1933. He remained with M-G-M in a succession of executive capacities until 1956. He won an Academy Award for his "Story of Boys Town" and is also the author of juveniles in book form.*]

For the cast listing, see page 313.

ACT I

INTO the living room of the Franklin D. Roosevelt summer home on Campobello Island—it is August 10, 1921—troops child after bathing-suited child. Eleanor Roosevelt, tall and willowy at thirty-six, calmly greets Anna, then Franklin junior, and finally Jimmy and Elliott. Picking up after them, she asks them not to drop their towels and sweaters. Next, seizing a megaphone, she shouts down to the dock for the stragglers: "Franklin! Johnny!" "Mother," says Jimmy, "I hate to say this, but your voice through there sounds like the call to judgment." "That's enough from you, Mr. James Roosevelt," she counters. "Now upstairs. All of you—upstairs!"

Going into a huddle, the boys lower their arms and shoot out their fingers in a game of "odds and evens." As victor, Franklin junior wins a ride upstairs on his brothers' hands, while Elliott complains loudly: "He's stuffed with lead—all lead."

The first to be dressed for dinner, Anna comes down to register several complaints. First, she tells her mother, she doesn't know why *Julius Caesar* had to be chosen for tonight's reading when all the good parts are for men. And, secondly, she'd appreciate it if

"Sunrise at Campobello": By Dore Schary. Copyright © 1957 as an unpublished work by Dore Schary. Copyright © 1958 by Dore Schary. Reprinted by permission of Random House, Inc., New York, N. Y.

tomorrow's picnic menu wouldn't consist of the everlasting fried chicken and hard-boiled eggs. But since it is her father who has the final say about casting, and Mrs. McGowan, in the kitchen, who has it about food, Anna is merely wasting her time.

"Eleanor," calls a tall, muscular, graceful, forty-year-old Franklin Roosevelt from the porch, "they heard you all the way across to Eastport." "Stand by, the Captain's home," Eleanor says. FDR lifts little Johnny through the window into the living room. Almost at once, Mademoiselle Marie materializes and wants to take Johnny off to get dressed for dinner. Johnny appeals to his father. FDR simply shakes his head; but when Johnny stalls in French, he wins a pickaback ride. FDR sweeps Johnny up to his back and races up the stairs with him to the noisy boys' world above.

ANNA—Boys are so loud and noisy. Mother, how you put up with the four of them, I don't know.
ELEANOR—The four boys are easy. It's the one girl.
ANNA—Do you think I'm difficult?
ELEANOR—I think you feel surrounded by the men in the family.
ANNA—Before Granny went to Europe she told me she thinks you're too severe with me.
ELEANOR—I'm aware of your chats with Granny.
ANNA—Actually, Granny spoils us. The boys can talk her out of anything—all they have to do is speak a little French or agree with her.
ELEANOR—And what about you?
ANNA—Oh, of course, so can I.
FDR (*just coming down the stairs*)—So can you what?
ANNA—What?
FDR—I heard you say "so can I."
ANNA—Oh, talk Granny out of anything I want—just like the boys. Especially if I agree with her when she says something about Mr. Howe.

Carrying his copy of *Julius Caesar,* James, coming downstairs, asks if Mr. Howe is coming back here again. Knowing James has a reason for his question, Eleanor insists that he tell what it is. "Well," says Jimmy, "usually he rooms next to me and that coughing and—" he illustrates—"wheezing he does so much keep me up at night. And if he burns that incense to stop the coughing—that's worse than anything." Remarking that he doesn't appear to suffer from a lack of sleep, FDR ordains that there will be no criticism or complaints of Mr. Louis Howe from Jimmy or anyone else. Anna slips in: "Granny always says that Mr. Howe—" FDR well knows Granny's opinions of Mr. Howe and has no wish to hear them from Anna. Abruptly changing the subject, he asks his two eldest to go elsewhere to rehearse *Julius Caesar*.

Alone with Eleanor, FDR asks for a drink. "I feel rather tired and achy—that's the first swim I've had in years that didn't refresh me." Eleanor thinks he should be more careful. "Eleanor," her husband says, "I am not catching another cold and I am not becoming an alcoholic." Glancing at the newspaper while Eleanor fixes him a drink, FDR comments on Harding's playing his tuba while six million people remain unemployed, and remembers something Woodrow Wilson once said to him: "It is only once in a generation that a people can be lifted above material things. That is why conservative government is in the saddle for two-thirds of the time."

Louie Howe's name crops up again. Howe hardly thinks that Wall Street is a place for a dedicated progressive. Eleanor questions this too. FDR explains away his banking job: "I've weathered battles with Tammany Hall, seven years in the Navy Department, and *Mama's* massive objection to politics—which she rates one step higher than garbage collecting. I am quite sure that Wall Street will not corrupt my political convictions." "That's a comfort," says his wife.

Dressed, hungry for dinner, the rest of the children troop down into the living room. They first receive their assignments for to-night's reading of *Caesar,* then hear parts of Granny's letter from London—and how she expects that they will be speaking perfect French on her return. "So," says FDR, "you had better be speaking perfect French. *Ici on parle français.*"

Timing it to coincide with the announcement of dinner, Jimmy challenges his father to some Indian arm wrestling. FDR takes him on, quickly beats him, and proclaims to his cheering children: "Undefeated and still champion."

As the children proceed to the dining room, their father looks appreciatively at the sun's last light on the water. The next minute he clutches his back in pain. "Must be a spot of lumbago," he says as Eleanor feels his forehead. "No, I don't feel feverish. Just suddenly"—he snaps his fingers—"like that . . ."

Eleanor, as FDR had hoped, orders him to bed and promises to bring him a tray. As the children can be heard cheering Mrs. McGowan, FDR pauses in amusement to listen to their yells, then slowly goes upstairs.

Scene II

September 1, 1921. Late at night, as the kerosene lamps burn not too brightly, small, asthmatic Louie Howe comes down from the sickroom. Encountering a bathrobe-clad Jimmy who is unable to sleep and unwilling to disturb his mother, Louie comforts the boy.

Jimmy—Sometimes I get frightened. So does Anna.

Howe—Well, stop being frightened. Those germs never ran into anybody as tough as your father. They'll be yelling for help by the time he gets through with them.

Jimmy—He's strong, all right.

Howe—He's a strong and big man in many ways. Jimmy, when I first got up here I was scared, too. I was worried about your father being so sick. But now he's beginning to fight back—and when he fights—well, sir, you know the first time I saw him was in Albany in 1911. He was fighting a tough battle with Tammany Hall. Believe me, they can fight like roughnecks. Well, he won that one going away—like Dempsey did to Carpentier. And, Jimmy, he's going to win this one.

Jimmy (*relieved*)—I hope you're right.

Howe—I've never been wrong in my life. Only once, when I figured the ice on the pond in Saratoga was thick enough to skate on. Well, sir, it took three days to wring me out.

As his mother comes down with a tray, Jimmy takes it to the kitchen, then comes back to say good night. He promises to get some sleep and asks Eleanor to get some, too. As Jimmy leaves, Howe exclaims irrelevantly: "Eleanor, why the hell can't we get some electric lights in here?" What he's really thinking about has to do with a different kind of power. "Where's Mrs. Roosevelt?" he asks.

Eleanor—Mamá's in her room. She'll probably be down in a few minutes. Louie, be understanding. It's been a desperately unhappy day for her.

Howe—I am understanding, Eleanor. I like the old lady. She fascinates me. Monumental and impregnable as the Rock of Gibraltar.

Eleanor—I know the problem that you have with Mamá.

Howe—It's no problem. She just hates the sight of me. She considers me the ward-heeler in Franklin's life.

ELEANOR—Louie, don't quarrel with her.

HOWE—Eleanor—I promise to shinny on my side if she shinnies on hers. (*A pause.*) It's going to be rough, but you're going to have to tell her the truth.

ELEANOR (*wearily*)—Louie, if we can only get him well enough to move him into New York. Each day with him here is like—(*Controlling herself.*) He should be in a hospital, getting the best care, the most modern treatment.

HOWE—Now you just remember this—nobody could have done more than you, or done it better.

Sara Delano Roosevelt, the Lady of the Manor, still elegantly dressed at such a late hour, comes down the stairs and accepts Eleanor's offer of a cup of tea. Alone, while Eleanor is getting the tea, with Howe and his chain-smoking, Mrs. Roosevelt first graciously asks after his wife, then sniffs and remarks: "The air is rather stuffy, don't you think?" Taking it in his stride, Howe answers: "We had the door open, but it's damn cold outside."

Though she professes to admire the way they have all behaved, Mrs. Roosevelt would undoubtedly like to be free of Howe's company, but he stays on. He stays on through the whole conversation Eleanor has with her mother-in-law about Franklin's illness, and he praises Eleanor's efforts. "Mrs. Roosevelt," he says, "this girl has worked like a squad of trained nurses. Dr. Lovett was amazed at how she had done it all." "Couldn't you get any nurses, dear?" Mrs. Roosevelt asks. "We tried," says Eleanor, "but none were available. Campobello is quite remote."

Howe stays on in spite of further hints from the old lady. Tired as she is, Eleanor tells her mother-in-law of these past three weeks. Critical of the specialist and of the island's isolation, Mrs. Roosevelt is in full control of her emotions until Eleanor reports that Dr. Lovett believes the infantile paralysis is mild, and that Franklin will recover "almost completely." "Almost?" his mother asks.

ELEANOR—Well, Mamá—at first Franklin lost control even of his hands. He couldn't write—or hold a spoon. Now his arms and hands are almost all well. We still don't know about his legs—or—his back.

SARA (*slowly*)—He can't sit up?

ELEANOR—No, dear, not yet. (SARA *puts down her cup, takes a handkerchief and puts it to her lips, stifling a desire to cry.*)

HOWE—The doctors feel his back muscles will be all right.

SARA—His legs—those wonderful legs—what about them?
ELEANOR—The doctors don't know.

Mrs. Roosevelt cries for her boy, then regains her composure, and says she certainly can help with the children. "That," says Eleanor, "would be wonderful."

Seeing Eleanor pass her hand over her tired eyes, Howe suggests that they all get some sleep. As he starts upstairs he trips on the landing and curses the lack of electricity. "He's a vulgar little man," Mrs. Roosevelt remarks. Eleanor, who considers Howe a "dear little man," informs her that he left a good Washington job to rush to Franklin's bedside. "There's nothing in life more important to him than Franklin," she says, and the least they can do is recognize that they all share this sense of devotion. Having never understood the relationship between her son and Howe, Mrs. Roosevelt suggests: "It's possible Mr. Howe merely enjoys riding along on Franklin's coattails."

This last is overheard by Howe as he comes back to get Eleanor. He controls his anger, and as Eleanor goes to her husband, he remains for a moment with her mother-in-law. Determined to be polite, Mrs. Roosevelt says: "You suffer a great deal from asthma, don't you?" Equally determined to maintain his position, Howe lights up. "A great deal," he says. "I'd be lonesome without it." "You know," Mrs. Roosevelt says, "that smoking isn't very good for you . . . you know that." "I do," he says.

Having her own definite ideas on the subject, she would like to hear of the plans for Franklin after he can be moved.

HOWE—Well, I'm sure that as soon as Franklin's well enough, he and Eleanor will decide where he would like to recuperate.
SARA—If Franklin's to have any permanent injury, the best place for him is Hyde Park. We can make a full life for him there. He can write, take care of the estate, raise his family as he was raised, and there will be enough to keep him active without overtaxing him or spending his energy.
HOWE—Mrs. Roosevelt, I've heard Franklin say that in public service a man must be prepared to spend and be spent. He may not be willing to accept a sedentary life in the country.
SARA—Mr. Howe, we must do everything that is possible to discourage him from remaining active in politics.
HOWE—Mrs. Roosevelt, Hyde Park or Timbuktu, Franklin's po-

litical future is ordained. That sounds mystical, I know. But I feel it as sure as I feel my heart beating.

SARA (*the politeness is wearing thin*)—Believe me, Mr. Howe, I respect your devotion, but Franklin is more to me than a prospective candidate for public office. He's my son.

HOWE—He is also Eleanor's husband, the father of five children and my dearest friend.

SARA (*the hard fist*)—Then he is blessed indeed to be the subject of so much affection.

HOWE (*losing his temper*)—But he is above all himself, Mrs. Roosevelt, and he happens to be the best damned progressive in the country.

SARA (*closing the iron door*)—My only interest is in his getting well—not his status as a politician. I am grateful for the care and devotion you have given Franklin. I am less grateful for your untimely and grandiose schemes.

HOWE—Mrs. Roosevelt, for the next few months Franklin may have need for some grandiose schemes. So may we all.

SARA—Good night, Mr. Howe.

SCENE III

Two weeks later—September 13th, 1921—preparations for the departure are everywhere evident. While Missy LeHand types some last-minute notes in the corner of the living room, luggage is carried out of the house, and Anna balks at having to wait outside. Little Johnny, dying to be a stretcher-bearer, asks Missy why all the boys can't carry their father's stretcher. Missy agrees it's a wonderful idea. "But," she adds, "you see, your father has made other plans, and it's too late to change." "He's a cute one," Missy says to Howe as Johnny leaves obediently. "They're all cute," Howe answers, "but there sure are a helluva lot of them."

With the children packed and waiting for the first of the two boats, Howe figures that they have about half an hour before FDR's boat leaves for Eastport.

MISSY (*putting papers into a brief case*)—You're going to have a lot of angry newspapermen breathing down your collar. They all want to see Mr. R.

HOWE—They'll see him—after he's on the train all propped up in his berth—a grin on his face. Once we get to Eastport—I'll flash the other dock, tell the newspapermen to come over, and explain there was a change of plans due to the tide or currents or something.

MISSY (*glancing at some notes before she packs them*)—When do we break the news that the Boss has infantile?

HOWE—Later. When we get to New York. Some time tomorrow. (*Reading from a release.*) "After thorough examinations, doctors today revealed Franklin D. Roosevelt recently suffered a mild attack of infantile paralysis. His legs have been temporarily affected, but it is anticipated he will have a complete recovery." Missy—where are those usual radiantly hopeful thoughts?

MISSY—Louie—I've been here for two weeks taking dictation and trying to act as he does—as if nothing is the matter. Sometimes it seems a sad and foolish game. He lies there, rattling on with plans for business conferences and meetings. Overhaul the Democratic Party—select the candidates for '22 and '24—organize this charity and reorganize that. I listen with wonder and I want to cry.

HOWE—Missy . . . maybe he doesn't mean one word of what he's planning or trying to do—but he wants us to believe it—so, Missy, believe . . .

Ready for travel, the elder Mrs. Roosevelt enters filled with comments about arrangements. She does not deem it wise that the children see their father on the stretcher. "Well," says Howe, "I'm afraid that will be unavoidable," and turns his attention to FDR's island neighbors, who have constructed and brought him a stretcher. Dr. Bennet, who is in charge of the expedition, praises their efforts: "Look at the stretcher they made. They've even fixed up a back rest." "Wonderful—really," Howe says, and means it.

Eleanor, carrying a bag, an extra blanket and FDR's old felt hat, joins the others—as tense as they are—at the foot of the stairs. Again her mother-in-law questions the wisdom of the children's seeing their father like this. "They may have to learn to see a lot of things," Eleanor answers in tired tones. "Perhaps," says Mrs. Roosevelt, "but it may be a shock, particularly to the younger ones." "They'll grow older," Howe snaps. Mrs. Roosevelt does not see why the day of FDR's departure could not have been kept from the press, nor does she want him placed on exhibition. "This is not a pleasant time for any of us," says Eleanor, "particularly Franklin."

The men, with Dr. Bennet supervising, carry a cocky FDR down the stairs. As Sara, Eleanor, and Missy watch, the men set down the stretcher safely on the floor. Thanking them, FDR asks: "How about a look around, Doc?" Doctor Bennet props up the back of the stretcher and FDR peers about. Digging into the pocket

of his robe, he brings forth a pack of cigarettes and his holder.
Howe lights his cigarette. "Thanks, Louie, my boy," says FDR,
adding: "How have you planned the logistics?"

HOWE (*knowing FDR loves these shenanigans*)—First, the children, Missy, your mother and Eleanor take off for the main dock.
That's where the sightseers and the press have congregated. A
goodly crowd has gathered and waits eagerly. (*Going into a heavy
Dutch burlesque accent.*) But, *mein Herr,* while all der peepuls is
vatching da von boat coming on der vater, vee go avay in da odder
boat for Eastport und get on der train. *Gut? Nicht wahr?*

FDR—Ah, a diversionary tactic.

HOWE—Precisely, *mein Herr.*

FDR—As Assistant Secretary of the Navy I used to rate a seven-
teen-gun salute. Have you arranged for that?

HOWE—You're just an ex-assistant—no guns. You're lucky we
got water.

Asking for his hat, FDR puts it on, grins and says: "How do I
look—snappy?" "Never better," his mother answers. Giving final
orders to Missy, he asks her to report to the hospital with everything typed up, and advises her to cancel his appearance at the Boy
Scout dinner: "I don't know if I'll feel up to making speeches until
after the New Year." He wishes his mother a gay "Bon Voyage!"
and asks Eleanor to let Duffy ride with him.

As the doctor and Eleanor go for the scottie, FDR kids Howe—
tells him he looks perfectly wretched and advises him to cut out those
cigarettes. "Look who the hell is talking about cigarettes," Howe
answers. "I haven't got asthma!" FDR grins.

Howe leaves as Eleanor gives Duffy to FDR and reports to him
concerning the condition of the sea. Approving of the man who is
to run his boat, Franklin reassures Eleanor in turn. As she goes
to the door to wave for the men, Franklin sags back against the
stretcher, lowers his head, and lets the hat drop from his hand.
He strains hard to retrieve it, but as he is unable to move his back,
the hat is beyond his reach. Realizing what has happened, Eleanor
hands it to him. "Are you sure that you can manage this trip?" she
asks. "I'm going to make a damn good try," he answers. He puts
his hat on, holds Duffy in one arm and perkily clamps the cigarette
holder in his mouth. The men reach down and lift the stretcher.
As they start out, Franklin says: "Gentlemen—thank you for the
sedan chair. By gosh—I feel like the Caliph of Bagdad."

ACT II

Nine months have passed. In the 65th Street New York house, in a wheel chair of his own design, FDR busies himself none too happily. Berating Missy for some small oversight in her work, he confesses that he's having a perfectly wretched day: his braces don't fit; he's tired of the everlasting kind hints in the mail; and he wants none of Missy's sweetness and light.

Later, under Eleanor's forbearing kindness, he unburdens himself. Pushing himself around, he says the exercise is stimulating—it takes some of the loneliness away.

ELEANOR—Loneliness, dear?

FDR—Invalidism (*quickly*)—even temporary—is very lonely. I remember reading: "A sick man wishes to be where he is not." (*After a moment.*) When you're forced to sit a lot—and watch others move about—you feel apart—lonely—because you can't get up and pace around. I find myself irritated when people come in here and parade all over the place. I have to keep exercising self-control to prevent screaming at them to sit down—quiet down—stand still.

ELEANOR—I'll remember.

FDR—You're quiet and restful.

They talk of other matters, but Eleanor suggests that there may be more that Franklin would care to tell her. It comes out that he, who has had scarcely any fear of fire, now finds himself on occasion overwhelmed by fear. To counter this sense of helplessness, he has lately begun to practice crawling. Holding onto herself, Eleanor answers that she hadn't known he had been crawling. Again they talk of other things, but suddenly wheeling himself close to Eleanor, Franklin takes her hand in his. The words he speaks are wrenched from him.

FDR—Eleanor, I must say this—once to someone. Those first few days at Campobello when this started, I had despair—deep, sick despair. It wasn't the pain—there was much more of that later on when they straightened the tendons in my legs. No, not the pain—it was the sense that perhaps I'd never get up again. Like a crab lying on its back. I'd look down at my fingers and exert every thought to get them to move. I'd send down orders to my legs and my toes—they didn't obey.

ELEANOR (*as he halts his speech for a moment, she goes to him, her head on his lap*)—Darling—

FDR—I turned to my faith, Babs—for strength to endure. I feel I have to go through this fire for some reason. Eleanor, it's a hard way to learn humility—but I've been learning by crawling. I know what is meant—you must learn to crawl before you can walk. (*They embrace.*)

Without a by-your-leave, Anna breaks in on them. Hastily withdrawing to go after Missy, Franklin leaves Eleanor alone with their daughter. As Eleanor wanders about straightening up, Anna haughtily registers a complaint against Mr. Howe's being given her room. Although she was moved weeks ago to the upstairs cubbyhole, when her grandmother spoke to her about it yesterday, Anna suddenly felt the indignity of such a move. Telling Anna that she is behaving badly, Eleanor refuses to discuss the matter. When Louis Howe makes a buoyant entrance, Anna flounces directly past him. "Marie Antoinette could not have been more noble on her way to the guillotine," he remarks. "It's a busy house, Louie," sighs Eleanor, "a busy house." "A busy world," Howe replies.

To bolster Franklin's morale, Howe consistently plants all sorts of items in the papers, such as the one he now reads in the *Chicago Tribune:* that the New York Democratic Party's choice for Governor is FDR. Eleanor regards this kind of thing as pointless. Noticing how depressed she is, Louie asks her to dine with him at Mouquin's. The splendid dinner he proposes does nothing to brighten her mood. Nor does her having to make a speech help her morale. "Louie," says Eleanor, "I'm no good at it. I can't lecture. I giggle at all the wrong times. I can't control my voice . . . When I shout, I think I'm whispering."

Howe won't let her off the hook. "The work has to be done. You are, for a while, Franklin's eyes, ears—and legs. You must go places he can't go." Eleanor, though tired and worn, promises to do what she can. When Franklin next breaks the news that without consulting her he has invited his law partners for dinner, Eleanor accepts the fact uncomplainingly. It is, as she has said, a busy household.

As Louis Howe argues that Franklin must cut down on some of his personal and business activities to conserve his energies for politics, it turns out that the odd business ventures seem to be increasing. When Howe kids him about these impractical schemes, Franklin says: "Caution, my friend, is the refuge of cowards." "And your refuge, Franklin," announces Eleanor, "is bed. You must rest before dinner."

FDR starts out obediently for bed, but on his own terms and under his own steam. With Eleanor and Howe frozen to the spot, FDR demonstrates the crawling he has been doing during solitary practice sessions. Sliding backwards on his haunches out the door, he directs his cocky grin at Eleanor. "Well, Eleanor?" he asks. "Good?" She manages: "Wonderful, Franklin, wonderful." As Howe, with the wheel chair, follows the disappearing feet out of the door, Eleanor is ready to crack. As she sinks into a chair and passes a hand over her tired eyes, she hears her mother-in-law's voice at the door.

Having brought Franklin junior and Johnny home from school, their grandmother inquires after Franklin. Eleanor informs her that Franklin has just crawled upstairs. Horrified, thinking of the appearance of things, his mother hastily goes to talk with her son.

Eleanor now has to make good a promise to read to Johnny and Franklin. In the midst of the reading, her control snaps. Turning away from the boys, she begins to sob. Missy and Howe come to the rescue: Missy removes the boys, and Howe quietly closes the door.

HOWE—Eleanor, if I can do anything—

ELEANOR (*shouting through her tears*)—No—nothing—and, Louie, I hate Mouquin's and I hate snails and I'm not going.

HOWE—Nobody ever lived who is more entitled to a good cry.

ELEANOR (*stopping her crying*)—I must have terrified the children. I won't ever do that again. Not ever.

SCENE II

Another nine months have passed. In a wrestling match on the floor with his sons, Elliott and Franklin junior, pinning them both down with his powerful arms, FDR has them both yell "uncle." Allowed to escape, the boys bring over the wheel chair, and from long experience and proper timing shoot FDR up onto its seat. He tells them cheerfully: "Boys—today I felt a little more power from my legs." Pointing to his thighs, he explains: "Down these heavy frontal muscles—the quadriceps. The bad spots we're still working on are in these thick muscles that run from the hips and buttocks—the gluteus maximus—and then these hamstring muscles on the back of the knees—the gastrocs. Without those I can't get balance or purchase." But he warns them that when he gets those all working together, they'd better start running.

When Missy enters with the inevitable stack of mail and notes, FDR tells the boys to vamoose. Wheeling himself to his desk, he starts reading and signing the mail, as Missy hands him a framed object that arrived by messenger. Examining it and admiring the typography, FDR says: "I sometimes regret having told the newspapers one of my favorite poems was 'Invictus.'" This is the fourteenth copy he has received, but since, in his opinion, it is the most beautiful, he tells Missy that he'll have it hung in his bedroom. Placing it on a table, Missy gets on with the answers to polio victims, and to Mr. McAdoo, who is already counting votes for himself in 1924. Says Missy: "He can taste the nomination." "He's in for a large and bitter disappointment," FDR answers. "It's going to be Al Smith."

Coming in from the icy cold, with a bundled-up Howe in tow, Eleanor seems actually to have enjoyed talking to hundreds of enthusiastic ladies. This is much appreciated by her husband, who says: "Between your speeches, Howe's shenanigans and my statements, we're keeping my head above water."

Though complicated business deals continue to take time, and waste money, family life has turned peaceful. Alone with Franklin, Eleanor notices how quiet the house is. "The children," she asks, "are they all home?" "Can't tell the players without a score card, ma'am," answers FDR. Counting on his fingers, he ticks off: "Anna is in her room, reading. Johnny is being read to by Mademoiselle. Jimmy ostensibly is still at Groton. Elliott and Franklin have retired to lick their wounds after a wrestling match." Though she can't stop him from wrestling, Eleanor does wish he would be careful.

Pulling himself onto the couch from his chair, Franklin says that his legs are coming along fine: "All four of them. I spent some time on those today. Soon it will be canes. First I want to handle those crutches without braces—or vice versa." And he is willing to heed Eleanor's advice to be patient.

FDR—Eleanor, when I first took ill I planned and dreamed about a bright future—half believing, half pretending, like a child on a carousel imagining himself a general in command of armies. But for weeks now something has been changing inside of me. I don't know when it began. What minute or day or hour—but today I was suddenly aware that, despite everything, I feel sure-footed.

ELEANOR—"A patient man shall bear for a time and afterward joy shall spring up unto him."

FDR—Shall spring up unto us. I sometimes wonder how many of your cousins are still confounded that we married. Do you think they still consider me a feather-duster?

ELEANOR (*smiling*)—Darling—there are undoubtedly some of your family who still believe that you didn't get much of a bargain.

FDR—I imagine they're reconciled to the truth that I did better than you did. Actually, I think Mamá's only objection to you was that your family said *Rusevelt* while we said *Rosevelt*.

ELEANOR—Could not a *Rusevelt* by any other name be just as sweet?

FDR (*laughing*)—Not to Mamá. Thinking back, I can hardly blame some of your relatives. I had a lot to learn, but I didn't want anyone to know it. So the truth is I was an awfully mean cuss in those early days.

ELEANOR—Never mean. Perhaps inexperienced.

FDR—I was snobbish—haughty. I had the Roosevelt name—the Teddy tradition (*imitates Teddy's broad smile*)—sauced in with ambition. (*He pats her hand.*) I had to learn something about the human heart. (*He smiles at her.*) I've been learning . . .

But when Anna barges in once again, FDR speaks so sharply to her that she runs crying from the room. Though he promises to make it up later Eleanor realizes that she had better talk with Anna before Anna runs to her grandmother. On the other hand, Franklin plans having an overdue talk with his mother. "Usually your talks with Mamá last for fifteen minutes—then they become quarrels," says Eleanor. FDR promises: "I'll time it. Make sure it's a talk."

Entering to dress for out-of-doors and a rare dinner with his family, Howe reports on Anna's sad state of mind. As Eleanor goes to soothe her daughter, Franklin watches Howe swathe most of his face in a muffler.

FDR—Can you breathe through all that?

HOWE—You know me. If I'm on my feet I assume I'm breathing.

FDR—Louie, I'm being reflective.

HOWE—Well, that's probably because you're heading for another birthday.

FDR—Having made this one, everything after is velvet. Part of my reflections had to do with you.

HOWE—Ah—I'm fired?

FDR (*he takes* HOWE's *hand*)—My good friend, as much as you loathe a sentimental moment, thank you for everything.

Heading towards the door, seeing the framed copy of "Invictus," Howe picks it up. Striking a mock-heroic pose, he gives a burlesque reading of the poem in a thick Dutch accent. But as he gets to the last stanza, he drops the comedy. He reads clearly and beautifully:

> "It matters not how strait the gate,
> How charged with punishment the scroll,
> I am the master of my fate:
> I am the captain of my soul."

Having paid this tribute to FDR, he says good night and leaves. Made more considerate of others through Eleanor's talk, Anna comes to apologize. She has a real rapprochement with her father, who compliments her for having grown ten years wiser in two minutes' time. When Mrs. Roosevelt arrives for dinner, Anna is polite to her grandmother, but it is obvious that she no longer sides with her against her parents.

She neither speaks French to her grandmother, nor defers to her opinions. When her grandmother advises: "Nurse should be very careful with the young ones in weather like this," Anna merely remarks: "I heard Mother telling Nurse that this morning." Both her grandmother and her father recognize Anna's new attitude. "Very sensible," murmurs Mrs. Roosevelt.

Her new-found tact successfully launched, Anna leaves the room. Sara at once starts telling Franklin that he is doing too much. He wishes he could do more: "It's only my legs that are temporarily bothered. The rest of me is as healthy as ever." While conceding this, his mother contends that Eleanor and that "ugly little man" push FDR far too rapidly. FDR answers that he never wants to hear Louis Howe referred to in this manner again. He would like to have a quiet talk with his mother but she must realize that though he is confident of recovery from his present condition, if he doesn't, he must get used to braces, canes and wheel chairs, and so must she.

FDR—Please let me finish. Louie Howe— (*His mother makes an involuntary grimace.*) Mamá, stop that. Louie Howe told me, while I was in the hospital after Campobello, that I had one of two choices. I could lie on my back, be a country squire and write books —*or*—get up and become President of the United States. *Now*— I believe Louie's dreams are far too bright—but I've no intention of retiring to Hyde Park and rusticating.

SARA (*quietly*)—Franklin, when you were a little boy, your dear father took you for a visit to the White House to see President Cleveland.

FDR (*fidgets*)—Mamá, I know.

SARA (*firmly*)—Let me finish. And President Cleveland said, "I make a strange wish for you. It is that you may never be President of the United States."

FDR—Well, he was playing the odds in wishing that.

His mother maintains that his cousin Teddy died because he didn't know when to stop, and because he failed to realize that one can't make the world the same for all people. It seems to FDR that as a human being he is at least obliged to try. But to his mother, this is not a bad world. FDR should not be self-conscious about being rich. "Advantages of birth," she says, "should be worn like clothes, with grace and comfort." FDR knows all about *noblesse oblige*—they went all through that when he sold the mining stock. "On reflection," says his mother, "you must admit that was a childish gesture." "I would not hang onto stock bringing me an income over the tortured bodies of miners who lived as though they were in the middle ages," Franklin answers. "These are different times. The attitude of *noblesse oblige* is archaic." "Franklin!" says his mother. "It's another name for indifference," he finishes.

He refuses to go into hiding at Hyde Park, which he loves. He wants to use it, not let it bury him. He won't allow himself to go down the drain. Angrily he tells his mother: "A bad beating either breaks the stick or the student. Well, I'm not broken. I'm not settling for the life of an ailing invalid. And I will no longer abide implications, innuendoes or insinuations that I do so." Appealing to his sense of caution, Mrs. Roosevelt asks him to ride out the storm. Then using her final weapon, she says: "I don't want to see you hurt." After this, he refuses to continue the discussion.

As Eleanor enters and sees at a glance what's been going on, her mother-in-law says that she will not stay for dinner. With gentle tact, Eleanor says: "Mamá, you may have quarreled with Franklin— but not with the rest of the family. Please?" Reluctantly agreeing to stay, Mrs. Roosevelt excuses herself and leaves the room. Eleanor then asks FDR if he needs anything. He needs nothing, he answers. Alone and in low spirits, he suddenly decides to accept his mother's challenge. He rolls his chair to his crutches, then placing them over his knees, moves the chair to a clear part of the room.

He puts up one crutch, then the other. Confident and determined, he is half out of the chair when the crutch slips. Crumpling to the floor, he lies there in pain and in sickening defeat. Then, slowly and painstakingly, he manages to get back into the wheel chair. After a pause, he stretches and bends over to recover each crutch from the floor. Exhausted, his head dejectedly bent forward, he creates the image of a man who has lost an important battle. But then he raises a grimly determined face, and prepares stubbornly to start the operation all over again.

ACT III

In May of 1924, Roosevelt, with Howe in quiet attendance, listens to a certain Mr. Lassiter. This gentleman has not come to the 65th Street house on some crackbrained business scheme, but to discuss Roosevelt's chairmanship of Al Smith's campaign for the presidential nomination. Immediately aware of the issues, Roosevelt in cat-and-mouse fashion draws out Mr. Lassiter. "You must certainly be aware of the fears that many Americans have, when they contemplate the election of a Catholic to the Presidency of the United States," says Mr. Lassiter. "The domination of the Church over its members is well known. And Governor Smith is a devout Catholic." "Would it be more acceptable if he were a renegade Catholic?" queries Howe from his perch on the couch. Chiding Howe, offering Lassiter and his following a personal statement of his views on this subject, Roosevelt asks how many copies he would like. "Oh," says Lassiter, "one or two would be sufficient, Mr. Roosevelt. We would print it and circulate it for the best effect." Preparing to dictate to Missy, FDR says that he too will see that it gets properly circulated in other quarters. "I am not worried," he dictates, "that the Roosevelt name will be tarnished by any association with Governor Smith. If a Catholic who has the ability, broadness of view and fine record that entitled him to be considered Presidential timber, cannot be nominated or elected President because of his religion, then we might just as well be consistent and say he cannot be Governor or Congressman or Mayor or hold any other public office or be called upon to serve in the Army or Navy in defense of his country in war." Twisting his chair around, FDR asks: "Is that what you had in mind, Mr. Lassiter?" With a furious "Good day," Lassiter stalks out of the room.

Missy says that unfortunately there are a lot of people who feel like Lassiter. Roosevelt repeats that Governor Smith is better equipped than anyone else to be the nominee of the Democratic Party. Howe retorts: "In this year of our Lord 1924, even if Al Smith were Protestant and 'Dry,' he couldn't be elected President on the Democratic ticket. If he's the right man, he's running at the wrong time." "Right or wrong," says Missy, "the Governor is twenty minutes late."

As Missy goes to her office, Howe has some second thoughts on Al Smith's seeking out Roosevelt today. Smith still needs upstate New York. And FDR is Protestant, rural and "Dry"—the logical cowcatcher. Howe has another thought: Ever since Bourke Cockran died, Smith has been trying to find a successor to place his name before the Convention. Roosevelt thinks that if Smith has finally got around to him, it must have been reluctantly. In the past, Al has always been patronizing. Imitating Smith, Roosevelt says: "Listen, kid, let me teach you the facts of life in the big city."

Howe now wonders whether FDR would be up to the job. Roosevelt himself sometimes wonders whether he could be equal to doing much active work. Maybe, he concedes, his dreams of public service would disappear in the hard light of practice. Howe believes that God has an eye on Roosevelt's future. "God has an infinite variety of tasks," says FDR sharply, "and I don't believe He's available as campaign manager."

Howe bears down: FDR might be able to carry off the speech wonderfully and put the party on notice that he's ready for active service. On the other hand, he could fail and be headed for the political boneyard.

When Eleanor stops by on her way to a meeting, the men ask her opinion. FDR tells of Louie's hunch. "Well," says Eleanor, "I have heard that he's been shopping around for a speaker." "She hears everything," says Louie.

Eleanor leaves the decision entirely up to her husband. Only he can decide if he's ready. "What about the risks or advantages politically?" asks Howe. "I am no politician," says Eleanor; "I have the naive point of view that in public service one should pursue principles without calculating the consequences." "She's right," says Howe; "she's no politician."

On her way out, Eleanor encounters and exchanges greetings with Smith. Missy announces the Governor. Shaking hands, Smith finds Roosevelt's hand a veritable vise. Answering Missy's offer of cold refreshments, Smith says: "Why, Missy—there's a law in this country against strong refreshment—an obnoxious law, but nevertheless a law." "I know," says Missy. "Scotch or rye?" "Scotch, thanks. And don't kill it with soda," says Governor Smith.

After a few mutual compliments, they get down to business. Admitting that he wants the nomination, Smith asks how FDR sizes it up. Roosevelt doesn't think Smith can make it on the first ballot. Nodding, Smith says that that's his opinion too. "But neither can

McAdoo," adds FDR. "I'll tell you one thing, Frank," says Smith. "If it isn't going to be me, it'll never be McAdoo. I'll fight him with my last breath. Any man who can take the support of an organization like the Ku Klux Klan—he's not my kind of man." At this point, Roosevelt shows Smith a letter from Babe Ruth saying that most everybody he talks to is for Al Smith. Chuckling, Smith asks: "How many ball players are there?"

As was anticipated, Smith now gets round to how much he misses Bourke Cockran. "For days now," he says, "I've been trying to think what Bourke would have wanted to say in a nominating speech." Playing right along, Roosevelt tells him.

FDR—It seems to me he'd have argued for you as a progressive. He certainly would have been aware of the issues—the Klan—the Volstead Act—and the latent issue of your faith. He might have been willing to point out that the obligation above any one candidate was to keep the party together.

SMITH—I'm all for party unity, but I don't intend to temporize on the issue of the Klan. And Bourke wouldn't have, either.

FDR—I agree that it ought to be burned out once and for all. But if we can't get through a resolution condemning the Klan, we still mustn't break up the party.

SMITH—Frank, I remember all my early lessons. One of them was that the first objective of a politician is to be elected. Then he can fight for causes. But in the case of the Klan, I'm willing to forget an early lesson.

FDR (*nods*)—There's another issue, Al. Even more important than the Klan. That's the issue of world politics and America's place in it. Bourke would have talked of that, perhaps.

SMITH—Frank, if you're talking about the League of Nations, that's a dead dodo.

FDR—I think if the Democratic Party is going to stand, it has to stand for something big and noble.

SMITH—I suppose there's nothing wrong with mankind having a vision of world organization. But it's only a vision.

FDR—Newton Baker wants to submit a resolution to support the League of Nations at the Convention.

SMITH—It hasn't got a chance.

FDR—Perhaps not. But I think you ought to support it. Woodrow Wilson's in his grave only three months, and I don't think we ought to let his convictions about the League be buried with him.

SMITH (*grudgingly*)—It's all right with me.

Howe—I'll speak to the Program Committee and have Baker put it on the schedule.

Smith—Frank, got any other notions about what Bourke Cockran would have to say?

FDR (*with a smile*)—Finally, I think he'd make up his own speech, a large part of which would have to do with the fine record of the man he'd be nominating.

Smith (*returning the smile*)—I suppose a few kind words about me would be in order. Frank, Bourke had a theory that no nominating speech ought to run more than thirty to forty minutes.

FDR—You can read the Bill of Rights in that time.

Smith—That's a long time for any man to be on his feet.

FDR—You certainly can't make an effective speech sitting down.

Smith—You can be sure of that.

FDR—After all the months I've spent in this chair, I've come to love the time I spend each day standing on my crutches.

Smith—Uh-huh. (*There is a pause.* Smith *looks at his glass, which is empty.*)

Howe—Fresh one, Governor?

Smith—No thanks. (*Puts glass down.*) Frank, I'd like you to put me in nomination.

Roosevelt and Howe couldn't seem more surprised. Roosevelt says that certainly he will do it. "I'll want to have a look," says Al Smith, "at what you're going to say, and Joe Proskauer may have an idea or two. He's a good phrase-maker." Roosevelt is amenable to the addition of a few phrases, but otherwise insists on saying what he wants to say. That being understood, Smith thanks FDR appreciatively, and receives FDR's thanks in turn. At the door, he does mention—as if he'd just thought of it—that FDR and Howe were both too surprised to be surprised.

Without a wasted minute, Roosevelt asks Missy to get him a blueprint of the Garden platform. He wants to know just how far it is from where he'll be sitting to the lectern. Howe figures it as about ten steps—no more. Roosevelt now plans that Jimmy, the largest of his children, will be with him; and as if measuring the exact distance, rolls his chair across the room. "Work hard, Franklin," says Howe. "They are liable to be the ten biggest steps you ever took in your life." "Perhaps," says Roosevelt. "Or, to be clinical—I may fall smack on my gluteus maximus."

SCENE II

On the night of June 26, 1924, the Garden swarms and roars with delegates. In an anteroom, Roosevelt, bronzed and beaming, sits waiting for his cue, while his family and staff manifest, during these tense few moments, an increasing nervousness.

Jimmy goes with his father behind a screen to help him put on his braces. Mrs. Roosevelt senior, somewhat harried by the howling mobs, arrives in time to give Franklin her blessing. FDR says simply: "He has given me many blessings." "And," says his mother, "Franklin, speak out loudly and clearly." As she leaves, Howe says: "Franklin, if I know Mamá, in a couple of months she'll be working on a political primer." He looks at his watch. "I know this is awful—but I'm getting nervous." Trying to knit, Eleanor announces that she's dropped three stitches. Roosevelt thinks the current seconding speech has taken a long time. Then Senator Walsh sends word by an hysterically excited worker that it's time for Roosevelt to appear.

FDR receives last minute good wishes. "Jimmy, are you all set?" he asks. "Yes, Father," Jimmy answers. "In my mind I have gone over it a hundred times." He smiles. "You make the speech, and I'll worry about everything else." "That's my son—" laughs Roosevelt "—man of iron." Checking his braces, clicking them into place, turning them with his hands, he then releases them: "They should be fine. Jimmy, if I slip, pick me up in a hurry." Eleanor comes to Franklin and they embrace. "I'm ready, Jimmy," Roosevelt cries. "Battle stations!"

SCENE III

Surrounded by the deafening noise of the convention, the Roosevelt family and retinue are seated on the speakers' platform. In this pre-microphone age, everyone has to yell to be heard, and waves of noise roll from all sides.

Over the cheering and screaming, over the banging of Walsh's gavel, a voice shouts: "Connecticut, the Nutmeg State, yields to the great Empire State of New York." Banging for quiet, Walsh bellows: "Ladies and Gentlemen! The chair recognizes the Honorable Franklin D. Roosevelt of the State of New York!"

Jimmy hands Roosevelt his crutches. Getting to his feet, smiling and confident, the smile always to the audience, FDR slowly walks those ten great steps. Reaching the lectern FDR—to a cacophony of rebel yells and of bands playing "The Sidewalks of New York"—gives his crutches to Jimmy, who steps down. Holding the lectern with one hand, and basking in the cheers of the crowd, a smiling FDR waves his other hand toward the crowd with a gesture that will someday be famous.

THE ENTERTAINER

A Play in Thirteen Scenes

BY JOHN OSBORNE

[*For a biographical sketch of John Osborne, see "Look Back in Anger."*]

For the cast listing, see page 317.

USING English music hall stage techniques throughout, *The Entertainer* is set in the dirty, run-down quarter of an English seaside resort.

The *overture,* consisting of "the latest, the loudest, and the worst" music, precedes:

NUMBER ONE

As the gauze front cloth of the theatre, featuring enormous naked young ladies over the words ROCK'N ROLL NEW'D LOOK, rises, Billy Rice, a slim, spruce man in his seventies, enters his house. Hearing roomers fighting, he yells over the stairs in powerful, Edwardian tones: "Will you kindly stop making all that noise?" With the slam of a door, a woman's crying and sobbing stops. Placing beer, newspaper, and a telegram on a table, Billy, while singing "Rock of Ages," slips into a woolen cardigan. Sitting down to take off his shoes, which he puts in tissue paper in a box, he makes himself comfortable. Between sips of beer, he cleans his already immaculate nails and gets ready to read his newspaper. When the sound of roomers' fighting resumes, Billy says with conviction: "Bloody Poles and Irish!"

In the midst of his singing "Nearer My God to Thee," the doorbell rings. As it rings again, Billy sings all the louder. Finally, grumbling, he opens the door for his granddaughter.

Jean, bespectacled and plain, greets Billy and studiously apolo-

"The Entertainer": By John Osborne. Copyright © 1958 by John Osborne. Published by Criterion Books, Inc. Reprinted by permission of Criterion Books, Inc., New York.

gizes for disturbing him. *Disarmed by this, Billy loses his irritation. Saying it's good to see her, he kisses her, goes back to his chair and his beer, and offers some to Jean. With a shake of her head, Jean refuses but listens quietly when Billy starts to talk.*

BILLY—You haven't been to the Club. Oh, I must take you then. It's very quiet, mind you. Except at week-ends. You get some of the wives then. But they're mostly oldtimers like me.

JEAN—Sounds fun.

BILLY—Well, it's somewhere to go when you're fed up with the place. Don't suppose it would appeal much to youngsters like yourself. I expect you go in more for these jazz places.

JEAN—I'd like to go. You must take me.

BILLY—Would you really? Would you? All right. But I warn you, there's none of your boogie-woogie. How long are you here for?

JEAN—Just the week-end.

BILLY—We'll go tomorrow night. It's a good night, Sunday. I sing them some of the old songs, sometimes, when I feel like it. Haven't done it lately, not for a long time. Don't seem to feel like it.

JEAN—Where's Dad?

BILLY—He's at the theatre. He's playing here—at the Grand this week, you know.

JEAN—Oh, yes, of course.

BILLY—I don't seem to feel like it these days. You get a bit depressed sometimes sitting here. Oh, then there's the Cambridge down the road. I go there, of course. But there's not the old crowd there, you know. What about the news, eh? That's depressing. What d'you make of all this business out in the Middle East? People seem to be able to do what they like to us. Just what they like. I don't understand it. I really don't. Archie goes to that damned place down by the clock tower.

JEAN—The Rockliffe.

BILLY—Yes, the Rockliffe. Every tart and pansy boy in the district are in that place at a week-end. Archie tried to get me there the other day. No, thank you. It's just a meat-market.

JEAN—How is Dad?

Billy complains that Archie has put money into a road-show. He himself hasn't seen it and wouldn't. "These nudes," *Billy says.* "They're killing the business. Anyway, I keep telling him—it's dead already. Has been for years. It was all over, finished, dead when I got out. . . . They don't want real people any more." *And even the nudes, those third-class sluts, haven't got figures nowadays.*

Half the time, Billy says, you can't tell the women from the men. That sounds like the Government and the Opposition to Jean, a subject Billy certainly doesn't want to talk about. Billy complains that Archie won't ever listen to him, and foresees his coming a cropper very soon. And it turns out that Archie isn't really putting money into the show; he has no money. He is doing it all on credit. "Do you know," Billy asks Jean, "I spent thousands of pounds on his education? Went to the same school as me. And his brother. Thousands of pounds. He wasn't one of these scholarship people, like you. And where's it got 'em?" He takes a drink. "That Rockliffe . . ." As he elaborates on the Rockliffe, it occurs to him that Jean doesn't look too well. He guesses that she's been on too many parties, something he doesn't entirely disapprove for the young. Still, sensing that things aren't right with her, Billy begs her to come to him if she's in any trouble. Getting slightly carried away with old-fashioned gallantry, Billy offers to pay her fare down from London. Knowing that he has only a few coins in his pocket, Jean says: "Darling, you'll need that for the week-end. There's cigarettes and papers, and you're taking me to the Club, remember?" Billy feels strongly that one must look after one's own kind. It's not the Government's job. He begs Jean not to waste her life. He repeats that she should do something good with it. He asks her to sit down and talk to him. "I don't get much chance to talk to anyone," Billy says. "They think you're a bit soft. Just because you can remember things when they were a bit different." Noticing that Jean isn't really listening, Billy notices, too, that she's been drinking. When she blurts out that she's had four large gins, Billy in his most understanding way advises her to put her feet up, close her eyes and relax. "I like listening to you," Jean says. "I always have." Billy remembers she always enjoyed being with him when she was a little girl: "You were a pretty little thing. With your dark curls and your little dresses. (*Quickly.*) Not that looks are everything. Not even for a woman. Don't you believe it. You don't look at the mantelpiece when you poke the fire. (JEAN *sits down and leans back.*) No, I'll say this for Archie—he always saw that you looked nicely turned out. You looked a little picture always. Spent too much I daresay. He was a smart little boy himself. Used to dress them in sailor suits then. He was a pretty little boy. Funny how they all turn out. (*Pause, then softly sincerely—*) I feel sorry for you people. You don't know what it's really like. You haven't lived, most of you. You've never known what it was like, you're all miserable really. You don't know what life can be like."

Number Two

The music strikes up, and Archie Rice—with his hat cocked at an angle and sporting a cane—makes his entrance. Against the gauze curtain of naked ladies, Archie performs: "Good evening, ladies and gentlemen—Archie Rice is the name. Archie Rice. Mrs. Rice's favorite boy. We're going to entertain you for the next two and a half hours and you've really had it now. All the exit doors locked. Talking about being locked in, some of these people ought to be locked up. Locked up. They did, honest. I'll give you a case in point. A case in point. My wife—my wife. Old Charlie knows her, don't you, Charlie? Old Charlie knows her. A real road-mender's job she is—isn't she, Charlie? It's all right. I've taken his drill away from him now. I have. Haven't I, Charlie? He's the only boy soprano in the Musician's Union. I know what you're waiting for. I know what you're waiting for and who isn't? Just keep your peckers up—they'll be on in a minute. You've got to put up with me first. And now—now, to open the show. I'm going to sing a little song I wrote myself. I hope you like it.

> "Why should I care?
> Why should I let it touch me!
> Why shouldn't I, sit down and try
> To let it pass over me?
> Why should they stare,
> Why should I let it get me?
> What's the use of despair,
> If they call you a square?
> You're a long time dead—
> Like my pal Fred,
> So why, oh why should I bother to care?"

Archie goes into his dance routine, finishing:

> "If they see that you're blue, they'll
>   —look down on you
> So why should I bother to care?   (Thank
>   God I'm normal!)
> So why should I bother to care?"

He exits.

Laurence Olivier in "The Entertainer"

NUMBER THREE

Coming home from the pictures, Jean's stepmother Phoebe is flushed with excitement at her daughter's unexpected arrival. Blonde and sixtyish, always talking and not listening, Phoebe is delighted with the gin Jean brought to her. Not wanting to have a drink on her own, she pours one for Jean, too. Billy sticks to his beer. "Well, this is nice," says Phoebe. "What a shame—I'd have been in earlier but I stayed and saw a bit of the big picture round again." She hardly remembers who was in the picture or what it was about. "What was the picture called?" Jean asks politely. Phoebe laughs. "Blimey, you should know better than to ask me that! You know what a rotten memory I've got. Well, cheerio!" She drinks up. "Oooh," Phoebe says, "that's a nice drop of gin—

some of the muck they give you nowadays—tastes like cheap scent. . . ." She rattles on and on. She tells of her job at Woolworth's that's not too bad though she does find the girls common. Finding Jean looking "peaky," Phoebe does a bit of prying.

PHOEBE—Graham's all right, is he?

JEAN—Yes, he's all right.

PHOEBE—There's nothing wrong there, is there?

BILLY—Why don't you mind your bloody business? She'll tell you if she wants to.

PHOEBE—All right, I know. She doesn't mind telling me if there's anything, do you?

JEAN—We had a slight disagreement. Nothing more, that's all.

PHOEBE—After all, she may not be my own, but I did help to bring her up a little, didn't I? After all, she's Archie's daughter. Be a bit strange if I wasn't interested whether she was happy or not. Oh, well, dear, don't take any notice. You'll soon make it up. Men are funny. You don't want to take any notice of them.

JEAN (smiling)—Wish I didn't.

PHOEBE—That's right. Have another drink. You'll soon feel better. What did you have a row about? Something silly, I'll bet. You haven't broken off your engagement?

JEAN—I don't know. Probably.

PHOEBE—Oh dear, I'm sorry.

JEAN—I went to the Rally in Trafalgar Square last Sunday.

BILLY—You did what?

JEAN—I went to the Rally in Trafalgar Square.

BILLY—What for, for God's sake?

JEAN—Because, Grandad, somehow—with a whole lot of other people, strange as it may seem—I managed to get myself steamed up about the way things were going.

BILLY—And you went to Trafalgar Square?

PHOEBE—Well, she said so, didn't she?

BILLY—Well, I should think you want your bloody head read!

JEAN—That was more or less Graham's feeling about it. Only he happens to be about fifty years younger than you, and he put it a bit differently. It all really started over something I wanted to do, and then it all came out, lots of things. All kinds of bitterness— things I didn't even know existed.

Graham didn't care for her teaching art to a tough bunch of Youth Club kids, either. He wants her to marry him right away before he's qualified. He wants her to stop threatening his world, and stop trying things for herself, and now she's refused on all counts. Still, it had never occurred to Jean that "you could love somebody, want them twenty-four hours a day and then suddenly find that you're neither of you even living in the same world." She apologizes for drinking the gin meant for Phoebe, and changes the subject to Mick —who's out "there."

Phoebe doesn't mind saying that she's lost some sleep this week over Mick, and though Archie doesn't talk about it, he's worried, too.

BILLY—He's a fine boy. When they called him, he went. No arguments, nothing. He just went.

JEAN (*suddenly*)—And when they called Frank, he refused, and he went to jail for it—for six months. Young Frank full of doubts about himself, and everybody, with a cold in his head half the year, and a weak chest. Lucky to pass C3. Poor Frank. (*To* PHOEBE.) He's not very strong, you always said. You went without to buy him little luxuries to eat, why, you wouldn't let him even clean his own shoes. No, you'd do it for him. But he went and said no and, what's more, he went to jail for it. Oh, he gave in eventually, but he said no for six months of his poor protected life—he said no! I think that's something. You don't have to measure up young Mick against Frank, Grandad. Now don't look hurt. I'm not getting at you. I love you very much—both of you, but I probably shouldn't have started drinking gin on the train.

Billy tells Jean that she can't turn against her own people, but she merely wonders who those people are. With her concern over Mick's safety, Phoebe, whistling in the dark, suggests that the Army does look after them. "Oh, yes, they look after them all right," Jean says. "Look after them better now than they did, when I was in it," Billy assures them. "I haven't read the evening paper yet. The Dardanelles—I went through that without a scratch. Not a scratch on me." "They're looking after us. We're all right, all of us," Jean cries. "Nothing to worry about. *We're* all right. God save the Queen!"

Archie, at the microphone, cracks wise, suggestive and low, has some homosexual banter with the orchestra leader, then launches into his version of a patriotic song, against an unfurled Union Jack.

NUMBER FIVE

As Billy reminisces about women of the nineties, Archie—weighted down with bag and bottles—enters briskly. A man in his fifties, with sleeked-down gray hair, he has an absent-minded quality that derives from his comedian's technique of throwing away lines. After teasing Billy, he greets Jean with a kiss and asks how she is. "Thank you," Jean answers, "I have had too much gin waiting for you." "Never mind," says Archie, "you can have some more in a minute. . . ." And without drawing a breath, Archie tells of his encounter with the big colored roomer, a ballet dancer, who told him about what they can expect at the Winter Garden.

ARCHIE—He was telling me if you drop your hat outside there now, you have to kick it down to the promenade before you can pick it up. (*Pauses quickly, then goes on expertly.*) They're not all colored, I saw a couple of 'em on the bus on the way home yesterday. They were talking together all the way, everybody listening. I just got up to press the bell, and a woman shouted out, "I lost two boys in the war for the likes of you!" I thought she meant me for a moment, so I turned round, and there she was, beating them with her umbrella like crazy.

BILLY—Don't like to see a man dancing like that.

ARCHIE—I was in a show with a couple of male dancers once. And wherever we went, on the Monday night some woman used to complain about their tights bulging. Wherever we went. Every Monday night. I'm sure it was the same woman each time. I used to call her the Camp Follower. Now, what are we going to have? Let's see what we've got. (*Rummages in carrier and pockets.*)

Billy, reminding Archie of the telegram that came for him, becomes tired and irritable when Archie disregards it. Instead of opening it, Archie, saying it's probably from one of his creditors, tosses it aside and dispenses liquor. Gin for the crowd and Dubonnet for Phoebe. "Old Phoebe," Archie says, "likes that, don't you, dear! She thinks she's being awfully U when she drinks that." This, announces Archie, is a celebration: he is celebrating his twentieth anniversary of not paying his income tax. To Billy's dour warning that they'll get him in the end, Archie breezes: "All right, love, you can sing us a hymn later. I think that is a very significant achievement, and I deserve some kind of tribute for it. Don't you think your old man deserves a tribute?" Jean answers: "I was just wondering how you came to pay income tax in 1936."

Through gin and anguish, Phoebe blurts out that Jean's engagement is broken, then cries: "Oh, I wish I knew what's going to happen." Archie has an answer: "Old Mick can look after himself, he's a boy without problems, that one. I expect he's screwing himself silly. I hope he is anyway. What's happened with you and Graham?" Billy reports indignantly that Jean attended the Trafalgar Square Rally. "Oh, really?" Archie says. "Are you one of those who don't like the Prime Minister? I think I've grown rather fond of him. I think it was after he went to the West Indies to get Noel Coward to write a play for him. Still, perhaps only someone of my generation could understand that. Does he bring you out in spots?" "Oh, Christ," wails Phoebe, "I wish I knew what was going to happen to us." As Archie continues his joking, Phoebe continues to wail.

PHOEBE—I don't want to always have to work. I mean you want a bit of life before it's all over. It takes all the gilt off if you know you've got to go on and on till they carry you out in a box. It's all right for him, he's all right. He's still got his women. While it lasts anyway. But I don't want to end up being laid out by some stranger in some rotten stinking little street in Gateshead, or West Hartlepool or another of those dead-or-alive holes!

JEAN—Phoebe, don't upset yourself, please. Let's enjoy ourselves—

PHOEBE—Enjoy myself! D'you think I don't want to enjoy myself! I'm just sick of being with down and outs, I'm sick of it, and people like him. (*She is crying.*)

ARCHIE—I wish women wouldn't cry. I wish they wouldn't. Try and say something to her, Jean.

JEAN (*going to* PHOEBE)—Why don't you?

Jean offers to take Phoebe up to bed. Pulling herself together with a sort of game dignity, Phoebe, after asking Archie to come up and say good-night, leaves docilely with Jean.

Allotting Billy one hymn before retiring, Archie listens pleasantly until the old man tires. When Jean comes back, Billy says his good-nights. Jean, left alone with her father, asks: "What is it? I've had a strange feeling in my stomach all day. As if something was going to happen. . . ." Since nobody here seemed to have read in the newspaper that Mick had been taken prisoner, Archie had refrained from telling them. Opening the telegram that he had purposely left unopened all evening, Archie decides that tomorrow is soon enough for them to find out.

Pouring drinks, Archie hopes to God that Mick will manage some-how. This time, starting one of his stories, Archie lets his voice trail off in fatigue. Pushing the bottle towards Jean, he says pleadingly: "Talk to me."

(End of Act I)

NUMBER SIX

Sitting around the table, drinking gin with Billy and Jean, Phoebe simply can't believe that Mick will be home in a couple of days. Billy remembers the rogues from the days when he played out there. In pre-war tones, he insists they wouldn't dare to keep Mick. "Well," says Jean, "the name of Rice is famous once again."

The newspapers report that a specially allocated plane is standing by to bring Mick home. Jean reads further: "Lieut. Pearson, of Leicester, who had been with Sergeant Rice until a few minutes before he was captured, said he must have killed at least seven of the attackers." After a pause Phoebe says that it's Archie whom she doesn't want disappointed. "He's had enough of disappoint-ments. I don't think he ever really gets used to them." Feeling you should never build things up, Phoebe says that Archie always builds everything up and it never turns out. For instance, the theatre business. Phoebe is afraid to answer the door for fear of a police-man with another summons. One unpleasant matter suggesting an-other, she gets on the subject of Archie's women, who also don't turn out. "They come back here a few times, and that's that." Billy bursts with indignation that she can speak that way in front of Jean: "She's used to being with people who know how to behave. She doesn't want to hear about your troubles." "No, of course she doesn't," Phoebe says. "Well then—the trouble with you people is you don't know how to carry on properly, that's your trouble," says Billy. "Give the girl a chance. She's got her own life to lead."

Contributing a new bottle of gin, Jean hears more and more about Archie's women. She suggests that Phoebe have something to eat, and unwisely uses the phrase: "People have to eat." With a laugh, Phoebe says that's not all they have to do. "They have to do a whole lot of things, a lot of things you don't even know about, and it's nothing to do with being educated and all that. . . ." Phoebe is spoiling for a fight. Jean, to Phoebe, is separated from her in all sorts of ways. She and Mick, Phoebe says, are the only ones among them who have what it takes. "And the old man of course," she adds. "He had it. Not that it's any use to him now. He's just a has-been, I suppose. Still—it's better to be a has-been than a never-

was. His other son's the same—Old Bill. Archie's brother. Not
that you'd think he was. Now he's really a big pot. He's really
a big pot. There's no flies on brother Bill." Jean tries to change
the subject, but Phoebe goes right on. She likes Bill because he's a
gentleman and different from Archie. She thinks back to the early
days when Bill would come by to help Archie out of trouble. It
wasn't nearly so much the money or his helping Archie that she
appreciated as the way he spoke to her and patted her arm. Jean
lets slip: "Yes, I can see him doing it." Phoebe—as Archie
and Frank enter the room—wants to know just what Jean means
by that. Over Archie's easy interruption, Phoebe tries to tell Jean
that she can't afford not to like Bill. "Sounds a pretty good reason
for not liking anyone, I should say," says Archie. "He's something
you'll never be," Phoebe persists. "And I'm something he'll never
be—good Old Bill. He may be successful, but he's not a bad sort.
Do you know that my brother Bill had one wife, no love affair, he's
got three charming gifted children? Two of them have made what
these people call highly successful marriages." Phoebe interrupts
this flow: "Archie, I was talking to Jean." "Yes," he says, "I
thought that's what you were doing. I sized the situation up in a
flash." "Oh, it's easy for people like you to make fun," Phoebe
cries. "I left school when I was twelve years old." "Christ," exclaims Archie, "if she tells me that once more I shall get up on the
roof, drunk as I am, I shall get up on the roof and scream. I've
never done that before."

Frank is distressed to see his mother like this, but Archie doesn't
let her get a word in edgewise. He even tells Jean what Phoebe was
prepared to tell her: that Bill had footed all the bills for her education that the scholarship didn't cover. Having killed Phoebe's story,
Archie remarks that he could always kill anyone's punch line if he
wanted.

PHOEBE—She doesn't know about Mick and you and me. I know
she doesn't.

ARCHIE—She'll find out. We always find these things out in time.
(*To* FRANK *and* JEAN.) She's tired and she's getting old. She's
tired, and she's tired of me. Nobody ever gave her two pennyworth
of equipment, except her own pretty unimpressive self, to give anything else to the rest of the world. All it's given her is me, and
my God, she's tired of that! Aren't you, my old darling? You're
tired of that, aren't you?

PHOEBE (*fiercely*)—I tried to make something of myself. I tried,
I really did try. I was nothing much to look at, but what I was I

made myself. I was a plain kid—no, I wasn't. I wasn't even plain. I was the ugliest bloody kid you ever saw in your life. You've never seen anyone as ugly as I was. But I made something of myself. I did try to do something. I made him want me anyway.

FRANK—Everyone shouts! Please, somebody speak quietly, just for once. Those bloody Poles will be up here in a minute. Let's have a row. It looks as if we're going to have one anyway. But please can we have a *quiet* row!

ARCHIE—It was a long time ago. They knew it was a long time ago. (*To* FRANK.) I wish you'd stop yelling. I can't hear myself shout. Sing one of your songs, there's a good boy. Where's the old man?

JEAN—He's in the kitchen.

ARCHIE—Billy! Come out of there! Who's he got in there? Something you picked up in the Cambridge! Have you ever had it on a kitchen table? Like a piece of meat on a slab. Slicing pieces of bacon. Don't you wish you were back with old Graham?

PHOEBE—Frank, he's going to bring up one of those women, isn't he? In here, isn't he?

ARCHIE—Leave her alone, son.

PHOEBE—Do you think I don't lie awake upstairs, and hear it going on?

ARCHIE—Of course they know. They know what sort of a bastard I am, love. I think they know almost as well as you do. Well, almost as well. She'll be all right, won't you, love? Where's the old man? (*To* FRANK *and* JEAN.) Now don't pretend you're not used to it. . . .

When Billy comes out of the kitchen, and Phoebe finds that he's been at the cake she bought as her treat for Mick, she gives vent to all her pent-up feelings. In rising hysteria she shouts: "Couldn't you leave it alone? It wasn't for you. What's the matter with you? I feed you, don't I? Don't think you give me all that much money every week, because you don't!" She had bought the cake for thirty shillings because she wanted to give Mick when he got home something he'd like after all he had gone through. "And now," Phoebe screams, "that bloody *greedy* old pig—that old pig, as if he hadn't had enough of everything already—he has to go and get his great fingers in it!" She bursts into tears. Deeply ashamed and hurt, Billy goes to his room.

Jean is pretty glum. Archie says that it's just that with their being slewed, they're somewhat more sub-human than usual. Suddenly Phoebe isn't sure that Jean really likes Mick. Paying no attention, Archie proposes that just this once, for Mick's sake, they pretend to act like a respectable, decent family. And since Mick is coming home, they should get on with the party.

NUMBER SEVEN

When the music plays, a dead-behind-the-eyes Archie rises, grins, starts his act. For the flicker of a moment, he seems surprised to find himself where he is. At one point he remarks to the audience that they don't think he's real. "Well," he says, stumbling, "I'm not."

Introducing his song title as "My girl's always short of breath, but she don't mind a good blow through," Archie gives a refrain:

> ". . . Thank God I'm normal, normal, normal.
> Thank God I'm normal,
> I'm just like the rest of you chaps."

As a spotlight behind a gauze curtain picks up a nude in Britannia's helmet, and the music becomes "Land of Hope and Glory," Archie thanks God they're normal in "this dear old land."

NUMBER EIGHT

The party continues. Phoebe has grown quite meek. She inquires politely if anyone had noticed in today's paper the picture of the Duchess of Porth's daughter. Phoebe thought her magnificent. Frank makes a rude remark. "Phoebe's very keen," says Archie, "on the Duchess of Porth, aren't you, love? She says she thinks she's natural." "I suppose it's a bit silly but I've always taken an interest in her," Phoebe confesses. "Oh, ever since she was quite young. I feel she must be very nice somehow."

Straight man to his father, Frank follows Archie's orders and sings. He chooses a very British song, one of Billy's Boer War numbers. Coming out of a snooze, Billy recalls that the last time he sang that was in a Yorkshire pub. It's not so much the song as the Yorkshire pudding served with the beer that Billy remembers. Archie teases his father, then deliberately vulgarizes a favorite song of Phoebe's so that she feels compelled to sing the proper version.

Billy's had enough. Since he only sat up, he says, to toast young Mick, he wants to get to bed before those Bloody Poles come up to complain. Phoebe is tired too, but she has something she wants to show Jean before she goes up.

She takes out a letter from her niece in Canada. Archie interrupts irritably: "You don't have to look interested, dear. She's not interested in all that horse manure about Canada." Archie is cross at the very mention of Phoebe's letter, which contains an offer for him to run a hotel in Ottawa.

JEAN—What about the boys?
PHOEBE—They can come too if they want. I don't know about Mick, but Frank likes the idea, don't you?
JEAN—Do you, Frank?
FRANK—Look around you. Can you think of any good reason for staying in this cozy little corner of Europe? Don't kid yourself anyone's going to let you do anything, or try anything here, Jeannie. Because they're not. You haven't got a chance. Who are you— you're nobody. You're nobody, you've no money, and you're young. And when you end up it's pretty certain you'll still be nobody, you'll still have no money—the only difference is you'll be *old!* You'd better start thinking about number one, Jeannie, because nobody else is going to do it for you. Nobody believes in that stuff any more. Oh, they may say they do, and may take a few bob out of your pay packet every week and stick some stamps on your card to prove it, but don't believe it—nobody will give you a second look. They're all so busy, speeding down the middle of the road together, not giving a damn where they're going, as long as they're in the bloody middle! (*Chirpily, almost singing.*) *The rotten bastards!* "Oh, when there isn't a girl about you feel so lonely. When there isn't a girl about you're on your only."
ARCHIE—Ssh, you'll wake up the Poles.
FRANK—Somebody should wake you up. "You're on your only!"
ARCHIE—You should go to bed.
FRANK—You and that blonde bitch in the Cambridge. You and her. Like a monkey up a tree, I don't think! I'm going to bed.
ARCHIE—Good night, boy.
FRANK (*singing*)—

"Rock of Ages cleft for me,
Let me hide myself in thee!"

"Anyway," says Archie, "you can't buy draught Bass in Toronto." Carefully folding her letter while apologizing to Jean for being a bit silly, Phoebe says good night.

The minute he's alone with Jean, Archie says baldly: "Your mother caught me in bed with Phoebe." Jean says merely that she hadn't known. "All my children," Archie continues, "think I'm a bum. I've never bothered to hide it, I suppose—that's the answer."

At this point Jean too would prefer to go to bed, but Archie won't let her. Very drunk now, he wants an audience. He's prepared to talk on and on as only a drunken man can. "Did I ever tell you the most moving thing that I ever heard? It was when I was in Canada —I managed to slip over the border sometimes to some people I knew, and one night I heard some negress singing in a bar. *Now you're going to smile at this,* you're going to smile your educated English head off, because I suppose you've never sat lonely and half slewed in some bar among strangers a thousand miles from anything you think you understand. But if ever I saw any hope or strength in the human race, it was in the face of that old fat negress getting up to sing about Jesus or something like that. She was poor and lonely and oppressed like nobody you've ever known. Or me, for that matter. I never even liked that kind of music, but to see that old black whore singing her heart out to the whole world, you knew somehow in your heart that it didn't matter how much you kick people, the real people, how much you despise them, if they can stand up and make a pure, just natural noise like that, there's nothing wrong with them, only with everybody else. . . ." Archie's never heard anything like that though he knows Billy in his day heard it, and Archie supposes they'll never hear such a sound again. He wishes to God he could feel like that old black bitch. He wishes he was that old black bag, but he knows he'll never be able to sing that way because he doesn't give a damn about anything. As for Jean, she may really feel something, but she will have to sit on her hands like everyone else.

All this is a preamble to Archie's asking Jean: "What would you say to a man of my age marrying a girl of—oh, about your age? Don't be shocked. I told you—I don't feel a thing." Outraged, Jean says he couldn't do a thing like that to Phoebe. Working into his act, Archie says he doesn't look sexy, does he, but he had that barmaid in the Cambridge who upset old Billy—he had her when Billy wasn't looking. . . . Phoebe comes in. From the noise, she thought he had somebody here. "They called," she says, "from downstairs. There's a policeman at the door for you, Archie."

PHOEBE—I thought he had someone in here. What do you think he wants?

ARCHIE—Just me and my daughter Jean. Me and my daughter Jean—by my first love. Why don't you go back to London? Say, aren't you glad you're normal? I've always been a seven-day-a-week man myself, haven't I, Phoebe? A seven-day-a-week man. I always needed a jump at the end of the day—and at the beginning too usually. Just like a piece of bacon on the slab. Well, it's every-body's problem. Unless you're Mick and have got no problem. Well, he had a problem, but now he's on his way. Yes, that's a boy without problems. I'm a seven day-a-week man myself, twice a day. Poor old Phoebe, don't look so scared, love. Either they're doing it, and they're not enjoying it. Or else they're not doing it and they aren't enjoying it. Don't look so scared, love. Archie's drunk again. It's only the income tax man!

PHOEBE—Frank's down there—

FRANK (*in*)—The bastards! *The rotten bastards!* They've killed him! They've killed Mick! Those bloody wogs—they've murdered him. Oh, the rotten bastards!

ARCHIE (*slowly singing a blues*)—Oh, lord, I don't care where they bury my body, no, I don't care where they bury my body, 'cos my soul's going to live with God!

(End of Act II)

NUMBER NINE

With a spotlight on him at the piano, Frank plays a dirge, remi-niscent of St. James Infirmary, for Mick—and the British.

NUMBER TEN

Dressed in black, or wearing black armbands, the family has re-turned from Mick's funeral. Though Archie tells his stories, and Billy thinks of the good old days, everybody's tired. Jean cries: "Everybody's tired all right. Everybody's tired, everybody's stand-ing about, loitering without any intent whatsoever, waiting to be picked up by whatever they may allow to happen to us next." But it is on Archie that she makes her immediate attack. To Jean, he's a bastard on wheels. Frank can't imagine what's the matter with her. Archie says casually don't ask him: he's never solved a problem in his life. "You haven't got the nous," snarls Jean. "You've been too busy hating all those feckless moochers out there in the great darkness, haven't you? You've been really smart." Jean wants Frank to know the truth about his father, but Frank, with Mick just buried, wants no rows.

JEAN—What do you want, two minutes silence? Not only is your father generous, understanding and sympathetic—he doesn't give a damn about anyone. He's two pennorth of nothing.

George Relph in
"The Entertainer"

ARCHIE—Yes, I should say that sums me up pretty well.

JEAN—You don't need to look at me! I've lost a brother too. Why do people like us sit here, and just lap it all up, why do boys die, or stoke boilers, why do we pick up these things, what are we hoping to get out of it, what's it all in aid of—is it really just for the sake of a gloved hand waving at you from a golden coach?

PHOEBE—I think I'll go and lie down. (*To* JEAN.) He's always been good to me.

FRANK—Shall I bring you up an aspirin?

JEAN—Nobody listens to anyone.

PHOEBE—Thank you, dear. If you wouldn't mind. (*To* JEAN, *simply.*) He's always been good to me. Whatever he may have done. Always. (*Exits.*)

With Phoebe out of the room, Jean says straight out to Archie: "You can't do it to her, I won't let you." But before she can really let go on what a dirty thing Archie is doing to Phoebe, she smells out something worse. As Billy goes to his room, he asks Archie what time they are expected at the booking office the next day. Hearing they are to see Charlie Klein, whom Archie considers a tough bastard, Billy says Charlie should be all right. It was Billy who made him sign up Eddie Drummer. . . . "He always had style, Eddie, and never any real suggestion of offense in anything he did. We all had our own style, our own songs—and we were all English. What's more, we spoke English. It was different. We all knew what the rules were, and even if we spent half our time making people laugh at 'em we never seriously suggested that anyone should break them. A real pro is a real man, all he needs is an old backcloth behind him and he can hold them on his own for half an hour. . . ." He thinks of Eddie still up there. "Old Eddie. One of the really great ones, I should say he is. I should say he's probably the last. Yes, I should say he's probably the last." Billy exits.

Jean is incredulous that Archie would put the old man back to work, would kill him, in fact, just to save his no-good, washed-up show. Archie says it is not to save the show: it's so he himself won't have to go to jail. Jean can't believe that her grandfather has lost all sense of self-preservation. Archie passes that off by saying that Billy owes it to him. Jean knows that this isn't true, that Billy owes nothing to anyone. It now turns out that Billy went to the young girl's parents and broke up Archie's plans. The girl hadn't known Archie was a married man with three grown-up children. "He scotched it!" Jean marvels. "So you see you weren't wrong, Jeannie, love," Archie says. "Not about Phoebe anyway— old Archie isn't going to get his oats after all."

NUMBER ELEVEN

ARCHIE—Ladies and gentlemen, Billy Rice will not appear to-night. Billy Rice will not appear again. I wish I could sing a song for him—in his place. A farewell. But, unfortunately, I can't. Nobody can. None of us, anyway.

NUMBER TWELVE

While Graham and Jean have it out on their own, brother Bill is behind his desk, dealing kindly but firmly with Archie. Bill has delivered an ultimatum to Archie: either he accepts the passage for himself and his family to Canada, and starts a new life there with his debts settled here, or Archie takes the consequences and goes to jail. The tickets for Canada are on the desk.

Jean, no longer wanting to marry Graham, insists that she must take care of Phoebe. Graham begs her to come back to him and the pleasant life they will lead together. Jean puts him off, as Archie makes his decision.

ARCHIE—You know, I've always thought I should go to jail. I should think it must be quite interesting. Sure to meet someone I know. D'you know what my landlady in Fulham used to say about you? She used to say: "He looks like a governor's man." Always said it—without fail.

GRAHAM—We're all in it for what we can get out of it. Isn't that what your father was supposed to say?

ARCHIE—You can never get anything at this Labour Exchange anyway. They must have more bums in this place than in any other town in England. Oh, well, thanks anyway, just two more performances. It's a pity though—I should have liked to notch up twenty-one against the income tax man. I'll never make my twenty-first now. It would have been fun to get the key of the door, somehow.

JEAN—Here we are, we're alone in the universe, there's no God, it just seems that it all began by something as simple as sunlight striking on a piece of rock. And here we are. We've got only ourselves. Somehow, we've just got to make a go of it. *We've only ourselves.*

BROTHER BILL—I'm sorry, Archie, but I've given up trying to understand.

NUMBER THIRTEEN

The Rock'n Roll. Nude tableau behind the first act gauze. Archie Rice's "one and only" music interrupts the program. He sings a few bars from his patriotic song, then goes into his spiel asking them not to clap too hard. They're all in a very old building, Archie says. Looking at Britannia, Archie reckons she's sagging a bit.

Archie is under a strain. When the curtain rises and he swaggers into his dance, the stage is dark and bare. He has a hard time singing "Why should I care—" He begins to falter; the music goes on without him. He picks up and continues, as Phoebe, carrying his raincoat and hat, appears. He stops without finishing; the music goes on as he walks over to Phoebe, who now helps him on with his coat. Archie hesitates, then comes downstage for the last time. "You've been a good audience," he says. "Very good. A very *good* audience. Let me know where you're working tomorrow night—and I'll come and see YOU." Archie Rice has gone. The music continues.

THE VISIT

A Play in Three Acts

By Friedrich Duerrenmatt

Adapted by Maurice Valency

[Friedrich Duerrenmatt *was born in 1921 in Konolfingen, a village near Berne. When he was 13 his father, a parson, took the family to Berne where young Duerrenmatt went to high school and then to the University. Later he attended the University of Zurich. His first play, "It Is Written," was produced in Zurich in 1947. His first real success was "The Marriage of Mississippi," produced in Germany in 1952 and recently staged Off Broadway as "Fools Are Passing Through." He has written six plays in all, seven radio scripts, one film and four novels.*

Maurice Valency, *professor of Comparative Literature at Columbia University, has a great knack for converting foreign plays into successful Broadway productions: witness "The Madwoman of Chaillot" and "The Enchanted." He has written several plays, notably "The Thracian Horses," which have been produced in other American cities and in Europe.*]

For the cast listing, see page 332.

A RAILWAY crossing bell starts ringing. A locomotive whistle sounds in the distance. In Güllen's dilapidated railway station, a scattered band of shabby men watch languidly as an express train rushes by.

Once upon a time, world-famous trains—the Emperor, the Diplomat, the Banker and the Flying Dutchman—all stopped here. Now only the local from Kaffingen and the 12:40 from Kalberstadt bother to come to this ruined town. "What with the Wagonworks shut down . . . the Foundry finished . . . the Golden Eagle Pencil Factory all closed up . . ." the men say, "it's life on the dole."

Before the mysterious blight descended, Güllen was a center of

"The Visit": By Maurice Valency, an English adaptation of "Der Besuch der alten Dame" by Friedrich Duerrenmatt. © 1956, 1958 by Maurice Valency. Reprinted by permission of Random House, Inc., New York.

industry, a cradle of culture where Goethe slept and Brahms composed a quartet. Now the men are pinning their hopes, their lives, on "Clara's" help. Last week they read of her giving a hospital in France; in Rome she founded a free nursery; in Leuthenau, a bird sanctuary. Clara owns oil companies, shipping lines, banks and even the biggest string of Geisha houses in Japan. "Is she coming?" they ask their shabby, sad-looking Burgomaster as he arrives on the platform.

Accompanied by a Pastor, a Teacher and Anton Schill—all equally shabby—the Burgomaster announces: "She's coming. The telegram has been confirmed. Our distinguished guest will arrive on the 12:40 from Kalberstadt. Everyone must be ready." The Burgomaster confirms all details for the little welcome Güllen can afford. The Teacher will lead the mixed choir and the children's choir; the church bells will ring (if the new ropes are fitted in time); the town band will play, and the Athletic Association will provide a human pyramid. At the lunch at the Golden Apostle, the Burgomaster will speak.

The man painting a banner of welcome for the station consults the Burgomaster who, in turn, asks Schill's advice. Once tall and handsome, now sloppy and gone to seed, Schill looks at the sign. He decides that it simply won't do. It is much too intimate with its "Welcome, Claire": it should read "Welcome, Madame." The Painter, remembering the lady as Clara Wascher, the carpenter's daughter, agrees to put "Welcome, Madame" on the other side. "Then," he says, "if things go well, we can always turn it around." "Well, anyway it's safer," says Schill. "Everything depends on the first impression."

The whole town is relying on Anton Schill, who alone knew Claire very well, to present their case.

SCHILL—Close? Yes, we were close, there's no denying it. We were in love. I was young—good looking, so they said, and Claire—you know—I can still see her in the great barn coming towards me—like a light out of the darkness there. And in the Konradsweil Forest, she'd come running to meet me—barefooted—her beautiful red hair streaming behind her, like a witch. I was in love with her all right. But you know how it is when you're twenty—life came between us.

BURGOMASTER—You must give me some points about her for my speech.

SCHILL—I think I can help you there.

TEACHER—Well, I've gone through the school rolls. And the

young lady's marks were, I'm afraid to say, absolutely dreadful. Even in deportment. The only subject in which she was even re- motely passable was natural history.

BURGOMASTER—Good in natural history. (*He makes a note.*)

SCHILL—She was an outdoor girl. Wild. Once, I remember, they arrested a tramp, and she threw stones at the policeman. She hated injustice passionately.

BURGOMASTER—Strong sense of justice. Excellent.

SCHILL—And generous . . .

The Burgomaster appreciates these pointers. Marking down Claire's generosity, he feels that all this has given him enough for his speech. "The rest, my friend," he tells Schill, "is up to you." Though not sure that he can part Claire from some of her millions, or that she will even remember him, Schill promises that at the first opportunity he will discuss Güllen's misery with her.

Wishing to go over the welcoming details with only two hours left for preparation, the Burgomaster is interrupted by the ringing of the station bell, and next by the thunder of an approaching train. As the men crane their necks to see it pass, the Station Master advances down the platform to give it his cursory salute. Instead of whizzing by, the train comes to a screaming stop.

PAINTER—But the Flying Dutchman never stops!

1ST MAN—It's stopping.

2ND MAN—In Güllen!

3RD MAN—In the poorest—

1ST MAN—The dreariest—

2ND MAN—The lousiest—

4TH MAN—The most God-forsaken hole between Venice and Stockholm. . . .

Over a hubbub of confusion, Claire's voice can be heard: "Is this Güllen?" She is accused of pulling the emergency cord. "I always pull the emergency cord," she says. The Station Master hurries off to ask what is going on. "And who the hell are you?" Claire asks. ("An extraordinary woman in her fifties—red haired, remarkably dressed—her face as impassive as an ancient idol, yet beautiful still"), Claire moves forward on the platform with singular grace. Her retinue—consisting of an old butler who wears dark glasses and a handsome young fiancé dressed for fishing—follows; and following them, the irate conductor of the Flying Dutchman.

As Schill says: "My God, Clara!" the Burgomaster, Teacher and Pastor try frantically to organize the unorganized welcome.

Claire orders her butler to pacify the conductor: "Bobby, give him a thousand marks." The townspeople gasp. Claire adds three thousand more for the Railway Widows Relief Fund. The bewildered conductor says: "But we have no such fund, Madame." "Now you have," Claire answers. Discovering this is Claire Zachanassian, the conductor falls all over himself. "Would you like the train to wait, Madame, while you visit the town? The Administration will be delighted. The cathedral porch is worth seeing, they say. Gothic. With the Massacre of the Innocents." "Take the train away," Claire answers. "I don't need it any more." Her fiancé reminds her of the reporters left in the dining car. Claire does not wish them in Güllen. "Later," she says, "they will come by themselves."

The train leaves, and in leaving, quite drowns out the Burgomaster's welcome. "Thank you, Mr. Burgomaster," Claire says. She bows to each citizen in turn, and fails to recognize Schill. "Clara!" he says. "Anton?" Claire turns.

SCHILL—Yes. It's good that you've come back.

CLAIRE—Yes. I've looked forward to this moment. All my life. Ever since I left Güllen.

SCHILL (*a little embarrassed*)—That is very kind of you to say, Clara.

CLAIRE—And have you thought about me?

SCHILL—Naturally. Always. You know that.

CLAIRE—Those were happy times we spent together.

SCHILL—Unforgettable. (*He smiles reassuringly at the* BURGOMASTER.)

CLAIRE—Call me the name you used to call me.

SCHILL (*whispers*)—My kitten.

CLAIRE—What?

SCHILL (*louder*)—My kitten.

CLAIRE—And what else?

SCHILL—Little witch.

CLAIRE—And I used to call you my black panther. You're gray now, and soft.

SCHILL—But you are still the same, little witch.

CLAIRE—I am the same? (*She laughs.*) Oh, no, my black panther. I am not at all the same.

Claire introduces Schill to her fiancé, her future eighth husband, who sulks. She plans to be married here in the cathedral. It was her dream when she was seventeen to be married in the Güllen Cathedral. Now, just as she wishes to see the town, the belated welcome overtakes her. The choir, the children, all with flowers and sashes, arrive. Amused, Claire tells them to proceed. They start to sing, but a passing express train drowns them out.

Police Chief Schultz, with a click of heels, puts himself at Claire's service. Looking at him through her lorgnette, Claire says: "Thank you, I have no need for you at the moment. But I think there will be work for you by and by. Tell me, do you know how to close an eye from time to time?" "How else," says the Police Chief, "could I get along in my profession?" "You might practice closing both," she says. "What a sense of humor, eh?" laughs Schill.

Claire accepts flowers from the Burgomaster's children and meets the Pastor. "Do you give consolation," she asks, "to the dying?" The Pastor is puzzled. "And to those who are condemned to death?" "Capital punishment has been abolished in this country," the Pastor answers. "I see," Claire says. "Well, it could be restored, I suppose." Again Schill laughs.

When the Burgomaster offers her his arm, Claire refuses. She never walks, nor does she ride in motor cars. She claps her hands and two huge bodyguards, bearing a sedan chair, come onto the platform. She seats herself.

CLAIRE—I travel this way—a bit antiquated, of course. But perfectly safe. Aren't they magnificent? Mike and Max. I bought them in America. They were in jail, condemned to the chair. I had them pardoned. Now they're condemned to my chair. I paid fifty thousand dollars apiece for them. You couldn't get them now for twice the sum.

SCHILL—No. Of course not.

CLAIRE—The sedan chair comes from the Louvre. I fancied it so much that the President of France gave it to me. The French are so unexpected, don't you think so, Anton? . . . Go. (MIKE *and* MAX *start to carry her off.*)

BURGOMASTER—You wish to visit the cathedral? And the old town hall?

CLAIRE—No. The great barn. And the forest of Konradsweil. I wish to go with Anton and visit our old haunts once again.

PASTOR—Very touching.

CLAIRE (*to the* BUTLER)—Will you send my luggage and the coffin to the Golden Apostle?

BURGOMASTER—The coffin?

CLAIRE—Yes. I brought one with me. Go.

When the great mass of luggage and the townspeople bearing it disappear, the Policeman is startled by the sight of two identically dressed blind men coming down the station platform. When he approaches them, they speak in high flute-like childish voices, repeating each other. The blind men say they are with the lady they belong to. They have no trade: they amuse the lady and look after the beast. They feed it raw meat; she feeds them chicken and wine. "Rich people have strange tastes," says the Policeman. They echo him. When he offers to take them to the lady, the Little Men chorus: "We know the way—we know the way."

The station disappears. In its place stands—in the last stages of decay—the Golden Apostle. As the procession of luggage, coffin and caged panther passes before him, the Burgomaster, drinking wine with the Teacher, pronounces it all too much for him. The Teacher agrees: "When this woman suddenly appeared on the platform, a shudder tore through me. . . ." A moment later, however, when the Policeman comes to tell them of Claire and Schill revisiting their old haunts, the Teacher, profoundly moved, is reminded of the poetry of Shakespeare. The Burgomaster finds himself so moved that he proposes a toast to the best-loved citizen of Güllen. An unearthly scream tears through the building. "Good God, what's that?" the Burgomaster cries. The Teacher says: "The black panther." "Oh!" The Burgomaster finishes his toast: "My successor—Anton Schill."

In the forest, having dismissed her sedan chair and told her fiancé where to fish, Claire is alone with Schill. Ill at ease, wanting to make a favorable impression, Schill speaks of their love for one another, but he is rather inexact about the details. Listening to him, asking to hear more, Claire corrects him where he is confused. She was seventeen and Schill was not yet twenty and, she remembers, they "were made for each other." "So we were," Schill says. "And," Claire continues, "you married Mathilde Blumhard and her store, and I married Old Zachanassian and his oil wells. He found me in a whorehouse in Hamburg. It was my hair that entangled him, the old golden beetle."

Clapping her hands for her butler, Claire asks for a cigar. Choosing one carefully, she also offers one to Schill. As they smoke, Schill asks Claire not to be angry at his having married Mathilde. "What a lucky thing for you that I did!" Schill says. "You were so young, so beautiful. You deserved a far better fate than to settle in this wretched town without any future." If she had stayed in Güllen

John Wyse, Lynn Fontanne a

fred Lunt in "The Visit"

and married him, her life would be as wasted as his—a shopkeeper in a bankrupt town. "But," she says, "you have your family, after all." Schill shrugs off his family who never let him forget his failure or poverty. His wife depresses him and his children, nice as they are, have no interest whatsoever in the higher things. "How sad for you," Claire says. He is full of self-pity for his life in Güllen. He has hardly ever been able to get away: "A trip to Berlin years ago. Five and a half days in the Swiss Alps. That's all." "The world is much the same everywhere," Claire answers. Claire has seen the world. She has lived in it. "The world and I," she says, "have been on very intimate terms."

Schill hopes that now, since Claire has returned, things will change. Claire has no intention of leaving her native town in its present impoverished condition. Schill, in raptures, taking Claire's hand in his, finds it all the way it was. "Just as it was years ago. If only we could roll back time and be together always!" "Is that your wish?" asks Claire.

In the dining room of the Golden Apostle, the tables are spread with ragged cloths, cracked china and chipped glass. The band plays and the people clap their hands, as Claire, followed by Bobby the butler, makes her entrance. "The applause is meant for you, gracious lady," says the Burgomaster. "The band deserves it more than I, Burgomaster," Claire answers. "They blow from the heart. And the human pyramid was beautiful. . . . You—show me your muscles." The Athlete kneels before her. "Superb. Wonderful arms—powerful hands. Have you ever strangled a man with them?" "Strangled?" gasps the Athlete. "Yes," Claire says, "it's perfectly simple. A little pressure in the proper place, and the rest goes by itself, as in politics."

The women, simpering, are presented to Claire, who remembers them well. She meets Anton Schill's wife and children. When the town physician is introduced, Claire, peering through her lorgnette, asks: "Do you sign the death certificates?" Startled, the man replies that it is his duty. "And when the heart dies," Claire asks, "what do you put down? Heart failure?" "What a golden sense of humor!" Schill laughs. "Bit grim, wouldn't you say?" answers the Doctor. "Not at all, not at all," Schill whispers. "She's promised us a million."

Claire sits patiently through the Burgomaster's flowery remembrance of things past. When her turn comes, she rises. Addressing the Burgomaster and her fellow townsmen, Claire says she is moved by the nature of their welcome and their disinterested joy. She was not the good girl described by the Burgomaster; nevertheless, she hopes to deserve their good opinion of her, and in memory of the seventeen years spent among them Claire proposes to make a gift of one billion marks. Five hundred million to the town, and five hundred million to the townspeople. There is a dead silence. "On one condition," adds Claire, and sits down.

Through the joyous bedlam, and over Anton Schill's gushes, Claire adds further: "I wish to buy justice." "But justice cannot be bought, Madame," says the Burgomaster. "Everything can be bought," Claire answers, as she summons Bobby.

Taking off his black glasses, Bobby turns out to be a former magistrate who was presiding judge in Güllen's criminal court for many years. Twenty-five years ago Madame Zachanassian persuaded him at a phenomenal salary to be her butler. Ordering Anton Schill to stand, Bobby conducts a court. In magisterial tones he recalls a bastardy case that had been tried before him. In it Anton Schill was charged by Clara Wascher with being the father of her illegitimate child. Schill at the time not only denied the charge, but he produced two witnesses in his support. Schill now loudly calls the whole thing an absurd business that happened when they were children. "Who remembers?" he says.

Calling the two blind men forth, Bobby shows that they were Schill's two witnesses. They had sworn falsely to having slept with Clara Wascher. Anton Schill had bribed them with a bottle of schnapps. "And now," Bobby orders them, "tell the people what happened to you." Hesitating and whimpering, the blind men tell the townspeople how Claire tracked them down. She found one in Australia and one in Canada. She turned them over to Mike and Max, who made them what they are today. "And there you have it," Bobby says. "We are all present in Güllen once more. The plaintiff. The defendant. The two false witnesses. The judge. Many years have passed. Does the plaintiff have anything further to add?"

CLAIRE—There is nothing to add.

BOBBY—And the defendant?

SCHILL—What's the use of all this? It's all dead and buried. It's mad to rake up this old rubbish again.

BOBBY—And what happened to the child that was born?

CLAIRE (*in a low voice*)—It lived a year.

BOBBY—And what happened to you?

CLAIRE—I became a whore. The judgment of the court left me no alternative. No one would trust me—no one would give me work.

BOBBY—So. And now, what is the nature of the reparation you demand?

CLAIRE—I want the life of Anton Schill.

Frau Schill, shouting "No, no!," rushes to her husband's side. Schill says it's a joke. All that's forgotten. Clara has forgotten nothing. She remembers that this morning he wished that time might be rolled back. It has been, and now she will buy justice, and is willing to pay a billion marks. Pale and dignified, the Burgomaster stands and addresses Claire: "Madame Zachanassian, we are not in the jungle. We are in Europe. We may be poor but we are not heathens. In the name of the town of Güllen, I decline your offer. In the name of humanity. We shall never accept." Everyone applauds wildly. Rising, Claire says: "Thank you, Burgomaster. I can wait."

ACT II

In his small, scantily stocked store opposite the Golden Apostle, Schill and his children are sweeping and singing away. Before the store opens for the day, a man making his delivery of eggs announces that butter will be going up again the first of the month. With no one to buy it, Schill feels that he will just have to cancel his order. "There's nothing else to do," he says. "And how's the family?" "Oh, scraping along," the delivery man says. "Maybe now things will get better." "Maybe," Schill answers.

When the man departs, Schill has his own announcement for his children. He wants them to know, that in spite of everything, it is settled and "official" that he is to be Güllen's next burgomaster. Impressed by this honor and the money involved, the son shakes his father's hand while the daughter kisses him. "You see, you don't have to be entirely ashamed of your father. Not everyone thinks alike," Schill says. Honor or no honor, the children pass up breakfast with Schill to make an early job-hunting start.

The business day begins with a man ordering expensive cigarettes and, even more surprisingly, buying them on credit. "On account," says the man. "Well, all right, just this once," Schill agrees. "Seeing it's you—Hofbauer." The blind men can be heard playing their fiddles. Commenting on their playing, the man asks Schill if it makes him nervous. Schill shrugs.

Women enter the store. They order milk—"whole milk," an unheard of thing. What's more, they ask for butter—instead of their usual drippings of lard—and bread, "white" bread, and a *whole* loaf. Schill is incredulous: "But a whole loaf would cost . . ." "On account," says one woman while the other thinks up a new extravagance. She orders chocolate; then the other woman orders chocolate also.

1ST WOMAN—We'll eat it here if you don't mind.
SCHILL—Yes, please do.
2ND WOMAN—It's so cool at the back of the shop.
SCHILL—On account?
WOMEN—Of course.
SCHILL—All for one, one for all.

A third man, entering and greeting Schill, remarks on the hot weather and asks how business is.

SCHILL—Fabulous. For a while no one came and now all of a sudden I'm running a luxury trade— Oh, I'll never forget the way you all stood by me at the Golden Apostle in spite of your need, in spite of everything. That was the finest hour of my life.
1ST MAN—We're not heathen, you know.
2ND MAN—We're behind you, my boy; the whole town's behind you.
1ST MAN—As firm as a rock.
1ST WOMAN (*munching her chocolate*)—As firm as a rock.
BOTH WOMEN—As firm as a rock, Herr Schill. As firm as a rock.
2ND MAN—There's no denying it—you're the most popular man in town.
1ST MAN—The most important.
2ND MAN—And in the spring, God willing, you will be our Burgomaster.
1ST MAN—Sure as a gun.
2ND MAN—Sure as a gun.

It now occurs to the second man to splurge a bit: he passes over his usual schnapps for some French cognac, and instead of ordinary stuff, asks for English tobacco. "English," Schill repeats. "But that makes twenty-three marks eighty." "Chalk it up," says the man. Suddenly noticing the man's new shoes, Schill, looking around his store, sees that each and every "on-account" customer is wearing shiny new shoes. One of the women explains that shoes wear out, and that they bought these on credit.

SCHILL—On credit? And where all of a sudden do you get credit?
2ND MAN—Everybody gives credit now.
1ST WOMAN—You gave us credit yourself.
SCHILL—And what are you going to pay with? Eh? (*They are*

all silent. He advances upon them threateningly.) With what?
Eh? With what? With what? (SCHILL *takes off his apron and leaves.*)

On her balcony at the Golden Apostle, Claire enjoys the autumn morning air with her fiancé. Having just caught another fish, Pedro finds Claire's birthplace charming. He tries for the right word to describe the townspeople. Claire suggests: "Simple, decent, hard-working, honest." Pedro is delighted to see that she knows what he meant. Another thing amazes him: on their arrival the town was dirty and run-down. Today it is spick and span and in perfect shape. Pedro feels that Claire's return has given the townspeople a new— Again he is at a loss for the right word. Claire supplies it: "Lease on life?" "Precisely," Pedro answers. "The town was dying, it's true," Claire says. "But a town doesn't have to die. I think they realize that now. People die, not towns. . . . Bobby! A cigar."

Arriving at the police station, Schill, in his role of future burgo-master, demands that the police arrest Madame Zachanassian. The Policeman answers coolly: "You're not elected yet, as far as I know." He considers this request extraordinary and pours himself a glass of beer. Schill insists that it's the Policeman's duty. "Sit down, sit down, Schill," says the Policeman. "Let's examine the case soberly and calmly. The lady offered us a billion marks. But that doesn't entitle us to take police action against her." He continues that, in order to arrest a person, the person must first commit a crime. Schill says it's "incitement to murder." Laughing this off, the Policeman says: "The price is much too high. For a case like yours, one might pay a thousand marks, at the most two thousand. But not a billion! That's ridiculous. And even if she meant it, that would only prove she was out of her mind. And that's not a matter for the police." Whether or not she is out of her mind, Schill feels the danger to him is the same. The Policeman tells him to pull himself together; everyone is on his side. Schill says: "No. All of a sudden my customers are buying white bread, whole milk, butter, imported tobacco. . . ." People who have been living on the dole suddenly are buying French cognac—and they all have new shoes. Holding out his foot with its shiny new boot, the Policeman asks what Schill has against new shoes. "You, too," Schill breathes, and notices next that the Policeman's beer is imported, not the poor local brew.

SCHILL—And you, Schultz, with your new shoes and your imported beer—how are you going to pay for them?

POLICEMAN—That's my business. (*His telephone rings. He picks it up.*) Police Station, Güllen. What? What? Where? Where? How? Right, we'll deal with it. (*Hangs up.*)
SCHILL (*said during telephone conversation*)—Schultz, listen. No. Schultz, please listen to me! Don't you see they're all . . . Listen, please! Look, Schultz. They're all running up debts. And out of those debts comes this sudden prosperity. And out of this prosperity comes the absolute need to kill me.

The Policeman insists that he's imagining things. Schill knows that all Claire has to do is sit on her balcony and wait. The Policeman says he's hysterical. Schill then notices the Policeman's new gold tooth. At this point the Policeman, calling him "crazy," says he has no time to waste—Madame Zachanassian's panther has escaped. While loading his gun, the Policeman says that it's at large: "I've got to hunt it down." "You're not hunting a panther and you know it!" Schill cries. "It's me you're hunting!" Telling him coldly to follow his advice, the Policeman advises: "Go home—lock the door, and keep out of everyone's way."

On Claire's balcony, Pedro confesses that her little town has begun to bore him. There's nothing doing here. These provincial people fear nothing, desire nothing, and strive for nothing. "They have everything they want," Pedro says. "They're asleep." Before he goes back to his fishing, Claire suggests that he telephone her Bank president to transfer a billion marks to her current account. "A billion," says Pedro. "Yes, my love."

Rushing into the Burgomaster's office, Schill finds himself facing a loaded revolver. "Is that a gun?" he asks. "Yes," says the Burgomaster. "Madame Zachanassian's black panther's broken loose. It's been seen near the cathedral. It's as well to be prepared." Schill says suspiciously that they're making quite a thing of it. Observing the Burgomaster's expensive cigar and new silk tie, he asks: "And have you also bought new shoes?" "Why, yes," says the Burgomaster, "I ordered a new pair from Kalberstadt. Extraordinary. However did you guess?" "That's why I'm here," Schill cries. And at that moment the arrival of a new typewriter for the office increases Schill's horror. "What's the matter with you?" says the Burgomaster. "My dear fellow, aren't you well?" Schill counters that it is the Burgomaster who is pale and trembling. "Are you frightened?" Schill asks.
Having come to claim protection of the authorities, Schill runs into bland hypocrisy. The Burgomaster can't imagine what he means.

Schill says the woman has put a price on his head. He has already appealed unavailingly to the Police—Policeman Schultz has a new gold tooth.

BURGOMASTER—Oh, Schill, really— You're forgetting. This is Güllen, the town of humane traditions. Goethe slept here. Brahms composed a quartet here. You must have faith in us. This is a law-abiding community.

SCHILL—Then arrest this woman who wants to have me killed.

BURGOMASTER—What an extraordinary idea! Look here, Schill. God knows the lady has every right to be angry with you. What you did there wasn't very pretty. You forced two decent lads to perjure themselves and had a young girl thrown out on the streets.

SCHILL—That young girl owns half the world. (*A moment's silence.*)

The Burgomaster thinks it's time to be frank: "Man to man, just as you said. After what you did, you have no moral right to say a word against this lady. And I advise you not to try. Also—I regret to have to tell you this—there is no longer any question of your being elected Burgomaster." This is official. But Schill will have, as before, the town's esteem and friendship, though the Burgomaster wishes that silence could now be drawn about the whole miserable business. Schill realizes that he will have to keep silent while they arrange his murder.

The Burgomaster resumes his noble role. He asks for the names of the people who are arranging Schill's murder and promises a thorough investigation.

SCHILL—You.

BURGOMASTER—I resent this. Do you think we'd kill you for money?

SCHILL—No. You don't want to kill me. But you want to have me killed.

In the dark, men prowl about with guns, while Claire, on her balcony, asks Bobby what the men are hunting. Discovering that her black panther has escaped, Claire observes: "They seem very excited. There may be shooting." Bobby thinks this possible.

Running to the cathedral, Schill begs sanctuary of the Pastor. After insisting that the men are hunting him down like a wild beast and making him go through hell, Schill listens to the Pastor's quiet reasoning: "The hell you are going through exists only within your-self. Many years ago you betrayed a girl shamefully, for money. Now you think that we shall sell you just as you sold her. No, my friend, you are projecting your guilt upon others. It's quite natural —but remember, the root of our torment lies always within ourselves, in our hearts, in our sins. When you have understood this, you can conquer the fears that oppress you; you have the weapons with which to destroy them." Advising Schill to worry only about his im-mortal soul, the Pastor says that there is great comfort in prayer. Schill seems to find relief as he kneels in front of the altar. Saying he must now go to a baptism, the Pastor starts to leave. The church bell rings. Then another bell chimes in. The bells peal together. Schill, lifting his head, hears the new bell. "Yes," says the Pastor with pride, "its tone is marvelous, don't you think? Full. Sonorous." Stepping back in horror, Schill cries: "A new bell! You, too, Pastor? You too?" Falling to his knees, the Pastor prays: "Oh, God, God forgive me. We are poor weak things, all of us. Do not tempt us any further. Go, Schill, go while there is still time."

In the fading light, men and guns swarm all over the streets. Claire, on her balcony, asks Bobby about the shooting she heard— had they caught her panther? "He's dead, Madame," Bobby an-swers. Claire had counted two shots.

Escorting two girl students, the Teacher arrives to offer the gra-cious lady on the balcony his condolences for the loss of her panther. "But what could we do?" the Teacher tells Claire. "The panther was savage—a beast. To him our human laws could not apply. . . ."

Schill comes out of the darkness carrying a gun. Scaring the children away, and the Teacher with them, Schill aims the gun at Claire. "Anton, why are you frightening the children?" Claire asks. "Go away, Claire," Schill warns her. Claire, with the gun pointed at her, quietly recalls that their first meeting took place on a bal-cony: that was the beginning and everything else had to follow. Ignoring the gun leveled at her and saying "There is no escape," Claire leaves the balcony. The shutters close behind her.

Anton Schill, carrying a suitcase, arrives furtively at the cleaned-up, shiny station. As if by chance, townspeople crowd in from all sides. Hesitating, Schill stops. He acknowledges the people's greet-ings and answers their questions with a ghastly, sick fear. Where is he taking his little trip? To Kalberstadt—and after that, Schill thinks he might go on to Australia. The townspeople exclaim at this. Why Australia? Schill mumbles that you can't always live in the same town. In the Doctor's opinion that's a risky trip for a man of

Schill's age; and the Burgomaster reminds Schill that one of the lady's Little Men ran off to Australia. Schill, says the Policeman, would be much safer here.

Cowering in anguish, Schill says through dry lips that he wrote a letter to the administration at Kaffingen but they didn't answer. The townspeople laugh. "They didn't answer," Schill explains, "because our postmaster held up my letter." Everyone exclaims that a man of the postmaster's integrity, a member of their council, doesn't hold up letters.

The crossing bell rings. As the Station Master announces the local to Kalberstadt, Schill manages to squeak out: "What are you all doing here? What do you want of me?" "We don't like to see you go," the Burgomaster says. "We've come to see you off." As the sound of the train grows louder, all the men casually hem in Schill. As the train stops, they press jovially around him.

A dark wall of men separates Schill from the train. Schill shrills they're going to push him under the train, or hold him back. "No, no," all the men answer. In terror, Schill crouches against the station wall. They crowd around him and urge him onto the train, until it starts to move, gathers speed and disappears. "There," says the Policeman, "it's gone without you." The crowd dissolves. The hysterical man is left alone on the platform.

Looking for water for his truck, a truck driver approaches Schill. "Missed your train?" he asks. "To Kalberstadt?" "Yes," says Schill. "Well, come with me," the driver invites him, "I'm going that way." Schill refuses. "This is my town," he decides. "This is my home. I've changed my mind. I'm staying." Shrugging, the truck driver leaves. Picking up his suitcase, looking first to the right, then to the left, Schill slowly walks straight ahead.

ACT III

Within the dim cavernous structure of the old barn Claire, dressed in magnificent wedding finery, sits like an idol in her sedan chair. Covered with the old barn's dust, the Doctor and Teacher are ushered into her presence. Claire hears out their elaborate compliments on her sumptuous wedding, and their apologies for intruding when her husband must be waiting impatiently. "No, no," Claire says, "I've packed him off to Brazil." "To Brazil, Madame?" says the Doctor. "Yes, he's gone for his honeymoon." As for the wedding guests that have come from all over the world, Claire has prepared such a delightful dinner that they will never miss her. "Now," she says, "what was it you wished to talk about?"

They've come about Anton Schill. "Is he dead?" Claire asks. "Madame," the Teacher answers, "we may be poor. But we have our principles." "I see," Claire says. "Then what do you want?" Both Teacher and Doctor explain that Güllen, so very long poor, in anticipation of Claire's well-known munificence has gone into debt. "In spite of your principles?" Claire says. "We're human, Madame," the Teacher replies. "I see," says Claire. "The question is," says the Doctor, "how are we going to pay?" Claire answers: "You already know."

The Teacher makes a courageous effort to explain how he and the Doctor feel about their town. They had both refused important posts elsewhere that they might serve their impoverished Güllen. They were born here; it is their life. The Teacher pleads with Claire, not for the billion marks, but for ten million to invest in their factories. He urges Claire to buy these plants. "Save us, Madame. Save us, and we will not only bless you, we will make money for you." The Teacher insists that this would not be charity, but good business. Claire concedes that it is a good idea, but finds it completely out of the question. She can't buy these plants, she says, because she already owns them. In fact, she has had her agents buy up this "rubbish" piece by piece over the years until she owns it all. "Your hopes," Claire says, "were an illusion, your vision empty, your self-sacrifice a stupidity, your whole life's completely senseless." *She* is "that mysterious blight." The day Claire was forced out of Güllen, she determined she would come back to settle all accounts.

Pleading with her that one injustice cannot cure another, the Teacher blocks the path of Mike and Max as they man the sedan chair. She has taught Güllen a terrible lesson, the Teacher says. He urges her to have pity—that highest form of justice. "The highest form of justice has no pity," Claire answers. "It is bright and pure and clear. The world made me into a whore; now I make the world into a brothel. Those who wish to go down, may go down. Those who wish to dance with me, may dance with me." To Mike and Max, Claire says: "Go."

The sanctimonious language of the townspeople can no longer screen their intention. In Anton Schill's store, his own wife prates of sympathy for poor Madame Zachanassian. Announcing that the reporters are on their way, the Butcher Hofbauer hopes that Schill, who hasn't come out of his room for a week, won't try to talk to them. "If he tries to throw dirt at our Clara," he says, "and tell a lot of lies, how she tried to get us to kill him, which anyway she never meant—" "Of course not," Frau Schill says. "Then," Hof-

bauer continues, "we'll really have to do something! And not because of the money"—he spits—"but out of ordinary human decency. God knows Madame Zachanassian has gone through enough
on his account already." "She has indeed," sympathizes Frau Schill.

Decidedly drunk, the Teacher comes into the store for another
small one. With the arrival of the reporters, the townspeople hover
about to see that Schill doesn't blurt out the story. Liquor having
given him unusual courage, the Teacher decides that he will go tell the
Press the truth about Claire's offer to Güllen. He doesn't get far; his
fellow townspeople gang up on him. Frau Schill and her son and
daughter say that the Teacher should be ashamed of himself. Wasting no words, the men spring at him. Only Schill's interference pre-
vents the Teacher from being mauled. Ordering the Teacher to say
nothing when the lone reporter enters the shop, Schill lies that
"Schill" has gone to Kalberstadt for the day.

After the reporter leaves, one of the men walks up to Schill. "That
was pretty smart of you to keep your mouth shut," he snarls. "You
know what to expect if you don't." Another, asking for a Havana,
tells Schill: "You know, to do what you did a man must be a
bastard!" Having had their say, the men leave the store. Frau
Schill and her children pointedly leave after them. Only the Teacher
remains. He apologizes to Schill for making a disturbance. He
had wanted to help, but it was obviously no use. Beginning to sober
up, the Teacher knows that he too will call Schill a bastard. He
knows that the townspeople are going to kill Schill—he had known
it all along. Their need was too strong, the temptation too great.
Equally the Teacher knows that he himself is hardening into one of
them. Schill answers all of this: "It can't be helped." Wavering,
the Teacher cries: "Pull yourself together, man. Speak to the reporters, you've no time to lose." Schill answers flatly: "No. I'm
not going to fight any more." He made Claire what she is and himself what he is: "Give me a lesson, Teacher. . . . Should I pretend
that I'm innocent?" The Teacher answers that he is getting what he
deserves, that he is guilty as hell. Schill agrees. "And you are a
bastard," the Teacher adds. Schill says: "Yes." Having got all
this off his chest, the Teacher orders a bottle "on account" and
shuffles off.

The Burgomaster now enters. He has come to ask Schill to prepare for the town meeting that night, when his case will be discussed
and final action taken. The lady's offer will be rejected. Schill
says: "Possibly." "Of course," says the Burgomaster, "I may be
wrong." "Of course," says Schill. The town meeting—now that
Claire's wedding has made Güllen famous—will be covered by the

Press, television and radio. Güllen's ancient democratic institutions are now of great interest to the world.

Claire's terms will not be made public; the matter will be put to a vote that only those involved will understand. Schill's character has been completely whitewashed to the Press, not for his sake but for the sake of his decent, honest family.

SCHILL—Oh.

BURGOMASTER—So far we've all played fair. You've kept your mouth shut and so have we. Now can we continue to depend on you? Because if you have any idea of opening your mouth at tonight's meeting, there won't be any meeting.

SCHILL—I'm glad to hear an open threat at last.

BURGOMASTER—We are not threatening you. You are threatening us. If you speak, you force us to act—in advance.

Schill says that he will abide by the town's decision. The Burgomaster, greatly relieved, says he is glad there is still a spark of decency left in him. The situation having been so much eased this far, the Burgomaster hopes that things will be made still easier. He has bought a gun for Schill, and thinking how much better it would be not to have to have a meeting at all, gives it to him. Schill doesn't want it, nor does he need it.

BURGOMASTER (*he clears his throat*)—You see? Then we could tell the lady that we had condemned you in secret session and you had anticipated our decision. I've lost a lot of sleep getting to this point, believe me.

SCHILL—I believe you.

BURGOMASTER—Frankly, in your place, I myself would prefer to take the path of honor. Get it over with, once and for all. Don't you agree? For the sake of your friends! For the sake of our children, your own children—you have a daughter, a son—Schill, you know our need, our misery.

SCHILL—You've put me through hell, you and your town. You were my friend, you smiled and reassured me. But day by day I saw you change—your shoes, your ties, your suits—your hearts. If you had dealt with me frankly, perhaps I would feel differently toward you now. I might even use that gun you brought me. For the sake of my friends. But now I have conquered my fear. Alone. It was hard, but it's done. And now you will have to judge me. And I will accept your judgment. For me that will be justice. How it will be for you, I don't know. (*He turns away.*) You may kill me if you like. I won't complain, I won't protest, I won't defend myself. But I won't do your job for you either.

BURGOMASTER (*takes up his gun*)—There it is. You've had your chance and you won't take it. Too bad. I suppose it's more than we can expect of a man like you.

Schill's family returns. All decked out in new "on-account" finery, they plan to take a ride in the son's new "on-account" car. Schill yearns to join them for a last ride through the forest. A horrified Frau Schill rejects the idea: "I don't think that will look very nice," she says. "No, perhaps not," says Schill. "I'll walk all the way." He says good-bye to each in turn. Barely acknowledging his farewells, the family departs.

For one brief, dreamlike moment, Schill and Claire meet in a golden forest. At peace, they speak affectionately to each other. Sitting on their bench and listening to the birds, Claire asks Schill if he would like some music. "Oh, yes," says Schill gratefully, "that would be very nice." Claire remembers his favorite songs and has them played for him.

They talk of children—his and theirs. Schill would like to know what *their* baby was like. Claire tells simply of the child's birth and death. Claire then asks how she was at seventeen in the days when he loved her. Schill remembers her beauty, and she remembers his strength.

SCHILL—Here we are, Clara, sitting together in our forest for the last time. The town council meets tonight. They will condemn me to death and one of them will kill me. I don't know who and I don't know where. I only know that soon a useless life will be brought to an end.

CLAIRE—Your love for me died years ago, Anton. But my love for you would not die. It turned into something strong like the hidden roots of the forest, something evil like white mushrooms that grow unseen in the darkness. And slowly it reached out for your life. Now I have you, you are mine. Alone. At last, and forever, a peaceful ghost in a silent house.

The music ends; Claire kisses Schill, who says: "Adieu."

With cameras trained on them and reporters taking down their every word, the townspeople conduct their meeting. Madame Zachanassian's desire to re-establish justice in Güllen by means of her gift is the theme of speeches made by the Burgomaster, and at even greater length, by the Teacher. With Christian charity, and through no desire for worldly goods—but out of love for the right and to reaffirm their faith—the townspeople, raising their hands, pass a unanimous vote.

The meeting thus concluded, the Press is ushered downstairs for refreshments, the doors are locked and the lights turned down. Schill and the townspeople alone remain in the dark council chamber.

With a nasty shove, the Policeman tells Schill this is it. The Burgomaster instructs a well-drilled group to form a lane, the Pastor to pray. As the Policeman acts in S.S. style, Schill, unafraid, slowly moves into the lane of silent men, where the Athlete awaits him. The lane closes in.

When the job is done, the Teacher's mantle covers Schill's body. Taking off his stethoscope, the Doctor pronounces: "Heart failure," which the Burgomaster alters to "Died of Joy." Claire enters, followed by Bobby, looks at the corpse a long moment, sighs and leaves. Taking a check from his wallet, Bobby holds it out to the Burgomaster's outstretched hand.

The Güllen-Rome express stops at the brilliantly lit railway station. As the Station Master calls, "All aboard, please," a procession of men, carrying trunks and bags, passes in front of the well-dressed crowd. After the last piece of luggage, men carry the coffin. Claire, impassive as a stone idol, follows the coffin to the train. The Station Master whistles " 'Board," and the train moves off while the band plays and the townspeople cheer.

A GRAPHIC GLANCE

Morris Carnovsky, Katharine Hepburn, Richard Waring, Donald Harron, John Colicos and Lois Nettleton in the American Shakespeare Festival's "The Merchant of Venice"

In "Say, Darling" Vivian Blaine rehearses for: (clockwise) David Wayne, Jerome Cowan, Johnny Desmond, Horace McMahon and Robert Morse

Abbe Lane, Tony Randall, Jacquelyn McKeever and Paul Valentine in "Oh Captain!"

Eddie Foy, Jerome Cowan, Gretchen Wyler, Barbara Perry and Stephen Douglass in "Rumple"

*They Who Get Slapped: (upper left) Ina Balin and Dean Stockwell;
(upper right) Vivienne Drummond and Kenneth Haigh; (center)
Jo Van Fleet and Arthur Hill; (lower left) Ellen McRae and Robert
Webber; (lower right) Art Carney and Siobhan McKenna*

S. J. Perelman in CBS-TV's Seven Lively Arts program, "The Changing Ways of Love"

Marcel Marceau returns to the City Center

Anne Baxter, Jean Dixon, Williams Smithers and Martine Bartlett in "The Square Root of Wonderful"

Lena Horne and Ricardo Montalban in "Jamaica"

278

Basil Rathbone and Faye Emerson in two straw-hat versions of "Witness for the Prosecution"

Troubled fathers on Broadway: George Relph, Chester Morris, Hugh Griffith, Pat Hingle, Cameron Prud'homme and Art Carney

Nancy Walker in "Copper and Brass"

PLAYS PRODUCED IN NEW YORK

PLAYS PRODUCED IN NEW YORK

June 1, 1957—May 31, 1958

(Plays marked "Continued" were still running on June 1, 1958)

(For summaries of the plays, see "Season on Broadway.")

SIMPLY HEAVENLY

(62 performances)

Musical comedy in two acts, with book and lyrics by Langston Hughes; music by David Martin. Produced by the Playhouse Heavenly Company at the Playhouse Theatre, August 20, 1957.

Cast of characters—

Simple	Melvin Stewart
Madam Butler	Wilhelmina Gray
Boyd	Stanley Greene
Mrs. Caddy	Dagmar Craig
Joyce Lane	Marilyn Berry
Hopkins	Duke Williams
Bar Pianist	Willie Pritchett
Mamie	Claudia McNeil
Bodiddly	Charles A. McRae
Character	Allegro Kane
Melon	John Bouie
Gitfiddle	Brownie McGhee
Zarita	Anna English
Arcie	Josephine Woods
John Jasper	Charles Harrigan
Big Boy, Cop	Maxwell Glanville
Nurse, Party Guest	Dagmar Craig

The action takes place in Harlem, U.S.A. Act I.—Scene 1—Simple's room on an early spring evening. Scene 2—Joyce's room, same evening. Scene 3—Paddy's Bar, just before midnight. Scene 4—Hospital room, next day. Scene 5—Paddy's Bar on Saturday night. Scene 6—Joyce's room, Sunday evening. Scene 7—Simple's room, a month later. Act II.—Scene 1—Paddy's Bar a week later, evening. Scene 2—Joyce's room, an evening two weeks later. Scene 3—Simple's room, a week later. Scene 4—Paddy's Bar, next morning. Scene 5—Lenox Avenue, that evening. Scene 6—Joyce's room, same evening. Scene 7—Simple's room, same evening. Scene 8—Paddy's Bar on a winter evening. Scene 9—A phone booth, Christmas Eve. Scene 10—Simple's room, same evening.

Staged by Joshua Shelley; setting and lighting by Raymond Sovey; orchestration by David Martin; production stage manager, Larry Parker; stage manager, Laurence Olvin; press representatives, David Lipsky and Phillip Bloom.

Musical numbers—

ACT I

"Love Is Simply Heavenly"	Joyce
"Let Me Take You for a Ride"	Zarita and Simple

283

"Broken String Blues" ....Gitfiddle
"Did You Ever Hear the Blues?" ..Mamie, Melon and Bar Characters
"I'm Gonna Be John Henry" ....Simple

ACT II

"When I'm in a Quiet Mood" ....Mamie and Melon
"Look for the Morning Star" ....Zarita
"Let's Ball Awhile" ....Zarita and Ensemble
"The Men in My Life" ....Zarita
"I'm a Good Old Girl" ....Mamie
"Look for the Morning Star" (Reprise) ....Ensemble

(Closed October 12, 1957)

MASK AND GOWN

(39 performances)

Musical revue in two acts, conceived by Leonard Sillman; continuity by Ronny Graham and Sidney Carroll; new music and lyrics by Ronny Graham, June Carroll, Arthur Siegel and Dorothea Freitag. Produced by Leonard Sillman and Bryant Haliday at the John Golden Theatre, September 10, 1957.

Principals—

T. C. Jones

Betty Carr   Gaby Monet
John Smolko   Rod Strong

Staged by Leonard Sillman; musical numbers staged and choreographed by Jim Russell; lighting by Lee Watson; musical direction and arrangements by Dorothea Freitag; production associate, Jacqueline Adams; production stage manager, Peter Pell; press representative, Bill Doll; accompaniment by Arthur Siegel and Dorothea Freitag (pianos), Ralph Roberts (drums).

Sketches and musical numbers—

ACT I

The Circus Is Over
T. C. on T. C.
T. C. on T. V.
Make Friends
Catch
Hesitation Waltz
T. C. A Dance
Bolero
T. C. on Hollywood
T. C. on Taps Topside—
   Don't Give Up the Ship
On Their Own
T. C. on Certain Singers

ACT II

Setting the Stage
T. C.—on—Avon
You Better Go Now
I'll Be Seeing You
T. C.

(Closed October 12, 1957)

CAROUSEL

(24 performances)

Musical in two acts, with book and lyrics by Oscar Hammerstein II and music by Richard Rodgers. Revived by the New York City Center Light Opera Company (Jean Dalrymple, Director) at the New York City Center, September 11, 1957.

Cast of characters—

Carrie Pipperidge	Pat Stanley
Julie Jordan	Barbara Cook
Mrs. Mullin	Kay Medford
Billy Bigelow	Howard Keel
First Policeman	Evans Thornton
David Bascombe	Robert Eckles
Girl with Bear	Elisa Monte
Nettie Fowler	Marie Powers
June Girl	Evelyn Taylor
Enoch Snow	Russell Nype
Jigger Craigin	James Mitchell
Hannah	Joan Eheman
Boatswain	Robert Pagent
Second Policeman	James Gannon
Captain	Sam Kirkham
Heavenly Friend (Joshua)	Leo Lucker
Starkeeper	Victor Moore
Louise	Bambi Linn
Carnival Boy	Robert Pagent
Enoch Snow, Jr.	Larry Fuller
Principal	Bruce Baggett

Townspeople: Jane Burke, Shirley Chester, Faith Compo, Cherry Davis, Elizabeth Edwards, Lindsay McGregor, Beth Parks, Basha Regis, Jeanne Shea, Joy Lynne Sica, Bruce Baggett, Don Becker, Jack Eddleman, James E. Gannon, Sam Kirkham, David London, Vincent B. McMahon, Bob Newkum, Ted Otis, Robert D. Reim.

Dancers: Patricia Birsh, Verna Cain, Dorothy Etheridge, Mickey Gunnerson, Sally Gura, Ruby Herndon, Catherine Horn, Reba Howells, Rosemary Jourdan, Eloise Milton, Kiki Minor, Evelyn Taylor, Jim Albright, Charles J. Carow, Gerald Fries, Larry Fuller, William T. Inglis, Donald Martin, Glenn Olson, Robert St. Clair, Gerald M. Teijolo, Jr.

Staged by John Fearnley and Robert Pagent; musical director, Julius Rudel; settings by Oliver Smith; lighting by Peggy Clark; costume supervisor, Florence Klotz; choreography by Agnes de Mille, restaged by Robert Pagent; assistant to Miss Dalrymple, Alan Green; choral director, Charles Smith; hair styles by Ernest Adler; production stage manager, Herman Shapiro; stage manager, Kermit Kegley; press assistant, Shelly Secunda.

Carousel was first produced by the Theatre Guild at the Majestic Theatre, April 19, 1945, for 890 performances; was revived by the Theatre Guild at the New York City Center, January 25, 1949, for 48 performances, and by the New York City Center Light Opera Company at the New York City Center, June 2, 1954, for 79 performances.

(Closed September 29, 1957)

FOUR WINDS

(21 performances)

Play in three acts by Thomas W. Phipps. Produced by Worthington Miner and Kenneth Wagg at the Cort Theatre, September 25, 1957.

Cast of characters—

Lee	Harry Shaw Lowe
Doctor Cazalet	Harry Mehaffey
Gage	Conrad Nagel
Audrey Pender	Luella Gear
Axel Doorn	Carl Esmond
Garrett Scott	Peter Cookson
Jeremy Paget	Robert Hardy
Mademoiselle	Ludmilla Toretzka
Davina Mars	Ann Todd
Tad Willis	James Rennie

The action of the play takes place in the patio of "Four Winds," Davina Mars' home in Palm Beach, Florida. Act I.—Late afternoon. Act II.—Scene 1—The following morning. Scene 2—Late afternoon the same day. Act III.—Scene 1—Two hours later. Scene 2—Three hours later.

Staged by Guthrie McClintic; production designed by Donald Oenslager, assisted by Klaus Holm (scenery and lighting) and Patton Campbell (costumes); production stage manager, Keene Curtis; press representatives, Richard Maney and Martin Shwartz.

(Closed October 12, 1957)

WEST SIDE STORY

(284 performances)
(Continued)

Musical in two acts, based on a conception of Jerome Robbins; book by Arthur Laurents; music by Leonard Bernstein; lyrics by Stephen Sondheim. Produced by Robert E. Griffith and Harold S. Prince (by arrangement with Roger L. Stevens) at the Winter Garden, September 26, 1957.

Cast of characters—

The Jets:

Riff, the leader	Mickey Calin
Tony, his friend	Larry Kert
Action	Eddie Roll
A-Rab	Tony Mordente
Baby John	David Winters
Snowboy	Grover Dale
Big Deal	Martin Charnin
Diesel	Hank Brunjes
Gee-Tar	Tommy Abbott
Mouth Piece	Frank Green
Tiger	Lowell Harris

Their Girls:
Graziella ....Wilma Curley
Velma ....Carole D'Andrea
Minnie ....Nanette Rosen
Clarice ....Marilyn D'Honau
Pauline ....Julie Oser
Anybodys ....Lee Becker

The Sharks:
Bernardo, the leader ....Ken Le Roy
Maria, his sister ....Carol Lawrence
Anita, his girl ....Chita Rivera
Chino, his friend ....Jamie Sanchez
Pepe ....George Marcy
Indio ....Noel Schwartz
Luis ....Al De Sio
Anxious ....Gene Gavin
Nibbles ....Ronnie Lee
Juano ....Jay Norman
Toro ....Erne Castaldo
Moose ....Jack Murray

Their Girls:
Rosalia ....Marilyn Cooper
Consuelo ....Reri Grist
Teresita ....Carmen Guiterrez
Francisca ....Elizabeth Taylor
Estella ....Lynn Ross
Marguerita ....Liane Plane

The Adults:
Doc ....Art Smith
Schrank ....Arch Johnson
Krupke ....William Bramley
Gladhand ....John Harkins

The action takes place on the West Side of New York City during the last days of summer. Act I.—Prologue: the Months Before; 5:00 P.M., the street; 5:30 P.M., a back yard; 6:00 P.M., a bedroom; 10:00 P.M., the gym; 11:00 P.M., a back alley; midnight, the drugstore. The Next Day—5:30 P.M., the bridal shop; 6:00 to 9:00 P.M., the neighborhood; 9:00 P.M., under the highway. Act II.—9:15 P.M., the bedroom; 10:00 P.M., another alley; 11:30 P.M., the bedroom; 11:40 P.M., the drugstore; 11:50 P.M., the cellar; midnight, the street.

Staged and choreographed by Jerome Robbins; co-choreographer, Peter Gennaro; production associate, Sylvia Drulie; scenic production by Oliver Smith; costumes by Irene Sharaff; lighting by Jean Rosenthal; musical director, Max Goberman; orchestrations by Leonard Bernstein, with Sid Ramin and Irwin Kostal; production stage manager, Ruth Mitchell; stage manager, Harry Howell; press representative, Reuben Rabinovitch.

Musical numbers—

ACT I

Prologue ....Danced by Jets and Sharks
Jet Song ....Riff, Baby John, A-Rab, Diesel and Jets
"Something's Coming" ....Tony
The Dance at the Gym ....Jets and Sharks
"Maria" ....Tony
"Tonight" ....Tony and Maria
"America" ....Anita and Shark Girls
"Cool" ....Riff and the Jets
"One Hand, One Heart" ....Tony and Maria
"Tonight" (Quintet and Chorus) ....Company
The Rumble ....Danced by Riff, Bernardo, Jets and Sharks

ACT II

"I Feel Pretty" ....Maria, Rosalia, Teresita and Francisca
"Somewhere" ....Danced by Company; sung by Consuelo
"Gee, Officer Krupke" ....Action, Snowboy and Jets
"A Boy Like That" ....Anita and Maria
"I Have a Love" ....Anita and Maria
Taunting ....Anita and the Jets
Finale ....Company

I KNOCK AT THE DOOR

(48 performances)

Stage reading, adapted by Paul Shyre from the first of six autobiographical novels by Sean O'Casey.   Produced by Lucille Lortel, Paul Shyre and Howard Gottfried at the Belasco Theatre, September 29, 1957.

Principals—

Rae Allen   Paul Shyre
George Brenlin   Roy Poole
Aline MacMahon   Staats Coatsworth
    Staged by Stuart Vaughan; setting and lighting by Lester Polakov; flutist, Frances Blaisdell; stage manager, Robert Paschall; press representative, Sol Jacobson.

(Closed November 10, 1957)

LOOK BACK IN ANGER

(279 performances)
(Continued)

Play in three acts by John Osborne.   Produced by David Merrick at the Lyceum Theatre, October 1, 1957.

Cast of characters—

Jimmy Porter ....Kenneth Haigh
Cliff Lewis ....Alan Bates
Alison Porter ....Mary Ure
Helena Charles ....Vivienne Drummond
Colonel Redfern ....Jack Livesey
    The action of the play takes place in the Porters' one-room flat in a large town in the Midlands, England; the time is the present.   Act I.— Early evening, April.   Act II.—Scene 1—Two weeks later.   Scene 2— The following evening.   Act III.—Scene 1—Several months later. Scene 2—A few minutes later.
    Staged by Tony Richardson; setting by Alan Tagg; costumes by Motley; setting, lighting and costumes supervised by Howard Bay; music for songs by Tom Eastwood; stage manager, Howard Stone; press representatives, Harvey Sabinson and Lewis Harmon.

See page 67.

MISS LONELYHEARTS

(12 performances)

Play in two acts by Howard Teichmann, based on the novel by Nathanael West.   Produced by Lester Osterman and Alfred R.

Glancy, Jr. (in association with Diana Green) at the Music Box,
October 3, 1957.

Cast of characters—

Ned Gates ....Henderson Forsythe
Goldsmith ....William Hickey
William Spain ....Pat O'Brien
A Boy ....Fritz Weaver
Sick-of-it-All ....Anne Meara
Gladys H. ....Marian Reardon
Desperate ....Jo Anna March
Betty ....Pippa Scott
Claude ....Maurice Ellis
Adele Farnum ....Irene Dailey
Mary Spain ....Ruth Warrick
Fay Doyle ....Janet Ward
Peter Doyle ....Dan Morgan
        Staged by Alan Schneider; setting and lighting by Jo Mielziner;
café music by Jule Styne; costumes by Patricia Zipprodt; production
associate, George Hamlin; production stage manager, John Drew
Devereaux; stage manager, William Dodds; press representative, Wil-
liam Fields.

(Closed October 12, 1957)

A BOY GROWING UP

(17 performances)

Stage reading, arranged by Emlyn Williams, from the stories of
Dylan Thomas. Produced by S. Hurok, in association with Roger L.
Stevens, at the Longacre Theatre, October 7, 1957.

Principal—

Emlyn Williams
        Stage manager, Robert Abbot; press representative, Martin Feinstein.

Program—

Introducing Dylan Thomas
Memories of Childhood (from "Quite Early One Morning")
Cousin Gwilym (from "Portrait of the Artist as a Young Dog")
"Who Do You Wish Was with Us?" (from the above)
The Outing (from "A Prospect of the Sea")
The Hand
Reminiscence of a Schoolmaster (from "Quite Early One Morning")
The Fight (from "Portrait of the Artist as a Young Dog")
"Just Like Little Dogs" (from the above)
Self-Portrait (from "Quite Early One Morning")
Adventures in the Skin Trade (fantasy)
A Memory of Older Youth (from "Quite Early One Morning")
A Note to Close On

(Closed October 20, 1957)

MARY STUART

(56 performances)

Play by Friedrich Schiller, in a new adaptation in two acts by Jean Stock Goldstone and John Reich. Produced by the Phoenix Theatre (T. Edward Hambleton and Norris Houghton) at the Phoenix Theatre, October 8, 1957.

Cast of characters—

```
Mary Stuart ........................................Irene Worth
Hannah Kennedy, her servant ....................Dorothy Sands
Sir Amyas Paulet, her guardian at Fotheringay ......Robert Goodier
Sir Edward Mortimer, his nephew ..................John Colicos
Lord Burleigh, Lord High Treasurer ................Max Adrian
Queen Elizabeth ................................Eva Le Gallienne
Count L'Aubespine, Ambassador from the Court
    of France .......................................James Neylin
The Earl of Leicester ..........................Douglas Campbell
The Earl of Shrewsbury ..........................William Hutt
Sir William Davison, Secretary of State .............Ellis Rabb
Sir Andrew Melvil ...............................Michael Hogan
O'Kelly ..............................................David Ford
Captain of the Guard ..............................Dario Barri
Guards ......................Dalton Dearborn, Vincent Dowling
    Act I.—Scene 1—Fotheringay Castle. Scene 2—Westminster Pal-
ace. Scene 3—Park at Fotheringay. Act II.—Scene 1—Westminster
Palace. Scene 2—Fotheringay Castle. Scene 3—Westminster Palace.
    Staged by Tyrone Guthrie; scenery and lighting by Donald Oens-
lager; costumes by Alvin Colt; incidental music by Michael Colicchio;
production stage manager, Robert Woods; stage manager, Jack Meri-
gold; press representative, Ben Kornsweig.
```

(Closed November 24, 1957)

THE EGGHEAD

(21 performances)

Play in three acts by Molly Kazan. Produced by Hope Abelson at the Ethel Barrymore Theatre, October 9, 1957.

Cast of characters—

```
Jackie Parson .....................................Kevin Drohan
Sally Parson .......................................Phyllis Love
Martin Donahue ...................................Biff McGuire
Gottfried Roth ....................................Eduard Franz
Harvey Robbins ................................Richard Robbins
Madeline Robbins ................................Helen Shields
Finney ...........................................Graham Jarvis
Hank Parson .......................................Karl Malden
Roger Parson ....................................Nicholas Pryor
Annie Grierson ...................................Marion Sweet
Perry Hall .......................................Lloyd Richards
Essie ..............................................Ruth Attaway
    The action takes place in the living room and study of the Parsons'
home in a small town in northern New England. Act I.—Late after-
noon, October. Act II.—Afternoon, December. Act III.—Two hours
later.
```

Staged by Hume Cronyn; settings by Richard Sylbert; costumes by Anna Hill Johnstone; production stage manager, Porter Van Zandt; stage manager, Jack Betts; press representatives, Harvey Sabinson and David Powers.

(Closed October 26, 1957)

ROMANOFF AND JULIET

(268 performances)
(Continued)

Comedy in three acts by Peter Ustinov. Produced by David Merrick at the Plymouth Theatre, October 10, 1957.

Cast of characters—

First Soldier	Phil Leeds
Second Soldier	Jack Gilford
The General	Peter Ustinov
Hooper Moulsworth	Fred Clark
Vadim Romanoff	Henry Lascoe
Igor Romanoff	Gerald Sarracini
Juliet	Elizabeth Allen
The Spy	Carl Don
Beulah Moulsworth	Natalie Schafer
Evdokia Romanoff	Marianne Deeming
Jr. Captain Marfa Zlotochienko	Sylvia Daneel
Freddie Vandestuyt	William Greene
The Archbishop	Edward Atienza

The action takes place in the main square in the capital city of the smallest country in Europe. Act I.—Dawn to morning. Act II.—Noon to afternoon. Act III.—Evening to night.

Staged by George S. Kaufman; setting by Denis Malcles; costumes by Helene Pons; settings and lighting supervised by Howard Bay; incidental music by Harold Rome; ballads by Anthony Hopkins and Peter Ustinov; production stage manager, Joseph Olney; stage manager, Ben Janney; press representative, Harvey Sabinson.

UNDER MILK WOOD

(39 performances)

Play in two acts by Dylan Thomas. Produced by Gilbert Miller, Henry Sherek and Roger L. Stevens at Henry Miller's Theatre, October 15, 1957.

Cast of characters—

Onlooker	Donald Houston
Captain Cat	Francis Compton
First Drowned	Pirie MacDonald
Second Drowned	Richard Longman
Rosie Probert	Catherine Dolan
Third Drowned	Charles Tyner
Fourth Drowned	Walter Thomson
Fifth Drowned	Donald Ewer
Myfanwy Price	Olive Dunbar
Mog Edwards	Alastair Duncan
Jack Black	Donald Ewer

Mr. Waldo ....Guy Spaull
Waldo's Mother ....Muriel Ault
Waldo's Wife ....Christine Thomas
First Neighbor ....Joan Newell
Second Neighbor ....Buddug-Mair Powell
Third Neighbor ....Pauline Flanagan
Fourth Neighbor ....Catherine Dolan
Little Boy Waldo ....Carson Woods
Matti Richards ....Suzanne Shell
Matti's Mother ....Peggy Turnley
Rev. Eli Jenkins ....Powys Thomas
Mrs. Ogmore-Pritchard ....Audrey Ridgwell
Mr. Ogmore ....Donald Moffat
Mr. Pritchard ....Tom Clancy
Gossamer Beynon ....Lisa Daniels
Organ Morgan ....Charles Tyner
Mrs. Organ Morgan ....Christine Thomas
Utah Watkins ....,...Alastair Duncan
Mrs. Utah Watkins ....Muriel Ault
Willy Nilly ....Walter Thomson
Mrs. Willy Nilly ....Joan Newell
P. C. Attila Rees ....Donald Ewer
Sinbad Sailors ....Pirie MacDonald
Lily Smalls ....Patricia Devon
Mae Rose Cottage ....Dorothy Rice
Bessie Bighead ....Buddug-Mair Powell
Ocky Milkman ....Richard Longman
Cherry Owen ....Tom Clancy
Butcher Beynon ....Guy Spaull
Mr. Pugh ....Richard Longman
Mrs. Pugh ....Pauline Flanagan
Mary Ann Sailors ....Muriel Ault
Dai Bread ....Tom Clancy
Polly Garter ....Diana Maddox
Nogood Boyo ....Donald Moffat
Lord Cut-Glass ....Alastair Duncan
The Guide Book ....Alastair Duncan
Mrs. Dai Bread One ....Christine Thomas
Mrs. Dai Bread Two ....Catherine Dolan
Mrs. Cherry Owen ....Buddug-Mair Powell
Mrs. Beynon ....Joan Newell
Maggy Richards ....Toby Stevens
Ricky Rees ....Raymond McHugh
Our Sal ....Katharine Dunfee
Nasty Humphrey ....Tony Atkins
Billy Swansea ....Carson Woods
One of Mr. Waldo's ....Ina Beth Cummins
Jackie with the Sniff ....Suzanne Shell
First Woman ....Patricia Devon
Second Woman ....Peggy Turnley
Third Woman ....Muriel Ault
Evans the Death ....Charles Tyner
Fishermen ....Donald Ewer, Tom Clancy
Gwenny ....Ina Beth Cummins
Child ....Katharine Dunfee
Mother ....Peggy Turnley
    The action of the play takes place in Llareggub, South Wales, in
the spring.
    Staged by Douglas Cleverdon; setting by Raymond Sovey; costumes
by Kathryn Miller; production stage manager, Richard Bender; stage
manager, Bert Gruver; press representatives, Richard Maney and
Martin Shwartz.

See page 86.

(Closed November 16, 1957)

NATURE'S WAY

(61 performances)

Comedy in two acts by Herman Wouk. Produced by Alfred de Liagre, Jr., at the Coronet Theatre, October 16, 1957.

Cast of characters—

Billy Turk	Orson Bean
Butler	Godfrey M. Cambridge
Maggie Turk	Betsy von Furstenberg
Mr. Chaney	James Arenton
Nadine Fesser	Beatrice Arthur
Vivian Voles	Scott McKay
Gilbert Price	Edmond Ryan
Mrs. Fawcett	Audrey Christie
Dr. Bacher	Robert Emhardt
The Waiter	Joe Silver
The Musician	Barry Newman
Rip Voorhees	Sorrell Booke
Mrs. Voorhees	Renee Roy
Dr. Blimber	Ronald Long

Action takes place in the penthouse apartment of the Billy Turks, in the East Sixties, New York City. Act I.—Morning. Act II.—Scene 1—Evening, two months later. Scene 2—The following evening.

Staged by Alfred de Liagre, Jr.; setting and lighting by Donald Oenslager; costumes by Frank Thompson; stage manager, Arthur Marlowe; press representative, Ben Washer.

(Closed December 7, 1957)

COPPER AND BRASS

(36 performances)

Musical comedy in two acts, with book by Ellen Violett and David Craig; lyrics by David Craig; music by David Baker. Produced by Lyn Austin and Thomas Noyes at the Martin Beck Theatre, October 17, 1957.

Cast of characters—

Experts	Byron Mitchell, David Gold, Stanley Papich, Jeff Duncan, John Dorrin, Bob Roman, Kevin Carlisle, Sam Greene
Katey O'Shea	Nancy Walker
Commissioner	Beau Tilden
Captain	Alan Bunce
Sergeant	Bruce Mackay
Ethel Potts	Michele Burke
Mary Potts	Evelyn Russell
Estelle O'Shea	Benay Venuta
Mrs. Zimmer	Alice Nunn
Mr. Morphky	Michael Roberts
Mrs. Morphky	Doreen McLean
Piggy	Byron Mitchell
Brawn	Norma Douglas

Brains ....Peter Conlow
Boy ....Stanley Papich
Principal ....Alice Pearce
Instructor ....Clyde Turner
George ....Dick Williams
Limey ....Hank Jones
Slam ....Doug Rogers
Professor ....Ernie Furtado
Traintime ....Frank Rehak
Slam's Girl ....Elmarie Wendel
Limey's Wife ....Elton Warren
Professor's Girl ....Bette Graham
Rookie Cops ....Sam Greene, Michael Roberts, John Darrin,
                    Bob Roman, Nat Wright, Larry Mitchell,
                                                   Jack Moore
Roderick ....David Gold
Policewomen ....Dorothy Aull, Joy Lane, Bette Graham
Woman in the Window ....Joy Lane
Guard ....Michael Roberts
   Dancers: Shawneequa Baker, Eve Beck, Judith Coy, Anita Dencks,
Kate Friedlich, Ellen Hubel, Coco Ramirez, Tina Ramirez, Ella
Thompson, Kevin Carlisle, Jeff Duncan, David Gold, Donald McKayle,
Jack Moore, Stanley Papich, Harold Pierson, Willard Nagel.
   Singers: Dorothy Aull, Laurie Franks, Bette Graham, Buzz Halli-
day, Joy Lane, Joanne Spiller, Elton Warren, Elmarie Wendel, John
Dorrin, Sam Greene, Bruce Mackay, Byron Mitchell, Larry Mitchell,
Michael Roberts, Bob Roman, Clyde Turner, Nat Wright.
   The action takes place in and around the island of Manhattan.
   Staged by Marc Daniels; choreography by Anna Sokolow; settings
and lighting by William and Jean Eckart; costumes by Alvin Colt;
musical direction and vocal arrangements by Maurice Levine; orchestrations by Ralph Burns; dance arrangements by John Morris; production stage manager, Jean Barrere; stage manager, Harry Young;
press representative, Barry Hyams.

Musical numbers—

ACT I

"Career Guidance" ....Career Guides, Katey
"Wearing of the Blue" ....Katey and Company
"I Need All the Help I Can Get" ....Katey
"Cool Combo Mambo" ....The Kids
"You Walked Out" ....George
"Cool Credo" ....George, Katey, Combo,
                                          Bandannies and Kids
"Bringing Up Daughter" ....Estelle
"Don't Look Now" ....Katey, George and Dancers
"Baby's Baby" ....Brawn, Brains and Dancers
   (Dance by Bob Fosse)
"You Walked Out" (Reprise) ....Katey

ACT II

"Call the Police" ....Katey and Policewomen
"Unmistakable Sign" ....Katey and Estelle
"Why Her?" ....George
"Me and Love" ....Katey
"Remember the Dancing" ....Company
   "Hong Kong" ....Estelle and Company
   "Argentine Tango" ....Principal and Captain
   "Sweet William" ....Estelle and Company
"Don't Look Now" (Reprise) ....George
"Little Woman" ....Katey
"Call the Police" (Finale) ....Entire Company

(Closed November 16, 1957)

THE CAVE DWELLERS

(97 performances)

Play in two acts by William Saroyan. Produced by Carmen Capalbo and Stanley Chase at the Bijou Theatre, October 19, 1957.

Cast of characters—

The Duke	Wayne Morris
The Queen	Eugenie Leontovich
The Girl	Susan Harrison
The King	Barry Jones
An Arab Chief	Ivan Dixon
Woman with Dog	Vergel Cook
The Young Queen	Francine Amdur
A Young Man	John Alderman
The Factory Foreman	Ronald Weyand
The Young Opponent	Ivan Dixon
Gorky	Ronald Weyand
The Father	Gerald Hiken
The Mother	Vergel Cook
The Silent Boy	John Alderman
Wrecking Crew Boss	Clifton James
Jamie, a workman	Ivan Dixon

The entire action of the play happens on the stage of an abandoned theatre on the lower East Side of New York, in the midst of a slum-clearing project. The time is the present. Act I.—Scene 1—Early afternoon. Scene 2—A little later. Scene 3—Early that evening. Scene 4—That Night. Scene 5—Late that night. Act II.—Scene 1—The same, several hours later. Scene 2—Early that afternoon. Scene 3—Later that afternoon. Scene 4—A little later. Scene 5—An hour or two later. Scene 6—Early Monday evening.

Staged by Carmen Capalbo; designed by William Pitkin; costumes by Ruth Morley; lighting by Lee Watson; music composed by Bernardo Segáll; production stage manager, Chuck Smith; stage manager, John Weaver; press representative, Samuel J. Friedman.

(Closed January 11, 1958)

MONIQUE

(63 performances)

Play in two acts by Dorothy and Michael Blankfort, based on a novel by Pierre Boileau and Thomas Narcejac. Produced by Shepard Traube (in association with Stephen W. Sharmat) at the John Golden Theatre, October 22, 1957.

Cast of characters—

Fernand Ravinel	Denholm Elliott
Lisette	Deirdre Owen
Lucienne Ravinel	Maureen Hurley
Henriette	Julie Bovasso
Dr. Monique Rigaud	Patricia Jessel
Desiré Merlin	Percy Waram
Gouttez	Neil Fitzgerald
Messenger	William Myers
Andre	Guy Sorel

The entire play takes place in the living room of the Ravinel home. The time is the present. Act I.—Scene 1—An afternoon in late March. Scene 2—A week later, evening. Scene 3—Two days later, late afternoon. Act II.—Scene 1—An hour later. Scene 2—That night. Scene 3—Two weeks later, around noon.

Staged by Shepard Traube; setting by John Robert Lloyd; lighting by Tharon Musser; costumes by Helene Pons; production stage manager, Bill Ross; stage manager, Perry Bruskin; press representative, George Ross.

(Closed December 14, 1957)

COMPULSION

(140 performances)

Play in two acts by Meyer Levin (Producer's Version), based on the novel by Mr. Levin. Produced by Michael Myerberg (in association with Len S. Gruenberg) at the Ambassador Theatre, October 24, 1957.

Cast of characters—

Judd Steiner (today)	Chris Gampel
A Prison Guard	Joseph Beruh
Sid Silver (today)	Gerald Gordon
Judd Steiner (1924)	Dean Stockwell
Artie Straus	Roddy McDowall
Charles Kessler	Ben Astar
Elsie Kessler	Gina Petrushka
A Drugstore Clerk	Joseph Beruh
Horn, the Prosecuting Attorney	Howard Da Silva
Sid Silver (1924)	Gerald Gordon
Al, owner of a speakeasy	Michael Constantine
Myra Seligman	Barbara Loden
Ruth Goldenberg	Ina Balin
A Waiter	Joseph Beruh
A Bartender	Mark Gordon
Oliver Steger	Ben Yaffee
McNamara, a detective	Elliott Sullivan
Padua, assistant to the Prosecutor	Paul Stevens
A Girl on the Telephone	Patricia Roe
Mr. Farmer	James Greene
A Medium	Dorothy Raymond
Billy Straus	Luchino Solito de Solis
Mrs. Straus	Joan Croydon
James Straus	Earl Hammond
Jonathan Wilk, the Defense Attorney	Michael Constantine
First Girl	Muriel Higgins
Second Girl	Patricia Roe
Third Girl	Barbara Miners
Fourth Girl	Suzanne Pleshette
Judah Steiner, Jr.	Bernard Lenrow
Aunt Bertha	Dorothy Raymond
Ferdinand Feldscher	Roger De Koven
Max Steiner	Stefan Gierasch
Sandra Mannheimer	Helen Baron
Swasey, a detective	Ted Gunther
Tom Daly, a reporter	James Bender
Mike Prager, another reporter	John Marley
Lyman, a third reporter	James Ray
Prison Guard	Mark Gordon
Danny Mines, a reporter	Joseph Beruh
Peg Sweet, a newspaper woman	Maybelle Wright

Willie Weiss ....Julian Barry
Raphael Goetz ....James Ray
Milt Lewis ....D. J. Sullivan
Emil, the Steiners' chauffeur ....Chris Gampel
Dr. Stauffer ....Reynolds Evans
Dr. Allman ....Ben Astar
Dr. McNarry ....Lloyd Gough
Dr. Ball ....Michael Constantine
Dr. Vincenti ....James Greene
Judge Matthewson ....Edward Cullen

Act I.—Scene 1—A prison, today. (Chicago, 1924)—Scene 2—Hegewisch Swamp. Scene 3—The Kessler home. Scene 4—The railway station and the Kessler home. Scene 5—A telephone booth and Hartman's Drugstore. Scene 6—The Four Deuces, a speakeasy. Scene 7—A montage. Scene 8—Judd Steiner's room. Scene 9—Artie Straus' room. Scene 10—Judd Steiner's room. Scene 11—The Dunes. Scene 12—The Steiner home. Scene 13—Judd Steiner's room. Scene 14—Hotel rooms. Scene 15—A fraternity house. Scene 16—Hotel rooms. Act II.—Scene 1—A Chicago jail. Scene 2—Jonathan Wilk's study. Scene 3—A Chicago jail. Scene 4—A courtroom.

Staged by Alex Segal; assistant to the producers, Robert Thom; settings by Peter Larkin; costumes by John Boxer; lighting by Charles Elson; production stage manager, John Paul; stage manager, Joseph Kapfer; press representative, Samuel J. Friedman.

(Closed February 22, 1958)

THE SQUARE ROOT OF WONDERFUL

(45 performances)

Play in three acts by Carson McCullers. Produced by Saint Subber and Figaro, Inc., at the National Theatre, October 30, 1957.

Cast of characters—

Paris Lovejoy ....Kevin Coughlin
Mollie Lovejoy ....Anne Baxter
John Tucker ....Philip Abbott
Loreena Lovejoy ....Martine Bartlett
Mother Lovejoy ....Jean Dixon
Phillip Lovejoy ....William Smithers
Joey Barnes ....Kippy Campbell

The setting is an apple farm in Rockland County, N. Y. Act I.—An early spring midnight. Act II.—The next evening. Act III.—Some days later.

Staged by George Keathley; scenery and lighting by Jo Mielziner; costumes by Noel Taylor; production manager, Selma Tamber; stage manager, John Maxtone-Graham; press representative, Dorothy Ross.

(Closed December 7, 1957)

JAMAICA

(244 performances)
(Continued)

Musical in two acts, with book by E. Y. Harburg and Fred Saidy; lyrics by E. Y. Harburg; music by Harold Arlen. Produced by David Merrick at the Imperial Theatre, October 31, 1957.

Cast of characters—

Koli .... Ricardo Montalban
Quico .... Augustine Rios
Savannah .... Lena Horne
Grandma Obeah .... Adelaide Hall
Ginger .... Josephine Premice
Snodgrass .... Roy Thompson
Hucklebuck .... Hugh Dilworth
Island Women .... Ethel Ayler, Adelaide Boatner
The Governor .... Erik Rhodes
Cicero .... Ossie Davis
Lancaster .... James E. Wall
First Ship's Officer .... Tony Martinez
Second Ship's Officer .... Michael Wright
Joe Nashua .... Joe Adams
Dock Worker .... Allen Richards
Radio Announcer .... Alan Shayne
Lead dancers: Alvin Ailey and Christyne Lawson.

Islanders: Ethel Ayler, Adelaide Boatner, Jayne Craddock, Norma Donaldson, Patricia Dunn, Doris Galiber, Lavinia Hamilton, Sandra Hinton, Chailendra Jones, Audrey Mason, Sally Neal, Pearl Reynolds, Christine Spencer, Carolyn Stanford, Jacqueline Walcott, Barbara Wright, George Boreland, Hugh Bryant, Herb Coleman, Hugh Dilworth, Frank Glass, Harold Gordon, Nat Horne, Albert Johnson, Tony Martinez, Jim McMillan, Charles Moore, Allen Richards, Claude Thompson, Roy Thompson, Billy Wilson, Michael Wright, Ben Vargas.

Action takes place on Pigeon Island, a mythical island off Jamaica. The time is the present. Act I.—Scene 1—Grandma Obeah's shack; a day in spring. Scene 2—The knoll near Grandma's shack; next day. Scene 3—Ginger's hut; that evening. Scene 4—Grandma's shack; later that evening. Scene 5—Koli's boat; the same night. Scene 6—Dockside; next morning. Scene 7—The Governor's mansion; a few days later. Scene 8—A night club. Scene 9—The beach at night. Scene 10—Grandma's shack; early evening. Scene 11—Dockside; next morning. Act II.—Scene 1—A bluff on the coast; three days later. Scene 2—The Governor's mansion; next afternoon. Scene 3—A room in the Governor's mansion; a few days later. Scene 4—Koli's fish market; next day. Scene 5—The Governor's mansion; the same day. Scene 6—The knoll; later afternoon of the same day.

Staged by Robert Lewis; production designed by Oliver Smith; choreography by Jack Cole; costumes by Miles White; lighting by Jean Rosenthal; orchestrations by Philip J. Lang; musical direction, continuity and vocals by Lehman Engel; dance music and additional vocals by Peter Matz; production stage manager, Neil Hartley; stage manager, Charles Blackwell; press representative, David Powers.

Musical numbers—

ACT I

"Savannah" .... Koli and Fishermen
"Savannah's Wedding Day" .... Grandma Obeah and Islanders
"Pretty to Walk With" .... Savannah
"Push the Button" .... Savannah
"Incompatibility" .... Koli, Quico and Island Men
"Little Biscuit" .... Cicero and Ginger
"Cocoanut Sweet" .... Grandma and Savannah
"Pity the Sunset" .... Koli and Savannah
"Yankee Dollar" .... Ginger and Islanders
"What Good Does It Do?" .... Koli, Cicero and Quico
"Monkey in the Mango Tree" .... Koli and Fishermen
"Take It Slow, Joe" .... Savannah
Beach at Night (Dance) .... Koli and Islanders
"Ain't It the Truth" .... Savannah

ACT II

"Leave the Atom Alone" .... Ginger and Islanders
"Cocoanut Sweet" (Reprise) .... Savannah
"For Every Fish" .... Grandma and Fishermen
"I Don't Think I'll End It All Today" .. Savannah, Koli and Islanders
"Napoleon" .... Savannah
"Ain't It the Truth" (Reprise) .... Savannah and Islanders
"Savannah" (Reprise) .... Savannah, Koli and Islanders

FAIR GAME

(217 performances)

Comedy in three acts by Sam Locke. Produced by Joseph M. Hyman at the Longacre Theatre, November 2, 1957.

Cast of characters—

Harry Bohlan ....Robert Webber
Lucille Bohlan ....Mary Alice Bayh
Susan Hammarlee ....Ellen McRae
Lou Winkler ....Sam Levene
A Waiter ....Ed Bryce
Arlene ....Sally Gracie
Irene ....Shirley Ballard
Janet ....Diana Millay
Speed Meyers ....Joseph Leon
Professor Spencer Thornton ....Hugh Reilly
Marian Thornton ....Sarah Cunningham
Rush Potter ....Earl George
A Second Waiter ....Paul Marin
Frank Salinder ....Herbert Evers
    Action takes place in New York City. The time is the present.
Act I.—Scene 1—A West Side apartment; early afternoon, late in
January. Scene 2—Dining room and Powder Room of Jimmy's Steak
House; that evening. Scene 3—The apartment; later that night. Act
II—Scene 1—Dressing Room and Office of Winkler Frocks, Inc.;
early in June, late afternoon. Scene 2—The apartment; one hour
later. Scene 3—Professor Thornton's study; immediately after. Act
III.—Scene 1—The Rose Room Supper Club; late that evening.
Scene 2—The apartment; next morning.
    Staged by Paul Roberts; settings by Frederick Fox; costumes by
Robert Mackintosh; production stage manager, Sterling Mace; stage
manager, Martha Handley; press representatives, Nat Dorfman and
Irvin Dorfman.

(Closed May 10, 1958)

RUMPLE

(45 performances)

Musical comedy in two acts, with book by Irving Phillips, lyrics by Frank Reardon and music by Ernest G. Schweikert. Produced by Paula Stone and Mike Sloan at the Alvin Theatre, November 6, 1957.

Cast of characters—

The Chief of Oblivia ....Clayton Coots
Judy Marlowe ....Lois O'Brien
Ginny ....Ginny Perlowin
Judy Marlowe's Friends ....Bonnie West, Janice Wagner,
                                          Sally Wile, Sari Clymas
Nelson Crandal ....Stephen Douglass
Kate Drew ....Gretchen Wyler
Rumple ....Eddie Foy
Anna ....Barbara Perry
J. B. Conway ....Milo Boulton
The Photographers ....Elliott Gould, Larry Stevens

```
Brannigan .......................................Ken Harvey
Barney ..........................................Jackie Warner
Dr. Wellington Winslow .........................Jerome Cowan
Nurse ...........................................Sari Clymas
The Weird Ones .................Elliott Gould, Doris Lorenz,
                                   Pat White, Lila Popper,
                                   Gail Kuhr, William Milié
The Dissenter ..................................George Martin
The Match Box ..............................Claire Gunderman
He Who Gets Slapped ...........................Elliott Gould
Reporter .......................................Eddie Weston
The Powder Room ...................................Pat White
The Unravelled .................................Bonnie West
Girls on a Bench .....................Doris Lorenz, Lila Popper
Lt. Mallory          }
The Voice of Oblivia }..........................Ken Harvey
```

Ensemble: Sari Clymas, Claire Gunderman, Gail Kuhr, Doris Lorenz, Lila Popper, Janice Wagner, Bonnie West, Pat White, Sally Wile; Bill Carter, Elliott Gould, Larry Howard, George Martin, William Milié, Roy Palmer, Larry Stevens, Eddie Weston.

Act I.—Prologue—Somewhere in Oblivia. Scene 1—Nelson Crandal's New York studio apartment; evening. Scene 2—Barney's Bar; later that night. Scene 3—Nelson's apartment; next morning. Scene 4—Central Park; later that morning. Scene 5—Nelson's apartment; that night. Act II.—Scene 1—Office of Dr. Winslow, psychiatrist; afternoon. Scene 2—Barney's Bar; later that afternoon. Scene 3—Nelson's apartment; early evening. Scene 4—Central Park; that night. Scene 5—Nelson's apartment; later that night.

Staged by Jack Donohue; choreography by Bob Hamilton; settings and lighting by George Jenkins; costumes by Alvin Colt; orchestrations by Ted Royal; musical director, Frederick Dvonch; dance music arranged by Robert Atwood; production stage manager, Edward Padula; stage manager, Chet O'Brien; press representative, Samuel J. Friedman.

Musical numbers—

ACT I

```
"It's You for Me" ................Stephen Douglass, Lois O'Brien
"In Times Like These" ...............Eddie Foy, Barbara Perry
"Red Letter Day" .................Gretchen Wyler, Ensemble and
                                                  Jackie Warner
"The First Time I Spoke of You" ...Stephen Douglass, Lois O'Brien
"Oblivia" ...........................Eddie Foy, Barbara Perry,
                                   Cartoon Characters, Holiday Girls
"Peculiar State of Affairs" ...........Eddie Foy, Gretchen Wyler
"How Do You Say Goodbye?" ....................Lois O'Brien
"Gentlemen of the Press" ..............Stephen Douglass, Cartoon
                                     Characters, Holiday Girls
```

ACT II

```
"To Adjust Is a Must" .............Jerome Cowan, Weird Ones
"Coax Me" .....................................Gretchen Wyler
"How Do You Say Goodbye?" (Reprise) ........Stephen Douglass
"All Dressed Up" ..................Gretchen Wyler, Ensemble
"In Times Like These" (Reprise) ...Gretchen Wyler, Jerome Cowan
"Peculiar State of Affairs" (Reprise) ..............Barbara Perry
"Wish" ............................................Eddie Foy
Finale ......................................Entire Company
```

(Closed December 14, 1957)

TIME REMEMBERED

(231 performances)
(Continued)

Comedy in two acts by Jean Anouilh, with English version by Patricia Moyes. Produced by the Playwrights' Company (in association with Milton Sperling) at the Morosco Theatre, November 12, 1957.

Cast of characters—

Amanda, a milliner ....Susan Strasberg
The Duchess of Pont-au-Bronc ....Helen Hayes
Theophilus, a butler ....Frederick Rolf
Lord Hector ....Glenn Anders
The Ice Cream Man ....Le Roi Operti
The Taxi Driver ....George Ebeling
Prince Albert ....Richard Burton
Ferdinand, a headwaiter ....Sig Arno
The Singer ....Stanley Grover
The Pianist ....Edmund Horn
The Violinist ....Seymour Miroff
The Cellist ....Emil Borsody
The Landlord ....Frederic Warriner
Germain, a ghilly ....Truman Gaige
Footmen and Waiters ....E. W. Swackhamer, Fred Starbuck,
                                                George Landolf
    The action takes place in the chateau and park of the Duchess of Pont-au-Bronc. Act I.—Scene 1—A study in the chateau; late afternoon. Scene 2—A clearing in the park; immediately afterward. Scene 3—The study; the following morning. Act II.—Scene 1—The Blue Danube Nightclub; the following evening. Scene 2—Outside the Chime of Bells; the next morning.
    Staged by Albert Marre; music composed by Vernon Duke; production designed by Oliver Smith; costumes by Miles White; lighting by Feder; production stage manager, George Hamlin; stage manager, Robert Fitzsimmons; press representative, William Fields.

See page 99.

NUDE WITH VIOLIN

(86 performances)

Comedy in three acts by Noel Coward. Produced by the Playwrights' Company, Lance Hamilton and Charles Russell at the Belasco Theatre, November 14, 1957.

Cast of characters—

Sebastien ....Noel Coward
Marie-Celeste ....Therese Quadri
Clinton Preminger, Junior ....William Traylor
Isobel Sorodin ....Joyce Carey
Jane ....Angela Thornton
Colin ....John Ainsworth
Pamela ....Iola Lynn

```
Jacob  Friedland .............................Morris  Carnovsky
Anya  Pavlikov .....................................Luba  Malina
Cherry-May  Waterton .........................Mona  Washbourne
Fabrice ........................................Robert  Thurston
Obadiah  Lewellyn ..................................Cory  Devlin
George .........................................Robert  Wark
Lauderdale .....................................Bobby  Alford
```
    The action of the play takes place in Paul Sorodin's studio in Paris.
The time is the present.   Act I.—Afternoon.   Act II.—Scene 1—A
few hours later.   Scene 2—The following afternoon.   Act III.—Scene
1—A few hours later.   Scene 2—The following morning.
    Staged by Noel Coward; production designed by Oliver Smith; cos-
tumes by Frank Thompson; lighting by Peggy Clark; production stage
manager, Keene Curtis; press representative, William Fields.

During the last two weeks of its run, *Nude with Violin* alternated
with performances of Mr. Coward's play, *Present Laughter* (opened
January 31, 1958).

(Closed February 8, 1958)

THE ROPE DANCERS

(189 performances)

Play in three acts by Morton Wishengrad.   Produced by the Playwrights' Company and Gilbert Miller at the Cort Theatre, November
20, 1957.

Cast of characters—
```
Lizzie  Hyland ................................Beverly  Lunsford
Margaret  Hyland .............................Siobhan  McKenna
The  Moving  Man .............................William  Edmonson
Mrs.  Farrow .....................................Joan  Blondell
Clementine ...............................Barbara  Ellen  Myers
James  Hyland ....................................Art  Carney
Lameschnik .....................................Joseph  Julian
The  Cop .........................................Joseph  Boland
Dr.  Jacobson .....................................Theodore  Bikel
```
    The scene of the play is New York City, at the turn of the century.
Act I.—An afternoon in early October.   Act II.—Scene 1—Immediately thereafter.   Scene 2—Half an hour later.   Scene 3—Half an
hour later.   Act III.—Two hours later.
    Staged by Peter Hall; production designed by Boris Aronson; cos-
tumes by Patricia Zipprodt; production stage manager, Lucia Victor;
stage manager, Frank Dudley; press representative, William Fields.

See page 117.

(Closed May 3, 1958)

THE COUNTRY WIFE

(45 performances)

Comedy in three acts by William Wycherly. Produced by the Playwrights' Company, Malcolm Wells and Daniel Blum at the Adelphi Theatre, November 27, 1957.

Cast of characters—

Mr. Horner	Laurence Harvey
Quack	George Tyne
Boy	Willie Wade
Sir Jasper Fidget	Ernest Thesiger
Lady Fidget	Pamela Brown
Mrs. Dainty Fidget, sister of Sir Jasper	Ludi Claire
Mr. Harcourt	Richard Easton
Mr. Dorilant	Peter Donat
Mr. Sparkish	John Moffatt
Mr. Pinchwife	Paul Whitsun-Hones
Mrs. Margery Pinchwife	Julie Harris
Alithea, sister of Pinchwife	Maureen Quinney
Mrs. Squeamish	Colleen Dewhurst
Lucy, Alithea's maid	Joan Hovis
Old Lady Squeamish	Cynthia Latham
Parson	David Vaughan

The scene of the play is London in 1675. Act I.—Scene 1—Horner's lodging. Scene 2—Pinchwife's house. Scene 3—The same. Scene 4—The Royal Exchange. Act II.—Scene 1—Pinchwife's house. Scene 2—Horner's lodging. Scene 3—Pinchwife's house. Act III.—Scene 1—Horner's lodging. Scene 2—The Piazza of Covent Garden. Scene 3—Horner's lodging.

Staged by George Devine; scenery and costumes by Motley; music by Thomas Eastwood; associate producer, Don LaSusa; production stage manager, Howard Whitfield; stage manager, Fred Baker; press representative, William Fields.

(Closed January 4, 1958)

LOOK HOMEWARD, ANGEL

(212 performances)
(Continued)

Play in three acts by Ketti Frings, based on the novel by Thomas Wolfe. Produced by Kermit Bloomgarden and Theatre 200, Inc., at the Ethel Barrymore Theatre, November 28, 1957.

Cast of characters—

Ben Gant	Arthur Hill
Mrs. Marie "Fatty" Pert	Florence Sundstrom
Helen Gant Barton	Rosemary Murphy
Hugh Barton	Leonard Stone
Eliza Gant	Jo Van Fleet
Will Pentland	Tom Flatley Reynolds
Eugene Gant	Anthony Perkins
Jake Clatt	Joseph Bernard

```
Mrs. Clatt .......................................Mary Farrell
Florry Mangle ...............................Elizabeth Lawrence
Mrs. Snowden ...................................Julia Johnston
Mr. Farrell ...................................Dwight Marfield
Miss Brown ......................................Susan Torrey
Laura James ...................................Frances Hyland
W. O. Gant .......................................Hugh Griffith
Dr. McGuire .....................................Victor Kilian
Tarkinton .......................................Jack Sheehan
Madame Elizabeth ..............................Bibi Osterwald
Luke Gant .......................................Arthur Storch
```
The action of the play takes place in the town of Altamont, in the State of North Carolina, in the year 1916. Act I.—Scene 1—A fall afternoon. Scene 2—That evening. Act II.—Scene 1—One week later. Scene 2—Two days later. Act III.—Two weeks later.

Staged by George Roy Hill; settings and lighting designed by Jo Mielziner; costumes by Motley; production stage manager, Kermit Kegley; stage manager, Clifford Cothren; press representatives, James D. Proctor and Merle Debuskey.

See page 136.

THE MAKROPOULOS SECRET

(33 performances)

Play in three acts by Karel Capek, in a new adaptation by Tyrone Guthrie. Produced by the Phoenix Theatre (T. Edward Hambleton and Norris Houghton) at the Phoenix Theatre, December 3, 1957.

Cast of characters—

```
Vitek (a clerk) ...................................Conrad Bain
Berthold Gregor .................................Whitfield Connor
Kristina (Vitek's daughter) ........................Nancy Malone
Dr. Kolonaty ....................................William Hutt
Emilia Marty ....................................Eileen Herlie
Baron Prus .....................................Karel Stepanek
Janek Prus (his son) ...........................Richard Morse
Official of the Opera House .........................Boris Aplon
Opera Manager .................................Taylor Graves
Conductor .....................................Dalton Dearborn
Hauck-Sendorf Ollendorf ...........................Eric House
Servant ........................................Dalton Dearborn
Frantz (Prus's groom) ...........................Taylor Graves
Doctor............................................Boris Aplon
```
The action takes place in the year 1911 in a city in central Europe. Act I.—Dr. Kolonaty's office. Act II.—Backstage of the Opera House next day. Act III—A hotel suite the following day.

Staged by Tyrone Guthrie; settings by Norris Houghton; lighting by Tharon Musser; costumes by Patton Campbell; production stage manager, Robert Woods; stage manager, Jack Merigold; press representative, Ben Kornsweig.

(Closed December 31, 1957)

THE DARK AT THE TOP OF THE STAIRS

(204 performances)
(Continued)

Play in three acts by William Inge. Produced by Saint Subber and Elia Kazan at the Music Box, December 5, 1957.

Cast of characters—

Rubin Flood ....Pat Hingle
Cora Flood ....Teresa Wright
Sonny Flood ....Charles Saari
Boy Offstage .... Jonathan Shawn
Reenie Flood ....Judith Robinson
Flirt Conroy .... Evans Evans
Morris Lacey ....Frank Overton
Lottie Lacey ....Eileen Heckart
Sammy Goldenbaum ....Timmy Everett
Punky Givens ....Carl Reindel
Chauffeur ....Anthony Ray
    The scene is the home of Rubin Flood, his wife and two children in a small Oklahoma town close to Oklahoma City. The time is the early 1920s. Act I.—A Monday afternoon in early spring. Act II.—After dinner, the following Friday. Act III.—The next day, late afternoon.
    Staged by Elia Kazan; setting by Ben Edwards; costumes by Lucinda Ballard; lighting by Jean Rosenthal; production stage manager, Burry Fredrik; stage manager, Bernard Pollock; press representatives, Harvey B. Sabinson, David Powers, Bernard Simon.

See page 161.

THE GENIUS AND THE GODDESS

(7 performances)

Play in three acts by Aldous Huxley and Beth Wendel, in collaboration with Alec Coppel, based on Mr. Huxley's novel. Produced by Courtney Burr, in association with Liska March, at Henry Miller's Theatre, December 10, 1957.

Cast of characters—

Timmy Maartens ....Billy Quinn
Ruth Maartens ....Nina Reader
Dr. Henry Maartens ....Alan Webb
Katy Maartens ....Nancy Kelly
Bertha ....Olga Fabian
John Rivers ....Michael Tolan
    The entire action of the play takes place in the living room of the Henry Maartens' home in St. Louis during the years 1921 and 1922. Act I.—Scene 1—Evening, early spring, 1921. Scene 2—Morning, some months later. Act II.—Scene 1—Night, two weeks later. Scene 2—Two nights later. Act III.—Scene 1—The next morning. Scene 2—A week later. Scene 3—The next morning.

Production staged and designed by Richard Whorf; costumes by Virginia Volland; produced by arrangement with Malcolm Pearson; stage managers, Jose Vega, Robert H. Paschall; press representative, George Ross.

(Closed December 14, 1957)

A SHADOW OF MY ENEMY

(5 performances)

Play in two acts by Sol Stein. Produced by Nick Mayo at the ANTA Theatre, December 11, 1957.

Cast of characters—

A Man	Leon Janney
Augustus Randall	Ed Begley
Holly Randall, the wife	Anne Hegira
The Second Interrogator, an employee of the Congress	Mason Adams
The First Interrogator, a member of the Congress	William Harrigan
Horace Smith, the friend	Gene Raymond
The Lawyer, Smith's defense counsel	Howard Wierum
The Prosecutor	William Zuckert
Dr. Hans Eberhart, the psychiatrist	John McGovern
Jasper Colgrove, an FBI man	Tom Gorman
Gretchen Muller, a former Communist	Ulla Kazanova
Delilah Franklin, the maid	Alma Hubbard

The Singers: Morris Gesell, Gordon Myers, Charles Bressler, Brayton Lewis.

Act I.—Scene 1—A prologue in the present. Scene 2—August, 1948. Act II.—Some days later.

Staged by Daniel Petrie; production designed and lighted by Donald Oenslager; choral music by Seymour Barab; conducted by Noah Greenberg; assistant to Mr. Mayo, Michael Shurtleff; production stage manager, Ross Bowman; press representatives, Harvey Sabinson, David Powers, Bernard Simon.

(Closed December 14, 1957)

THE MUSIC MAN

(188 performances)
(Continued)

Musical comedy in two acts, with book, music, and lyrics by Meredith Willson; story by Meredith Willson and Franklin Lacey. Produced by Kermit Bloomgarden, with Herbert Greene (in association with Frank Productions, Inc.), at the Majestic Theatre, December 19, 1957.

Cast of characters—

Traveling Salesmen	Russell Goodwin, Hal Norman, Robert Howard, James Gannon, Robert Lenn, Vernon Lusby, Robert Evans
Charlie Cowell	Paul Reed
Conductor	Carl Nicholas

Harold Hill ....Robert Preston
Mayor Shinn ....David Burns
                  ⎧ Ewart Dunlop ....Al Shea
"The Buffalo Bills" ⎨ Oliver Hix ....Wayne Ward
                  ⎨ Jacey Squires ....Vern Reed
                  ⎩ Olin Britt ....Bill Spangenberg
Marcellus Washburn ....Iggie Wolfington
Tommy Djilas ....Danny Carroll
Marian Paroo ....Barbara Cook
Mrs. Paroo ....Pert Kelton
Amaryllis ....Marilyn Siegel
Winthrop Paroo ....Eddie Hodges
Eulalie Mackecknie Shinn ....Helen Raymond
Zaneeta Shinn ....Dusty Worrall
Gracie Shinn ....Barbara Travis
Alma Hix ....Adnia Rice
Maud Dunlop ....Elaine Swann
Ethel Toffelmier ....Peggy Mondo
Mrs. Squires ....Martha Flynn
Constable Locke ....Carl Nicholas
    River City townspeople and kids: Pamela Abbott, Babs Delmore,
Martha Flynn, Janet Hayes, Peggy Mondo, Barbara Williams, Elaine
Swann, Marie Santella, Marlys Watters, James Gannon, Russell
Goodwin, Robert Howard, Peter Leeds, Robert Lenn, Hal Norman,
Carl Nicholas, Joan Bowman, Alice Clift, Nancy Davis, Penny Ann
Green, Lynda Lynch, Jacqueline Maria, Marilyn Poudrier, Pat Mari-
ano, Elisabeth Buda, Babs Warden, Tom Panko, Ronn Cummins,
Robert Evans, Vernon Lusby, Gary Menteer, John Sharpe, Roy Wil-
son, Gerald Teijelo, Bob Mariano, Vernon Wendorf.
    Act I.—Scene 1—A railway coach on the morning of July 4, 1912.
Scene 2—River City, Iowa, center of town, immediately following.
Scene 3—The Paroos' house, that evening. Scene 4—Madison Gym-
nasium, thirty minutes later. Scene 5—Exterior of Madison Library,
immediately following. Scene 6—Interior of Madison Library, immediately following. Scene 7—A street, the following Saturday noon.
Scene 8—The Paroos' porch, that evening. Scene 9—Center of town,
noon on the following Sunday. Act II.—Scene 1—Madison Gymna-
sium, the following Tuesday evening. Scene 2—The Hotel porch, the
following Wednesday evening. Scene 3—The Paroos' porch, immediately following. Scene 4—The footbridge, fifteen minutes later. Scene
5—A street, immediately following. Scene 6—Madison Park, a few
minutes later. Scene 7—River City High School assembly room, immediately following.
    Staged by Morton Da Costa; settings and lighting by Howard Bay;
choreography by Onna White; costumes by Raoul Pene du Bois; orchestration by Don Walker; dance arrangements by Laurence Rosenthal; production associate, Sylvia Drulie; hair styles by Ronald de
Mann; musical direction and vocal arrangements by Herbert Greene;
production stage manager, Henri Caubisens; stage manager, Herman
Magidson; press representative, Arthur Cantor.

Musical numbers—

ACT I

"Rock Island" ....Charlie Cowell and Traveling Salesmen
"Iowa Stubborn" ....Townspeople of River City
"Trouble" ....Harold and Townspeople
"Piano Lesson" ....Marian, Mrs. Paroo, Amaryllis
"Goodnight My Someone" ....Marian
"Seventy Six Trombones" ....Harold, Boys and Girls
"Sincere" ....Olin, Oliver, Ewart, Jacey
"The Sadder-but-Wiser Girl" ....Harold and Marcellus
"Pickalittle" ....Eulalie, Maud, Ethel, Alma,
                        Mrs. Squires, Ladies of River City
"Goodnight Ladies" ....Olin, Oliver, Ewart, Jacey
"Marian the Librarian" ....Harold, Boys and Girls
"My White Knight" ....Marian
"Wells Fargo Wagon" ....Winthrop and Townspeople

ACT II

"It's You" ....Olin, Oliver, Ewart, Jacey, Eulalie,
                                 Maud, Ethel, Alma and Mrs. Squires
"Shipoopi" ....Marcellus, Harold, Marian, Tommy,
                                 Zaneeta and Kids
"Pickalittle" (Reprise) ....Eulalie, Maud, Ethel, Alma,
                                 Mrs. Squires and Ladies
"Lida Rose" ....Olin, Oliver, Ewart, Jacey
"Will I Ever Tell You" ....Marian
"Gary, Indiana" ....Winthrop
"It's You" (Reprise) ....Townspeople, Boys and Girls
"Till There Was You" ....Marian and Harold
"Seventy Six Trombones" and "Goodnight My
   Someone" .... Harold and Marian
"Till There Was You" (Reprise) ....Harold
Finale ....Entire Company

MISS ISOBEL

(53 performances)

Play in three acts by Michael Plant and Denis Webb. Produced by Leonard Sillman and John Roberts at the Royale Theatre, December 26, 1957.

Cast of characters—

Mrs. Ackroyd ....Shirley Booth
Ellen ....Kathleen McGuire
Mrs. Ling ....Edith King
Miriam Ackroyd ....Nancy Marchand
Robin ....Peter Lazer
Howard ....John Randolph
Nurse ....Dinnie Smith
Andrew McNeil ....Robert Duke
   The action takes place in the Ackroyd house in San Francisco. The time is the present. Act I.—An evening in July. Act II.—Scene 1—The following evening. Scene 2—The next morning. Scene 3—An evening in August. Act III.—A morning in September.
   Staged by Cedric Hardwicke; setting by Peter Larkin; lighting by Lee Watson; costumes by Audre; production associate, Jacqueline Adams; entire production supervised by Mr. Sillman; production stage manager, Morty Halpern; stage manager, William Krot; press representative, Samuel J. Friedman.

(Closed February 8, 1958)

THE CHAIRS and THE LESSON

(22 performances)

Two plays by Eugene Ionesco, translated by Donald Watson. Produced by the Phoenix Theatre (T. Edward Hambleton and Norris Houghton) at the Phoenix Theatre, January 9, 1958.

THE CHAIRS
(a "tragic farce")

Cast of characters—

The Old Man ....Eli Wallach
The Old Woman ....Joan Plowright
The Orator ....Kelton Garwood

THE LESSON
(a "comic drama")

Cast of characters—

The Maid ....Paula Bauersmith
The Student ....Joan Plowright
The Professor ....Max Adrian
    Staged by Tony Richardson; settings by Jesse Beers (setting for
"The Chairs" based on original designs by Jocelyn Herbert); lighting
by Tharon Musser; music and sound effects by John Addison; production stage manager, Robert Woods; stage manager, William Armitage; press representative, Ben Kornsweig.

(Closed January 26, 1958)

TWO FOR THE SEESAW

(156 performances)
(Continued)

Play in three acts by William Gibson. Produced by Fred Coe at
the Booth Theatre, January 16, 1958.

Cast of characters—

Jerry Ryan ....Henry Fonda
Gittel Mosca ....Anne Bancroft
    The action takes place this past year, between fall and spring, in
two rooms—Jerry's and Gittel's—in New York City. Act I.—Scene
1—Both rooms; September, late afternoon. Scene 2—Gittel's room;
midnight, the same day. Scene 3—Both rooms; daybreak following.
Act II.—Scene 1—Jerry's room; October, at dusk. Scene 2—Both
rooms; December, at noon. Scene 3—Gittel's room; a Saturday night
in February. Act III.—Scene 1—Gittel's room; midday in March.
Scene 2—Jerry's room; May, at dusk. Scene 3—Both rooms; afternoon, a few days later.
    Staged by Arthur Penn; scenery and lighting by George Jenkins;
costumes by Virginia Volland; production stage manager, Porter Van
Zandt; stage manager, Phillip Pruneau; press representatives, Arthur
Cantor and Ted Goldsmith.

MARCEL MARCEAU

(32 performances)

Program of pantomimes performed by Marcel Marceau and his
partners, Gilles Segal and Pierre Verry. Produced by the New York

City Center Theatre Company (Jean Dalrymple, Director), by arrangements with Ronald A. Wilford Associates, Inc., and Jean de Rigault, at the New York City Center, January 21, 1958.

Repertoire of Marcel Marceau—

PART I

New Style-Pantomimes of Marcel Marceau: Skating, Optical Distances, Racing, The Apache 1900, The Flea Market, The Fair, The Circus Showman, The Drug Store, The Policeman, At the Café, Bird in Flight.
Style-Pantomimes of Marcel Marceau: Walking, Walking Against the Wind, The Staircase, The Bureaucrat, The Dandy, Tug of War, The Tight Rope Walker, At the Clothier, The Sculptor, The Dice Player, The Public Garden, Youth, Maturity, Old Age and Death.
Style-Pantomimes of Gilles Segal: Underwater Fishing, The Watchmaker, The Shower, The Roosters, The Puppeteer, The Letter, The Pianist, The Hairdresser.
Style-Pantomimes of Marcel Marceau and Gilles Segal: The Tug of War, Bicycle Racing, The Tight Rope Walkers, Up and Down a Hill with Handcart.

PART II

BIP—New Repertoire: BIP and the Bumble Bee, BIP in the Subway, BIP as a Baby Sitter, BIP at the Rodeo, BIP Goes to the Moon, BIP as a Violin Virtuoso, BIP at a Society Party, BIP Commits Suicide, BIP as a Fireman.
BIP: BIP as a Lion Tamer, BIP as a Painter, BIP has a Sore Finger, BIP the Tragic Actor, BIP as a Skater, BIP Goes Traveling, BIP Hunts Butterflies, BIP as the Botany Professor, BIP Has a Date, BIP at the Dance Hall, BIP Plays David and Goliath.

Presentation of cards by Pierre Verry; stage manager, Walter Russell; press representatives, Jean Dalrymple and Tom Trenkle.

(Closed February 16, 1958)

SUMMER OF THE 17TH DOLL

(29 performances)

Play in three acts by Ray Lawler. Produced by the Theatre Guild and the Playwrights' Company (by arrangement with the Australian Elizabethan Theatre Trust and St. James's Players, Ltd.) at the Coronet Theatre, January 22, 1958.

Cast of characters—

Pearl Cunningham ....Madge Ryan
Bubba Ryan ....Fenella Maguire
Olive Leech ....June Jago
Emma Leech ....Ethel Gabriel
Barney Ibbot ....Ray Lawler
Roo Webber ....Kenneth Warren
Johnnie Dowd ....Richard Pratt
   The action takes place in the home of Olive Leech and her mother, Emma, in a suburb of Melbourne. The time is December, 1952, during an Australian summer, the five-month lay-off holiday for sugarcane workers. Act I.—Scene 1—Sunday, late afternoon. Scene 2—Next morning. Act II.—Scene 1—New Year's Eve. Scene 2—The following Friday evening. Act III.—Next morning.

Staged by John Sumner; setting by Anne Fraser, supervised by
Marvin Reiss; production associate, Warren Caro; production stage
manager, John Cornell; stage manager, Alan North; press representatives, Walter Alford and Reginald Denenholz.

See page 182.

(Closed February 15, 1958)

THE BODY BEAUTIFUL

(60 performances)

Musical comedy in two acts, with book by Joseph Stein and Will
Glickman; music by Jerry Bock; lyrics by Sheldon Harnick. Produced by Richard Kollmar and Albert Selden at the Broadway Theatre, January 23, 1958.

Cast of characters—

Dave ....Jack Warden
Albert ....William Hickey
Harry ....Lonnie Sattin
Bob ....Steve Forrest
Ann ....Mindy Carson
Dominic ....Edward Becker
Eddie ....Tom Raskin
Richie ....Bob Wiensko
Florence ....Jane Romano
Boxer ....Bill Richards
Handler ....Knute Sullivan
Frank ....Richard Chitos
Nicky ....Tony Atkins
Trainer ....Albert Popwell
Boxer ....Bob Wiensko
Marge ....Barbara McNair
Jane ....Helen Silver
Kathy ....Kathie Forman
Danny ....Tommy Halloran
George ....Armand Bonay
Artie ....Jeff Roberts
Josh ....Alan Weeks
Pete ....Richard De Bella
Phil ....Edmund Gaynes
Announcer ....Jack DeLon
Referee ....Bill Richards
Reporters ....Mace Barrett, Harry Lee Rogers,
                            Mitchell Nutick, Stanley Papich
Gloria ....Mara Lynn
Campbell ....Mark Allen
Two Men ....Jack DeLon, Knute Sullivan
Ben ....Joe Ross
Singers: Dorothy Aull, Mace Barrett, Edward Becker, Jack DeLon,
Bette Graham, Buzz Halliday, Mary Louise, Broc Peters, Tom Raskin,
Joe Ross, Knute Sullivan, Bob Wiensko.
Dancers: Bob Daley, Ethelyne Dunfee, Shellie Farrell, Jeanna
Belkin, Patti Karr, Patsi King, Louis Kosman, Ralph McWilliams,
Mitchell Nutick, Stanley Papich, Albert Popwell, Nora Reho, Bill
Richards, Harry Lee Rogers, Yvonne Othon, James McAnany.
The action takes place in and around New York City at the present
time. Act I.—Scene 1—Dave Coleman's office and the Gym. Scene 2
—Corridor of the Jersey City Arena, next night. Scene 3—The Gym,

the following day. Scene 4—The office. Scene 5—Community Center Playground and nearby street. Scene 6—Several stadiums. Scene 7— Another section of the Gym, a few weeks later. Scene 8—The office. Scene 9—Dressing rooms in the Hartford Arena. Scene 10—The Arena.   Act II.—Scene 1—Summer training camp, a few days later.   Scene 2—Several stadiums.   Scene 3—The office, three months later.   Scene 4—A steam bath.   Scene 5—The street.   Scene 6—Terrace and ballroom of the Stockton home.   Scene 7—Dressing rooms. Scene 8—A stadium corridor.

Staged by George Schaefer; settings and lighting by Jean and William Eckart; costumes by Noel Taylor; dances and musical numbers by Herbert Ross; musical direction and vocal arrangements by Milton Greene; ballet music by Genevieve Pitot; orchestrations by Ted Royal; production stage manager, Michael Ellis; stage manager, Paul Leaf; press representative, Frank Goodman.

Musical numbers—

ACT I

"Where Are They?" ....Jack Warden, Boy Dancers and Singers
"The Body Beautiful" ....Mindy Carson with Bob Daley, Louis Kosman, Mitchell Nutick, Bill Richards, and Harry Lee Rogers
"Pffft'" ... . Steve Forrest and William Hickey
"Fair Warning" ...Barbara McNair and Lonnie Sattin with Dorothy Aull, Bette Graham, Buzz Halliday, Mary Louise, Mace Barrett, Jack DeLon, Tom Raskin, and Knute Sullivan
"Leave Well Enough Alone" ....Mindy Carson
"Blonde Blues" ....Jack Warden
"Blonde Blues Dance" ....Mara Lynn and Jack Warden
"Uh-Huh, Oh Yeah!".......Tony Atkins, Armand Bonay, Richard Chitos, Richard De Bella, Edmund Gaynes, Tommy Halloran, Jeff Roberts and Alan Weeks
"All of These and More" ....Mindy Carson, Steve Forrest and the Ensemble
"Nobility" ....Edward Becker, Bob Daley, Jack DeLon, Broc Peters, Albert Popwell, Tom Raskin, Knute Sullivan and Bob Wiensko
"The Body Beautiful" (Reprise) ....Mindy Carson

ACT II

"Summer Is" ....Singers and Dancers with Kathie Forman
"The Honeymoon Is Over" ....Mara Lynn, Jane Romano and Helen Silver
"Just My Luck" ....Mindy Carson and the Kids
"All of These and More" (Reprise) ....Barbara McNair and Lonnie Sattin
"Art of Conversation" ....William Hickey, Singers and Dancers
"Gloria" ....Jack Warden, Mara Lynn and Dancers
"A Relatively Simple Affair" ...Mindy Carson and Barbara McNair
Finale ....Entire Company

(Closed March 15, 1958)

MAYBE TUESDAY

(5 performances)

Comedy in three acts by Mel Tolkin and Lucille Kallen. Produced by Ethel Linder Reiner and Jack Lawrence at the Playhouse Theatre, January 29, 1958.

Cast of characters—

Mildred ....Myra Carter
Florence ....Brett Somers
Jackie ....Midge Ware

```
Vivian ....................................................Sybil Lamb
Adelle ..............................................Zohra Lampert
Leonard ..........................................Louis Edmonds
Katy ..............................................Patricia Smith
Mark ..............................................Richard Derr
Dr. Roper ........................................Ralph Bell
Sherman ..........................................Robert Elston
Lois ..............................................Alice Ghostley
Arthur ............................................Wynn Pearce
Larry .............................................Barry Newman
Miss Kitchell (offstage voice) ....................Carol Gustafson
```

The play takes place in a West Side, New York City, apartment shared by seven girls working in New York. Act I.—Scene 1—The kitchen; Saturday about noon. Scene 2—The living room; immediately following. Scene 3—The living room; later that afternoon. Act II.—Scene 1—The living room; about 6:30 that night. Scene 2—The living room; a few minutes later. Act III.—Scene 1—The living room and the kitchen; about midnight. Scene 2—The living room; Sunday, about noon.

Staged by Elliot Silverstein; scenery and lighting by Paul Morrison; costumes by Ann Roth; production stage manager, Paul Patrick; stage manager, Robert Livingston; press representative, Ben Washer.

(Closed February 1, 1958)

SUNRISE AT CAMPOBELLO

(140 performances)
(Continued)

Play in three acts by Dore Schary. Produced by the Theatre Guild and Dore Schary at the Cort Theatre, January 30, 1958.

Cast of characters—

```
Anna Roosevelt ....................................Roni Dengel
Eleanor Roosevelt .................................Mary Fickett
Franklin D. Roosevelt, Jr. ........................Kenneth Kakos
James Roosevelt ...................................James Bonnet
Elliott Roosevelt .................................Perry Skaar
Edward ............................................James Earl Jones
Franklin Delano Roosevelt .........................Ralph Bellamy
John Roosevelt ....................................Jeffrey Rowland
Marie .............................................Ethel Everett
Louis McHenry Howe ................................Henry Jones
Mrs. Sara Delano Roosevelt ........................Anne Seymour
Miss Marguerite (Missy) Le Hand ...................Mary Welch
Doctor Bennet .....................................James Reese
Franklin Calder ...................................William Fort
Mr. Brimmer .......................................Clifford Carpenter
Mr. Lassiter ......................................Richard Robbins
Governor Alfred E. Smith ..........................Alan Bunce
Daly ..............................................Jerry Crews
Policeman .........................................Floyd Curtis
Senator Walsh .....................................Vincent Dowling
A Speaker .........................................Edwin Phillips
Stretcher Bearers ....Edwin Phillips, Vincent Dowling, Floyd Curtis
```

Act I.—Scene 1—The living room of the Franklin D. Roosevelt home at Campobello, New Brunswick, Canada, August 10, 1921. Scene 2—The same, September 1, 1921. Scene 3—The same, September 13, 1921. Act II.—Scene 1—The living room of the Franklin D. Roosevelt room in New York, May, 1922. Scene 2—The same, January, 1923. Act III.—Scene 1—The same, May, 1924. Scene 2—Madison

Square Garden (an anteroom), June 26, 1924. Scene 3—The Platform, moments later.
    Staged by Vincent J. Donehue; setting and lighting by Ralph Al-
swang; costumes by Virginia Volland; production stage manager, Jean
Barrere; stage manager, Kenneth Mays; press representatives, Irving
Dorfman and Marjorie Barkentin.

See page 203.

PRESENT LAUGHTER

(6 performances)

Comedy in three acts by Noel Coward. Revived by the Playwrights' Company and Lance Hamilton and Charles Russell at the
Belasco Theatre, January 31, 1958.

Cast of characters—

Daphne Stillington..............................Angela Thornton
Miss Erikson ....Avril Gentles
Fred ....Robert Thurston
Monica Reed ....Mona Washbourne
Garry Essendine ....Noel Coward
Liz Essendine ....Joyce Carey
Roland Maule ....William Traylor
Morris Dixon ....John Ainsworth
Henry Lyppiatt ....Winston Ross
Joanna Lyppiatt ....Eva Gabor
Contesse de Vriac ....Therese Quadri
    The action of the play passes in Garry Essendine's studio in London.
Time: the present. Act I.—Morning. Act II.—Scene 1—Evening,
three days later. Scene 2—The next morning. Act III.—Evening,
a week later.
    Staged by Noel Coward; production designed by Oliver Smith;
costumes by Frank Thompson; lighting by Peggy Clark; production
stage manager, Keene Curtis; stage manager, John Dutra; press representative, William Fields.

For two weeks *Present Laughter* alternated performances with
Nude with Violin. It was first produced in New York by John C.
Wilson at the Plymouth Theatre, October 29, 1946, for 158 per-
formances.

(Closed February 8, 1958)

THE INFERNAL MACHINE

(40 performances)

Play in two acts by Jean Cocteau, in a new adaptation by Albert
Bermel. Produced by the Phoenix Theatre (T. Edward Hambleton
and Norris Houghton) at the Phoenix Theatre, February 3, 1958.

Cast of characters—

The Voice	Claude Dauphin
The Young Soldier	Peter Brandon
The Soldier	Albert Paulson
The Captain of the Patrol	Gene Saks
Queen Jocasta	June Havoc
Teiresias, the High Priest	Philip Bourneuf
Ghost of Laius	Earle Hyman
The Sphinx (The Goddess of Vengeance)	Joan McCracken
Anubis (The Egyptian God of the Dead)	Roberts Blossom
A Theban Mother	Clarice Blackburn
Her Son	Joey Renda
Oedipus	John Kerr
The Drunk	Byrne Piven
The Messenger from Corinth	Bill Penn
Creon, Jocasta's Brother	Martin Rudy
The Old Shepherd	Jacob Ben-Ami
Antigone, daughter of Jocasta and Oedipus	Kimetha Laurie

Act I.—Scene 1—The Ghost. Scene 2—The Sphinx. Act II.—Scene 1—The Wedding. Scene 2—The King.

Staged by Herbert Berghof; scenery by Ming Cho Lee; costumes by Alvin Colt; lighting by Tharon Musser; production stage manager, Robert Woods; stage manager, William Armitage; press representative, Ben Kornsweig.

(Closed March 9, 1958)

OH CAPTAIN!

(135 performances)
(Continued)

Musical comedy in two acts, based on an original screen play by Alec Coppel, with book by Al Morgan and José Ferrer; music and lyrics by Jay Livingston and Ray Evans. Produced by Howard Merrill and Theatre Corporation of America at the Alvin Theatre, February 4, 1958.

Cast of characters—

Captain Henry St. James	Tony Randall
Mrs. Maud St. James	Jacquelyn McKeever
Enrico Manzoni	Edward Platt
The Crew, S.S. Paradise	George Ritner, Bruce MacKay, Louis Polacek, Nolan Van Way
A Clerk	Jack Eddleman
The Neighbors	Betty McGuire, Dee Harless, Jean Sincere
Lisa	Alexandra Danilova
Bobo	Abbe Lane
The Guide	Stanley Carlson
A Spaniard	Paul Valentine
Mae	Susan Johnson

English Townspeople, Dockworkers, Tourists, Parisians: Cherie Burgess, Shirley De Burgh, Sally Gura, Birgitta Kiviniemi, Asia Mercoolova, Kiki Minor, Adriane Rogers, Mona Pivar, Sybil Scotford, Mona Tritsch, Joyce Carroll, Dee Harless, Sheila Matthews, Betty McGuire, Alice Nunn, Jean Sincere, Helene Whitney; Bill Atkinson, Alvin Beam, Kevin Carlisle, Allen Conroy, David Lober, Gordon Marsh, Doug Springer, Ken Urmston, Eddie Verso, Jack Eddleman, Bruce MacKay, Louis Polacek, George Ritner, Tony Rossi, Charles Rule, James Stevenson, Nolan Van Way.

The action is continuous in suburban London, on board the S.S.
Paradise and in Paris.
Staged by José Ferrer; scenery and lighting by Jo Mielziner; cos-
tumes by Miles White; dances and musical numbers created by James
Starbuck; musical direction, vocal and ballet arrangements by Jay
Blackton; production associate, Sylvia Drulie; hair styles by Ernest
Adler; production stage manager, George Quick; stage manager, Doris
Einstein; press representatives, David Powers and Bernard Simon.

Musical numbers—

ACT I

"A Very Proper Town" ....The Captain and the Company
"Life Does a Man a Favor (When It Gives Him
    Simple Joys)" ....Maud and the Captain
"A Very Proper Week" ....The English Townspeople
"Life Does a Man a Favor (When It Leads Him
    Down to the Sea)" ....The Captain, Manzoni and the Crew
"Captain Henry St. James" ....The Crew of the S.S. Paradise
"The Dock Dance" ....The Dockworkers
"Three Paradises" ....The Captain
"Surprise" ....Maud and the Neighbors
"Life Does a Man a Favor (When It Puts Him in
    Paree)" ....The Captain
"Hey Madame" ....Sung and danced by the Captain and Lisa
"Femininity" ....Bobo
"It's Never Quite the Same" ....Manzoni and the Crew
"It's Never Quite the Same" (Reprise)..Maud, Manzoni and the Crew
"We're Not Children" ....Maud and the Spaniard
"Give It All You Got" ....Mae and the Tourists
"Love Is Hell" ....Mae and the Ladies of the Ensemble
"Keep It Simple" ....Bobo and Her Dancing Companions

ACT II

"The Morning Music of Mont-
    martre" ....Mae and the People of Montmartre
"You Don't Know Him" ....Bobo and Maud
"I've Been There and I'm Back" ....Manzoni and the Captain
"Double Standard" ....Bobo and Maud
"All the Time" ....The Captain
"You're So Right for Me" ....Manzoni and Bobo
"All the Time" (Reprise) ....Maud
Finale ....The Entire Company

WINESBURG, OHIO

(13 performances)

Play in three acts by Christopher Sergel, based on the novel by
Sherwood Anderson. Produced by Yvette Schumer, S. L. Adler and
the Saba Company at the National Theatre, February 5, 1958.

Cast of characters—

Mary ....Claudia McNeil
Elizabeth Willard ....Dorothy McGuire
Hop Higgins ....Roland Wood
Seth ....Lee Kinsolving
Turk ....Anthony Tuttle
Art ....Jeff Harris
George Willard ....Ben Piazza
Tom Willard ....James Whitmore
Salesman ....Joseph Sullivan
Ed Crowley ....Wallace Acton

```
Old Pete ........................................Arthur Hughes
Parcival .............................................Ian Wolfe
Will Henderson ................................Crahan Denton
Dr. Reefy ..........................................Leon Ames
Newsboy ..........................................Martin Fried
Mrs. Wilson ......................................Lois Holmes
Mr. Wilson ...................................Woodrow Parfrey
Helen White ...................................Sandra Church
```
The place is a small hotel in Winesburg, Ohio. The time is around the turn of the century. Act I.—An evening in spring. Act II.—The following summer. Act III.—The following fall.

Staged by Joseph Anthony; setting designed by Oliver Smith; lighting by Jean Rosenthal; costumes by Dorothy Jeakins; production stage manager, Bill Ross; stage manager, Leonard Patrick; press representatives, Richard Maney and Martin Shwartz.

(Closed February 15, 1958)

INTERLOCK

(4 performances)

Play in three acts by Ira Levin. Produced by Richard Myers, Julius Fleischmann and Walter N. Trenerry at the ANTA Theatre, February 6, 1958.

Cast of characters—
```
Hilde ..........................................Rosemary Harris
Paul .........................................Maximilian Schell
Lucille ..........................................Georgia Burke
Everett ..........................................John Marriott
Mrs. Price ........................................Celeste Holm
```
The action takes place in Mrs. Price's home in the Gramercy Park section of Manhattan, several years after the Second World War. There are two scenes in each act. Act I.—October. Act II.—November. Act III.—December.

Staged by Philip Burton; setting and lighting by Howard Bay; costumes by Robert Mackintosh; stage manager, Edmund Baylies; press representatives, Harvey B. Sabinson, David Powers and Bernard Simon.

(Closed February 8, 1958)

THE ENTERTAINER

(97 performances)

Play in fifteen scenes by John Osborne. Produced by David Merrick (by arrangement with the English Stage Company & L. O. P. Ltd.) at the Royale Theatre, February 12, 1958.

Cast of characters—
```
Billy Rice (Archie's father) ........................George Ralph
Jean Rice (Archie's daughter by first marriage).....Joan Plowright
Archie Rice .....................................Laurence Olivier
Phoebe Rice (Archie's second wife) .............Brenda de Banzie
Frank Rice (Archie & Phoebe's son) ................Richard Pasco
```

Britannia .... Jeri Archer
William Rice (Archie's older brother) .... Guy Spaull
Graham (Jean's fiancé) .... Peter Donat
    The action of the play takes place in a seaside resort in the north of
England during the Suez Crisis, fall of 1956. Scenes: 1—Overture;
2—Billy and Jean; 3—Archie Rice—"Don't Take Him Seriously"; 4—
Billy, Jean and Phoebe; 5—Archie Rice—"In Trouble Again"; 6—
Billy, Jean, Phoebe and Archie; 7—Overture; 8—Billy, Phoebe, Jean,
Archie and Frank; 9—Archie Rice—"Interrupts the Program"; 10—
Billy, Phoebe, Jean, Archie and Frank; 11—Overture; 12—Billy,
Phoebe, Jean, Archie and Frank; 13—"The Good Old Days Again";
14—Jean and Graham, Archie and Billy; 15—Archie Rice—"The One
and Only."
    Staged by Tony Richardson; music by John Addison; settings by
Alan Tagg; costumes by Clare Jeffery; lighting and design supervision
by Tharon Musser; musical director, Gershon Kingsley; stage manager, Don Wilson; press representative, Harvey Sabinson.

See page 225.

(Closed May 10, 1958)

CLOUD 7

(11 performances)

Comedy in three acts by Max Wilk. Produced by Milton Baron
and Marshall Earl at the John Golden Theatre, February 14, 1958.

Cast of characters—

D. Barstow Trumbull .... John McGiver
Secretary .... Alison Adams
Newton Reece .... Ralph Meeker
Commuter .... Richard McMurray
Sally Reece .... Anne Helm
Russ .... James Valentine
Mary Reece .... Martha Scott
Beismuller .... Richard Hamilton
William Doubleday .... Robert Eckles
Marlowe .... Charles C. Welch
Fiona Bostwick .... Mary Cooper
Delivery Boy .... Terry Doyle
Mrs. Potter .... Cele McLaughlin
Mrs. Doubleday .... Harriet MacGibbon
Mrs. Finch .... Mary Bell
Dudley R. Bostwick............................... Charles White
Helga Quinn .... Louise Hoff
    The action of the play takes place in the living room of Newton
Reece's home in Green Haven, Connecticut; also in and out of various
peripheral places that reveal themselves in the different scenes of the
three acts that continue from a Tuesday evening through Thursday
evening in the same week of the present time.
    Staged by Jed Horner; settings and lighting by Albert Johnson;
costumes by Alice Gibson; stage manager, John Drew Devereaux; press
representatives, James D. Proctor and Merle Debuskey.

(Closed February 22, 1958)

ANNIE GET YOUR GUN

(16 performances)

Musical comedy in two acts by Herbert and Dorothy Fields; music and lyrics by Irving Berlin. Revived by the New York City Center Light Opera Company (Jean Dalrymple, Director) at the New York City Center, February 19, 1958.

Cast of characters—

Children	Christopher Shea Trenkle, Diane Ramey
Charlie Davenport	Jack Whiting
Indians	Stuart Hodes, Edward Villella
Property Man	Jack Emrek
Foster Wilson	Leo Lucker
Coolie	Bert Wood
Dolly Tate	Margaret Hamilton
Winnie Tate	Rain Winslow
Tommy Keeler	Richard France
Frank Butler	David Atkinson
Annie Oakley	Betty Jane Watson
Her Sisters	Dorleen Thomas, Elaine Lynn, Penny Grayam
Brother	Flip Mark
Buffalo Bill	James Rennie
Mrs. Little Horse	Hertha Shea
Mrs. Black Tooth	Jan Canada
Trainman	Laurence Watson
Porters	John Bouie, Walter P. Brown
Riding Mistress	Ruthanna Boris
Pawnee Bill	William LeMassena
Sitting Bull	Harry Bellaver
Indian Dancer	Stuart Hodes
Majordomo	John Bouie
Waiters	Walter P. Brown, Laurence Watson
Schuyler Adams	Jack Rains
Mrs. Adams	Basha Regis
Dr. Ferguson	Jack Irwin
Mrs. Ferguson	Barbara Saxby
Sylvia Potter-Porter	Clare Waring

Singers: Jane Burke, Janet Canada, Naomi Collier, Patricia Finch, Bonnie Lawrence, Nancy Radcliffe, Basha Regis, Barbara Saxby, Kenneth Ayers, Ralph W. Farnworth, Jack Irwin, Sam Kirkham, Stanley Page, Edgar Powell, Jack Rains, Casper Roos, Van Stevens, Ralph Vucci, Wendell Lynn.

Dancers: Joan Dubrow, Beverly Gaines, Lida Gaschke, Dorothy Hill, Iva March, Miriam Pandor, Fleur Raup, Renee Slade, Carolee Winchester, Doris Wright, Allen Byrns, Marvin Gordon, Charles Jackson, Daniel Jogalsky, Edward Monson, James Moore, Harold Pittard, Parker Wilson, Vic Vallaro.

Staged by Daniel Burr; dances and musical numbers staged by Helen Tamaris; settings by George Jenkins; lighting by Peggy Clark; costume supervisor, Florence Klotz; musical director, Frederick Dvonch; general stage manager, Herman Shapiro.

Annie Get Your Gun was first produced by Richard Rodgers and Oscar Hammerstein II at the Imperial Theatre, May 16, 1946, for 1,147 performances.

(Closed March 2, 1958)

THE DAY THE MONEY STOPPED

(4 performances)

Play in two scenes by Maxwell Anderson and Brendan Gill, based on the novel by Mr. Gill. Produced by Stanley Gilkey and the Producers Theatre at the Belasco Theatre, February 20, 1958.

Cast of characters—

Boaz Bridges	William Hansen
Richard Morrow	Kevin McCarthy
Ellen Wells	Collin Wilcox
Kathie Morrow	Mildred Natwick
Charles Morrow	Richard Basehart

The action takes place in the law offices of Morrow and Morrow in a Connecticut town. The time is not so long ago. Scene 1—A spring morning. Scene 2—A moment later.

Staged by Harold Clurman; setting and lighting by Jo Mielziner; costumes by Betty Coe Armstrong; production stage manager, Frederic de Wilde; press representative, Barry Hyams.

(Closed February 22, 1958)

PORTOFINO

(3 performances)

Musical comedy in two acts, with music by Louis Bellson and Will Irwin; book and lyrics by Richard Ney; additional lyrics by Sheldon Harnick. Produced by Richard Ney at the Adelphi Theatre, February 21, 1958.

Cast of characters—

Nicky	Georges Guetary
Kitty	Helen Gallagher
Padre, Guido	Robert Strauss
Angela	Jan Chaney
Sandro	Wallace Eley
Tullio	Darryl Richard
Tavern Keeper	Webb Tilton

Singers: Patricia Greenwood, Louise Pearl, Joy Marlene, Joy Lynne Sica, Lynne Stuart, Marvin Goodis, Mitchell May, Charles Aschmann, Bill Ryan, Pat Tolson, Jim Fullerton.

Dancers: Kenley Hammond, Leslie Snow, Sally Wile, Barbara Richman, Gerrie Still, Sari Clymas, Patricia Ann White, Karen Sargent, Roy Palmer, Diki Lerner, Harvey Jung, Jimmy Kirby, Stuart Fleming, John Foster, Hilbert Rapp, Tom Hester.

The time is today. The scene is a piazza in Portofino, a lovely Italian resort town. Act I.—Early evening. Act II.—Scene 1—Immediately following. Scene 2—The next morning.

Staged by Karl Genus; choreography by Charles Weidman and Ray Harrison; scenery by Wolfgang Roth; costumes by Michael Travis; lighting by Lee Watson; orchestrations by Philip Lang; vocal arrangements by Joseph Moon; musical director, Will Irwin; assistant to Mr. Ney, Teresa Calabrese; production stage manager, Jerry Leider; stage manager, Morgan James; press representative, David Lipsky.

THE BEST PLAYS OF 1957–1958

Musical numbers—

Prologue .... Padre

ACT I

Opening—"Come Along"
"No Wedding Bells for Me" ....Company
Festa—"Come Along" (Reprise) ....Nicky
"Red-Collar Job" ....Company
"Here I Come" ....Guido
"New Dreams for Old" ....Kitty
"A Dream for Angela" ....Nicky
"Isn't It Wonderful?" ....Angela
"Dance of the Whirling Wimpus" ....Kitty, Nicky and Company
"Under a Spell" ....Nicky and Girls

ACT II

"Under a Spell" (Reprise) ....Nicky and Girls
"That's Love" ....Nicky and Company
"Too Little Time for Love" ....Tavern Keeper
"Guido's Tango" ....Guido and Kitty
"It Might Be Love" ....Nicky
"Here I Come" (Reprise) ....Kitty
"Bacchanale" ....Company
"Morning Prayer" ....Company
"Kitty Car Ballet" ....Kitty and Boys
"The Grand Prix of Portofino" ....Company
"Portofino" ....Nicky
"I'm in League with the Devil" ....Kitty
"Why Not for Marriage" ....Nicky
"Portofino" (Reprise) ....Company

(Closed February 22, 1958)

BLUE DENIM

(108 performances)
(Continued)

Play in three acts by James Leo Herlihy and William Noble. Produced by Barbara Wolferman and James Hammerstein at the Playhouse Theatre, February 27, 1958.

Cast of characters—

Arthur Bartley ....Burt Brinckerhoff
Major Bartley ....Chester Morris
Lillian Bartley ....Pat Stanley
Jessie Bartley ....June Walker
Ernie Lacey ....Warren Berlinger
Janet Willard ....Carol Lynley

The entire action of the play takes place in the Bartley home in Detroit. The time is the present. Act I.—An early May evening, after dinner. Act II.—Scene 1—July, a Tuesday evening. Scene 2—The following Thursday evening. Act III.—Friday evening.

Staged by Joshua Logan; setting by Peter Larkin; lighting by Charles Elson; costumes by Alvin Colt; production stage manager, Edward Whitfield; press representatives, Sol Jacobson, Lewis Harmon and Helen Hoerle.

WHO WAS THAT LADY I SAW YOU WITH?

(104 performances)
(Continued)

Comedy in two acts by Norman Krasna. Produced by Leland Hayward at the Martin Beck Theatre, March 3, 1958.

Cast of characters—

David Williams	Peter Lind Hayes
Michael Haney	Ray Walston
Schultz	Wallace Rooney
Ann Williams	Mary Healy
Robert Doyle	William Swetland
Secretary	Joan Morgan
Harry Powell	Roland Winters
Waiter	Stephen C. Cheng
Lee Wong	Richard Kuen Loo
Gloria Coogle	Roxanne Arlen
Florence Coogle	Virginia de Luce
Joe Bendix	Pete Gumeny
Evans	Robert Burr
Parker	Frank Milan
Orlov	Larry Storch
Belka	Gregory Morton
First Tenant	Pete Gumeny
Second Tenant	Pamela Curran
Building Employee	W. Edgar Rooney
Third Tenant	Joan Morgan
McCarthy	Dan Frazer

Act I.—Scene 1—An office in Columbia University, four P.M. Scene 2—A shop of the Columbia Broadcasting System, five P.M. Scene 3—The Williams' living room, seven P.M. Scene 4—The New York office of the Federal Bureau of Investigation, next day, ten A.M. Scene 5—The office in Columbia University, four P.M. Scene 6—The Williams' living room, five minutes later. Scene 7—A telephone booth; the F.B.I. office; fifteen minutes later. Scene 8—The Williams' living room, six P.M. Scene 9—A Chinese restaurant off Broadway, six-thirty P.M. Act II.—Scene 1—The F.B.I. office, midnight. Scene 2—The Williams' living room, next day, nine A.M. Scene 3—The F.B.I. office, ten A.M. Scene 4—Inside the Empire State Building, four P.M.

Staged by Alex Segal; settings by Rouben Ter-Arutunian; costumes by Ruth Morley; music by Bernard Green; production stage manager, David Gray, Jr.; stage manager, Bert Gruver; press representative, Abner D. Klipstein.

THE WALTZ OF THE TOREADORS

(31 performances)

Comedy in three acts by Jean Anouilh, with an English version by Lucienne Hill. Revived by Robert Whitehead at the Coronet Theatre, March 4, 1958.

Cast of characters—

Mme. St. Pé ....Lili Darvas
General St. Pé ....Melvyn Douglas
Gaston, his secretary ....John Stewart
Sidonia, his daughter ....Martha Orrick
Estelle, another daughter ....Mary Grace Canfield
Doctor Bonfant ....George Macready
First Maid ....Miriam Phillips
Mlle. de Ste-Euverte ....Betty Field
Mme. DuPont-Fredaine ....Patricia Falkenhain
Father Ambrose ....Robert Geiringer
New Maid ....Patricia Fay

   The action of the play takes place in the home of General St. Pé in
France, about 1910. Act I.—In two scenes. Act II.—In two scenes.
Act III.

   Staged by Harold Clurman; designed by Ben Edwards; production
stage manager, Paul A. Foley; stage manager, Norman Kean; press
representative, Barry Hyams.

The Waltz of the Toreadors was first produced January 17, 1957,
by the Producers Theatre (Robert Whitehead) at the Coronet Theatre, for 132 performances.

(Closed March 29, 1958)

WONDERFUL TOWN

(16 performances)

Musical comedy in two acts, based on the play *My Sister Eileen*
by Joseph Fields and Jerome Chodorov and the stories by Ruth Mc-
Kenney; book by Joseph Fields and Jerome Chodorov; music by
Leonard Bernstein; lyrics by Betty Comden and Adolph Green. Revived by the New York City Light Opera Company (Jean Dalrymple, Director) at the New York City Center, March 5, 1958.

Cast of characters—

Guide ....Wayne Sherwood
Appopolous ....George Givot
Lonigan ....Jack Rains
Helen ....Betsy von Furstenberg
Wreck ....Jordan Bentley
Violet ....Paula Wayne
Valenti ....Ted Beniades
Eileen ....Jo Sullivan
Ruth ....Nancy Walker
A Strange Man ....Don Grusso
Drunks ....Daniel P. Hannafin, Jack Fletcher
Robert Baker ....Peter Cookson
Associate Editors ....Bill Walker, Mark Zeller
Mrs. Wade ....Cris Alexander
Chef ....Mark Zeller
Waiter ....Robert Grant
Delivery Boy ....Alan Johnson
Chick Clark ....Frank Maxwell
Shore Patrolman ....Bill Walker
First Cadet ....Rudy del Campo

Second Cadet ....Gerald Fries
Policeman ....Daniel P. Hannafin
Ruth's Escort ....Jack Fletcher
Greenwich Villagers:
    Singers: Joan Fagan, Pat Hall, Jane A. Johnston, Barbara A. Lock-
ard, Sadie McCollum, Genevieve Owens, Laine Roberts, Susan Terry,
Paula Wayne, Elmarie Wendel, Robert Atherton, Robert Grant, Dan-
iel P. Hannafin, Bob Maxwell, Jack Rains, Wayne Sherwood, Bill
Walker, Millard Williams, Mark Zeller.
    Dancers: Nora Bristow, Barbara Giné, Bettye Jenkins, Jeannie
Jones, Svetlana McLee, Odette Phillips, Carol-Sue Shaer, Gina Tri-
chonis, Rudy del Campo, Ted Forlow, Jerry Fries, Alan Johnson,
John Ira Moore, Eddie Pfeiffer, Marc Scott, Larry Stevens.
    The play takes place in Greenwich Village in the 30s. Staged by
Jerome Chodorov; choreography by Ralph Beaumont; entire production
supervised by Herbert Ross; scenery and costumes by Raoul Pene du
Bois; costume supervision by Ruth Morley; lighting by Peggy Clark;
musical direction and vocal arrangements by Lehman Engel; associate
conductor, Gino Smart; orchestrations by Don Walker; production
stage manager, John Scott; stage manager, Chet O'Brien; press representative, Tom Trenkle.

Wonderful Town was first produced by Robert Fryer at the Winter
Garden Theatre, February 25, 1953, for 559 performances.

(Closed March 16, 1958)

TWO GENTLEMEN OF VERONA

(28 performances)

Comedy by William Shakespeare. Produced by the Phoenix The-
atre (T. Edward Hambleton and Norris Houghton) in the Stratford
Festival Company of Canada's production, at the Phoenix Theatre,
March 18, 1958.

Cast of characters—

Valentine ⎫
Protheus ⎬ The Two Gentlemen ....{ Eric House / Lloyd Bochner }
Speed (servant to Valentine) ....Douglas Rain
Julia ....Ann Morrish
Lucetta ....Helen Burns
Sir Eglamour ....Eric Christmas
Antonio (father to Protheus) ....George McCowan
Panthino (servant to Antonio) ....Powys Thomas
Silvia ....Diana Maddox
Thurio ....Eric Berry
Launce (servant to Protheus) ....Bruno Gerussi
Duke of Milan (father to Silvia) ....Douglas Campbell
Hostess of the Inn ....Amelia Hall
Ursula (maid to Silvia) ....Roberta Maxwell
Artist ....Bill Cole
Well-Bred Outlaws ....Powys Thomas, Bill Cole, John Gardiner
Low-Class Brigands ....George McCowan, Jeremy Wilkin
Ladies ....Helen Burns, Amelia Hall, Gladys Richards, Lois Shaw
Officers ....Powys Thomas, Jeremy Wilkin
Sailors ....Jeremy Wilkin, John Gardiner, Julian Flett
Flunkeys ....John Gardiner, Julian Flett
    Scene: Verona, Milan and a forest near Mantua.

Staged by Michael Langham; designed by Tanya Moiseiwitsch; dances arranged by Tom Brown; music by Louis Applebaum; production stage manager, Robert Woods; press representative, Ben Kornsweig.

(Closed April 20, 1958)

OKLAHOMA!

(16 performances)

Musical in two acts, based on the play *Green Grow the Lilacs* by Lynn Riggs; book and lyrics by Oscar Hammerstein II; music by Richard Rodgers. Revived by the New York City Center Light Opera Company (Jean Dalrymple, Director), by arrangement with Rodgers and Hammerstein, at the New York City Center, March 19, 1958.

Cast of characters—

Aunt Eller	Betty Garde
Curly	Herbert Banke
Laurey	Lois O'Brien
Will Parker	Gene Nelson
Jud Fry	Douglas Fletcher Rodgers
Ado Annie Carnes	Helen Gallagher
Ali Hakim	Harvey Lembeck
Gertie Cummings	Patricia Finch
Sylvie	Gemze de Lappe
Andrew Carnes	Owen Martin
Cord Elam	Sheppard Kerman

Singers: Jane Burke, Jan Canada, Naomi S. Collier, Patricia Finch, Bonnie Lawrence, Wendy Martin, Nancy Radcliffe, Barbara Saxby, Lois Van Pelt, Lynn Wendell, Kenneth Ayers, Ralph Farnworth, Jack Irwin, Barney Johnston, Sam Kirkham, Stanley Page, Edgar Powell, Casper Roos, Van Stevens, Ralph Vucci.

Dancers: Patricia Birsh, Isabelle Farrell, Ruby Herndon, Marilyn Kessler, Naomi Marritt, Ellen Matthews, Elicia Miller, Ilona Murai, Nana Predente, Evelyn Taylor, Toodie Wittmer, Jenny Workman, Richard Colacino, Marvin Gordon, Thomas W. Hasson, James Maher, Gene Neal, David Neuman, William Ross, Eddie Weston.

The time is just after the turn of the century; the place is Indian Territory, now Oklahoma.

Staged by John Fearnley (originally directed by Rouben Mamoulian); dances by Agnes de Mille restaged by Gemze de Lappe; settings by Lemuel Ayers; lighting by Peggy Clark; costume supervisor, Florence Klotz; musical director, Frederick Dvonch.

Oklahoma! was first produced March 31, 1943, by the Theatre Guild. It set the long-run record for American musicals with 2,248 performances. It was revived by Rodgers and Hammerstein at the New York City Center, August 31, 1953, for 40 performances.

(Closed March 30, 1958)

BACK TO METHUSELAH

(29 performances)

Play by Bernard Shaw, in a new two-act version by Arnold Moss. Produced by the Theatre Guild, in association with Arnold Moss, at the Ambassador Theatre, March 26, 1958.

Cast of characters—

Bernard Shaw	Arnold Moss
Adam	Tyrone Power
Eve	Faye Emerson
The Serpent	Valerie Bettis
Cain	Richard Easton
Dr. Conrad Barnabas	Arthur Treacher
Parlourmaid	Faye Emerson
Rev. William Haslam	Tyrone Power
The Accountant General	Arthur Treacher
The Archbishop	Tyrone Power
Mrs. Lutestring	Faye Emerson
Fusima	Valerie Bettis
Elderly Gentleman	Arthur Treacher
Zozim	Tyrone Power
Zoo	Faye Emerson
Strephon	Richard Easton
Chloe	Valerie Bettis
The Ancient	Tyrone Power
The Newly Born	Deirdre Owen
Lilith	M'el Dowd

Act I.—Scene 1—The Garden of Eden; in the Beginning. Scene 2—An oasis in Mesopotamia; a few centuries later. Scene 3—The study of Dr. Barnabas; in the early 1920s. Act II.—Scene 1—The Thing Happens; the office of the Accountant General, 2108 A.D. Scene 2—The Tragedy of an Elderly Gentleman; Galway Bay, Ireland, a summer day, 3000 A.D. Scene 3—As Far as Thought Can Reach; 31,958 A.D.

Staged by Margaret Webster; scenery and lighting by Marvin Reiss; costumes by Patricia Zipprodt; electronic effects created by Vladimir Ussachevsky and Otto Luening; production stage manager, Marshall Young; stage manager, William Ball; press representatives, Bernard Simon and Nat Dorfman.

Back to Methuselah was first produced by the Theatre Guild at the Garrick Theatre, February 27, 1922.

(Closed April 19, 1958)

THE BROKEN JUG

(12 performances)

Comedy by Donald Harron, based on the German play by Heinrich von Kleist. The Stratford Festival Company of Canada's production presented by the Phoenix Theatre (T. Edward Hambleton and Norris Houghton) at the Phoenix Theatre, April 1, 1958.

Cast of characters—

Bridget Turkeyfoot	Amelia Hall
Margaret	Diana Maddox
Judge Adam	Douglas Campbell
Dermot Huish (Adam's clerk)	Douglas Rain
Quant (constable)	Eric Christmas
Georges de Moulinville	Bruno Gerussi
Jessie Gillick	Helen Burns
Achille de Moulinville	Powys Thomas
Eva Gillick	Ann Morrish
Sergeant	Jeremy Wilkin
Major Clovell	Eric Berry
Solomon Doolittle	Bill Cole
Joseph Baggot	John Gardiner
Abner Slee	Julian Flett
Humphrey (courier)	George McCowan

Scene: the house of the Magistrate of a small settlement of western upper Canada early in 1813, during the war between Canada and the States.

Staged by Michael Langham; designed by Tanya Moiseiwitsch; production stage manager, Robert Woods; press representative, Ben Kornsweig.

(Closed April 13, 1958)

SAY, DARLING

(68 performances)
(Continued)

Comedy in three acts by Richard Bissell, Abe Burrows and Marian Bissell, based on the novel by Mr. Bissell; with songs by Betty Comden, Adolph Green and Jule Styne. Produced by Jule Styne and Lester Osterman at the ANTA Theatre, April 3, 1958.

Cast of Characters—

Mr. Schneider	Gordon B. Clarke
Frankie Jordan	Constance Ford
Jack Jordan	David Wayne
Photographer	Jack Naughton
Pilot Roy Peters	Jack Manning
Ted Snow	Robert Morse
June, the secretary	Eileen Letchworth
Schatzie Harris	Horace McMahon
Richard Hackett	Jerome Cowan
Irene Lovelle	Vivian Blaine
Rudy Lorraine	Johnny Desmond
Sidemen	Wendell Marshall, Peter Howard
Charlie Williams	Robert Downing
Maurice, a pianist	Colin Romoff
Arlene McKee	Wana Allison
Jennifer Stevenson	Jean Mattox
Earl Jorgeson	Elliott Gould
Cheryl Merrill	Virginia Martin
Accompanist	Peter Howard
Sammy Miles	Steve Condos
Rex Dexter	Mitchell Gregg
Boris Reschevsky	Matt Mattox
Waiter	Jack Naughton
Morty Krebs	Walter Klavun
Tatiana	Jean Mattox
Joyce	Kelly Leigh

Kids in the show: Wana Allison, Marcella Dodge, Barbara Hoyt, Kelly Leigh, Julie Marlowe, Jean Mattox, Carolyn Morris, Elliott Gould, Charles Morrell, Richard Tone, Calvin von Reinhold.

Act I.—Scene 1—An airport in the Corn Country. Scene 2—Hackett & Snow's office in the Big City. Scene 3—Stamford: the house that Jack took. Scene 4—The office. Act II.—Scene 1—The auditions. Scene 2—Stamford. Scene 3—Rehearsals. Scene 4—Stamford. Scene 5—Irene Lovelle's apartment. Scene 6—Stamford. Act III.—Scene 1—That hotel room in New Haven. Scene 2—Stamford. Scene 3—Back to that hotel room in New Haven. Scene 4—Idlewild Airport in New York. The time is the present.

Staged by Abe Burrows; costumes by Alvin Colt; lighting by Peggy Clark; dances by Mr. Mattox; Colin Romoff and Peter Howard at the pianos; associate producer, George Gilbert; production stage manager, Robert Downing; stage manager, Daniel S. Broun; press representative, John L. Toohey.

Musical numbers—

ACT I

"Try to Love Me"
"It's Doom"
"The Husking Bee"

ACT II

"It's the Second Time You Meet That Matters"
"Chief of Love"
"Say, Darling"
"The Carnival Song"

ACT III

"Try to Love Me"
"Dance Only with Me"
"Something's Always Happening on the River"

JOYCE GRENFELL

(24 performances)

A program of monologues and songs, written by Miss Grenfell, with music by Richard Addinsell. Produced by Roger L. Stevens and Laurier Lister at the Lyceum Theatre, April 7, 1958.

Program—

PART I

Opening Numbers
Wibberly
Songs of Many Lands
Writer of Children's Books
Piano Interlude
  (music by George Gershwin)
Artist's Room
Picture Postcard
Boat Train
Joyful Noise
  (music by Donald Swann)

PART II

The Woman on the Bus
Friend to Tea
Songs My Mother Taught Me
  (arranged by Viola Tunnard)
Committee
Three Brothers

Shirl's Girl Friend: the Giant Wheel
Piano Interlude
  (music by George Gershwin)
A Thought for Today
Time
Nursery School: Free Activity Period
It's Almost Tomorrow
   George Bauer at the piano; Miss Grenfell's dresses by Victor Stiebel; production stage manager, Constance Alderson; press representative, William Fields

(Closed April 26, 1958)

THE NEXT PRESIDENT

(13 performances)

A "musical salmagundi." Produced by Frank B. Nichols at the Bijou Theatre, April 9, 1958.

Principals—

Mort Sahl
The Jimmy Giuffre 3 (Mr. Giuffre, Bob Brookmeyer and Jim Hall)
Anneliese Widman
The Folk Singers (David Allen, Erik Darling, Robin Howard, Dylan Todd, Mary Allin Travers, Donald Vogel, Stan Watt, Caroly Wilcox)

Program—

PART I: THE STATUS QUO
1. The Chorus of Collective Conscience ....The Folk Singers
2. "Cry Holy" ....The Folk Singers
3. A Night-to-Night Report of the News
     with Complete Flexibility as to Foreign Policy ....Mort Sahl
4. The Jimmy Giuffre 3
5. "Gotta Dance" ....Anneliese Widman
6. "Deep Blue Sea" ....The Folk Singers
7. Mort Sahl
               PART II: A BRAND NEW ATTITUDE
                WITH THE SAME OLD PREJUDICES
1. "He's Gone Away"...........................The Folk Singers
2. "The Green Country" ....The Jimmy Giuffre 3
3. "Cloudy Morning" ....David Allen
4. Animation ....Anneliese Widman
5. Mort Sahl
6. Press Conference .. ..Mort Sahl and The Folk Singers
   Staged by Frank B. Nichols; production designed by Lee Watson; production stage manager, Robert Livingston; press representative, Arthur Cantor.

(Closed April 19, 1958)

LOVE ME LITTLE

(8 performances)

Comedy in two acts by John G. Fuller, adapted from the novel by Amanda Vail. Produced by Alexander H. Cohen at the Helen Hayes Theatre, April 15, 1958.

Cast of characters—

Emily Whittaker ....Susan Kohner
Amy ....Joan Hovis
Jean ....Sarah Hardy
Nancy ....Lin Pierson
Sally ....Marlene Cameron
Sue Fosburgh ....Avra Petrides
Father ....Donald Cook
Mother ....•...............Joan Bennett
Laurie Trumbull ....Meg Mundy
Lester ....Robert Dowdell
Stanley ....Hal England
William ....Nicholas Pryor
Greg ....Dana White
 At the dance: Joseph Cronin, June Deutsch, Marc Vinson.
 The action of the play takes place at the Woodley Hall School for Girls near Hartford, Connecticut, the Whittaker apartment in New York City, and at Stover Island.
 Staged by Alfred Drake; scenery designed by Ralph Alswang; clothes by Motley; production associate, Arthur C. Twitchell, Jr.; production stage manager, Mary Ellen Hecht; stage manager, Leonard Patrick; press representatives, Richard Maney and Martin Shwartz.

(Closed April 19, 1958)

LE THEATRE DU NOUVEAU MONDE

(16 performances)

Repertory of plays by Moliere, in French, presented in two programs. Le Theatre du Nouveau Monde productions presented by the Phoenix Theatre (T. Edward Hambleton and Norris Houghton) at the Phoenix Theatre, April 29, 1958, and May 6, 1958.

Repertoire—

 Le Malade Imaginaire, a comedy in three acts by Moliere; staged by Jean Gascon; sets by Robert Prevost; music by Clermont Pepin.
 An Evening of Three Farces by Moliere: "Le Mariage Force," "Sganarelle," and "La Jalousie du Barbouille"; staged by Jean Gascon and Jean Dalmain; sets by Robert Prevost; music by Pierre Phillipe and Jean-Baptiste Lully (arranged by Clermont Pepin).

Repertory Company—

Huguette Oligny	Guy Hoffman
Victor Desy	Jean-Louis Paris
Georges Groulx	Jean-Louis Roux
Gaetan Labreche	Denyse Saint-Pierre
Denise Pelletier	Jean Gascon
Gabriel Gascon	Jean-Paul Jeannotte

Louise Pichette

Production stage manager, Robert Woods; press representative, Ben Kornsweig.

(Closed May 11, 1958)

THE FIRSTBORN

(38 performances)

Play in seven scenes by Christopher Fry. Produced by Katharine Cornell and Roger L. Stevens (under the auspices of the America-Israel Cultural Foundation, in tribute to Israel's 10th Anniversary) at the Coronet Theatre, April 30, 1958.

Cast of characters—

Anath Bithiah, sister of the Pharaoh ....Katharine Cornell
Teusret, daughter of the Pharaoh ....Kathleen Widdoes
A Guard ....Jack Betts
Kef, a minister ....Chris Gampel
Seti the Second, the Pharaoh ....Torin Thatcher
Rameses, son of the Pharaoh ....Robert Drivas
Moses ....Anthony Quayle
Aaron, his brother ....Michael Strong
Miriam, his sister ....Mildred Natwick
Shendi, Miriam's son ....Michael Wager
Overseers ....Jack Betts, Philip Robinson
   The action of the play takes place in the summer of 1200 B.C., alternating between the palace of Seti the Second at Tanis, Egypt, and the tent of Miriam. The play is in seven scenes.
   Staged by Anthony Quayle; production designed by Boris Aronson; songs by Leonard Bernstein; costumes by Robert Fletcher; lighting by Tharon Musser; production stage manager, Keene Curtis; stage manager, Richard Blofson; press representative, William Fields.

(Closed May 31, 1958)

JANE EYRE

(36 performances)
(Continued)

Play in three acts by Huntington Hartford, based on the novel by Charlotte Bronte. Produced by Courtney Burr, in association with Sterling productions, at the Belasco Theatre, May 1, 1958.

Cast of characters—

Leah, a servant ....Carol Hebald
Mrs. Fairfax, the housekeeper ....Blanche Yurka
Adele Varens, Mr. Rochester's ward ....Susan Towers
Jane Eyre, a governess..............................Jan Brooks
Grace Poole....................................Adelaide Klein
Gregory ....Francis Compton
Edward Rochester, Master of Thornfield .... Eric Portman
Richard Mason, a gentleman from Jamaica ....Frank Silvera
Lady Ingram ....Norah Howard
Hon. Blanche Ingram, her daughter ....Iola Lynn
Lord Ingram, her son ....Adrian Foley
Reverend Wood ....Douglas Wood
Colonel Dent ....George Spelvin
Miss Wood ....Ann Stanwell

Mr. Green ....Richard Nicholls
Briggs ....John Malcolm
Bertha ....Jane White
Guests ....Tom McDermott, Nick Richards
                                               Dorothy Scott
    The entire action of the play takes place in Thornfield Hall, in Millcote, England, during the early part of the nineteenth century. Act I.—Scene 1—Early evening, January. Scene 2—One month later. Act II.—Scene 1—An evening in May. Scene 2—Four weeks later. Act III.—Early evening, one year later.
    Staged by Demetrios Vilan; scenery designed by Ben Edwards; costumes by Motley and Frank Spencer; music arranged by Lehman Engel; stage managers, Charles Durand, Bob Paschall and Tom McDermott; press representative, George Ross.

THE VISIT

(32 performances)
(Continued)

    Play in three acts by Friedrich Duerrenmatt, adapted by Maurice Valency. Produced by the Producers' Theatre at the Lunt-Fontanne Theatre, May 5, 1958.

Cast of characters—

Hofbauer ....Keneth Thornett
Helmesberger ....David Clarke
Wechsler ....Milton Selzer
Vogel ....Harrison Dowd
The Painter ....Clarence Nordstrom
Station Master ....Joseph Leberman
Burgomaster ....Eric Porter
Professor Muller ....Peter Woodthorpe
Pastor ....William Hansen
Anton Schill ....Alfred Lunt
Claire Zachanassian ....Lynn Fontanne
1st Conductor ....Jonathan Anderson
Pedro Cabral ....Myles Eason
Bobby ....John Wyse
Police Chief Schultz ....John Randolph
1st Grandchild ....Lesley Hunt
2nd Grandchild ....Lois McKim
Mike ....Stanley Erickson
Max ....William Thourlby
1st Blind Man ....Vincent Gardenia
2nd Blind Man..................................Alfred Hoffman
Frau Burgomaster ....Frieda Altman
Frau Block ....Gertrude Kinnell
Frau Schill ....Daphne Newton
Ottilie Schill ....Marla Adams
Karl Schill ....Ken Walken
Doctor Nusslin ....Howard Fischer
Athlete ....James MacAaron
Truck Driver ....John Kane
Reporter ....Edward Moor
Townsmen ....Robert Donley, Kent Montroy
    The action of the play takes place in and around the little town of Gullen, somewhere in Europe.
    Staged by Peter Brook; designed by Teo Otto; supervision and lighting by Paul Morrison; Miss Fontanne's costumes by Castillo; production stage manager, Frederic de Wilde; press representative, Barry Hyams.

See page 244.

FACTS AND FIGURES

VARIETY'S TABULATION
OF FINANCIAL HITS AND FLOPS

HITS

Back to Methuselah
Boy Growing Up
Dark at the Top of the Stairs
Entertainer
Look Back in Anger

Look Homeward, Angel
Music Man
Romanoff and Juliet
Two for the Seesaw
West Side Story

STATUS NOT YET DETERMINED

Blue Denim
Jamaica
Jane Eyre
Oh Captain
Say, Darling

Sunrise at Campobello
Time Remembered
The Visit
Who Was That Lady I Saw You
    With?

FAILURES

Body Beautiful
Cave Dwellers
Cloud 7
Compulsion
Copper and Brass
Country Wife
The Day the Money Stopped
The Egghead
Fair Game
Four Winds
The Genius and the Goddess
I Knock at the Door
Interlock
Love Me Little
Mask and Gown
Maybe Tuesday

Miss Isobel
Miss Lonelyhearts
Monique
Nature's Way
Nude with Violin
Portofino
Present Laughter
Rope Dancers
Rumple
Shadow of My Enemy
Simply Heavenly
Square Root of Wonderful
Summer of the 17th Doll
Under Milk Wood
Winesburg, Ohio

SPECIAL, MISCELLANEOUS (UNRATED)

Annie Get Your Gun	Marcel Marceau
Carousel	Oklahoma
The Firstborn	Wonderful Town

CLOSED DURING TRYOUT TOUR

Carefree Heart	Soft Touch
One Foot in the Door	This Is Goggle
Plaintiff in a Pretty Hat	Ziegfeld Follies
Saturday Night Kid	

Holdovers from 1956-1957 Season, Since Clarified

HITS

Bells Are Ringing	New Girl in Town
Hole in the Head	Visit to a Small Planet
Li'l Abner	

FAILURES

Apple Cart	Moon for the Misbegotten
Happiest Millionaire	Potting Shed
Happy Hunting	Waltz of the Toreadors
Hotel Paradiso	Ziegfeld Follies
Major Barbara	

STATISTICAL SUMMARY

(Last Season Plays Which Ended Runs After June 1, 1957)

Plays	Number Performances	Closing Date
The Potting Shed	143	June 1, 1957
The Pajama Game (revival)	23	June 2, 1957
Ziegfeld Follies	123	June 15, 1957
The Diary of Anne Frank	717	June 22, 1957
Inherit the Wind	806	June 22, 1957
A Moon for the Misbegotten	68	June 29, 1957
Hotel Paradiso	108	July 13, 1957
The Happiest Millionaire	271	July 13, 1957
A Hole in the Head	156	July 13, 1957
No Time for Sergeants	796	September 14, 1957
Separate Tables	332	September 28, 1957
Damn Yankees	1,019	October 12, 1957
Happy Hunting	412	November 30, 1957
The Most Happy Fella	676	December 14, 1957
Visit to a Small Planet	388	January 11, 1958
The Tunnel of Love	417	February 22, 1958
Long Day's Journey into Night	390	March 29, 1958
New Girl in Town	431	May 24, 1958

LONG RUNS ON BROADWAY

To June 1, 1958

(Plays marked with asterisk were still playing June 1, 1958)

Plays	Number Performances
Life with Father	3,224
Tobacco Road	3,182
Abie's Irish Rose	2,327
Oklahoma!	2,248
South Pacific	1,925
Harvey	1,775
Born Yesterday	1,642
The Voice of the Turtle	1,557
Arsenic and Old Lace	1,444
Hellzapoppin	1,404
Angel Street	1,295
Lightnin'	1,291
The King and I	1,246
Guys and Dolls	1,200
Mister Roberts	1,157
Annie Get Your Gun	1,147
The Seven Year Itch	1,141
Pins and Needles	1,108
Kiss Me, Kate	1,070
Pajama Game	1,063
The Teahouse of the August Moon	1,027
Damn Yankees	1,019
Anna Lucasta	957
Kiss and Tell	957
The Moon Is Blue	924
* My Fair Lady	923
Can-Can	892
Carousel	890
Hats Off to Ice	889
Fanny	888
Follow the Girls	882

Plays	Number Performances
The Bat	867
My Sister Eileen	865
White Cargo	864
Song of Norway	860
A Streetcar Named Desire	855
Comedy in Music	849
You Can't Take It with You	837
Three Men on a Horse	835
Inherit the Wind	806
No Time for Sergeants	796
Where's Charlie?	792
The Ladder	789
State of the Union	765
The First Year	760
Death of a Salesman	742
Sons o' Fun	742
Gentlemen Prefer Blondes	740
The Man Who Came to Dinner	739
Call Me Mister	734
High Button Shoes	727
Finian's Rainbow	725
Claudia	722
The Gold Diggers	720
The Diary of Anne Frank	717
I Remember Mama	714
Tea and Sympathy	712
Junior Miss	710
Seventh Heaven	704
Cat on a Hot Tin Roof	694
Peg o' My Heart	692

Plays	*Number Performances*	*Plays*	*Number Performances*
The Children's Hour ...	691	Brigadoon	581
Dead End	687	Brother Rat	577
The Lion and the Mouse .	686	Show Boat	572
Dear Ruth	683	The Show-Off	571
East Is West	680	Sally	570
The Most Happy Fella ..	676	One Touch of Venus	567
The Doughgirls	671	Happy Birthday	564
Irene	670	The Glass Menagerie	561
Boy Meets Girl	669	Wonderful Town	559
Blithe Spirit	657	Rose Marie	557
The Women	657	Strictly Dishonorable ...	557
A Trip to Chinatown ...	657	Ziegfeld Follies	553
Bloomer Girl	654	Floradora	553
The Fifth Season	654	Dial "M" for Murder ...	552
Rain	648	Good News	551
Witness for the Prosecu-		Let's Face It	547
tion	645	Within the Law	541
Call Me Madam	644	The Music Master	540
* Li'l Abner	644	Pal Joey	540
Janie	642	What a Life	538
The Green Pastures	640	The Red Mill	531
The Fourposter	632	The Solid Gold Cadillac .	526
* Bells Are Ringing	628	The Boomerang	522
Is Zat So?	618	Rosalinda	521
Anniversary Waltz	615	Chauve Souris	520
The Happy Time	614	Blackbirds	518
Separate Rooms	613	Sunny	517
Affairs of State	610	Victoria Regina	517
Star and Garter	609	The Vagabond King	511
The Student Prince	608	The New Moon	509
* Auntie Mame	605	Shuffle Along	504
Broadway	603	Up in Central Park	504
Adonis	603	Carmen Jones	503
Street Scene	601	The Member of the Wed-	
Kiki	600	ding	501
Wish You Were Here ...	598	Personal Appearance	501
A Society Circus	596	Panama Hattie	501
Blossom Time	592	Bird in Hand	500
The Two Mrs. Carrolls ..	585	Sailor, Beware!	500
Kismet	583	Room Service	500
Detective Story	581	Tomorrow the World ...	500

NEW YORK DRAMA CRITICS CIRCLE AWARDS

At their annual meeting, the New York Drama Critics Circle chose Ketti Frings' *Look Homeward, Angel* (adapted from the Thomas Wolfe novel) as the best new American play of the season. As the best foreign play, the Circle chose John Osborne's *Look Back in Anger,* and as the best musical, Meredith Willson's *The Music Man.*

Circle awards have been—

1935-36—Winterset, by Maxwell Anderson
1936-37—High Tor, by Maxwell Anderson
1937-38—Of Mice and Men, by John Steinbeck
1938-39—No award.
1939-40—The Time of Your Life, by William Saroyan
1940-41—Watch on the Rhine, by Lillian Hellman
1941-42—No award.
1942-43—The Patriots, by Sidney Kingsley
1943-44—No award.
1944-45—The Glass Menagerie, by Tennessee Williams
1945-46—No award.
1946-47—All My Sons, by Arthur Miller
1947-48—A Streetcar Named Desire, by Tennessee Williams
1948-49—Death of a Salesman, by Arthur Miller
1949-50—The Member of the Wedding, by Carson McCullers
1950-51—Darkness at Noon, by Sidney Kingsley
1951-52—I Am a Camera, by John van Druten
1952-53—Picnic, by William Inge
1953-54—The Teahouse of the August Moon, by John Patrick
1954-55—Cat on a Hot Tin Roof, by Tennessee Williams
1955-56—The Diary of Anne Frank, by Frances Goodrich and
          Albert Hackett
1956-57—Long Day's Journey into Night, by Eugene O'Neill
1957-58—Look Homeward, Angel, by Ketti Frings

PULITZER PRIZE WINNERS

For the sixth successive year the Pulitzer Prize went to the same play as the Critics Circle Award—in this case, *Look Homeward, Angel.*
Pulitzer awards have been—

1917-18—Why Marry?, by Jesse Lynch Williams
1918-19—No award.
1919-20—Beyond the Horizon, by Eugene O'Neill
1920-21—Miss Lulu Bett, by Zona Gale
1921-22—Anna Christie, by Eugene O'Neill
1922-23—Icebound, by Owen Davis
1923-24—Hell-bent for Heaven, by Hatcher Hughes
1924-25—They Knew What They Wanted, by Sidney Howard
1925-26—Craig's Wife, by George Kelly
1926-27—In Abraham's Bosom, by Paul Green
1927-28—Strange Interlude, by Eugene O'Neill
1928-29—Street Scene, by Elmer Rice
1929-30—The Green Pastures, by Marc Connelly
1930-31—Alison's House, by Susan Glaspell
1931-32—Of Thee I Sing, by George S. Kaufman, Morrie Ryskind, Ira and George Gershwin
1932-33—Both Your Houses, by Maxwell Anderson
1933-34—Men in White, by Sidney Kingsley
1934-35—The Old Maid, by Zoë Akins
1935-36—Idiot's Delight, by Robert E. Sherwood
1936-37—You Can't Take It with You, by Moss Hart and George S. Kaufman
1937-38—Our Town, by Thornton Wilder
1938-39—Abe Lincoln in Illinois, by Robert E. Sherwood
1939-40—The Time of Your Life, by William Saroyan
1940-41—There Shall Be No Night, by Robert E. Sherwood
1941-42—No award.
1942-43—The Skin of Our Teeth, by Thornton Wilder
1943-44—No award.
1944-45—Harvey, by Mary Coyle Chase
1945-46—State of the Union, by Howard Lindsay and Russel Crouse

1946-47—No award.
1947-48—A Streetcar Named Desire, by Tennessee Williams
1948-49—Death of a Salesman, by Arthur Miller
1949-50—South Pacific, by Richard Rodgers, Oscar Hammerstein
    II and Joshua Logan
1950-51—No award.
1951-52—The Shrike, by Joseph Kramm
1952-53—Picnic, by William Inge
1953-54—The Teahouse of the August Moon, by John Patrick
1954-55—Cat on a Hot Tin Roof, by Tennessee Williams
1955-56—The Diary of Anne Frank, by Frances Goodrich and
    Albert Hackett
1956-57—Long Day's Journey into Night, by Eugene O'Neill
1957-58—Look Homeward, Angel, by Ketti Frings

BOOKS ON THE THEATRE

1957-1958

Abbott, George. *New Girl in Town.* (Music and lyrics by Bob Merrill.) Random House. $2.95.

Adams, W. Bridges. *The Irresistible Theatre:* A History of the English Stage from the Conquest to the Commonwealth. World. $6.00.

Anouilh, Jean. *Five Plays* (Antigone, Eurydice, The Ermine, The Rehearsal, Romeo and Jeannette). Hill and Wang. $1.75 (paper).

Anouilh, Jean. *Time Remembered.* (Adaptation by Patricia Moyes.) Coward-McCann. $2.95.

Beckett, Samuel. *Endgame.* Grove. $1.25 (paper).

Bentley, Eric (Editor). *Let's Get a Divorce! and Other Plays.* (Six French farces.) Hill and Wang. $1.75 (paper).

Blum, Daniel. *Theatre World 1956-57.* Greenberg. $5.00.

Cantor, Eddie, and Ardmore, Jane K. *Take My Life.* Doubleday. $3.95.

Chapman, John (Editor). *Broadway's Best, 1956-57.* Doubleday. $4.50.

Clurman, Harold. *The Fervent Years.* Hill and Wang. $1.35 (paper).

Coward, Noel. *Nude With Violin.* Doubleday. $3.00.

Dryden, John. *Three Plays.* (Conquest of Granada, Marriage à la Mode, Aureng-Zebe.) Hill and Wang. $1.45 (paper).

Enck, John J. *Jonson and the Comic Truth.* University of Wisconsin Press. $5.00.

Ewen, David. *Richard Rodgers.* Holt. $4.95.

Freedley, George. *The Lunts.* Macmillan. $4.50.

Frings, Ketti. *Look Homeward, Angel.* Scribner. $2.95.

Gassner, John W. (Editor). *Best Plays of the Modern American Theatre:* Fourth Series, 1952-57. Crown. $5.75.

Goldsmith, Oliver. *Plays.* (Edited by George Pierce Baker.) Hill and Wang. $1.25 (paper).

Green, Paul. *Drama and the Weather.* Samuel French. $3.00.

Hainaux, Rene. *Stage Design Throughout the World Since 1935.* Theatre Arts. $17.50.

Hazlitt, William. *On Theatre.* Hill and Wang. $1.25 (paper).

Inge, William. *The Dark at the Top of the Stairs.* Random House. $2.95.

Inskip, Donald. *Jean Giraudoux:* The Making of a Dramatist. Oxford. $4.75.

Ionesco, Eugene. *Four Plays.* (The Chairs, The Lesson, The Bald Soprano, Jack or the Submission.) Grove. $3.50.

Knapp, Bettina L. *Louis Jouvet:* Man of the Theatre. Columbia University Press. $6.00.

Kronenberger, Louis (Editor). *The Best Plays of 1956-1957.* Dodd, Mead. $6.00.

Laurents, Arthur B. *West Side Story.* (Lyrics by Stephen Sondheim, music by Leonard Bernstein.) Random House. $2.95.

Lawrence, Jerome, and Lee, Robert E. *Auntie Mame.* Vanguard. $3.50.

Lind, L. R. (Editor). *Ten Greek Plays in Contemporary Translation.* (Aeschylus, Sophocles, Euripides, Aristophanes.) Houghton Mifflin. $4.00.

MacLeish, Archibald. *J.B.* (A Play in Verse.) Houghton Mifflin. $3.50.

Matthews, Brander (Editor). *Papers on Acting.* (Coquelin, Sarcey, Booth, Irving et al.) Hill and Wang. $1.45 (paper).

Matthews, Brander (Editor). *Papers on Playmaking.* (Pinero, Dumas fils, Lope de Vega, Goethe, Sardou, Coquelin, Goldoni et al.) Hill and Wang. $1.35 (paper).

Mayorga, Margaret (Editor). *Best Short Plays.* (20th Anniversary Edition: O'Neill, Saroyan, Tennessee Williams, Maxwell Anderson et al.) Beacon. $6.00.

Moody, Richard. *The Astor Place Riot.* Indiana University Press. $5.00.

Nicoll, Allardyce (Editor). *Shakespeare Survey 11.* Cambridge University Press. $5.50.

O'Neill, Eugene. *A Touch of the Poet.* Yale. $3.75.

Osborne, John. *The Entertainer.* Criterion. $2.75.

Osborne, John. *Look Back in Anger.* Criterion. $2.75.

Pearson, Hesketh. *Gilbert:* His Life and Strife. Harper. $4.50.

Priestley, J. B. *The Art of the Dramatist.* The Writer, Inc. $2.75.

Saroyan, William. *The Cave Dwellers.* Putnam. $3.50.

Schary, Dore. *Sunrise at Campobello.* Random House. $2.95.

Seyler, Athene, and Haggard, Stephen. *The Craft of Comedy.* (2nd edition.) Theatre Arts. $2.50.

Ustinov, Peter. *Romanoff and Juliet.* Random House. $2.95.

West, E. J. (Editor). *Shaw on Theatre.* (Uncollected essays, letters and articles.) Hill and Wang. $3.95.

Wilder, Thornton. *Three Plays.* (Our Town, The Skin of Our Teeth, The Matchmaker.) Harper. $4.95.

Willans, Geoffrey. *Peter Ustinov.* British Book Centre. $4.50.

Williams, Tennessee. *Orpheus Descending:* with *Battle of Angels.* New Directions. $3.75.

Williams, Tennessee. *Suddenly Last Summer.* New Directions. $2.50.

Willson, Meredith. *The Music Man.* Putnam. $2.95.

Wishengrad, Morton. *The Rope Dancers.* Crown. $3.00.

Wouk, Herman. *Nature's Way.* Doubleday. $3.50.

Wright, Edward A. *A Primer for Playgoers.* Prentice-Hall. $6.50.

Young, Stark. *The Theatre.* Hill and Wang. $0.95 (paper).

PREVIOUS VOLUMES OF BEST PLAYS

Plays chosen to represent the theatre seasons from 1899 to 1957 are as follows:

1899-1909

BARBARA FRIETCHIE, by Clyde Fitch. Life Publishing Co.
THE CLIMBERS, by Clyde Fitch. Macmillan.
IF I WERE KING, by Justin Huntly McCarthy. Samuel French.
THE DARLING OF THE GODS, by David Belasco. Little, Brown.
THE COUNTY CHAIRMAN, by George Ade. Samuel French.
LEAH KLESCHNA, by C. M. S. McLellan. Samuel French.
THE SQUAW MAN, by Edwin Milton Royle.
THE GREAT DIVIDE, by William Vaughn Moody. Samuel French.
THE WITCHING HOUR, by Augustus Thomas. Samuel French.
THE MAN FROM HOME, by Booth Tarkington and Harry Leon Wilson. Samuel French.

1909-1919

THE EASIEST WAY, by Eugene Walter. G. W. Dillingham and Houghton Mifflin.
MRS. BUMPSTEAD-LEIGH, by Harry James Smith. Samuel French.
DISRAELI, by Louis N. Parker. Dodd, Mead.
ROMANCE, by Edward Sheldon. Macmillan.
SEVEN KEYS TO BALDPATE, by George M. Cohan. Published by Bobbs-Merrill as a novel by Earl Derr Biggers; as a play by Samuel French.
ON TRIAL, by Elmer Reizenstein. Samuel French.
THE UNCHASTENED WOMAN, by Louis Kaufman Anspacher. Harcourt, Brace and Howe.
GOOD GRACIOUS ANNABELLE, by Clare Kummer. Samuel French.
WHY MARRY?, by Jesse Lynch Williams. Scribner.
JOHN FERGUSON, by St. John Ervine. Macmillan.

1919-1920

ABRAHAM LINCOLN, by John Drinkwater. Houghton Mifflin.
CLARENCE, by Booth Tarkington. Samuel French.
BEYOND THE HORIZON, by Eugene G. O'Neill. Boni & Liveright.

DÉCLASSÉE, by Zoë Akins. Liveright, Inc.
THE FAMOUS MRS. FAIR, by James Forbes. Samuel French.
THE JEST, by Sem Benelli. (American adaptation by Edward Sheldon.)
JANE CLEGG, by St. John Ervine. Henry Holt.
MAMMA'S AFFAIR, by Rachel Barton Butler. Samuel French.
WEDDING BELLS, by Salisbury Field. Samuel French.
ADAM AND EVA, by George Middleton and Guy Bolton. Samuel French.

1920-1921

DEBURAU, adapted from the French of Sacha Guitry by H. Granville Barker. Putnam.
THE FIRST YEAR, by Frank Craven. Samuel French.
ENTER MADAME, by Gilda Varesi and Dolly Byrne. Putnam.
THE GREEN GODDESS, by William Archer. Knopf.
LILIOM, by Ferenc Molnar. Boni & Liveright.
MARY ROSE, by James M. Barrie. Scribner.
NICE PEOPLE, by Rachel Crothers. Scribner.
THE BAD MAN, by Porter Emerson Browne. Putnam.
THE EMPEROR JONES, by Eugene G. O'Neill. Boni & Liveright.
THE SKIN GAME, by John Galsworthy. Scribner.

1921-1922

ANNA CHRISTIE, by Eugene G. O'Neill. Boni & Liveright.
A BILL OF DIVORCEMENT, by Clemence Dane. Macmillan.
DULCY, by George S. Kaufman and Marc Connelly. Putnam.
HE WHO GETS SLAPPED, adapted from the Russian of Leonid Andreyev by Gregory Zilboorg. Brentano's.
SIX CYLINDER LOVE, by William Anthony McGuire.
THE HERO, by Gilbert Emery.
THE DOVER ROAD, by Alan Alexander Milne. Samuel French.
AMBUSH, by Arthur Richman.
THE CIRCLE, by William Somerset Maugham.
THE NEST, by Paul Geraldy and Grace George.

1922-1923

RAIN, by John Colton and Clemence Randolph. Liveright, Inc.
LOYALTIES, by John Galsworthy. Scribner.
ICEBOUND, by Owen Davis. Little, Brown.
YOU AND I, by Philip Barry. Brentano's.
THE FOOL, by Channing Pollock. Brentano's.

MERTON OF THE MOVIES, by George Kaufman and Marc Connelly, based on the novel of the same name by Harry Leon Wilson.
WHY NOT? by Jesse Lynch Williams. Walter H. Baker Co.
THE OLD SOAK, by Don Marquis. Doubleday, Page.
R.U.R., by Karel Capek. Translated by Paul Selver. Doubleday, Page.
MARY THE 3D, by Rachel Crothers. Brentano's.

1923-1924

THE SWAN, translated from the Hungarian of Ferenc Molnar by Melville Baker. Boni & Liveright.
OUTWARD BOUND, by Sutton Vane. Boni & Liveright.
THE SHOW-OFF, by George Kelly. Little, Brown.
THE CHANGELINGS, by Lee Wilson Dodd. Dutton.
CHICKEN FEED, by Guy Bolton. Samuel French.
SUN-UP, by Lula Vollmer. Brentano's.
BEGGAR ON HORSEBACK, by George Kaufman and Marc Connelly. Boni & Liveright.
TARNISH, by Gilbert Emery. Brentano's.
THE GOOSE HANGS HIGH, by Lewis Beach. Little, Brown.
HELL-BENT FER HEAVEN, by Hatcher Hughes. Harper.

1924-1925

WHAT PRICE GLORY? by Laurence Stallings and Maxwell Anderson. Harcourt, Brace.
THEY KNEW WHAT THEY WANTED, by Sidney Howard. Doubleday, Page.
DESIRE UNDER THE ELMS, by Eugene G. O'Neill. Boni & Liveright.
THE FIREBRAND, by Edwin Justus Mayer. Boni & Liveright.
DANCING MOTHERS, by Edgar Selwyn and Edmund Goulding.
MRS. PARTRIDGE PRESENTS, by Mary Kennedy and Ruth Hawthorne. Samuel French.
THE FALL GUY, by James Gleason and George Abbott. Samuel French.
THE YOUNGEST, by Philip Barry. Samuel French.
MINICK, by Edna Ferber and George S. Kaufman. Doubleday, Page.
WILD BIRDS, by Dan Totheroh. Doubleday, Page.

1925-1926

CRAIG'S WIFE, by George Kelly. Little, Brown.
THE GREAT GOD BROWN, by Eugene G. O'Neill. Boni & Liveright.
THE GREEN HAT, by Michael Arlen.
THE DYBBUK, by S. Ansky, Henry G. Alsberg-Winifred Katzin translation. Boni & Liveright.
THE ENEMY, by Channing Pollock. Brentano's.
THE LAST OF MRS. CHEYNEY, by Frederick Lonsdale. Samuel French.
BRIDE OF THE LAMB, by William Hurlbut. Boni & Liveright.
THE WISDOM TOOTH, by Marc Connelly. George H. Doran.
THE BUTTER AND EGG MAN, by George Kaufman. Boni & Liveright.
YOUNG WOODLEY, by John van Druten. Simon & Schuster.

1926-1927

BROADWAY, by Philip Dunning and George Abbott. George H. Doran.
SATURDAY'S CHILDREN, by Maxwell Anderson. Longmans, Green.
CHICAGO, by Maurine Watkins. Knopf.
THE CONSTANT WIFE, by William Somerset Maugham. George H. Doran.
THE PLAY'S THE THING, by Ferenc Molnar and P. G. Wodehouse. Brentano's.
THE ROAD TO ROME, by Robert Emmet Sherwood. Scribner.
THE SILVER CORD, by Sidney Howard. Scribner.
THE CRADLE SONG, translated from the Spanish of G. Martinez Sierra by John Garrett Underhill. Dutton.
DAISY MAYME, by George Kelly. Little, Brown.
IN ABRAHAM'S BOSOM, by Paul Green. McBride.

1927-1928

STRANGE INTERLUDE, by Eugene G. O'Neill. Boni & Liveright.
THE ROYAL FAMILY, by Edna Ferber and George Kaufman. Doubleday, Doran.
BURLESQUE, by George Manker Watters and Arthur Hopkins. Doubleday, Doran.
COQUETTE, by George Abbott and Ann Bridgers. Longmans, Green.
BEHOLD THE BRIDEGROOM, by George Kelly. Little, Brown.
PORGY, by DuBose Heyward. Doubleday, Doran.
PARIS BOUND, by Philip Barry. Samuel French.
ESCAPE, by John Galsworthy. Scribner.

THE RACKET, by Bartlett Cormack. Samuel French.
THE PLOUGH AND THE STARS, by Sean O'Casey. Macmillan.

1928-1929

STREET SCENE, by Elmer Rice. Samuel French.
JOURNEY'S END, by R. C. Sherriff. Brentano's.
WINGS OVER EUROPE, by Robert Nichols and Maurice Browne. Co-
    vici-Friede.
HOLIDAY, by Philip Barry. Samuel French.
THE FRONT PAGE, by Ben Hecht and Charles MacArthur. Covici-
    Friede.
LET US BE GAY, by Rachel Crothers. Samuel French.
MACHINAL, by Sophie Treadwell.
LITTLE ACCIDENT, by Floyd Dell and Thomas Mitchell.
GYPSY, by Maxwell Anderson.
THE KINGDOM OF GOD, by G. Martinez Sierra; English version by
    Helen and Harley Granville-Barker. Dutton.

1929-1930

THE GREEN PASTURES, by Marc Connelly (adapted from "Ol' Man
    Adam and His Chillun," by Roark Bradford). Farrar & Rine-
    hart.
THE CRIMINAL CODE, by Martin Flavin. Horace Liveright.
BERKELEY SQUARE, by John Balderston.
STRICTLY DISHONORABLE, by Preston Sturges. Horace Liveright.
THE FIRST MRS. FRASER, by St. John Ervine. Macmillan.
THE LAST MILE, by John Wexley. Samuel French.
JUNE MOON, by Ring W. Lardner and George S. Kaufman. Scribner.
MICHAEL AND MARY, by A. A. Milne. Chatto & Windus.
DEATH TAKES A HOLIDAY, by Walter Ferris (adapted from the Ital-
    ian of Alberto Casella). Samuel French.
REBOUND, by Donald Ogden Stewart. Samuel French.

1930-1931

ELIZABETH THE QUEEN, by Maxwell Anderson. Longmans, Green.
TOMORROW AND TOMORROW, by Philip Barry. Samuel French.
ONCE IN A LIFETIME, by George S. Kaufman and Moss Hart. Far-
    rar & Rinehart.
GREEN GROW THE LILACS, by Lynn Riggs. Samuel French.
AS HUSBANDS GO, by Rachel Crothers. Samuel French.

ALISON'S HOUSE, by Susan Glaspell. Samuel French.
FIVE-STAR FINAL, by Louis Weitzenkorn. Samuel 'French.
OVERTURE, by William Bolitho. Simon & Schuster.
THE BARRETTS OF WIMPOLE STREET, by Rudolf Besier. Little,
Brown.
GRAND HOTEL, adapted from the German of Vicki Baum by W. A.
Drake.

1931-1932

OF THEE I SING, by George S. Kaufman and Morrie Ryskind; music
and lyrics by George and Ira Gershwin. Knopf.
MOURNING BECOMES ELECTRA, by Eugene G. O'Neill. Horace Live-
right.
REUNION IN VIENNA, by Robert Emmet Sherwood. Scribner.
THE HOUSE OF CONNELLY, by Paul Green. Samuel French.
THE ANIMAL KINGDOM, by Philip Barry. Samuel French.
THE LEFT BANK, by Elmer Rice. Samuel French.
ANOTHER LANGUAGE, by Rose Franken. Samuel French.
BRIEF MOMENT, by S. N. Behrman. Farrar & Rinehart.
THE DEVIL PASSES, by Benn W. Levy. Martin Secker.
CYNARA, by H. M. Harwood and R. F. Gore-Browne. Samuel
French.

1932-1933

BOTH YOUR HOUSES, by Maxwell Anderson. Samuel French.
DINNER AT EIGHT, by George S. Kaufman and Edna Ferber. Dou-
bleday, Doran.
WHEN LADIES MEET, by Rachel Crothers. Samuel French.
DESIGN FOR LIVING, by Noel Coward. Doubleday, Doran.
BIOGRAPHY, by S. N. Behrman. Farrar & Rinehart.
ALIEN CORN, by Sidney Howard. Scribner.
THE LATE CHRISTOPHER BEAN, adapted from the French of René
Fauchois by Sidney Howard. Samuel French.
WE, THE PEOPLE, by Elmer Rice. Coward-McCann.
PIGEONS AND PEOPLE, by George M. Cohan.
ONE SUNDAY AFTERNOON, by James Hagan. Samuel French.

1933-1934

MARY OF SCOTLAND, by Maxwell Anderson. Doubleday, Doran.
MEN IN WHITE, by Sidney Kingsley. Covici-Friede.
DODSWORTH, by Sinclair Lewis and Sidney Howard. Harcourt,
Brace.

AH, WILDERNESS, by Eugene O'Neill. Random House.
THEY SHALL NOT DIE, by John Wexley. Knopf.
HER MASTER'S VOICE, by Clare Kummer. Samuel French.
NO MORE LADIES, by A. E. Thomas.
WEDNESDAY'S CHILD, by Leopold Atlas. Samuel French.
THE SHINING HOUR, by Keith Winter. Doubleday, Doran.
THE GREEN BAY TREE, by Mordaunt Shairp. Baker International
Play Bureau.

1934-1935

THE CHILDREN'S HOUR, by Lillian Hellman. Knopf.
VALLEY FORGE, by Maxwell Anderson. Anderson House.
THE PETRIFIED FOREST, by Robert Sherwood. Scribner.
THE OLD MAID, by Zoë Akins. Appleton-Century.
ACCENT ON YOUTH, by Samson Raphaelson. Samuel French.
MERRILY WE ROLL ALONG, by George S. Kaufman and Moss Hart.
Random House.
AWAKE AND SING, by Clifford Odets. Random House.
THE FARMER TAKES A WIFE, by Frank B. Elser and Marc Connelly.
LOST HORIZONS, by John Hayden.
THE DISTAFF SIDE, by John van Druten. Knopf.

1935-1936

WINTERSET, by Maxwell Anderson. Anderson House.
IDIOT'S DELIGHT, by Robert Emmet Sherwood. Scribner.
END OF SUMMER, by S. N. Behrman. Random House.
FIRST LADY, by Katharine Dayton and George S. Kaufman. Random House.
VICTORIA REGINA, by Laurence Housman. Samuel French.
BOY MEETS GIRL, by Bella and Samuel Spewack. Random House.
DEAD END, by Sidney Kingsley. Random House.
CALL IT A DAY, by Dodie Smith. Samuel French.
ETHAN FROME, by Owen Davis and Donald Davis. Scribner.
PRIDE AND PREJUDICE, by Helen Jerome. Doubleday, Doran.

1936-1937

HIGH TOR, by Maxwell Anderson. Anderson House.
YOU CAN'T TAKE IT WITH YOU, by Moss Hart and George S. Kaufman. Farrar & Rinehart.
JOHNNY JOHNSON, by Paul Green. Samuel French.
DAUGHTERS OF ATREUS, by Robert Turney. Knopf.

STAGE DOOR, by Edna Ferber and George S. Kaufman. Doubleday, Doran.
THE WOMEN, by Clare Boothe. Random House.
ST. HELENA, by R. C. Sherriff and Jeanne de Casalis. Samuel French.
YES, MY DARLING DAUGHTER, by Mark Reed. Samuel French.
EXCURSION, by Victor Wolfson. Random House.
TOVARICH, by Jacques Deval and Robert E. Sherwood. Random House.

1937-1938

OF MICE AND MEN, by John Steinbeck. Covici-Friede.
OUR TOWN, by Thornton Wilder. Coward-McCann.
SHADOW AND SUBSTANCE, by Paul Vincent Carroll. Random House.
ON BORROWED TIME, by Paul Osborn. Knopf.
THE STAR-WAGON, by Maxwell Anderson. Anderson House.
SUSAN AND GOD, by Rachel Crothers. Random House.
PROLOGUE TO GLORY, by E. P. Conkle. Random House.
AMPHITRYON 38, by S. N. Behrman. Random House.
GOLDEN BOY, by Clifford Odets. Random House.
WHAT A LIFE, by Clifford Goldsmith. Dramatists' Play Service.

1938-1939

ABE LINCOLN IN ILLINOIS, by Robert E. Sherwood. Scribner.
THE LITTLE FOXES, by Lillian Hellman. Random House.
ROCKET TO THE MOON, by Clifford Odets. Random House.
THE AMERICAN WAY, by George S. Kaufman and Moss Hart. Random House.
NO TIME FOR COMEDY, by S. N. Behrman. Random House.
THE PHILADELPHIA STORY, by Philip Barry. Coward-McCann.
THE WHITE STEED, by Paul Vincent Carroll. Random House.
HERE COME THE CLOWNS, by Philip Barry. Coward-McCann.
FAMILY PORTRAIT, by Lenore Coffee and William Joyce Cowen. Random House.
KISS THE BOYS GOOD-BYE, by Clare Boothe. Random House.

1939-1940

THERE SHALL BE NO NIGHT, by Robert E. Sherwood. Scribner.
KEY LARGO, by Maxwell Anderson. Anderson House.
THE WORLD WE MAKE, by Sidney Kingsley.
LIFE WITH FATHER, by Howard Lindsay and Russel Crouse. Knopf.

THE MAN WHO CAME TO DINNER, by George S. Kaufman and Moss Hart. Random House.
THE MALE ANIMAL, by James Thurber and Elliott Nugent. Random House, New York, and MacMillan Co., Canada.
THE TIME OF YOUR LIFE, by William Saroyan. Harcourt, Brace.
SKYLARK, by Samson Raphaelson. Random House.
MARGIN FOR ERROR, by Clare Boothe. Random House.
MORNING'S AT SEVEN, by Paul Osborn. Samuel French.

1940-1941

NATIVE SON, by Paul Green and Richard Wright. Harper.
WATCH ON THE RHINE, by Lillian Hellman. Random House.
THE CORN IS GREEN, by Emlyn Williams. Random House.
LADY IN THE DARK, by Moss Hart. Random House.
ARSENIC AND OLD LACE, by Joseph Kesselring. Random House.
MY SISTER EILEEN, by Joseph Fields and Jerome Chodorov. Random House.
FLIGHT TO THE WEST, by Elmer Rice. Coward-McCann.
CLAUDIA, by Rose Franken Meloney. Farrar & Rinehart.
MR. AND MRS. NORTH, by Owen Davis. Samuel French.
GEORGE WASHINGTON SLEPT HERE, by George S. Kaufman and Moss Hart. Random House.

1941-1942

IN TIME TO COME, by Howard Koch. Dramatists' Play Service.
THE MOON IS DOWN, by John Steinbeck. Viking.
BLITHE SPIRIT, by Noel Coward. Doubleday, Doran.
JUNIOR MISS, by Jerome Chodorov and Joseph Fields. Random House.
CANDLE IN THE WIND, by Maxwell Anderson. Anderson House.
LETTERS TO LUCERNE, by Fritz Rotter and Allen Vincent. Samuel French.
JASON, by Samson Raphaelson. Random House.
ANGEL STREET, by Patrick Hamilton. Constable & Co., under the title "Gaslight."
UNCLE HARRY, by Thomas Job. Samuel French.
HOPE FOR A HARVEST, by Sophie Treadwell. Samuel French.

1942-1943

THE PATRIOTS, by Sidney Kingsley. Random House.
THE EVE OF ST. MARK, by Maxwell Anderson. Anderson House.

THE SKIN OF OUR TEETH, by Thornton Wilder. Harper.
WINTER SOLDIERS, by Dan James.
TOMORROW THE WORLD, by James Gow and Arnaud d'Usseau.
    Scribner.
HARRIET, by Florence Ryerson and Colin Clements. Scribner.
THE DOUGHGIRLS, by Joseph Fields. Random House.
THE DAMASK CHEEK, by John van Druten and Lloyd Morris. Ran-
    dom House.
KISS AND TELL, by F. Hugh Herbert. Coward-McCann.
OKLAHOMA!, by Oscar Hammerstein 2nd and Richard Rodgers.
    Random House.

1943-1944

WINGED VICTORY, by Moss Hart. Random House.
THE SEARCHING WIND, by Lillian Hellman. Viking.
THE VOICE OF THE TURTLE, by John van Druten. Random House.
DECISION, by Edward Chodorov.
OVER 21, by Ruth Gordon. Random House.
OUTRAGEOUS FORTUNE, by Rose Franken. Samuel French.
JACOBOWSKY AND THE COLONEL, by S. N. Behrman. Random
    House.
STORM OPERATION, by Maxwell Anderson. Anderson House.
PICK-UP GIRL, by Elsa Shelley.
THE INNOCENT VOYAGE, by Paul Osborn.

1944-1945

A BELL FOR ADANO, by Paul Osborn. Knopf.
I REMEMBER MAMA, by John van Druten. Harcourt, Brace.
THE HASTY HEART, by John Patrick. Random House.
THE GLASS MENAGERIE, by Tennessee Williams. Random House.
HARVEY, by Mary Chase.
THE LATE GEORGE APLEY, by John P. Marquand and George S.
    Kaufman.
SOLDIER'S WIFE, by Rose Franken. Samuel French.
ANNA LUCASTA, by Philip Yordan. Random House.
FOOLISH NOTION, by Philip Barry.
DEAR RUTH, by Norman Krasna. Random House.

1945-1946

STATE OF THE UNION, by Howard Lindsay and Russel Crouse.
    Random House.
HOME OF THE BRAVE, by Arthur Laurents. Random House.

DEEP ARE THE ROOTS, by Arnaud d'Usseau and James Gow. Scribner.

THE MAGNIFICENT YANKEE, by Emmet Lavery. Samuel French.

ANTIGONE, by Lewis Galantière (from the French of Jean Anouilh). Random House.

O MISTRESS MINE, by Terence Rattigan. Published and revised by the author.

BORN YESTERDAY, by Garson Kanin. Viking.

DREAM GIRL, by Elmer Rice. Coward-McCann.

THE RUGGED PATH, by Robert E. Sherwood. Scribner.

LUTE SONG, by Will Irwin and Sidney Howard. Published version by Will Irwin and Leopoldine Howard.

1946-1947

ALL MY SONS, by Arthur Miller. Reynal & Hitchcock.

THE ICEMAN COMETH, by Eugene G. O'Neill. Random House.

JOAN OF LORRAINE, by Maxwell Anderson. Published by Maxwell Anderson.

ANOTHER PART OF THE FOREST, by Lillian Hellman. Viking.

YEARS AGO, by Ruth Gordon. Viking.

JOHN LOVES MARY, by Norman Krasna. Copyright by Norman Krasna.

THE FATAL WEAKNESS, by George Kelly. Samuel French.

THE STORY OF MARY SURRATT, by John Patrick. Dramatists' Play Service.

CHRISTOPHER BLAKE, by Moss Hart. Random House.

BRIGADOON, by Alan Jay Lerner and Frederick Loewe. Coward-McCann.

1947-1948

A STREETCAR NAMED DESIRE, by Tennessee Williams. New Directions.

MISTER ROBERTS, by Thomas Heggen and Joshua Logan. Houghton Mifflin.

COMMAND DECISION, by William Wister Haines. Random House.

THE WINSLOW BOY, by Terence Rattigan.

THE HEIRESS, by Ruth and Augustus Goetz.

ALLEGRO, by Richard Rodgers and Oscar Hammerstein 2d. Knopf. Music published by Williamson Music, Inc.

EASTWARD IN EDEN, by Dorothy Gardner. Longmans, Green.

SKIPPER NEXT TO GOD, by Jan de Hartog.

AN INSPECTOR CALLS, by J. B. Priestley.
ME AND MOLLY, by Gertrude Berg.

1948-1949

DEATH OF A SALESMAN, by Arthur Miller. Viking.
ANNE OF THE THOUSAND DAYS, by Maxwell Anderson. Sloane.
THE MADWOMAN OF CHAILLOT, by Maurice Valency, adapted from
   the French of Jean Giraudoux. Random House.
DETECTIVE STORY, by Sidney Kingsley. Random House.
EDWARD, MY SON, by Robert Morley and Noel Langley. Random
   House, New York, and Samuel French, London.
LIFE WITH MOTHER, by Howard Lindsay and Russel Crouse.
   Knopf.
LIGHT UP THE SKY, by Moss Hart. Random House.
THE SILVER WHISTLE, by Robert Edward McEnroe. Dramatists'
   Play Service.
TWO BLIND MICE, by Samuel Spewack. Dramatists' Play Service.
GOODBYE, MY FANCY, by Fay Kanin. Samuel French.

1949-1950

THE COCKTAIL PARTY, by T. S. Eliot. Harcourt, Brace.
THE MEMBER OF THE WEDDING, by Carson McCullers. Houghton
   Mifflin.
THE INNOCENTS, by William Archibald. Coward-McCann.
LOST IN THE STARS, by Maxwell Anderson and Kurt Weill. Sloane.
COME BACK, LITTLE SHEBA, by William Inge. Random House.
THE HAPPY TIME, by Samuel Taylor. Random House.
THE WISTERIA TREES, by Joshua Logan. Random House.
I KNOW MY LOVE, by S. N. Behrman. Random House.
THE ENCHANTED, by Maurice Valency, adapted from a play by Jean
   Giraudoux. Random House.
CLUTTERBUCK, by Benn W. Levy. Dramatists' Play Service.

1950-1951

GUYS AND DOLLS, by Jo Swerling, Abe Burrows and Frank Loesser.
DARKNESS AT NOON, by Sidney Kingsley and Arthur Koestler. Ran-
   dom House.
BILLY BUDD, by Louis O. Coxe and Robert Chapman. Princeton
   University Press.
THE AUTUMN GARDEN, by Lillian Hellman. Little, Brown & Co.

BELL, BOOK AND CANDLE, by John van Druten. Random House.
THE COUNTRY GIRL, by Clifford Odets. Viking Press.
THE ROSE TATTOO, by Tennessee Williams. New Directions.
SEASON IN THE SUN, by Wolcott Gibbs. Random House.
AFFAIRS OF STATE, by Louis Verneuil.
SECOND THRESHOLD, by Philip Barry. Harper & Bros.

1951-1952

MRS. MCTHING, by Mary Coyle Chase.
THE SHRIKE, by Joseph Kramm. Random House.
I AM A CAMERA, by John van Druten. Random House.
THE FOURPOSTER, by Jan de Hartog.
POINT OF NO RETURN, by Paul Osborn. Random House.
BAREFOOT IN ATHENS, by Maxwell Anderson. Sloane.
VENUS OBSERVED, by Christopher Fry. Oxford.
JANE, by S. N. Behrman and Somerset Maugham. Random House.
GIGI, by Anita Loos and Colette. Random House.
REMAINS TO BE SEEN, by Howard Lindsay and Russel Crouse.
    Random House.

1952-1953

THE TIME OF THE CUCKOO, by Arthur Laurents. Random House.
BERNARDINE, by Mary Coyle Chase.
DIAL "M" FOR MURDER, by Frederick Knott. Random House.
THE CLIMATE OF EDEN, by Moss Hart. Random House.
THE LOVE OF FOUR COLONELS, by Peter Ustinov.
THE CRUCIBLE, by Arthur Miller. Viking.
THE EMPEROR'S CLOTHES, by George Tabori. Samuel French.
PICNIC, by William Inge. Random House.
WONDERFUL TOWN, by Joseph Fields, Jerome Chodorov, Betty
    Comden and Adolph Green. Random House.
MY 3 ANGELS, by Sam and Bella Spewack.

1953-1954

THE CAINE MUTINY COURT-MARTIAL, by Herman Wouk. Double-
    day & Company, Inc.
IN THE SUMMER HOUSE, by Jane Bowles. Random House.
THE CONFIDENTIAL CLERK, by T. S. Eliot. Harcourt, Brace and
    Company, Inc.
TAKE A GIANT STEP, by Louis Peterson.
THE TEAHOUSE OF THE AUGUST MOON, by John Patrick. G. P.
    Putnam's Sons.

THE IMMORALIST, by Ruth and Augustus Goetz. Ruth and Augustus Goetz. Dramatists' Play Service.

TEA AND SYMPATHY, by Robert Anderson. Random House.

THE GIRL ON THE VIA FLAMINIA, by Alfred Hayes.

THE GOLDEN APPLE, by John Latouche and Jerome Moross. Random House.

THE MAGIC AND THE LOSS, by Julian Funt. Samuel French.

1954-1955

THE BOY FRIEND, by Sandy Wilson.

THE LIVING ROOM, by Graham Greene. Viking.

BAD SEED, by Maxwell Anderson. Dodd, Mead.

WITNESS FOR THE PROSECUTION, by Agatha Christie.

THE FLOWERING PEACH, by Clifford Odets.

THE DESPERATE HOURS, by Joseph Hayes. Random House.

THE DARK IS LIGHT ENOUGH, by Christopher Fry. Oxford.

BUS STOP, by William Inge. Random House.

CAT ON A HOT TIN ROOF, by Tennessee Williams. New Directions.

INHERIT THE WIND, by Jerome Lawrence and Robert E. Lee. Random House.

1955-1956

A VIEW FROM THE BRIDGE, by Arthur Miller. Viking.

TIGER AT THE GATES, by Jean Giraudoux, translated by Christopher Fry. Oxford.

THE DIARY OF ANNE FRANK, by Frances Goodrich and Albert Hackett. Random House.

NO TIME FOR SERGEANTS, by Ira Levin. Random House.

THE CHALK GARDEN, by Enid Bagnold. Random House.

THE LARK, by Jean Anouilh, adapted by Lillian Hellman. Random House.

THE MATCHMAKER, by Thornton Wilder. Harper.

THE PONDER HEART, by Joseph Fields and Jerome Chodorov. Random House.

MY FAIR LADY, by Alan Jay Lerner and Frederick Loewe. Coward-McCann.

WAITING FOR GODOT, by Samuel Beckett. Grove.

1956-1957

SEPARATE TABLES, by Terence Rattigan. Random House.

LONG DAY'S JOURNEY INTO NIGHT, by Eugene O'Neill. Yale University Press.

A VERY SPECIAL BABY, by Robert Alan Aurthur. Dramatists Play Service.

CANDIDE, by Lillian Hellman, Richard Wilbur, John Latouche, Dorothy Parker and Leonard Bernstein. Random House.

A CLEARING IN THE WOODS, by Arthur Laurents. Random House.

THE WALTZ OF THE TOREADORS, by Jean Anouilh, translated by Lucienne Hill. Coward-McCann.

THE POTTING SHED, by Graham Greene. Viking.

VISIT TO A SMALL PLANET, by Gore Vidal. Little, Brown.

ORPHEUS DESCENDING, by Tennessee Williams. New Directions.

A MOON FOR THE MISBEGOTTEN, by Eugene O'Neill. Random House.

WHERE AND WHEN THEY WERE BORN

(Compiled from the most authentic records available)

Abbott, George	Forestville, N. Y.	1889
Abel, Walter	St. Paul, Minn.	1898
Addy, Wesley	Omaha, Neb.	1912
Adler, Luther	New York City	1903
Aherne, Brian	King's Norton, England	1902
Aldrich, Richard	Boston, Mass.	1902
Anderson, Judith	Australia	1898
Anderson, Maxwell	Atlantic City, Pa.	1888
Anderson, Robert	New York City	1917
Andrews, Julie	London, England	1935
Arthur, Jean	New York City	1905
Ashcroft, Peggy	Croydon, England	1907
Atkinson, Brooks	Melrose, Mass.	1894
Bainter, Fay	Los Angeles, Cal.	1892
Bankhead, Tallulah	Huntsville, Ala.	1902
Barrymore, Ethel	Philadelphia, Pa.	1879
Barton, James	Gloucester, N. J.	1890
Begley, Ed	Hartford, Conn.	1901
Behrman, S. N.	Worcester, Mass.	1893
Bellamy, Ralph	Chicago, Ill.	1904
Bergman, Ingrid	Stockholm, Sweden	1917
Bergner, Elisabeth	Vienna, Austria	1900
Berlin, Irving	Russia	1888
Bernstein, Leonard	Brookline, Mass.	1918
Best, Edna	Hove, England	1900
Blackmer, Sidney	Salisbury, N. C.	1898
Blaine, Vivian	Newark, N. J.	1923
Bolger, Ray	Dorchester, Mass.	1904
Bondi, Beulah	Chicago, Ill.	1892
Booth, Shirley	New York City	1909
Bourneuf, Philip	Boston, Mass.	1912
Boyer, Charles	Figeac, France	1899
Brando, Marlon	Omaha, Neb.	1924

Brent, Romney .... Saltillo, Mex. 1902
Brown, Joe E. .... Holgate, Ohio 1892
Burke, Billie .... Washington, D. C. 1895
Byington, Spring .... Colorado Springs, Colo. 1898

Cagney, James .... New York City 1904
Cantor, Eddie .... New York City 1892
Carnovsky, Morris .... St. Louis, Mo. 1898
Carradine, John .... New York City 1906
Carroll, Leo G. .... Weedon, England 1892
Carroll, Madeleine .... West Bromwich, England 1906
Channing, Carol .... Seattle, Wash. 1921
Chase, Ilka .... New York City 1905
Chatterton, Ruth .... New York City 1893
Claire, Ina .... Washington, D. C. 1895
Clark, Bobby .... Springfield, Ohio 1888
Clift, Montgomery .... Omaha, Neb. 1921
Clurman, Harold .... New York City 1901
Cobb, Lee .... New York City 1911
Coburn, Charles .... Macon, Ga. 1877
Collinge, Patricia .... Dublin, Ireland 1894
Collins, Russell .... New Orleans, La. 1897
Conroy, Frank .... London, England 1885
Cook, Donald .... Portland, Ore. 1902
Cook, Joe .... Evansville, Ind. 1890
Cooper, Gladys .... Lewisham, England 1888
Cooper, Melville .... Birmingham, England 1896
Corbett, Leonora .... London, England 1908
Cornell, Katharine .... Berlin, Germany 1898
Coulouris, George .... Manchester, England 1906
Coward, Noel .... Teddington, England 1899
Crawford, Cheryl .... Akron, Ohio 1902
Cromwell, John .... Toledo, Ohio 1888
Cronyn, Hume .... London, Ontario 1912
Crothers, Rachel .... Bloomington, Ill. 1878
Crouse, Russel .... Findlay, Ohio 1893
Cummings, Constance ...... Seattle, Wash. 1911

Dale, Margaret .... Philadelphia, Pa. 1880
Dana, Leora .... New York City 1923
Daniell, Henry .... London, England 1894
Derwent, Clarence .... London, England 1884
Douglas, Melvyn .... Macon, Ga. 1901

Gish, Dorothy .... Massillon, Ohio 1898
Gish, Lillian .... Springfield, Ohio 1896
Gordon, Ruth .... Wollaston, Mass. 1896
Green, Martyn .... London, England 1899
Greenwood, Joan .... London, England 1921
Guinness, Alec .... London, England 1914
Guthrie, Tyrone .... Tunbridge Wells, England 1900
Gwenn, Edmund .... Glamorgan, Wales 1875

Hagen, Uta .... Göttingen, Germany 1919
Hammerstein, Oscar, II ..... New York City 1895
Hardie, Russell .... Griffin Mills, N. Y. 1906
Hardwicke, Sir Cedric ...... Lye, Stourbridge, England 1893
Harris, Julie .... Grosse Point, Mich. 1925
Harrison, Rex .... Huyton, Lancashire, England .. 1908
Hart, Moss .... New York City 1904
Havoc, June .... Seattle, Wash. 1916
Haydon, Julie .... Oak Park, Ill. 1910
Hayes, Helen .... Washington, D. C. 1900
Hayward, Leland .... Nebraska City, Neb. 1902
Heflin, Frances .... Oklahoma City, Okla. 1924
Hellman, Lillian .... New Orleans, La. 1905
Helmore, Tom .... London, England 1912
Helpmann, Robert .... South Australia 1911
Henie, Sonja .... Oslo, Norway 1913
Hepburn, Audrey .... Brussels, Belgium 1929
Hepburn, Katharine .... Hartford, Conn. 1909
Herlie, Eileen .... Glasgow, Scotland 1920
Hiller, Wendy .... Bramhall, England 1912
Holliday, Judy .... New York City 1924
Holloway, Stanley .... London, England 1890
Holm, Celeste .... New York City 1919
Homolka, Oscar .... Vienna, Austria 1898
Hull, Henry .... Louisville, Ky. 1890
Hunt, Martita .... Argentine Republic 1900
Hunter, Kim .... Detroit, Mich. 1922
Hussey, Ruth .... Providence, R. I. 1917

Ives, Burl .... Hunt Township, Ill. 1909

Johnson, Harold J. (Chic) ... Chicago, Ill. 1891
Joy, Nicholas .... Paris, France 1889

McCracken, Joan .... Philadelphia, Pa. 1923
McDowall, Roddy .... London, England 1928
McGrath, Paul .... Chicago, Ill. 1900
McGuire, Dorothy .... Omaha, Neb. 1918
McKenna, Siobhan .... Belfast, Ireland 1923
Menotti, Gian-Carlo .... Italy 1912
Meredith, Burgess .... Cleveland, Ohio 1908
Merkel, Una .... Covington, Ky. 1903
Merman, Ethel .... Astoria, L. I. 1909
Middleton, Ray .... Chicago, Ill. 1907
Mielziner, Jo .... Paris, France 1901
Miller, Arthur .... New York City 1915
Miller, Gilbert .... New York City 1884
Mitchell, Thomas .... Elizabeth, N. J. 1892
Moore, Victor .... Hammonton, N. J. 1876
Moorehead, Agnes .... Clinton, Mass. 1906
Morgan, Claudia .... New York City 1912
Morley, Robert .... Semley, England 1908
Moss, Arnold .... Brooklyn, N. Y. 1910
Muni, Paul .... Lemberg, Austria 1895

Nagel, Conrad .... Keokuk, Iowa 1897
Natwick, Mildred .... Baltimore, Md. 1908
Neal, Patricia .... Packard, Ky. 1926
Nesbitt, Cathleen .... Cheshire, England 1889
Nugent, Elliott .... Dover, Ohio 1900

Odets, Clifford .... Philadelphia, Pa. 1906
Oenslager, Donald .... Harrisburg, Pa. 1902
Olivier, Sir Laurence .... Dorking, Surrey, England 1907
Olsen, John Siguard (Ole) ... Peru, Ind. 1892
O'Malley, Rex .... London, England 1906
O'Neal, Frederick .... Brookville, Miss. 1905
Osborn, Paul .... Evansville, Ind. 1901

Page, Geraldine .... Kirksville, Mo. 1925
Palmer, Lilli .... Posen, Austria 1914
Petina, Irra .... Leningrad, Russia 1900
Picon, Molly .... New York City 1898
Porter, Cole .... Peru, Ind. 1892
Portman, Eric .... Yorkshire, England 1903
Price, Vincent .... St. Louis, Mo. 1914

Quayle, Anthony .... Ainsdale, England 1913

Rains, Claude .... London, England 1889
Raitt, John .... Santa Ana, Cal. 1917
Rathbone, Basil .... Johannesburg, Africa 1892
Rattigan, Terence .... London, England 1911
Redgrave, Michael .... Bristol, England 1908
Redman, Joyce .... Newcastle, Ireland 1918
Reed, Florence .... Philadelphia, Pa. 1883
Rennie, James .... Toronto, Canada 1890
Rice, Elmer .... New York City 1892
Richardson, Sir Ralph .... Cheltenham, England 1902
Ritchard, Cyril .... Sydney, Australia 1898
Rodgers, Richard .... New York City 1902
Royle, Selena .... New York City 1905
Russell, Rosalind .... Waterbury, Conn. 1911

Sarnoff, Dorothy .... Brooklyn, N. Y. 1919
Saroyan, William .... Fresno, Cal. 1908
Schildkraut, Joseph .... Vienna, Austria 1895
Scott, Martha .... Jamesport, Mo. 1914
Segal, Vivienne .... Philadelphia, Pa. 1897
Sherman, Hiram .... Boston, Mass. 1908
Shumlin, Herman .... Atwood, Colo. 1898
Silvers, Phil .... Brooklyn, N. Y. 1911
Simms, Hilda .... Minneapolis, Minn. 1920
Skinner, Cornelia Otis .... Chicago, Ill. 1902
Slezak, Walter .... Vienna, Austria 1902
Smith, Kent .... Smithfield, Me. 1910
Stanley, Kim .... Tularosa, N. M. 1921
Stapleton, Maureen .... Troy, N. Y. 1926
Starr, Frances .... Oneonta, N. Y. 1886
Stickney, Dorothy .... Dickinson, N. D. 1903
Stone, Carol .... New York City 1917
Stone, Dorothy .... New York City 1905
Stone, Ezra .... New Bedford, Mass. 1918
Stone, Fred .... Denver, Colo. 1873
Straight, Beatrice .... Old Westbury, N. Y. 1918
Sullavan, Margaret .... Norfolk, Va. 1910

Tandy, Jessica .... London, England 1909
Tetzel, Joan .... New York City 1923
Thorndike, Sybil .... Gainsborough, England 1882

NECROLOGY

June 1, 1957—May 31, 1958

Alton, Robert, 51, dance director. He began his career as a dancer in "Take It from Me" and became one of Broadway's finest dance directors. He staged the dances for four Ziegfeld Follies —"Anything Goes," "Hooray for What," "Pal Joey" and "Hellzapoppin'." In 1935 he went to Hollywood and worked on such pictures as "Strike Me Pink," "The Harvey Girls" and "Annie Get Your Gun." Born Bennington, Vt.; died Hollywood, June 12, 1957.

Anglin, Margaret, 81, actress. One of America's finest actresses and a star for many years, she made her first professional appearance in 1894 in "Shenandoah." In October 1898, she made a personal hit as Roxane in "Cyrano de Bergerac" opposite Richard Mansfield. During her career she acted in about 80 plays. Among the most successful were "The Devil's Disciple," "Camille," "Joan of Arc," "Mrs. Dane's Defense," "The Great Divide," "As You Like It," "Twelfth Night," "Medea," "Green Stockings," "The Woman of Bronze" and "Diplomacy." Her last Broadway appearance was in "Fresh Fields" in 1936. She continued her career out of town and in summer stock until 1943. Born Ottawa, Canada; died Toronto, Canada, Jan. 7, 1958.

Ballard, Fred, 72, playwright. After attending the University of Nebraska, he was assistant property man at the Illinois Theatre and the Grand Opera House in Chicago. He then joined Prof. Baker's famous 47 Workshop at Harvard and won the Harvard Prize Play contest with "Believe Me, Xantippe." He wrote "Rainy Day," "Young America" and with Henry Beresford "Out of Luck." His "Ladies of the Jury," one of Mrs. Fiske's most popular vehicles, was twice made into a picture. His other plays include "When's Your Birthday?" and "What's Wrong?" Born in Nebraska; died Lincoln, Neb., Sept. 24, 1957.

Benatzky, Ralph, 73, composer. Popular in Europe as a composer and playwright, he was represented in America by "Meet My Sister," "The Apaches Cocktail" and the popular "White Horse Inn." He also did motion picture scoring, chorale music and art songs. He was recipient of the Austria Cross for Arts and

369

Sciences and Chevalier of the French Legion of Honor. Born Moravia; died Zurich, Switzerland, Oct. 17, 1957.

Brown, Lew, 64, song writer. As Louis Brownstein he was brought from Russia to the United States at the age of five. At 16 he was a lifeguard at the Rockaway beaches. His first song, "Please Don't Take My Lovin' Man Away," which he sold for $7, was introduced to the public by Belle Baker. In 1925 he formed a partnership with B. G. De Sylva and Ray Henderson and the three were so close that nobody ever really knew who actually wrote the music and the lyrics. In 1928 the team had five shows running simultaneously on Broadway—"Good News," "Manhattan Mary," "Three Cheers," "Follow Thru" and "George White's Scandals." Mr. Brown produced motion pictures for which he also wrote songs. In all he wrote, or collaborated on, about 7000 songs. In 1956 20th Century-Fox released a movie based on the De Sylva-Brown-Henderson partnership entitled "The Best Things in Life Are Free." Born Russia; died New York, Feb. 5, 1958.

Buchanan, Jack, 64, actor. His first success was in London in André Charlot's "Bubbly" in 1917. A well-known song-and-dance man in England, he won international fame with Beatrice Lillie and Gertrude Lawrence in "Charlot's Revue of 1924." He followed this with his New York appearance in "Charlot's Revue of 1926" and "Wake Up and Dream." In London he starred in "Sunny," "That's a Good Girl," "Stand Up and Sing," "This'll Make You Whistle" and many others. In New York in 1948 he followed Frank Fay as Elwood P. Dowd in "Harvey." He made several motion pictures in England and Hollywood. He was also a manager and director, staging most of his own productions. Born Helensburgh, Scotland; died London, Oct. 20, 1957.

Busby, Amy, 85, actress. This famed beauty of the nineties ran away from home to go on the stage, making her debut in 1889 in "London Assurance." Her final appearance was in 1896 with William Gillette in "Secret Service," after which she gave up the stage for marriage. In the brief span of her career she played leading roles with William H. Crane, Stuart Robeson, Richard Mansfield and Rose Coghlan. In 1940 she went to Hollywood and played small roles in several films including "Topper Takes a Trip." Born Rochester, N. Y.; died East Stroudsburg, Pa., July 13, 1957.

Colman, Ronald, 67, actor. He attended Hadley School at Littlehampton, Sussex, where he appeared in amateur theatricals. In

1916 he made his professional debut in London in "The Maharanee of Arakan." Four years later he came to this country and supported Robert Warwick in "The Dauntless Three." While supporting Ruth Chatterton in "La Tendresse" he was offered the male lead in the movie "The White Sister" starring Lillian Gish. This was the beginning of a long picture career ("Beau Geste," "Bulldog Drummond," "Lost Horizon," etc.): few Hollywood actors have for so long proved so popular. He was also extremely popular in radio and television. In 1948 he won an Oscar for his role in "Double Life." Born Richmond, Surrey, England; died Santa Barbara, Calif., May 19, 1958.

Cooke, Harry, 56, actor. He played his first role at the age of four. Upon graduating from high school he decided to make the theatre his career, and was in such plays as "The Good Earth," "I, Myself" and "The Children's Hour." He took over for Paul Douglas in the "Born Yesterday" lead. Born Manchester, N. H., died Forest Hills, N. Y., March 21, 1958.

Davenport, Butler, 87, actor, producer. As a teen-ager he understudied with Augustin Daly and played roles with Richard Mansfield. He later worked with Duse, Bernhardt, Belasco and John Drew. Beginning in 1908 he wrote a number of plays and in 1910 Lee Shubert produced his "Keeping Up Appearances." In 1912 he began opening little theatres of his own and in January 1913 opened the Davenport Theatre on 27th Street near Lexington Avenue, the first free theatre in the world. He never charged admission, money being collected by passing the hat. At this unique playhouse he was president, director, producer, treasurer, star, playwright, press agent and sometimes "charlady." Born New York; died New York, Apr. 7, 1958.

Day, Juliette, age not given, actress. Well-known in the twenties and thirties, she appeared in "Yellow Jacket," "Katy Did," "This Thing Called Love," "The Matinee Girl," "The Dark," and many others. Birthplace not given; died Northport, L. I., Sept. 18, 1957.

Devereaux, Jack, 76, actor. Educated at Georgetown University, he appeared on Broadway and acted in early motion pictures. He helped to form Devslick, Inc., a producing company for new and unusual plays. He married John Drew's daughter Louise. Among the plays in which he appeared were "A Pair of Sixes," "Brewster's Millions," "Baby Mine" and "The Famous Mrs. Fair." Birthplace not given; died New York, Jan. 19, 1958.

Dreiser, Edward M., 84, actor. Brother of the novelist Theodore Dreiser and the composer Paul Dresser, he appeared in such plays as "The Soldier of Fortune," "Within the Law," and "The Climbers," reaching his peak in "Paid in Full." An accident that nearly cost him his eyesight ended his career on the stage. Birthplace not given; died Springfield Gardens, L. I., Jan. 29, 1958.

Fenton, Frank, 51, actor. He made his Broadway debut after graduating from Georgetown University. Among his New York appearances were "The Philadelphia Story," "Susan and God" and "Boy Meets Girl." On tour he supported Katharine Cornell in "Alien Corn," "Romeo and Juliet" and "The Barretts of Wimpole Street." He made his screen debut in 1942 in "Lady of Burlesque." Born Hartford, Conn.; died Hollywood, July 24, 1957.

Fields, Herbert, 60, librettist. This son of the famous Lew Fields attended Columbia University, where he met Richard Rodgers and Lorenz Hart and collaborated with them in 1925 on the "Garrick Gaieties." They did a new edition the following year. He then teamed up with his sister Dorothy to write "Hello, Daddy!" for their father. Herbert did the librettos for Cole Porter's "Fifty Million Frenchmen" and "The New Yorkers." He was also the librettist for "Present Arms," "Panama Hattie" and "Du Barry Was a Lady." With his sister he wrote "Something for the Boys," "Mexican Hayride" and the big hit "Annie Get Your Gun." He did several film scenarios including "Love Before Breakfast," "Father Takes a Wife," "The Hot Heiress" and film versions of some of his Broadway plays. Born New York; died New York, March 24, 1958.

Geddes, Norman Bel, 65, designer. He ended his formal training at 16 after brief periods at Cleveland and Chicago art schools. Otto H. Kahn financed a trip to New York and introduced him to officials of the Metropolitan Opera. He subsequently did designs for three Met productions that aroused the interest of Broadway producers and he soon turned his attention to the theatre. In all he designed more than 200 productions ranging from opera to Ringling Brothers Circus. Among these were "The Truth About Blayds," "Lady Be Good," "The Rivals," "Ziegfeld Follies," "Fifty Million Frenchmen" and "Flying Colors." His "The Miracle" in 1923 was rated one of the major spectacles of the New York stage. His "Futurama" at the 1939-40 New York World's Fair gained him world-wide attention. He designed furniture, buildings and refrigerators. Though not a licensed architect, he was retained to redesign downtown Toledo. His influence was felt throughout the entire field of design. Born Adrian, Mich.; died New York, May 8, 1958.

Goetz, Augustus, 56, playwright. He attended the University of Pennsylvania. On a European trip he met and later married Ruth Goodman, daughter of the producer Philip Goodman. Together Mr. and Mrs. Goetz collaborated on plays and motion pictures for 27 years. Jed Harris' production of "The Heiress" was their first big success on Broadway and was later made into a picture. They also wrote "One Man Show," "The Immoralist" and "The Hidden River." Probably their best-known film play was "Sister Carrie." Born Buffalo, N. Y.; died New York, Sept. 30, 1957.

Green, Harry, 65, comedian. At 14 he left a successful vaudeville career to attend De Witt Clinton High School and later City College and New York University. Show business won him back from his law studies and he returned to vaudeville. For five years he toured as George Washington Cohen in his sketch "The Cherry Tree" and took it to London in 1920. He had made his London debut in 1914 in a Jewish lawyer skit. After appearing there in 1921 in "Welcome Stranger" he returned to New York and was seen in "Clubs Are Trumps," "Piper Paid," "All for All" and others. In the past 30 years he made over 60 films—"Be Yourself," "Mr. Skitch" and "The Kibitzer" among them. He was appearing in television in London at the time of his death. Born New York City; died London, May 31, 1958.

Guitry, Sacha, 72, actor, playwright. Son of Lucien Guitry, he was one of the leading players of the French stage and screen. He played his first role at the age of 17; his career as a playwright began a year earlier with "Le Page." He appeared in New York with his wife Yvonne Printemps. One of the best-known of his 105 plays, "Deburau," was produced on Broadway by David Belasco. Born St. Petersburg, Russia; died Paris, July 24, 1957.

Handy, W. C., 84, composer. Son of an ex-slave Methodist preacher, he went into a traveling minstrel at 15. He added to his musical education at the Negro Agricultural and Mechanical College near Huntsville, Ala. He then organized orchestras and minstrels. He was known as the "father of the blues" because of the tremendous and continuing success of his "St. Louis Blues," "Memphis Blues" and "Beale Street Blues." He also wrote some 60 others. Paramount pictures recently filmed the story of his life in "St. Louis Blues." Born Florence, Ala.; died New York, March 28, 1958.

Hay, Mary, 56, actress. One of Broadway's glittering personalities during the twenties, she was in "The Ziegfeld Follies of 1920" followed by roles in "Sunny" and "Marjolaine." In 1924 she was featured with Hal Skelly in "Mary Jane McKane." She was with Gertrude Lawrence in "Treasure Girl" and also appeared in "Greater Love," of which she was part author. Born Fort Bliss, Texas; died Inverness, California, June 4, 1957.

Haye, Helen, 83, actress. After touring the provinces for 12 years, she made her first appearance in London at the Shaftsbury Theatre. Two months later she played the Queen to Sir Herbert Tree's "Hamlet" and was Olivia in "Twelfth Night." In the next 40 years she played some 130 roles, acting in England, the United States and Canada. She was 78 when she appeared as the Dowager Empress in "Anastasia" in England. She was also an instructor at the Royal Academy of Dramatic Arts: among her pupils were Celia Johnson, Sir John Gielgud, Flora Robson and Charles Laughton. Born Assam, India; died London, Sept. 1, 1957.

Henson, Leslie, 66, actor. In 1910 he joined a company known as The Tatters and remained with them for five years. He played in New York in "Tonight's the Night" which later went to London's West End. Also in London he was in "Sally," "The Cabaret Girl," "The Beauty Prize" and "Kid Boots," followed by "Lady Luck," "Funny Face," "It's a Boy," "It's a Girl" and others. In 1939 he toured South Africa. He worked as producer and director. One of his greatest successes was "Tons of Money" which ran for 737 performances. Born London; died Harrow Weald, Middlesex, Dec. 2, 1957.

Herbert, F. Hugh, 60, playwright. Raised in England, he attended the Royal School of Mines at the University of London. After being invalided out of the British Army in 1917 he went to work in the advertising department of Selfridge's department store in London. When he came to the United States he took up playwriting with almost immediate success and in 1921 he wrote his first film scripts. For Broadway he wrote, among others, "Kiss and Tell," "For Love or Money" and "The Moon Is Blue." He was also a movie producer, director, novelist, poet and writer of magazine articles. Among his movie credits were "Sitting Pretty" and "Home Sweet Homicide." One of his most recent radio shows was "Meet Corliss Archer." Born Vienna; died Hollywood, May 17, 1958.

Hicks, Russell, 62, actor. After graduation from preparatory school in Maryland, he entered business and later acted in motion pictures. He had bit roles in "The Birth of a Nation" and "Intolerance." After World War I he was an executive with Famous Players and was then a surveyor for the city of Baltimore. His first stage role was in "It Pays to Smile." Others included "Goin' Home," "Torch Song," "Diamond Lil" and "As You Desire Me." His last Broadway appearance was in "The Caine Mutiny Court Martial." Born Baltimore; died Los Angeles, June 1, 1957.

Jackson, Ethel, 80, actress. Educated in Paris, Vienna and Dresden, she originally intended to be a pianist. She made her first appearance on the stage at the Savoy Theatre, London, in August 1897, in the chorus of "The Yeomen of the Guard," followed by parts in "The Grand Duchess," "The Gondoliers" and "The Beauty Stone." She came to America under Charles Frohman's management in 1898 to appear in "Little Miss Nobody." Later she was in "The Runaway Girl," "Little Red Riding Hood," "Miss Bob White" and others. In 1907 she made an enormous hit as the original "Merry Widow" in this country. After some years of retirement she returned to the stage in such plays as "The Purple Road," "A Pair of Sixes," "The Blue Bird," "Dodsworth" and "The Women." Her last appearance was with Paul Muni in "Key Largo" in 1939. Born New York; died East Islip, L. I., Nov. 23, 1957.

Kaufman, S. Jay, 71, playwright. Better known as a theatrical columnist he nevertheless wrote and produced more than 60 one-act plays and many sketches for acts at the Palace and other Broadway theatres. Among the revues to which he contributed were "The Streets of Paris" and "Keep Off the Grass." Birthplace not given; died New York, June 20, 1957.

Kingsford, Walter, 73, actor. He came here from England in 1912 and his first Broadway appearance was in "Fanny's First Play" in which he had previously appeared in London. He supported Ethel Barrymore in "The Constant Wife" and was in Lord Dunsany's "If." He played Polonius in a modern-dress version of "Hamlet" and was with Jane Cowl in "Art and Mrs. Bottle." He was also in "Children of Darkness," "Criminal at Large" and "After All." He made many films, including the "Dr. Kildare" series. Born England; died Los Angeles, Feb. 7, 1958.

Mather, Aubrey, 72, actor. Attended Trinity College and Cambridge University before making his stage debut as Bernardo in "Hamlet" in 1905. His first London appearance was in 1909 in "Brewster's Millions." He first came to America in 1919 in "The Luck of the Navy" and later toured Canada in "General Post." He also toured Australia and South Africa in several plays. In New York he was Polonius to Leslie Howard's "Hamlet." Also in New York he was in "Bachelor Born," "Good Hunting" and "Foolish Notion." His last appearance was in London in "Separate Tables." Among his movies were "The House of Fear," "The Lodger" and "The Importance of Being Earnest." Born Minchinhampton, Eng.; died Stanmore, Eng., Jan. 15, 1958.

Moeller, Philip, 77, author, producer. He was educated at New York public schools, New York University and Columbia University. His first production was "Helena's Husband" at the Bandbox Theatre, N. Y., in 1913. He was one of the founders and directors of both the Washington Square Players and the Theatre Guild. Among the more than 70 plays he directed are "Saint Joan," "Fata Morgana," "The Guardsman" and "They Knew What They Wanted." He was author of "The Roadhouse in Arden," "Madame Sand," "Molière," "Sophie" and others. Born New York; died New York, Apr. 26, 1958.

Morgan, Charles, 64, playwright. He was drama critic of the London "Times" from 1926 to 1939. In 1936 he wrote his first successful play, "The Flashing Stream." This was followed by an equally successful dramatized version of his novel "The River Line." His last effort was "The Burning Glass" produced in 1953. Among his novels were "The Fountain," which won the Hawthornden Prize in 1933, and "The Voyage," which won him the James Tait Black Memorial book prize in 1940. Born London; died London, Feb. 6, 1958.

Morrissey, Will, 72, actor, song writer, author, producer. He was one of the last shoestring producers: by 1940 he had produced more than 40 shows almost every one of which became stranded on the road. Martha Raye, Mickey Rooney, Bing Crosby and Hugh Herbert were all under his management. Birthplace not given; died Santa Barbara, Calif., Dec. 16, 1957.

Nathan, George Jean, 76, drama critic. He attended public school in Cleveland and received private instruction in French, Spanish, German and piano. At 11 he wrote dramas which he played in his father's barn. In 1904 he graduated from Cornell University, and later attended the University of Bologna in Italy. His uncle, the critic and playwright Charles Frederic Nirdlinger, got him a reporting job on the "New York Herald." He soon quit and became editor and critic of two magazines, "Outing" and "The Bohemian." Two years later he joined H. L. Mencken at "The Smart Set" and the two became famous. He wrote over 40 books. He was critic at one time or another for "Puck," "The American Mercury," "Judge," "Life," "Vanity Fair," "The Saturday Review of Literature," "Esquire," "Scribner's," "Newsweek," "Liberty," "The New York Journal-American" and King Features Syndicate. He helped H. L. Mencken found "The American Mercury." With Theodore Dreiser, James Branch Cabell, Eugene O'Neill and Ernest Boyd he founded a literary paper which lasted until 1937. A great opponent of the merely hackneyed and third-rate, and the champion of independent-minded playwrights, notably O'Casey and O'Neill, at his death he was the dean of American drama critics. Born Ft. Wayne, Ind.; died New York, Apr. 8, 1958.

Patson, Doris, 53, actress. She studied voice at the Guildhall School of Music in London. At 14 she was a concert pianist but abandoned the piano to dance with the famous Tiller Girls. Later she was in "Little Nellie Kelly" and "The Punch Bowl Revue." In 1925 she came to the United States to play the ingenue lead in "Louie the 14th" for Ziegfeld. She was in such musicals as "Katja," "Lovely Lady" and "Strike Up the Band," and was last seen playing lead in the road company of "Witness for the Prosecution." Born Islington, Eng.; died New York, June 12, 1957.

Percy, S. Esme, 69, actor. After running away from school at 15, he was befriended by and studied with Sarah Bernhardt. He studied in Paris and Brussels and made his stage debut at 17 with the F. R. Benson troupe in Nottingham, England. The following year he went to London in "Romeo and Juliet." He first appeared in the United States in 1932 in "Red Planet." Eighteen years later he came to New York in "The Lady's Not for Burning." To cover his more than 50-year stage career, "Who's Who in the Theatre" uses four columns. He also appeared in movies and on radio and television. Born London; died Brighton, Eng., June 16, 1957.

Taliaferro, Edith, 64, actress. She made her stage debut at the age of two with James A. Herne in "Shore Acres." During her early career she toured with such stars as Olga Nethersole and E. H. Sothern. Other plays included "The Evangelist," "Young Wisdom," "Mother Carey's Chickens," "Kissing Time" and "Private Lives." Her greatest success was doubtless "Rebecca of Sunnybrook Farm" which she played in New York in 1910. She was married to actor House Jameson and was the sister of

Mabel Taliaferro. She also played in London and toured Australia. Born Richmond, Va.; died Newtown, Conn., March 2, 1958.

Taylor, Estelle, 58, actress. She was picked from a Broadway chorus line for pictures where she made a name for herself as a featured player. She married boxer Jack Dempsey and with him was co-starred on Broadway in 1928 in "The Big Fight." She then returned to pictures. She was in "Dorothy Vernon of Haddon Hall," "Cimarron," the early version of "The Ten Commandments" and others. Born Wilmington, Del.; died Hollywood, Apr. 15, 1958.

Todd, Mike, 49, producer. His name was originally Avrom Hirsch Goldbogen. At five he helped a fruit peddler, at seven he sold papers and played in a boys' band. In 1918 the family moved to Chicago and he entered a trade school. Before he was 20 he made and lost his first million in real estate. Later he went to Hollywood and started a company that sound-proofed movie stages. His first successful attempt at show business was during the Chicago World's Fair in 1933 when he produced a flame dance. He then set out for Broadway where his first two shows, "Call Me Ziggy" and "The Man from Cairo," were flops. His first success was "The Hot Mikado." With Lowell Thomas he was one of the founders of the Cinerama film process, and later devoted his time to the Todd-AO process. In all he produced 21 Broadway shows, among them "Up in Central Park" and "Star and Garter." His movie "Around the World in 80 Days" created a sensation, and his flamboyant activities in and out of show business made him a Broadway legend. Born Minneapolis; died Grants, N. M., March 22, 1958.

van Druten, John, 56, playwright. He wanted to be a writer but his father insisted that he study law. He attended University College School and London University. His first hit in this country was "Young Woodley" in 1925. Altogether he wrote some 27 plays as well as many movie scenarios. Among his more important plays were "There's Always Juliet," "The Distaff Side," "The Voice of the Turtle," "I Remember Mama" and "I Am a Camera." Starting with "The Voice of the Turtle," he was his own director. In 1951 he staged the musical hit "The King and I." He became a naturalized citizen in 1943 and settled down on his ranch in California's Coachella Valley. Born London; died Indio, Calif., Dec. 19, 1957.

Vaughn, Hilda, 60, actress. She attended Vassar College and the American Academy of Dramatic Arts. Her first success on

Broadway was in "The Flood." In 1924 she won the lead in the road company of "Rain." This was followed by "The Seed of the Brute" and "Glory Hallelujah." She then did several films, among them "Dinner at Eight" and "Nothing Sacred." Later New York plays included "Get Away Old Man," "Jacobowsky and the Colonel" and "On Whitman Avenue." She toured Europe for six months in "Double Door." Born Baltimore; died Baltimore, Dec. 28, 1957.

Vermilyea, Harold, 68, actor. Broadway first saw him in 1914 in "The Lion and the Mouse," the first of 32 plays in which he appeared in New York. He was in such hits as "It Pays to Advertise," "Get-Rich-Quick Wallingford," "A Tailor Made Man," "Captain Applejack," "The Enemy" and "Boy Meets Girl." After World War II he spent most of his time in pictures and was also on television. His last plays on Broadway were "Jacobowsky and the Colonel" and "Deep Are the Roots." Born New York; died New York, Jan. 8, 1958.

Vincent, James, 74, actor, director. After studying oratory and dramatic art, he became a leading man in various stock companies. He was in "The Man Stood Still," "As a Man Thinks," "The Trail of the Lonesome Pine" and "Criminal at Large." He directed many films for the Sterling Film Corp. and Fox Films. Theda Bara, Stuart Holmes, Bertha Kalish and Virginia Pearson all worked under his direction. Born Springfield, Mass.; died New York, July 12, 1957.

Vokes, May, in her 70's, actress. She made her first impression in "My Friend from India" in 1896 and was later seen in "A Fool and His Money," "A Pair of Sixes," "A Full House" and others. Her greatest success was in "The Bat" in 1920. She appeared in many revivals of this play, the last time in 1937. Birthplace not given; died Stamford, Conn., Sept. 13, 1957.

Walker, Charlotte, 81, actress. She made her stage debut while in her teens and at 19 appeared in London in "The Mummy." Later she was with Richard Mansfield. One of her best-remembered roles was in "The Trail of the Lonesome Pine" in 1911. David Belasco saw her in "On Parole" and engaged her for "The Warrens of Virginia," "Just a Wife" and "Call the Doctor." She made several early movies. In 1923 she was in the Players Club revival of "The School for Scandal." Born Texas; died Kerrville, Texas, March 23, 1958.

Welch, Mary, 35, actress. She was raised in San Diego and attended U.C.L.A. where she won an award as the outstanding drama student. She made her Broadway debut as Jo in "Little Women" in the City Center production in 1944 and later supported Ethel Barrymore on tour in "The Joyous Season." In 1948 she appeared on Broadway with Alfred Drake in "Joy to the World." She was Stella in the national company of "A Streetcar Named Desire." Other plays include "Dream Girl," "The House of Bernarda Alba" and "The Solid Gold Cadillac." She was active in films and television and for the last three years ran the Welch Workshop, an acting school. Her last appearance was as Missy Le Hand in "Sunrise at Campobello." Born Charleston, S. C.; died New York, May 31, 1958.

Williams, E. G. Harcourt, 77, actor. One of England's better-known actors, he appeared in more than 200 plays by, among others, Shakespeare, Sheridan, Goldsmith, Ibsen, Chekhov and Shaw. He made pictures and was on radio and television. In 1929 he joined the Old Vic and in four years produced 50-odd plays. His activities occupy four columns in "Who's Who in the Theatre." Born Croyden, Eng.; died England, Dec. 13, 1957.

Witherspoon, Cora, 67, actress. She was educated in New Orleans and Paris, and made her first stage appearance in New Orleans in 1905 in "Janice Meredith." Her first Broadway appearance was in "The Concert" with Leo Ditrichstein. She appeared in such hits as "Daddy Long-Legs," "The Great Lover," "Three Faces East," "The Awful Truth," "Grounds for Divorce," "The Fall of Eve," "The Constant Wife," "Camille" and "Jezebel." She was also in innumerable motion pictures. Born New Orleans; died Las Cruces, New Mexico, Nov. 17, 1957.

THE DECADES' TOLL

(Prominent Theatrical Figures Who Have Died in Recent Years)

	Born	Died
Adams, Maude	1872	1953
Anderson, John Murray	1886	1954
Arliss, George	1869	1946
Bennett, Richard	1873	1944
Bernstein, Henri	1876	1953
Calhern, Louis	1895	1956
Carroll, Earl	1893	1948
Carte, Rupert D'Oyly	1876	1948
Christians, Mady	1900	1951
Cochran, Charles B.	1872	1951
Collier, Willie	1866	1943
Cowl, Jane	1884	1950
Craven, Frank	1890	1945
Crosman, Henrietta	1865	1944
Davis, Owen	1874	1956
Digges, Dudley	1879	1947
Duncan, Augustin	1872	1954
Errol, Leon	1881	1951
Fields, W. C.	1879	1946
Gaige, Crosby	1883	1949
Garfield, John	1913	1952
Golden, John	1874	1955
Hampden, Walter	1879	1955
Hart, Lorenz	1895	1943
Hart, William S.	1870	1946
Hooker, Brian	1881	1947
Howard, Willie	1883	1949
Jolson, Al	1886	1950
Jouvet, Louis	1887	1951
Kane, Whitford	1882	1956
Kern, Jerome D.	1885	1945
Lawrence, Gertrude	1898	1952

	Born	*Died*
Lehar, Franz	1870	1948
Loftus, Cecilia	1876	1943
Lord, Pauline	1890	1950
Mantle, Burns	1873	1948
Marlowe, Julia	1866	1950
Merivale, Philip	1886	1946
Molnar, Ferenc	1878	1952
Moore, Grace	1901	1947
Nazimova, Alla	1879	1945
Nethersole, Olga	1870	1951
O'Neill, Eugene	1888	1953
Patterson, Joseph Medill	1879	1946
Perry, Antoinette	1888	1946
Pinza, Ezio	1895	1957
Powers, James T.	1862	1943
Reinhardt, Max	1873	1943
Romberg, Sigmund	1887	1951
Scheff, Fritzi	1879	1954
Selwyn, Edgar	1875	1944
Shaw, G. B.	1856	1950
Sheldon, Edward	1886	1946
Sherwood, Robert E.	1896	1955
Shubert, Lee	1875	1953
Tarkington, Booth	1869	1946
Tauber, Richard	1890	1948
Tyler, George C.	1867	1946
Ward, Fannie	1872	1952
Warfield, David	1866	1951
Webster, Ben	1864	1947
Whitty, Dame May	1865	1948
Woods, Al H.	1870	1951
Woollcott, Alexander	1887	1943
Youmans, Vincent	1899	1946

INDICES

INDEX OF AUTHORS AND PLAYWRIGHTS

INDEX OF PLAYS AND CASTS

Bold face page numbers refer to pages on which
Cast of Characters may be found.

INDEX OF PRODUCERS, DIRECTORS, DESIGNERS, STAGE MANAGERS, COMPOSERS, LYRICISTS AND CHOREOGRAPHERS

135631

LIBRARY
OF
MOUNT ST. MARY'S
COLLEGE
EMMITSBURG, MARYLAND

NOV 2 8 1978